Whitney Straight

Whitney and Daphne, upon their return from honeymoon, 5 September 1935. (Author's collection)

Whitney Straight

Racing Driver, War Hero, Industrialist

The Authorised Biography

Paul Kenny

In fond memory of the very finest of fellows,
Bert Flower

Front cover and spine illustration: Whitney breaking the three-year old record on the Shelsley Walsh hill climb, 30 September 1933 (Midland Automobile Club).
Back cover quotes: Whitney's diary, 6 November 1942; Churchill Archive Centre, CHAR 20/200/59, Whitney Straight, letter to Winston Churchill, 5 March 1945; HSBC Archives, London, UK GCS-0101, File relating to W. Straight, Kenneth Barber, Secretary of Midland Bank, letter to Lord Alanbrooke, 5 October 1956.

First published 2025
Reprinted 2026

The History Press
97 St George's Place, Cheltenham,
Gloucestershire, GL50 3QB
www.thehistorypress.co.uk

© Paul Kenny, 2025

The right of Paul Kenny to be identified as the Author of this work has been asserted in accordance with the Copyright, Designs and Patents Act 1988.

All rights reserved. No part of this book may be reprinted or reproduced or utilised in any form or by any electronic, mechanical or other means, now known or hereafter invented, including photocopying and recording, or in any information storage or retrieval system, without the permission in writing from the Publishers.

British Library Cataloguing in Publication Data.
A catalogue record for this book is available from the British Library.

ISBN 978 1 80399 111 5

Typesetting and origination by The History Press
Printed and bound in Great Britain by TJ Books, Padstow, Cornwall.

The History Press proudly supports

Trees for Life
www.treesforlife.org.uk

EU Authorised Representative: Easy Access System Europe
Mustamäe tee 50, 10621 Tallinn, Estonia
gpst.request@easproject.com

Contents

Acknowledgements 7
Prologue 11

1. New York 13
2. After Willard 27
3. Dartington 39
4. Cambridge or Racing? 55
5. A Brief, Busy Attempt at Both 73
6. Racing Wins Out 99
7. The Straight Stable 117
8. From Brooklands to Bremgarten 129
9. Facing Facts 145
10. Daphne 163
11. High Flyer 169
12. War 197
13. Captivity 213
14. Expanding Horizons 229
15. To BOAC, Via BEA 251
16. Breaking Up 285

17.	Non-Exec	305
18.	Liquidation	323
19.	A Good Sport and Afraid of Nothing	339

Notes	343
Bibliography	357
Index	365

Acknowledgements

My heartfelt thanks go to Whitney's daughters, Camilla Bowater and Amanda Opinsky, and their respective husbands, Michael and Jim, for their very considerable help and support throughout this project. The willingness of Camilla and Amanda to let me read their father's diaries and to quote extensively from them was of crucial importance, as it enabled Whitney's observations to infuse my text. They also kindly contributed to the transcription of the diaries and to the acquisition of certain archival photographs.

Their late mother, Lady Daphne Straight, deserves special mention. After Whitney's untimely death, she found the courage and patience to ensure his papers went to good homes – his motor racing material to Beaulieu, his logbook and wartime photo albums to the RAF Museum, his travel papers to the Royal Geographic Society and so on. She made my job as her husband's biographer a great deal easier.

Whitney's son, Barney Walker, was one of the first people I approached about the book, and I shall always be grateful to him and his wife Helen for the support they gave me.

Special thanks go to the woman who made a much better job than me of deciphering the appalling handwriting Whitney employed in his diaries – the queen of transcribers, Maureen Moran.

The staff at Cornell University's Division of Rare and Manuscript Collections, home to the archives of Whitney's father Willard and of his mother Dorothy in respect of her New York years, were enormously helpful. My thanks and best wishes go to them, and to the team at Devon

Heritage Centre, custodian of the great bulk of Dartington's archives. I wish to pay particular tribute to the late Yvonne Widger, Archives & Collection Administrator at The Dartington Hall Trust, in whose little office behind Dartington's cinema screen I read Whitney's school reports and correspondence with his stepfather. Local historian Kevin Mount provided expert insight on various Dartington points.

Jeremy Vaughan, Head of Motoring at the Royal Automobile Club, kindly permitted me to use the Clubhouse library to research contemporary accounts of Whitney's years as a racing driver, and Clubhouse Librarian Trevor Dunmore was a most helpful host. Special thanks also go to Leif Snellman, proprietor of goldenera.fi, *The Golden Era of Grand Prix Racing*. He has scoured contemporaneous accounts of the important Continental races of the inter-war years in British, French, German and Italian magazines to provide a balanced, objective account of those meetings. He saved me many weeks of research time. Maserati historian Adam Ferrington deserves special mention too.

The British Airways Heritage Collection houses meticulous records of BEA and BOAC. Jim Davies and Adrian Constable were expert and considerate hosts throughout my lengthy stay with them, and Adrian kindly read my aviation chapters and provided many valuable insights. I also want to credit Gavin McGuffie and Mathilde Jourdan, respectively Senior Archivist and Archives Assistant at the Postal Museum, and Helen Ceci, Archivist at HSBC History. Well-maintained corporate archives are a joy to work with.

By contrast, I acknowledge that I might have done a better job of narrating Whitney's time at Rolls-Royce, and his Girobank work for the Post Office. Sadly, I was unable to access either the Rolls-Royce Heritage Trust or Santander archives.

My two pre-readers, David Hanley and David Lowe, read each draft chapter as it came off the production line and helped me avoid numerous clunks and typos. My productivity was also helped by Rich Thomas and my son, Ben Kenny, who ensured that all three screens on my desk kept working to optimal effect.

Dr James Hansell made diagnoses from contemporary accounts, demystified medical terminology and provided valuable insight on medical matters.

Emily Clegg and Nicolai Holst of CACI went to enormous trouble to accurately map Whitney's week on the run in occupied and Vichy France. My thanks and compliments also go to Ian Dewsbery, Louisa Keyworth

Acknowledgements

and Symon Porteous of Lovell Johns for the other maps in the book, and for the assiduous way they created the plans of the Brooklands track layouts Whitney raced over.

I owe so much to my agent, Tom Cull, most notably for introducing me to The History Press. It has been a great pleasure working with The History Press, and I want to thank in particular Mark Beynon, the commissioning editor who signed me up; his successor Amy Rigg; project editor Jezz Palmer; designers Martin Latham and Anita Pumfrey; campaigns executive Graham Robson; editor Paul Middleton; proofreader James Ryan; and indexer Joanna Luke.

Others who kindly gave of their time and knowledge include Sabu Advani; Rupert Allason; Peter Amos; Beth Astridge, University Archivist, and Christine Davies, Special Collections and Archives Co-ordinator in the University of Kent's Special Collections and Archives department; Malcolm Barber; Frank Bowles of the Department of Archives and Modern Manuscripts at Cambridge University Library; Sophie Bridges, Archivist at Churchill Archives Centre, Churchill College, University of Cambridge; John Brinkmann; Keila Bruggar, AHHA Intern at the Manuscript Division of the Library of Congress; Anna Bühler, Legal Secretary at the Public Prosecutor's Office of the Canton of Bern; Dean Butler; Pamela Clark, former Senior Archivist at the Royal Archives and her successor, Julie Crocker; Tom Clarke; Patrick Collins, Curator, Vehicles and Research at the National Motor Museum Trust, Beaulieu; Jacqueline Cox, Keeper of Cambridge University Archives; Athena Demetriou, Bodleian Libraries' Admissions Officer; Stephen Dorril; Svenja Duppenbecker; David Elliot; the late Bill Elmhirst; the late Mike Evans, Chairman Emeritus of the Rolls-Royce Heritage Trust; Paul Fearnley; Adam Ferrington; Malcolm Fillimore; Rupert Finch Hatton; Fergus Fleming; David K. Frazier and Zach Downey of Indiana University's Lilly Library; Bryan Gable, Special Collections, Revs Institute; Ivor Game; Jon Gilbert of the Adrian Harrington bookshop; Jennifer Govan, Senior Librarian in Research and Information Services, Gottesman Libraries of Teachers College, Columbia University; Adam Green, Senior Assistant Archivist at Trinity College Library, Cambridge; Nina Hadaway, Archive, Library and Research Manager at the RAF Museum; Mark Hawkins; Tim Healey; Glyn Hughes, Honorary Archivist of the Alpine Club; Gillian Humphreys, Library Assistant at Weston Library, Oxford; the late Chris Jacques; Wolfgang

Kaese; Tomas Karlsson; Helen Keen of Surrey History Centre; Mark Knights of Beaulieu Film and Video; Howard Kroplick, Co-President of the Roslyn Landmark Society; Jane Lagesse; Beatrice Meecham, Engagement & Heritage Project Officer at Brooklands Museum; Dr Anne McLaughlin, Digitisation Services Manager, Trinity College Library, Cambridge; Robin McCullagh of the Royal Irish Automobile Club; Kim and Mitch McCullough; Gabrielle Mihaescu, former Cemetery Associate of the American Battle Monuments Commission, Suresnes American Cemetery, Paris; David Moore, Midland Automobile Club Archivist; David Morys, Archivist of the Bugatti Trust; Tom Moulson; Micah Musheno, Licensing Manager of the Whitney Museum of American Art; the late Mary Bride Nicholson; Doug Nye; Nick Opinsky; Adrian Porter and Sophia Elek; Christine Reynolds, Assistant Keeper of the Muniments, the Library, Westminster Abbey; Jonathan Rishton, former editor of *The Automobile*; Chris Royle; Dr Benjamin Ryser of the State Archives of the Canton of Bern; Christiane Salecker of Audi Tradition; April Sankey, Operations Director of Awards Intelligence; Erwin Schöllkopf; Martin Scröder; Mickaël Simon; Quentin Spurring; Philip Strickland; David Swig at RM Sotheby's; Corinne Turner, former Managing Director of Ian Fleming Publications; Jan Turner, Deputy Librarian at the Royal Geographical Society; Laurent Viton; Lin Watson, Senior Archivist at Teign Heritage – Teignmouth and Shaldon Museum; Maurice Wickstead; Richard Williams; and Anne Williamson.

Last but the very opposite of least, I thank my extraordinary wife, Jane. I could not conceivably have completed this project without her love and support.

My thanks go to all of the above, and my apologies to those who helped me and whom I have not acknowledged.

Any errors or omissions are entirely mine.

Paul Kenny, Teddington
January 2025

Prologue

Cornell University's Willard Straight Hall is one of America's oldest purpose-built students' union buildings. Opened in 1925, and designed by New York architects Delano & Aldrich, it makes highly effective use of the steep contours of the campus' Libe Slope – walk the thirty paces or so from the front door to the Memorial Room, and there are now five further floors beneath you. Long banners depicting the insignia of each of the University's fifteen colleges and schools hang from the ceiling of the Memorial Room, and an imposing stone fireplace dominates its right-hand wall.

The inscription above it reads:

> Treat all women with chivalry ** The respect of your fellows is worth more than applause ** Understand and sympathise with those who are less fortunate than you are ** Make up your own mind but respect the opinions of others ** Don't think a thing right or wrong just because someone tells you so ** Think it out yourself, guided by the advice of those whom you respect ** Hold your head high and your mind open, you can always learn ** Extracts from Willard Straight's letter to his son

Before departing for France to join the American Expeditionary Force in December 1917, Major Willard Straight had written the letter to his elder son, and sealed it in an envelope addressed to 'Master Whitney Straight ... if anything happens to me'. Though Willard survived the First World War, he died just weeks after the Armistice, cut down by pneumonia brought on by Spanish Flu, and thus 6-year-old Whitney came to read the words that his father had hoped he never would.

This book is the story of the young American boy who read that letter, the English gentleman he became and the extent to which he heeded his father's advice.

1

New York

Outside on the streets of New York, horseless carriages were vying for supremacy over horse-drawn buggies. Inside the five-storey townhouse on East 67th Street, near the corner with Madison Avenue, Dr Cragin's attempts to induce the baby had failed. It was clear now that the expectant parents would not get their wish – their first child would not be born on election day. Nor would their great friend, Theodore Roosevelt, be returning to the White House. His decision to run against its current occupant, William Taft, had split the Republican vote and assured Woodrow Wilson of becoming the twenty-eighth president of the United States. An anxious night ensued, and it was not until 4.45 the following afternoon, Wednesday, 6 November 1912, that the baby arrived, weighing 7lb 14oz. He was nicknamed 'Bill' but at a simple service, held at home in the new year, he was christened Whitney Willard Straight. In the tradition of the time, his given names were drawn from each side of his family – Whitney was his mother Dorothy's maiden name, and Willard the first name of his father.

Dorothy Whitney's christening, twenty-six years earlier, had been a much grander affair. It was held in Washington's St John's Church, across Lafayette Square from the White House. Among the congregation of 500 sat President Grover Cleveland and his entire cabinet. Dorothy's father, William, had been influential in Cleveland's presidential campaign, and at the time of her birth was busy rebuilding the US fleet as secretary of the navy. When Cleveland was defeated in the 1888 election, William left politics and the family moved to New York, where he invested in railroads. Young Dorothy and her friend Gladys Vanderbilt chatted on a private telephone line rigged up between their nurseries on opposite sides of Fifth Avenue.

She was just 6 when she was told she was going on a journey, and led in to say goodbye to her mother, Flora, who lay reclining on a sofa. Only later did she learn that Flora had died while she was away. In January 1904, William was taken ill at the opera. He failed to have his appendicitis treated until too late, and died five days later of peritonitis. Dorothy, aged 17, became one of New York's most prominent heiresses, and moved back to her childhood home on Fifth Avenue, now owned by her brother Harry. Just two years later, she established her own household at Applegreen, a large, three-storey, shingle-style house on her late father's estate at Old Westbury, on Long Island's North Shore. Harry had recently become vice president of Long Island Motor Parkway Inc. When the road opened in 1908, it passed south of Applegreen, and Dorothy lived in rural splendour with her companion-cum-chaperone, Beatrice Bend, daughter of the late George Bend, who had served on the governing body of the New York Stock Exchange.

Dorothy exploited her independence to the full. Away from the usual dinners, theatre visits and book clubs, she studied political economy at Columbia, left Applegreen at 5 a.m. to take her seat in the grandstand for a Vanderbilt Cup race and enjoyed a grand tour of Europe with just Beatrice and Beatrice's mother Elizabeth for company. She was clear in what she expected from marriage. She had seen many 'matches' result in unsatisfactory unions, and was confident about what ultimately counted: 'Perfect faith in each other — that above all things is the truest, surest foundation, and I can't imagine anything more wonderful than this sort of understanding between two people. Nothing then could really go wrong.'[1] Thus far, none of her suitors, whether from the New York world of politics and the professions, or among the lords and counts across the Atlantic, had come close to meeting her criteria.

In January 1909, she was invited to Washington to attend the social events marking the end of Roosevelt's second term in office. Sitting next to her at dinner one evening was someone quite unlike the other young men she had met. His name was Willard Straight. He had been born in January 1880 in Oswego, on the New York shore of Lake Ontario. His mother, Emma Dickerman, had met Henry Straight while teaching at the Nebraska school where he was principal. Sadly, Henry contracted tuberculosis and died in 1886, and Emma suffered the same fate four years later. Aware that her condition was terminal, she arranged for Willard and his sister Hazel to be raised by friends of hers in Oswego.

Willard found the arrangement frustrating and ended up being expelled from school, but a year at a military academy in Bordentown, New Jersey, helped him adopt a more disciplined approach to life, and he went on to read Architecture at Cornell University in Ithaca, some 200 miles northwest of New York City. After graduating in 1901, he joined China's maritime operations, helping to maintain an orderly customs function and manage commercial traffic along the coast and on the Yangtze River. He took on direct representation of America's overseas interests in 1905, when he became a vice consul, first in Korea, and then in Cuba. There, he formed a lifelong friendship with an architect, Bill Delano, and took personal responsibility for arranging the honeymoon of Roosevelt's daughter Alice and Nicholas Longworth, a future speaker of the House of Representatives. Alice's father took note, and influenced Willard's next role, supporting US trade in what was then Manchuria, as Consul-General in Mukden, modern-day Shenyang.

Now fluent in Mandarin, Willard's engagements with China grew more commercial and, shortly after meeting Dorothy in Washington, he became the representative of a group of US banks negotiating a large international loan to China. The objective was to make the country more resilient to Russian and Japanese influence, and more receptive to trade with the West. In May 1909, while in New York for meetings with the banks, he saw Dorothy again, and she invited him out for an afternoon riding at Applegreen. She was fascinated by his work and his tales of the Orient, and he was delighted to learn that she would be visiting China on her forthcoming world tour. They agreed to meet in Beijing. Dorothy's intrepid band of women on the tour comprised her maid, Louisa Weinstein, and Beatrice and Elizabeth Bend. They sailed from San Francisco to Japan, and when they reached Seoul, Willard took responsibility for their safe passage to Beijing. He sent two of his staff to translate and cook for them in a private railway carriage, and he and his housemate, a diplomat named Henry Fletcher, moved out to the US legation and made their home available to Dorothy and her party.

A blissful fortnight of walks, rides, dinners, late-night conversations and serenading ensued. Dorothy was swept along by it all, and when she wrote to thank Willard, it was in the most glowing of terms. 'Oh Wise Man of the East,' she began, and wrote of 'two of the happiest weeks I have ever known'.² But she bid him 'goodbye' more than once and, in wishing him 'true happiness in the future, for you deserve the best there is',³ she had no expectation that she would be part of that future. Willard, however, was in no doubt where his future lay, and four months later, when Dorothy and her party arrived in Cairo, she was greeted by thirty of his letters that made his feelings for her quite clear. While in Cairo, she met Roosevelt and his family, who had arrived from a hunting trip, and when Willard came up in conversation, she learned that the former president rated him highly. It left her hoping that Roosevelt would serve a third term, and make Willard his secretary of state. As things stood, however, Willard could hardly be considered a suitable match. When he saw her briefly, on his way to London to update banker J.P. Morgan on the state of the loan negotiations, she rejected his marriage proposal.

But Willard kept up his long-distance campaign, and his prospects brightened considerably when he returned to New York in the spring of 1911, having played a significant role in the successful conclusion of the loan negotiations with China. Now he had the status and respect to complement the trust that had shone through in his many letters. When he next proposed to her, Dorothy accepted. The engagement was only announced after the couple had sailed from New York, in the company of both Bends, and the wedding took place in Geneva, far from the prying eyes of the New York press corps.

They honeymooned in Venice, then travelled up to Paris to begin the two-week rail journey to Beijing. They arrived on 11 October, the very day on which the city of Wuhan, 700 miles to the south, fell to revolutionaries – 2,000 years of Chinese imperial rule was drawing to a violent end. An early visitor to their first marital home was a major with the local contingent of US marines, with a present of two revolvers. By the beginning of March 1912, looting and executions had become commonplace in Beijing, but Willard and Dorothy still felt safe enough to dine one evening at the nearby home of George Morrison, Chinese correspondent of *The Times*. Violence erupted outside, and Willard dashed back to rescue Dorothy's maid, Louisa, and bring her to Morrison's house. It took twenty marines to escort the group to the safety of the US legation, Dorothy in a rickshaw, with Louisa in her lap, and a few belongings tied on behind.

With the international loans signed, there clearly was little value in Willard and Dorothy continuing to live in such danger, and they set off for London in late March. Dorothy found the Trans-Siberian Railway more arduous this time. She was pregnant with Whitney, and suffering from morning sickness. England proved a welcome respite. They stayed with Dorothy's elder sister, Pauline, and her husband, Almeric Paget, 1st Baron Queensborough. Dorothy enjoyed her time with Pauline, and followed from afar the many twists and turns in the US presidential election campaign, while Willard commuted to and from the London offices of Morgan Grenfell. It was not until August that they headed for home, and leased the East 67th Street townhouse where Whitney would be born.

On 14 October, Roosevelt was shot before he was due to speak at a rally in Milwaukee, Wisconsin. His glasses case and a folded copy of the address prevented the bullet from doing much damage, and he still gave his speech before being taken to hospital, but Dorothy rushed the following morning to New York's Hotel Manhattan to comfort his wife, Edith. From there she visited her doctor, and after that there would be no more rushing. At her next consultation, on 28 October, he ordered her straight home to bed. Two nights later, Willard played host to their dinner guests without her, and left her at home while he led them down to Madison Square Garden to hear Roosevelt's first speech since Milwaukee. At the end of the week, Dorothy received a visit from one of her father's former lawyers, William Page, so that she could update her will. Given what she was about to go through, her caution was well-placed. Whitney was born fit and well after a 27-hour labour, but Dorothy was left in great pain from complications of the bladder and kidneys. Three weeks passed before she was well enough to go downstairs for dinner, and Whitney was a month old before she had her first post-natal bath. They finally left the city for Applegreen on 11 December.

Christmas was a quiet affair, notable to baby Whitney only for being put on Borden's condensed milk. Nurse Bates was his primary carer early on, but his parents were actively involved with him from the start. Dorothy often bathed him, and Willard regularly sketched him in a special book, which sadly has not survived. By early February, Whitney was sitting on his mother's lap, 'laughing & cooing & talking to himself & really enjoying life. He holds his head up by himself.'[4] A regular feature of family life was the weighing of 'Bill' each Sunday. At six months, he was up to 19lb 4oz.

Whitney Straight

The family's first summer holiday together was spent in Manhasset, just a few miles west of Applegreen, though they took the more scenic trip around Sands Point aboard a chartered boat. Amid all the lunches, dinners, tennis and golf, Dorothy regularly strolled into the village with Whitney in his pram. She was the proudest of mothers, and found her son 'sweet and dignified and proud of himself. People turned around to look at him wherever he went and his little serious pink face seemed to call for the smiles from passers-by.'[5]

Wilson's defeat of Roosevelt not only jeopardised Willard's political aspirations, but also meant his work on the international loans to China had been in vain. The country was still in turmoil, and the Wilson administration was opposed to dollar diplomacy. This led to a period of uncertainty for Willard. He was now an American banker with little experience of American banking. Nevertheless, while Roosevelt remained on the political sidelines, Willard and Dorothy put her wealth to effective use. They founded a new, pro-Roosevelt, magazine, *The New Republic*, and installed as its editor Herbert Croly, the political philosopher whose book, *The Promise of America*, they had read to each other while travelling.

They called in Willard's architect friend, Bill Delano, to turn the old Cotton Exchange in Hanover Square into India House, a club for businessmen interested in foreign trade. They also employed Delano to design an impressive stable block at Applegreen, and a superb new mansion, inspired by the Wren-designed wing at Hampton Court Palace. It stands to this day at 1130 Fifth Avenue, on the corner with 94th Street. There was even a garage built in complementary style, two blocks south. 'If I do say so,' Delano wrote later, 'it's a well-planned and lovely house; once inside, it seems much larger than it really is.'[6]

In early July 1914, Dorothy, heavily pregnant with her second child, found Whitney, now 20 months old, upset and agitated. Within days, he was very unwell indeed with what she feared was dysentery. Doctors visited him frequently and Miss Barker, who had attended the infant Whitney while Dorothy recovered from her labour, re-joined the team as night nurse. For more than three weeks, he moved his bowels a dozen times a day and bled heavily from his rectum. To make matters worse, Willard came home from a polo match with a cracked bone in his ankle. But Dorothy had still more pressing concerns to attend to. On Sunday, 2 August, after another long labour, she gave birth to a daughter, named Beatrice after Miss

Bend, but nicknamed Biddy. Across the Atlantic, the lamps were going out all over Europe. The day before Biddy's birth, the Germans declared war on Russia. The day after it, they declared war on France. Britain entered the war the next day. Back home, Beatrice Bend left for the family cottage in Onteora in the Catskills, to prepare the way for Nurse Bates' arrival the next day with Whitney. His mother, baby sister and entourage joined him three weeks later. By then, he was well again, but he would suffer with rectal bleeding in adulthood too.

Two years later, on 1 September 1916, Willard and Dorothy's third child, Michael, was born. At the time, the family was holidaying in Southampton, on the South Shore of Long Island, and Whitney was enjoying his first swims in the ocean with his father, but the holiday was curtailed when a German U-boat sank several ships off Nantucket. Knowing that America's entry into the war was only a matter of time, Willard lobbied for a role in the State Department. He wrote directly to President Wilson, and spoke also with Wilson's adviser on Europe, the self-styled Colonel Edward House. Willard had first met House in 1915, and impressed him by being able to speak on his behalf to France's hawkish foreign minister, Théophile Delcassé. But Willard's politics blocked his way to a role in Wilson's administration, and instead he sat his officers' examination. In May 1917, a month after the US entered the war, he was commissioned a major in the Adjutant General's reserve corps.

Willard's last weekend before departing for France was spent with his family. He posed for photographs on the lawn at Applegreen, young Whitney standing proudly beside him in a little soldier suit, then took Dorothy and the children back into town for a service at the cathedral. He wrote a letter the next day and sealed it in an envelope addressed to 'Master Whitney Straight ... if anything happens to me'. Early on Wednesday, 12 December, he sailed for Europe, arriving in Paris on Boxing Day. He and Dorothy slipped back into the long-distance correspondence of their early days. Whitney joined in, and offered up a little prayer each night: 'Dear God – please keep my Daddy safe tonight. Keep him safe till morning light.'[7]

Willard was indeed kept safe. Keen though he was to lead a battalion into action, his organisational skills were far too prized to have him exposed to danger. His first task was to implement the War Risk Insurance Bureau's new life insurance policy for US servicemen. Within seven weeks, he and a complement of fewer than 100 men, utilising vehicles borrowed from the Red Cross and huts from the YMCA, wrote $1.25 billion of policies on the lives of a quarter of a million personnel scattered across France. It was an extraordinary achievement.

In March, Willard was sent to Langres, an old cathedral town 190 miles south-east of Paris, to study operations at the Army Staff College. The town had once been the hillside stronghold of the Gauls in their wars against the Romans, and Willard sent a charming, illustrated letter to Whitney, telling him about the legend of the Gallic chieftain, Sabinus. One sketch was of Sabinus brandishing a spear at a *sanglier* (wild boar): 'It is dark brown in colour and has long bristles and little beady black eyes – and tusks ... which he sometimes uses when he's being hunted – to cut the people who are chasing him.'[8] In his letters to his children, Willard was quite happy to bend the truth to suit the moral of his tale. In this case, he claimed that the deaths of Sabinus and his family had inspired the Gauls to defeat the Romans. 'So you see that although Sabinus and Mrs Sabinus and their children didn't live to see it – their bravery and heroism in the end saved their country. That's what people who are fighting today are trying to do.'[9]

Whitney's letters to his father were brief and to the point: 'Dear Daddy-addy, I love you very much and want you to come back home ... Beatrice sends you a big kiss. Do make haste and come home again to your little boy Bill.'[10] Willard sent him a collection of postcards from Langres, for him to share with Biddy and Michael. They showed naïve depictions of a little American boy in uniform with a little French girl. On the back of each, Willard composed a short verse, like this one:

> In olden days the armoured knights
> Kept vigil here, and had their fights
> Between the hours of lunch and four
> And then they went to eat some more[11]

Willard completed his course at the Army Staff College in June, and joined 3rd Corps HQ, where he took responsibility for logistics. His manual on the subject was adopted by GHQ, and he was sent back to Langres to lecture on it.

Meanwhile, Whitney's busiest summer yet had begun with a visit to Roosevelt's Oyster Bay home. The former president was an entertaining host and gave his young guest some hunting knives. Whitney played with the largest of them, terrifying his mother. Next came another short trip, to the Roslyn water works. Whitney was transfixed by the machinery. 'Each engine had three big pistons', he dictated to Dorothy to forward to Willard:

> and then when the man wanted to stop it, do you know what he did? Each engine had 3 oil tanks at each side – and then the man when he wanted to stop it he turned each of these little oil taps around – and then turned two little taps off – and then he put the clutch off – and then he went to the boiler room and put the break back and forth – and then the engine stopped – and after that he turned a little wheel![12]

Whitney was given a new soldier suit to replace the one he had worn for the photographs with his father, but perhaps the uniform of a US Army Air Service pilot would have been more appropriate. He had seen a triplane bomber flying on exercise, or in his own words, 'a bomb dropping plane and it had 3 wings',[13] and he found it even more thrilling than the Roslyn water works. He and his cousin, Bobby Sandborne, collected some boxes and planks and built and painted their own biplane. They called it the Sandborne Straight and, while it may have lacked the comfort of the Miles Whitney Straight of eighteen years later, it is clear that Whitney had already become obsessed with flying.

The family returned to Southampton for their 1918 summer holiday. It suited Dorothy – being by the Atlantic made her feel closer to Willard. She told him, 'Here by this great ocean your spirit seems actual, one with mine.'[14] It suited Whitney too, for the long beach and the many children visiting it each day enabled him to conduct war games with his friends. Young Charlie Potter told his mother that, 'Whitney Straight is a good sport and afraid of nothing',[15] while Dorothy's friend Edith Bates considered him 'the manliest little boy she has ever seen'.[16] He grew stronger and braver as a swimmer, troubling Dorothy when he swam far out into the water. He was maturing too – one morning on the beach, he asked his mother if she could buy some sweets and charge them to her. 'That's a new game,'[17] she thought.

A brutal reminder of the hazards facing those serving in Europe came when news reached New York of the death of Roosevelt's youngest son, Quentin, shot down near the village of Chamery, south-east of Reims, on

14 July, Bastille Day. He had been due to marry Dorothy's niece, Flora. 'He died game – dear boy,' wrote Willard, 'but it's a bad business, this airman's game.'[18] A month later, while on leave in Normandy, Willard sent his children another of his illustrated parables. This one explained how the Vikings in their long boats had behaved like pirates before colonising the north of France, and becoming first Normans, then kings of England. 'You must understand all these things, so that you can see how wonderful it is that French and English and Americans are all together fighting the Germans who are just like the pirates of the old days.'[19]

In October, Willard was sent to the château in Senlis, 35 miles north of Paris, which served as the headquarters of Marshal Ferdinand Foch, Supreme Allied Commander. Here, he reported to Colonel Thomas Mott, the liaison officer between Foch and the Commander of the American Expeditionary Force, General John 'Black Jack' Pershing. At the very centre of communications recording the final stages of the war, Willard wrote again to 'my dear Bill' on his 6th birthday:

> You are going to have fights. I hope you will. Never fight a boy smaller than you are. Never let a bigger boy bully a little fellow. That's the sort of thing we have been fighting for in France. Remember too that as you grow older you'll think more and fight less with your fists; but you must always fight with all your heart and all your ability for the same thing that you fight for, when you are a boy, with your fists ... Just remember this on your birthday, always. For as Beatrice was born on the day that war commenced, so the war comes to an end, really, on your birthday; and if this war is to be worth the great sacrifices that it has cost, you and I and all of us must try to be worthy of the men who have died so that we might live, and we must live in the same fine spirit that has enabled them to make the supreme sacrifice. Just remember that.[20]

Four days later, Mott drove to Paris with the text of the Armistice, leaving Willard at the château in Senlis. His task was to advise Allied HQ when it had been signed, or record any changes in the text and pass these on to Mott. As he sat in the library, waiting into the early hours, he resumed the letter to Dorothy he had begun a week earlier. 'I love you everything', he wrote, using the line he and Dorothy shared with young Whitney. In the last half inch of space, at the bottom of eight pages of tiny, spidery writing, he added this: '5.40 AM Nov 11th. General Destiches has telephoned that hostilities will cease on Nov. 11 – at 11 AM ... It is Peace – Best Beloved – think what it means!'[21] Thus did Major Willard Straight of the American Expeditionary Force record the end of the First World War, and his part in it.

As to what peace meant, he was clear about the role America must play in the forthcoming negotiations. He thought it critical that Britain and France did not extract too high a price from Germany, but he was not confident that Wilson was up to the job. 'It will be a catfight,' he wrote to Dorothy:

> WW is not a leader – not for a moment – he's no more ready for peace than he was for war ... We should have made our bargain with the Allies when we first came in – or at least when we began to send troops in such large numbers. Now we will be apt to get nothing – not even the peace we fight for, but a peace which will instead of being founded on a League of Nations, have the foundation for other wars.[22]

Colonel House arrived in Paris to lead the US peace delegation. Dorothy had hosted House and his wife at Applegreen several times, and also visited their New York apartment, pressing upon him how valuable Willard could be to the negotiations. Her efforts paid off, and when Willard returned to Paris and checked into the Hotel de Crillon, House added him to his team. Having seen at first hand the persuasiveness of Dorothy across the dinner table, House also proposed that she should come to Paris. Willard decided Whitney should come too, to have memories of such a historic moment.

On the evening of 17 November Willard added a few last lines to the letter to Dorothy he had started only hours after finishing the previous one in the library in Senlis. 'Dear Beloved – are you coming – that's all I'm thinking of.' He concluded, 'And now bed – I love you everything – Yours Willard.'[23] The last words he ever wrote fell, slanting down the page. The man who had maintained an even hand through thousands of words to his family over the previous eleven months was deeply exhausted.

He rose from his bed the next morning, but returned to it later in the day with a fever. He had contracted Spanish Flu, the contagion that would claim more lives than the war itself. Colonel House also went down with it, but rallied soon enough, while Willard's condition worsened. As the week wore on, his temperature rose ever higher, and pneumonia was diagnosed.

Delirium set in, and his breathing grew increasingly laboured. He died at 1 a.m. on Sunday, 1 December, aged just 38. His only contribution to the preparations for the peace talks he was so keen to influence was to tell President Clemenceau and General Pershing when Wilson would arrive in Paris. There would indeed be another war. When the Armistice was formally agreed, in a carriage of Marshall Foch's train in the Forest of Compiègne, Foch pointedly walked out as the Germans signed it. Adolf Hitler would have the same carriage drawn to the same forest glade twenty-two years later, and walk out as the French signed their surrender.

Incidentally, Dorothy's most recent biographer has queried why the 60-year-old Colonel House recovered swiftly from his encounter with Spanish Flu while the much younger Willard succumbed to it. She asks if, after the abandonment of Roosevelt's political aspirations, Wilson's cancellation of the international loans to China and the denial of any opportunity to become a war hero, 'poor Willard died of shame?'[24] That is to misunderstand both Spanish Flu and Willard. The US Centers (sic) for Disease Control and Prevention notes of Spanish Flu, 'Mortality was high in people younger than 5 years old, 20–40 years old, and 65 years and older. The high mortality in healthy people, including those in the 20–40 year age group, was a unique feature of this pandemic.'[25] As for Willard, the Versailles peace talks were about to give this most international of Americans the chance to make a real difference on the world stage, and provide the platform from which to mount a career in politics or diplomacy. Shame was the last thing on his mind.

Back in New York, the 6-year-old boy who should have been enjoying his first Thanksgiving recess from school was instead handed the letter his father had written almost a year earlier. It read:

My dear Bill
You may never see this letter. I hope you never will. But should anything happen to me, I want you to have a word – you as the oldest – that you may have it for yourself and your blithe young sister and your brother Michael. My father died when I was seven years old, and I had no word save such as my mother gave me. She was taken, too, before I knew what she meant. I trust for your sake, and the sake of all three of you, your mother will be there to guide you. All the best in you comes from her, and the finest in you will be brought out by her. You are blessed as no

other children have been blessed in your mother. May your worship for her – for it will be with you as it is with me, reverence and real worship – guide you and lead you to treat all women with real chivalry. Save yourself and tell Michael to save himself, that you may go clean and unashamed to her who will be your wife and the mother some day of your children. Many good men don't. They may laugh at you, but they will respect you, and the respect of your fellows is worth more than their applause. Sometimes you'll get both.

You are a fine honest lad. Be honest. Be honest and frank and generous even if others tell you you are quixotic. It is better to be quixotic than the opposite. Here again be like your mother.

Be gentle and strong. Defend those who are weak. Understand and sympathise with those who are less fortunate than you are. But do not let those who try to do so mistake your gentleness for weakness. Fight if you must and if you must, fight hard and fight fair.

Make up your own mind, but respect the opinion of others. Don't think a thing right or wrong because someone tells you so. Think it out yourself guided by the advice of those whom you respect.

Watch your mother; help her; comfort her. Don't let her tire herself out. Watch over your sister; protect her.

Hold your head high, and keep your mind open. You can always learn. God bless you.

Your Father.[26]

2

After Willard

SS *Leviathan* was due to sail from Brest on 8 December, carrying the first tranche of US troops to leave France, and Colonel House made arrangements for the ship to take Willard home too. But Dorothy would not hear of it – she wanted him buried among the fallen compatriots whom he had so admired. So it was that, on 3 December, a Cadillac bore Willard's flag-draped coffin away from the Hotel de Crillon and up to the American Military Cemetery being laid out to the west of Paris in Suresnes. Uniformed soldiers slow-marched on each side of it, and friends and associates followed behind on foot. The address was given by Bishop Charles Brent, senior chaplain to the US Forces: 'His organising genius was exactly what the moment needed. We had thought of him as one of those destined and prepared to make a valuable contribution to the reconstruction of life in the new era that is at its dawn. But it had been ordered otherwise …'[1]

Cables and letters of condolence rained in on Applegreen. Among them was a letter to Whitney, postmarked 11 December, yet clearly written by his father some time earlier. Willard had sent 'My Dear Jonny Soldier-Man'[2] some postcards of Napoleon's tomb at Les Invalides in Paris. Since 1915, the French had displayed captured German aircraft and artillery there, and Willard told his son, 'Some day when the war is over I'll bring you to see all these things yourself. Be a good boy and look after Mother and Beatrice & Michael.'[3] Many of Willard's letters to his son had ended like this, exhorting him to be a brave man and look after the family while he was away. Whitney was just 6, the only one of the children who really remembered their father, and all he could do was to bottle up his own emotions and try not to be too much of a nuisance to his grieving mother. On New Year's Day 1919, a month after Willard's death, even Louisa, Dorothy's maid, could see that Whitney 'felt real bad'.⁴

A sombre mood hung over the house. Willard's possessions arrived home over Christmas, and no one could summon the will to even inform Dorothy. He may have been away for a year, but the family had spent so much time writing to him and discussing his letters to them that he had remained a central presence in their lives. The abrupt end to this correspondence created a vacuum that made their sense of loss all the sharper. The entire household fell ill. The contagion may have been called Spanish Flu, but it was in the process of wiping a dozen years off US life expectancy, and the family and staff were lucky to survive their bouts with it. Sorrow mounted on sorrow when Theodore Roosevelt died of a pulmonary embolism on 6 January, aged just 60.

Returning to school after a grief-stricken Christmas was a welcome distraction for Whitney. He had joined first grade at The Lincoln School on Park Avenue just months earlier. The Lincoln was managed by Columbia University's Teachers College, but it had been created by the General Education Board, a philanthropic organisation focused on innovative education, and established and funded by oil magnate John D. Rockefeller. The creative friction between Teachers College and the GEB over just how innovative The Lincoln could be was a recurring feature of the relationship, and something that Dorothy observed from a unique position. Utterly passionate about education, she sat on The Lincoln's Administrative Board, and on the Executive Committee and Committee on Education at Teachers College, where she was also a trustee.

The Rockefeller connection and the school's location, a block from where Whitney had been born, might have led to an exclusive student population, but that would have gone against GEB principles, and a generous range of scholarships ensured that an eclectic cross-section of the city's young boys and girls attended. As the *New York Times'* Elmer Davis discovered, 'The children of a number of multi-millionaire households are balanced by the children of coachmen and butlers, and of mechanics and store-keepers, just as the children of old New York families are balanced by children whose parents brought them over in the steerage not very long ago.'⁵

This mixed environment led young Whitney to question the whole concept of wealth, and his right to it. He announced one year that he wanted no birthday presents at all, and Dorothy told him she was proud 'to have a son who was a rebel'.[6] She credited The Lincoln with developing his independence of thought. 'In that atmosphere he can't be content to be just a rich boy. The influence is all the other way.'[7]

Whitney thrived under the 'units of work' approach practised in The Lincoln's Elementary School. One early focus was on milk – the children considered its importance to diet, and drank and cooked with it; they visited a dairy farm and a pasteurisation plant; they learned how milk was transported into the city, and how it was marketed and sold there; they maintained records of how much milk was consumed at home; and they purchased milk for the classroom, paying for it from the school bank.

The Lincoln closed for the summer recess of 1919 in mid-June, and Dorothy took her children away for their first holiday without their father. Southampton, with its memories of Whitney's swimming lessons with his father, and of Dorothy's almost telepathic connection across the ocean to Willard in France, was out of the question. They headed north almost 300 miles, to Raquette Lake in the Adirondacks. Here, Whitney was taught the rudiments of sailing, and how to fish for trout and bass. He spent large portions of each day with his mother, who felt sufficiently recovered to pick up her diary for the first time as a widow. Her entries during her time at Raquette Lake are littered with phrases like 'too heavenly'[8] and 'most perfect day'.[9] Apart from the time Whitney almost lost his fingers in a mishap with an axe, the family was enjoying a wonderful, restorative holiday together.

Yet a week later, Dorothy was making plans to sail for France with her niece Flora, having received a cable from General Pershing inviting her to Paris. The children would stay in the company of a few household staff to enjoy the mountain life, but their mother sailed from New York on 14 August. It is not clear if she understood the true purpose of Pershing's invitation. Many contemplative vigils at Willard's grave, and 'a most wonderful and happy day'[10] in Langres visiting his old house, the Staff College and the Cathedral, clearly helped her in her grieving. She also supported Flora through the trip to Quentin's grave near Chamery. But the bulk of her time in France was spent in the company of politicians, officers and architects, agreeing to help fund the completion of a military cemetery fit for heroes at Suresnes.

Dorothy had always had a strongly philanthropic nature, and she became particularly keen to pursue it in memory of Willard. She was now sole proprietor of *The New Republic*, she had commitments to numerous educational establishments and she raised funds for causes like the Women's Trade Union League. It all meant that she saw less of her children, and lost sight of how they were coping with their own grief. Throughout his young life, Whitney had grown used to spending more time with governesses and tutors than with his parents, but with Willard dead, he felt Dorothy's absences more keenly. She did not return from France until the last weekend of September. There was just time to take the children to the nearby Mineola Fair on the Saturday. Then, on the Monday, Whitney returned to school.

Dorothy may have seen less of her elder son than he would have wished, but a most unlikely source demonstrates that she had some understanding of his nature, if not his feelings. The love she and Willard had shared for each other had been so spiritual that she was genuinely surprised not to be able to feel his guiding hand from beyond the grave, and in her isolation she turned to a Maryland spiritualist known only as Mary K. The woman filled more than a dozen notebooks in large, looping handwriting, purporting to be Willard's answers to Dorothy's questions. Given that these can only have come inadvertently from Dorothy talking to Mary K about her family, the observations concerning Whitney are most revealing. When asked what the future had in store for him, the answer recorded in one of the notebooks was, 'He will have a life of great worldly interest. He will mix in the world – stand out but more as a good businessman and good fellow – a companion – he will be restless and fond of pleasure as well as work.'[11] And when asked how Whitney should be prepared for such a life, the answer proved just as prescient: 'He will not be a literary type – he will be more of a sports and businessman, so fit him for that.'[12]

On 19 April 1920, 8-year-old Whitney looked neither sporty nor business-like at New York's first big social occasion since the war. The great and the good of New York society thronged into St Bartholomew's Church on Park Avenue to see Flora marry stockbroker Roderick Tower, an old friend of Quentin's from their pilot-training days. Whitney was the only page boy, bedecked in frilly shirt, white gloves and satin trousers, and carrying a larger posy than any of the flower girls.

He was much more in his element come July, when the family first visited the house that was to be their base for the next five summers – a clifftop idyll in Woods Hole, Massachusetts, overlooking Buzzards Bay. The waters there are protected from the Atlantic by Cape Cod, but the currents ripping between the Elizabeth Islands can make for treacherous conditions – the ideal environment for young Whitney to work on his sailing skills. There was also a summer camp for him to enjoy, run by the nearby Oceanographic Institute. This was just as well, for Dorothy spent much of the holiday sorting through Willard's papers and meeting with Herbert Croly of *The New Republic*. He was going to write Willard's biography, and Dorothy would be closely involved.

When Whitney returned to The Lincoln at the end of summer, he found to his delight that his passion for boats and the water made him the ideal pupil for his third-grade teacher, Nell Curtis. The curriculum she had chosen was based on her love of the Hudson River, and she led the twenty boys and girls in her charge through its piers, boatyards and docks, and taught them about the vessels plying the river and how they were built. In class, she used a reflectoscope, an early form of projector, to show the children artists' impressions of the Hudson a century and two centuries earlier. She took them to libraries and galleries to learn about ancient Egypt, and the millennia of traffic on the Nile, and oversaw their creation of a frieze that ran round the classroom, charting the development of the boat.

A pattern emerged in Whitney's life. Dorothy absorbed herself with her causes and committees, and based the family in the city each semester, Applegreen at the weekends and at Christmas, and Woods Hole for the summer. Biddy joined The Lincoln, then Michael. 'Never let a bigger boy bully a little fellow',[13] Whitney's father had taught him, and now he put the advice into practice – older boys waiting for Michael found Whitney waiting for them.

At Applegreen, he loved taking his brother and sister for a ride around the lawn in his Studebaker – not a car, but a goat-drawn carriage. Another vehicle he was fond of was the Marmon convertible Dorothy bought for his tutor, Albert Crystal. Whitney persuaded him to take the children out on to the Long Island Motor Parkway, leaving them gasping for breath at a joyous 60mph. Crystal also fed Whitney's love of aviation, taking him regularly on the short drive from Applegreen to Roosevelt Field. The airfield had been used for training purposes during the war, and was renamed in honour of Quentin in 1919. In 1927, Charles Lindbergh would take off from there in his *Spirit of St Louis*, on the first successful transatlantic solo flight, but for Whitney and Michael, Roosevelt Field was the place where they could marvel at the pilots giving acrobatic joyrides for a dollar. The hangars surrounding the field were full of Curtis JN-4 'Jenny' biplanes, now surplus to military requirements and the prized possessions of young men taking up flying as a pastime. Crystal would lift Whitney up into a cockpit so he could wiggle the control stick, stretch down to operate the rudder, and dream of being an aviator. 'For Mr Crystal and me,' recalled Michael many years later, 'those hours were a diversion. For Whitney they were a life unfolding.'[14]

On Saturday, 2 July 1921, while most of the country was fixated on the million-dollar prize fight between Jack Dempsey and Georges Carpentier, all seemed normal at Applegreen. The Lincoln had broken up for the summer, the children were looking forward to returning to Woods Hole, and Dorothy had another round of guests to entertain. What was unusual was that one of them agreed to Whitney's invitation to participate in an apple fight, then led Dorothy and the children on a bird's nest expedition. The following morning, the man followed Whitney down to the poultry shed and patiently explained to the 10-year-old why a bird could grow so much when part of its body was removed. He pointed out how the combs and spurs on a cockerel distinguished it from a pullet. Whitney wanted to know why the cockerels were to be put into the breeding pens, and the man was just explaining why this would ensure the eggs would hatch when Whitney's governess, Mme Colas, arrived and the conversation came to a halt. By the time Whitney and the man had burned their fingers on the Fourth of July fireworks they set off the next evening, Whitney had made a friend, if not for life, then at least for some considerable time.

Leonard Knight Elmhirst, or Jerry as the family would come to know him, was born in June 1893, and raised in the village of Laxton, in Yorkshire, England. He graduated with an MA in history from Trinity College Cambridge, and worked briefly for a missionary in India. In advance of being demobbed from the British army in 1919, he took a course in agriculture, and decided to study the subject in more depth in the US. A shipping strike in England meant he arrived late at Willard's old university, Cornell, but within a day he had arranged a tuition grant, a course in agricultural science, and accommodation at a club for overseas students called the Cosmopolitan. There, he ate for free and received an extra pumpkin pie a week in return for working in the kitchens early each morning. The other club members so respected Jerry's determination that in his second semester they elected him president, a role that brought with it an onerous responsibility. The Cosmopolitan owed creditors $80,000, and its insolvency would cause acute embarrassment for the Cornell lecturers keeping it afloat with promissory notes. As president, it fell to Jerry to avoid this at all costs, and he was advised there was only one person in the country who could help him – Dorothy.

In preparing assiduously for his audience with her, he learned that Willard had himself tried to help the Cosmopolitan during his undergraduate days, and had left provision in his will for anything that would make Cornell 'a more human place'.[15] When he met her, Jerry was canny enough not to ask her outright for financial support, as so many others did. He merely requested that she visit the university. During her trip, he went off to his lectures and left her with Cornell's Professor of History, George Burr, an old friend of Willard's. Jerry confined himself simply to escorting Dorothy back to Ithaca station. It was only upon running back up the hill to Burr that he learned she had agreed not only to save the Cosmopolitan Club but, in memory of Willard, and to help make Cornell a more human place, she would fund the construction of a union building too.

After the Applegreen weekend, Jerry took stock. Dorothy had sent him a Corona typewriter in a leather case stamped with his initials, so that he could keep her informed of developments with the building. She had also sent him money, and agreed to provide him with financial support for an ambitious project developing a school and farm in the Indian state of West Bengal. 'I am sorely puzzled,' he mused, 'to know how far Mrs Straight is ready to carry this developing relationship ... My thought and mind goes out to her across all barriers with an unbounded love, whilst my other and lower self, on the perpetual lookout for loot, metallic or fleshly, blunders along in the background. What will come of it all?'[16] He concluded he would invite her back to Cornell.

Dorothy interrupted another Woods Hole holiday to make the trip. Productive meetings about the union building filled the morning – it would be designed by Willard's old architect friend, Bill Delano – and in the afternoon Jerry took her for a picnic in Enfield Glen. It poured with rain, but she was impressed by the tent he rigged up for her with his old army rug, and it was not until 11 p.m. that she caught the train back to New York. Reunited the next day with her children, Whitney suggested she invite Jerry to join them in Woods Hole. By the end of those few days, when she left Jerry at Boston Station, bound for Montreal on his way to India, the parting was an emotional one. She thought he was leaving for good, while Jerry thought precisely the opposite, writing that he wanted to adopt her as his 'mother and sister and everything else'.[17]

As he waited aboard SS *Victoria* to sail from Montreal, Jerry sent a six-page letter to Whitney. 'I want to thank you very much for all the good times you gave me at Woods Hole. Try and think of the happiest few days you ever spent and then you'll realise a little of what I felt, the boating and bathing and all the rest of it. You were a very fine host.'[18] He thanked Whitney for his leaving present – a piece of chewing gum – and concluded, 'Will you say goodbye once more to Mother for me, and take care of her with your life.'[19] Three years after his father's death, someone else was now telling him to be a brave man for his mother.

Jerry's first proposal of marriage to Dorothy arrived from India a few months later, in January 1922. She rejected it outright, and sent out to him a social worker named Gretchen Green, whom she clearly hoped would do more than set up a social centre for the farm and school Jerry was developing. But Miss Green lacked the metallic and fleshly loot he knew lay elsewhere, and he returned to the more considered approach he had adopted when first seeking Dorothy's help over the Cosmopolitan. It was to be a very different kind of long-distance campaign than the one pursued by the romantic Willard. In a series of letters from the autumn of 1922 to the spring of the following year, what began as the sketch of an idea from Gretchen became an instruction from Gretchen and then Dorothy's plan – that she and the children should get away to England for a time. The suggestion was always someone else's, but the idea that Jerry should join them there, or even accompany them, was always his. In May, he wrote for the first time of replicating in England the kind of school he was running in India – but the staff would need to be American because they had such a lead over British thinking on education.

Dorothy invited Jerry back to Woods Hole that summer, a spell she described afterwards as 'that little span of nineteen days which brought me perfect harmony'.[20] She spent much of the next year gravely ill with a thyroid condition, but by the summer of 1924 she found 'the English experiment'[21] much on her mind. She was particularly keen that Jerry should meet Satis Coleman and study her methods. Coleman was The Lincoln's music teacher, and tutored Whitney and Michael outside school. Her approach was to teach young children music on instruments they had made. In fourth grade, Whitney made his own drum and decorated it in artwork inspired by the Native American designs he had seen on a trip to the Metropolitan Museum of Art. She directed older children to make xylophones and even fiddles. Her methods would become adopted widely, and her book, *Creative Music for Children*, became the definitive work on the subject.

That summer marked a rite of passage for Whitney, now rising 12. He spent part of it on his own, at a summer camp in Providence, Rhode Island, sailing and fishing. When Dorothy drove the 70 or so miles from Woods Hole to collect him, he was a changed boy. He was filthy, spoke 'practically a new language',[22] and had developed strong opinions on how children should be raised: 'If I had children I certainly wouldn't have them brought up by French governesses and English gardeners – I'd have my children brought up by a farmer.'[23]

That never came to pass, but he was about to acquire a stepfather with a degree in agriculture. Jerry proposed marriage and the English experiment again. Dorothy sought the agreement of her children, and they were in favour, Whitney explaining that Jerry and Albert Crystal were his best friends. Upon getting the all-clear from her doctor that she was well enough to bear Jerry's children, Dorothy agreed to marriage and England. They were married on the Applegreen lawn on 3 April 1925. She was 38, he 31. After honeymooning off the Florida Keys in her brother Payne's yacht, they returned briefly to Applegreen to see the children, then sailed for England to visit the place Jerry had chosen for the English experiment.

A month before the wedding, he had visited England, equipping himself with a new car, a driving licence, and membership of the Royal Automobile Club. He and his sister Irene took all day to travel the 175 miles south-west from London to Exeter, the county town of Devon. The next morning, he found that the first property on the list provided to him by estate agents Knight Frank & Rutley had little to recommend it, and drove on to the second. He would look no further. Dartington Hall lay in the wooded valley of the River Dart, some 10 miles inland from Dartmouth. Built in the late fourteenth century for John Holland, Earl of Huntingdon and half-brother to King Richard II, it had been in the continuous ownership of the Champernowne family for more than 350 years, but the latest generation had moved out four years earlier and the estate was in considerable disrepair. Jerry had a more immediate problem: he could not locate the entrance.

Finally we crept along a little cutting and came to a thatched lodge and gate with a bridge over a bubbling brooklet – in we went and up and down wonderful hills till we pulled up in a veritable fairy land – in winter too – what it would be like in spring or summer or autumn I dare not imagine. I wanted to kneel and worship the beauty of it all, and every fresh vista only seemed the more to recommend the handiwork of nature joined with the reverent hand of generations of men … I'm sorry, I've dreamt of it ever since as a fit home for you and the children and I've pictured you there – the squire's wife, and I've found local possibilities of all kinds and part of my heart remains there. But I've done nothing definite yet – merely paved the way so that at a moment's notice we can set the wheels in motion – yes – and there's good sailing within a mile and a half, sea bathing and boating down at Dartmouth and a mile of good fishing and wonderful river below – and I think the owner's so hard up and so hopeless of getting an offer that half the original offer will do.[24]

On first seeing Dartington, Dorothy found it 'too heavenly'[25] but thought the 'interiors difficult!'[26] – little wonder, since few had roofs over them, and there was no electricity. She and Jerry were obliged to base themselves first in the Seymour Hotel in nearby Totnes, and then in a Victorian house there named Elmsleigh. The Hall would take so long to renovate that when they first moved on to the estate, it was to live in the Old Parsonage, which they acquired from the Church. The purchase of Dartington was eventually concluded in August for £30,000. To put this in context, at the time Dorothy was worth some $25 million.

She headed back to the US in October, and was welcomed warmly by her children. She was pregnant, and they nicknamed her bump Chris, though Whitney was keen that the child be named Dick or Robert if it were a boy, and threatened to write to Jerry on the matter. Biddy was insistent that it be a girl, and she would prevail – Ruth Elmhirst would be born in London the following March. Dorothy made a point of having supper with her children each evening after school, and lunch and supper with them at Applegreen during the weekends. A houseful of boys helped Whitney celebrate his 13th birthday, though Biddy beat the lot of them to win the treasure hunt that weaved round Applegreen's gardens. The following weekend, an old friend came to stay, and Dorothy explained to Whitney that she would be dining with her. She was stunned by his reaction:

> 'You aren't going to have supper with us?' he exclaimed – and I saw a look on his face that was like a flash of lightning to me. Children are so difficult to fathom – perhaps they have no way of understanding themselves. They can be lonely and heart-sick and miserable without in the least knowing why – and without being able to express it to anyone else.[27]

Of course, the truth is that Whitney knew exactly how lonely, heart-sick and miserable he had been for much of the past seven years, but he had chosen not to express it directly to his mother. Dorothy was still more surprised after discussing the matter with her secretary, Anna Bogue:

> She feels that all this last summer he was really at heart very lonely. He seems to feel our absence rather keenly – and was apparently continually asking Miss Bogue when we were returning ... This morning he said to me again, 'When does Jerry sail?' There is something quite touching about it all, because outwardly he appears so fully occupied with the immediate interests of life which apparently absorb him.[28]

Whitney had grown adept at hiding his feelings – the man who ran the summer camp could not understand why such an apparently confident and sociable boy wanted to spend every afternoon on his own in a boat – and Dorothy was probably no worse a parent than any in her milieu. At least this episode made her consider whether she and Jerry should take Whitney with them when they headed back to Dartington after Christmas – without, apparently, extending the idea to Biddy and Michael. But these years left a mark on Whitney. He was a grown man when he suddenly raged at Dorothy for giving his teddy bear to his cousin Bobby when they were children, explaining with contempt that buying him another was not the answer.

Jerry finally re-joined the family in December. He and Dorothy went to Cornell for the formal dedication of Willard Straight Hall, then returned to Applegreen to celebrate Christmas with the children. Three days later, they sailed for England – without Whitney. He would spend another five months at The Lincoln, where at least Otis Caldwell, the school's founding director, could see that he and Biddy were 'outstanding leaders. You should see them handling groups of children.'[29]

It was not until the following May that Whitney joined Dorothy and Jerry at Dartington, a month ahead of his sister and brother. Dorothy welcomed him, exclaiming, 'Whitney is now a grown man!',[30] then left with Jerry to go shopping for furniture.

3

Dartington

Whitney enjoyed his first summer at Dartington. He swam and fished for trout in the Dart, he attended the ten-day scout camp held in fields by the river for the boys who would be joining the new school in September and he was particularly drawn to the estate's private roads. His first attempts at negotiating them at speed were in a chair to which he fitted wheels, and when this became too slow for him, he asked Dorothy and Jerry for a motorbike. They agreed to put up half the money, but he would have to earn the other half. Bricklayers were helping to renovate the old courtyard, and Whitney went to work alongside them. His reward for building a retaining wall was a 250cc Dunelt, and he roared happily round the estate on it.

The objectives of Dartington Hall School were set out boldly in the opening pages of its *Outline of an Educational Experiment*:

> This school is for adventure … nowhere does such a promising field exist as in the hearts of children, who, with their fresh powers of intelligence, invention, imagination and enterprise, embrace in themselves all the elements necessary for adventurous living. It is our aim to provide an environment in which children can exercise these powers, both as individuals and as members of a group, so that education and adventure may be hardly distinguishable.[1]

The prospectus made clear that the school, 'like all experiments must develop naturally. Its teaching methods, therefore, will be subject to modification, and in the light of experience may even have to be radically altered'.[2] Central to those methods were the projects that would bridge school and estate, and Jerry's hand was clearly at work here, for poultry farming was given as an example. The chicken farm would be run by children, or juniors as they were to be called, just as the teachers and estate staff would be called seniors. Under the guidance of a poultry expert, the juniors would take responsibility for cleaning, feeding and breeding. They would sell their produce to the kitchen at local market rates and keep accounts for their enterprise. Similar projects would be run by juniors in many of the departments being set up at Dartington, and this would necessitate a novel approach to school holidays. With livestock, gardens and fields to attend to, juniors could not all leave school at the same time. Rather, each would get two months off a year, including either Christmas Day or New Year's Day, plus camping trips, to be fitted around their projects and the wishes of their parents.

The prospectus also highlighted the eclectic mix of Dartington Hall School's initial team of seniors. Jerry headed the list, citing his Cambridge MA and Cornell BSc alongside his former position as 'Director of the Institute of Rural Reconstruction, Visca Bhasrati, Bengal',[3] where he had first formulated his plans for 'the English experiment'.[4] Wyatt Rawson was an old friend of Jerry's from Cambridge. Recorded alongside his Trinity College BA was his time as an instructor at Brown University, Rhode Island, when Jerry had been at Cornell and the two men had become reacquainted. Rawson had left his role as Headmaster of the Grange School in Hertfordshire to join Dartington, while Marjorie Wise had most recently taught at Clapham High School in London. A graduate of New York's Columbia University, she had been recommended to Dorothy by a Teachers College lecturer. Less academic credentials were provided for the fourth member of the teaching staff. He had been a prize cadet at what was then known as the Royal Military College in Sandhurst, and a lieutenant in the 3rd Battalion of the York and Lancaster Regiment. Most recently, he had been a 'Short Course Student'[5] at Cornell. He was Jerry's brother, Vic.

On Monday, 11 September 1926, all four attended the first morning of a five-day conference called to establish how the school would function. The forum was chaired by Professor Eduard Lindeman. He was based at the New School of Social Work, another New York educational establishment supported by Dorothy. His seminal work, *The Meaning of Adult Education*, would be published this same year. Seven others were in attendance. Maude Rigden had cared for Dorothy at the time of Ruth's birth, and was to be school matron. Accountant and secretary Douglas 'Doc' Watson would commence each school day at 7 a.m. with a sharp blast on his whistle and a yell of 'Rise and shine!' Head Gardener P.W. Woods joined the men brought in to set up the poultry unit, dairy farm and apple orchard and cider press. Dorothy, the woman paying for it all, completed the line-up.

The conference opened with Jerry seeking to define the line between estate and school. He saw them as being clearly separate at the outset, yet no one working on the estate was to think, 'The school is not my job.'[6] Lindeman raised the image of 'friends educating each other'.[7] Rawson spoke of 'drawing children into their own education, allowing them to choose subjects and plan projects.[8] When Lindeman asked what place democracy should have, Jerry defined it as doing without a headmaster. The reactions were telling. Rawson argued 'no school ever thus succeeded'[9] and Wise thought it would be a 'slower way of doing things',[10] but Jerry insisted that 'common combined intelligence'[11] would outweigh the 'authority of one'.[12] Thus were the seeds sown that would cause 'the English experiment' to stall within two years. Dorothy had barely spoken; Jerry had failed to justify his vision of a democratic school; Rawson and Wise would find it impossible, therefore, to articulate or maintain it; and the relationship between school and estate would rarely be easy.

The school opened on Friday, 26 September 1926, when Whitney – seven weeks short of his 14th birthday – Biddy, Michael and the son of the man planting Dartington's apple orchard, Oliver Morel, met the five juniors Rawson had collected from Totnes Station: Louis Heidinger, Keith and Mary Ponsford, Michael Preston and Lorna Nixon. After a game of football and tea, they gathered in the library of the Old Parsonage. Rawson explained how an advisor from among the teaching staff would help each of them devise a programme covering their academic and project work, and that the objective of this first meeting was for them to select their advisors. The girls all chose Wise, but Rawson offered the boys the option to vote on paper – the Equal Franchise Act still lay twenty-one months away – and their results were only made known the next day, when the juniors met to choose their projects.

At this session, when it was announced that Whitney had voted for Jerry, he was told that he would be getting Rawson, as his stepfather had other priorities to attend to for a month. When, inspired by the teaching of Nell Curtis at The Lincoln, Whitney informed the group that for his first project he wanted to build a boat, Jerry replied that lack of equipment made this impossible. Dorothy considered it 'a thoughtless request'[13] and watched him leave the room with tears in his eyes. The school was not yet two days old, and its oldest junior had not been granted his choice of advisor or project, or permitted to run his own learning. When Michael Preston was elected chairman of juniors' meetings and Oliver Morel secretary, Whitney made his first criticism of the experiment: 'We are having too many meetings.'[14] The following evening, another New York associate of Dorothy's, Ruth Morgan, gave a talk about the League of Nations. Michael asked what language was spoken there and Biddy wanted to know where the Ruhr was, but Whitney, bored and frustrated, lay on the floor throughout Morgan's talk with his back to her.

His confidence collapsed over the following week. After Rawson had given him some initial language and music tests, Whitney ran to Dorothy, again on the verge of tears. He was embarrassed that he could remember so little French and could no longer play an instrument. Worse, he was concerned that workmen may have overheard his discomfort. He forgot his party trick at a gathering that evening and Biddy shrieked at him that he was a fool. When Rawson took him to nearby Torquay to find cello and violin teachers, he was given four simple tasks and forgot to attend to any of them. It took him a week to grasp that field hockey was a team game.

The tide only turned when Whitney insisted that his first project would indeed be the construction of a boat. As Mr Harris, one of the carpenters mentoring him, noted, 'he has got some grit'.[15] It was a big undertaking, and took until the spring to complete. Dorothy recognised what was driving his zest and commitment – he could not wait to take his boat out on the Dart. Only in one respect did he take a short cut: he ignored Harris' advice to use movable boards, and screwed them directly into the ribs of the boat. Nevertheless, another of the estate carpenters, Mr Gill, told Dorothy that Whitney had done a very capable job.

Jerry acted as advisor on another of Whitney's early projects – maintaining and operating the generator that provided electricity to the Hall. He carried out his responsibilities diligently and effectively, but he found it less easy to write up his findings. What finally emerged was a twenty-page report, 'How to run a twenty-four horsepower oil engine'. Two versions of Whitney's diagram demonstrating the internals and flows of the engine survive. The first is a messy sketch with little detail and a large ink blot. The second is a much smarter, more detailed affair, with handwriting far neater and more decipherable than Whitney would ever employ in the diaries he kept for most of his adult life. Yet, even here, the legend describing the engine's internals, which runs from A to M, skips D and I. The twenty pages of text have not survived, but one can almost see Jerry's trim moustache bristling when he recorded that they were used 'as a training in style, in handwriting, in neatness and especially in the readiness to repeat work until something like perfection has been achieved.'[16]

Whitney's first Dartington Hall School report bears witness to the unique nature of his curriculum. He was slow in algebra but keen to grasp its principles, and his French was improving. He had cleaned and oiled the estate cars, and taken apart and reassembled a concrete mixer, but he did not allow sufficient time to put away his tools before the bell rang, and he had failed to keep accounts for the maintenance of his motorbike, or for his tobacco store, though he had at least taken out the appropriate government licence to run it!

January 1927 saw a welcome addition to the school staff. Rawson was a regular customer at A.H. Mayhew's bookshop on London's Charing Cross Road. So was the father of 23-year-old John Wales, who had received a classical education and (something of which Jerry surely approved) a diploma in agriculture. When Mayhew learned where Rawson was working, he arranged for him to meet Wales, and soon the young man had been appointed temporary librarian at Dartington. He was swiftly promoted to full-time teacher and school administrator, and Whitney became so fond of him that he called him 'Pop', as would generations of Dartington juniors to come.

Through that first academic year, a way of working evolved, and seniors and juniors jointly developed a series of rules aimed primarily at keeping them all safe. 'Red dangers' included pillion riding on public roads, and the areas that could only be visited with a senior, such as the sawmill, smithy, quarries and reservoirs. 'Pink dangers' could 'easily be avoided by the use of common sense'[17] and included inappropriate use of pickaxes, saws and knives, and the provocation of bulls and horses. Guns could be kept by any junior of 13 or over, and younger children could use them in the company of anyone above that age. There was to be no shooting within 200 yards of a building, but sparrows, rooks, rabbits, pigeons, rats, partridges and pheasants were all considered fair game.

The rules regarding swimming and boating also graded juniors. To be classified as a senior swimmer, one had to be capable of swimming 100 yards upstream, and carrying Biddy across the river. Only Whitney held this status to begin with, so unless a senior was in attendance, all swimming and boating activities by juniors were dependent on his presence. He could also penalise anyone breaking the rules – a first offence meant a week's ban from swimming, a second incurred a suspension of two weeks, and a third led to no swimming for a month. It was a considerable responsibility to give to a 14-year-old, and an indication of just how important Whitney was to the experiment.

Further evidence of this lies in the report the local doctor, S.R. Williams, made on the school shortly after Whitney left. After five pages of harrumphing about the children's 'chronic mental fatigue'[18] brought on by 'the hourly effort of making decisions about all sorts of things which might be decided for them',[19] Williams concluded by referring to the contributions made to the school by Whitney and by the matron, Maud Rigden. 'The sense of responsibility shown by Whitney during the first year or so was quite remarkable and the admirable way he set the pace beyond praise. The school owes much to these two.'[20]

The swimming rules made no mention of what was to be worn in the river, and in fact juniors were encouraged to swim naked, and to take showers together, on the grounds that it was perfectly natural, and reduced rather than encouraged furtive curiosity. It was all part of a liberal approach to sex education, and yet the usual Dartington contradictions applied. Dorothy was quite happy to talk frankly about any subject in her regular Question Club, including periods, birth control and prostitution. The younger the questioner, the better: 'It means that we won't have to undo misconceptions which I often find myself doing with the boys and girls of 10 and 11.'[21] Yet when Jerry found that the juniors had formed Kissing Club and were going off into the woods to practise, he called them together and told them he had not kissed Dorothy until he had married her.

During the spring of 1927, six of the elder boys were granted a break from their projects for the same two weeks. Whitney was among them, and Pop Wales led them off on a walking holiday in Normandy, armed with £40 in cash from Jerry. The group regularly marched 20 miles a day in glorious weather, and all went well until they reached Caen, and Whitney was struck down with abdominal pains. Wales thought it was appendicitis, and, with no knowledge of the French language and dwindling funds, was a worried man. But Whitney perked back up as quickly as he had fallen ill, and the group made it back across to Southampton and home to Dartington safe and sound, with one shilling and sixpence left between them.

The English experiment was working sufficiently well for Dorothy to sell the old family home on Fifth Avenue, yet she and Jerry recognised that an external review was warranted. They turned back to New York for this, and specifically to Dr Frederick Bonser of Teachers College. His recent paper, *Curriculum-Making in Laboratory or Experimental Schools*, made him the ideal person to consider Dartington's progress. It has previously been understood that Bonser brought his wife with him, but this is not so. She preferred not to make two Atlantic crossings in quick succession, and Bonser was accompanied on the trip by their daughter Virginia, who herself had experience of teaching and teacher training in US country schools. Their visit took place through the first three weeks of June 1928.

The Bonser Report, as it became known, cannot have made happy reading for Dartington's founders. Even though there were still only seventeen children in the school, the Bonsers felt there were too few teachers, and even fewer who understood how to apply Dorothy and Jerry's educational philosophy. The estate departments could not hope to meet the project needs of the younger children, and older children were suffering because no one was managing the link between school and estate: 'a third person who can see clearly in both directions is needed.'[22] The Bonsers drew damning conclusions about the poor punctuality endemic in the school. Simply inserting intervals between work periods would help address this, but the absence of any admonishment for being late meant children felt no shame in their tardiness. The abandonment of projects through boredom or unforeseen challenges was criticised too. The report posed the question some juniors' parents were asking: 'Are the children working up to their capacity for achieving reasonable normal mental growth, or are they learning habits of dawdling or wasting time?'[23]

Frederick and Virginia Bonser had recorded the results of the confusion and lack of leadership displayed in five days of debate under the chairmanship of Professor Lindeman two years earlier. The Dartington experiment as originally conceived by its founders was foundering. Rawson and Wise left within months, yet the radical alterations permitted by the school's first prospectus would not be implemented for another three years. For now, Pop Wales and Vic Elmhirst would be in charge, there would be a new teacher dedicated to the younger juniors, and more staff for the older ones, including a strong science teacher, and 'a young girl who will teach dancing, and help in the organising of folk activities'.[24]

Another change concerned the age of juniors arriving at Dartington. This most liberal of establishments was attracting more than its fair share of problematic children who had been expelled from schools elsewhere. The increasing tension between a school that encouraged mixed, naked swimming and an estate trying to generate a profit meant that estate staff sent their children elsewhere, and this only increased the proportion of difficult children at Dartington. Better, thought Wales, to recruit only younger children, in the hope that they could more easily be acclimatised to Dartington ways. This may have made sense for the school, but it left Whitney, who back in New York had counted his future stepfather and his tutor as his closest friends, still devoid of company his own age.

Still, he knuckled down and, now in his third year, was doing well in most of his academic work. In English, he had been impressed by André Maurois' fictionalised account of the life of Shelley, *Ariel*, and could recite Shelley's poetry. Now he was reading Byron and telling his new English teacher, Mr Gibbs, what to read. Gibbs also took him for French, and was impressed by the breadth of his vocabulary. Wales thought Whitney had started the new year 'splendidly'[25] and was delighted by the pride and pleasure he took in structuring his time, consistently spending about 21 hours a week on classwork, and between fifteen and eighteen on projects. He had set aside an afternoon a week to work in the garage, but since he now knew more about cars and engines than any of the estate mechanics, he focused instead on servicing his growing collection of motorbikes. One of these was an old Triumph with a sidecar, and Whitney persuaded office boy Roy Bolt to become a regular passenger. His ballast enabled Whitney to set even quicker times up and down Dartington's lower drive. Eventually, on the bend outside the garden superintendent's garage, the sidecar cried enough, parted company with the bike and sent Roy careering through a hedge. He was unhurt, but he declined further offers of rides from the aspiring racer.

As the autumn of 1928 progressed, Whitney's work improved to the point that Wales considered him 'exceedingly satisfactory all round'.[26] He had researched his essay on 'The History of Aviation' thoroughly, and had done such a good job of writing it that it was to be published in the school magazine. While most of his reading was on aircraft and engineering, he had also tackled Julian Huxley's *Essays of a Biologist* and Will Durant's *Story of Philosophy*. He was more than proficient on clarinet, saxophone, trombone and trumpet, and was running his own jazz band, made up of people from nearby Totnes. He was thinking of the future too, and considering a degree at Harvard or Yale. Another sign of his growing maturity, as he approached his 16th birthday, was the way in which he was beginning to act as a fulcrum between seniors and juniors. This had been prompted by his concerns about school discipline. He told Wales and Vic Elmhirst that the only answer was compulsion on the part of the seniors to oblige the juniors to behave better, but they encouraged him over the course of two meetings to support the concept of discipline by the group. Whitney went away and met with Biddy, Michael and three other juniors, and they concluded that they should act as representatives of 'public opinion'. They would run a weekly meeting with all the juniors, to discuss and agree upon what behaviour was and was not acceptable. Wales was most impressed: 'Without his help it is doubtful whether Vic and myself could have achieved what we desired in making the juniors see the necessity for self-discipline.'[27]

Wales' main concern for Whitney at this stage – aside from his consistently poor maths and the absence of science that might threaten him getting into Harvard or Yale – was that he was still only 15 years old. In the way he took full responsibility for planning and undertaking his academic and project work, he was behaving more like a university student than a schoolboy, yet his confidence was easily dented, and when he encountered problems he had a tendency to be fiercely critical, either of himself or those around him. Wyatt Rawson's parting gift to Dartington had been a frank report on each of its juniors. He admitted being impressed by Whitney's transition 'from a town life where he could do pretty well as he pleased and was toadied to by nearly everyone he came in contact with, to the country life of Dartington and a complete lack of position'.[28] Rawson was the first person to note that Whitney 'is unconsciously quite as ready to regard himself as English as he is to think of himself as American'.[29] His conclusion was particularly prescient: 'A brilliant and precious boy on one side of his character, but he will always find it difficult to unify his impulses.'[30]

But Whitney's impulses were about to find the perfect outlet. The boy whose favourite pastime in the US had been to watch the aerobatics over Roosevelt Field learned that an aerodrome had opened just 20 miles from Dartington. Bill Parkhouse had flown with the Royal Navy Air Service during the war, and was now a qualified air instructor. He ran a successful Fiat car dealership and repair shop in his hometown of Teignmouth and was keen to extend the business into aviation. He took a lease out on 80 acres of moorland some 3 miles inland from Teignmouth and almost 800ft above sea level. He installed a petrol pump, built a hangar for his Avro Avian biplane and declared Haldon Aerodrome open for business.

Parkhouse later recalled he first met Whitney one Saturday afternoon, but his logbook reveals he first flew the aspiring aviator on Wednesday, 17 April 1929:

> A young lad arrived on a rather old motorcycle and with a breathless enquiry asked if I taught people to fly, followed more anxiously by a question as to how much I charged. Being told, a searching of pockets produced about 20 shillings, all of which was thrust into my hand with a request to let him stay up as long as I could and in any case 'Mother would pay any extra.' His first trip in the air took us over Dartington Hall – his home.[31]

That same day, Parkhouse received an invitation to Dartington, to agree with Dorothy and Jerry the incorporation of twice-weekly flying lessons at Haldon Aerodrome into Whitney's syllabus.

Parkhouse called him 'my most apt pupil, with a most amazing knowledge of all aircraft matters',[32] and within a couple of months Jerry asked Parkhouse to quote for an aircraft that Whitney could call his own. Discussions initially focused on a new de Havilland Moth with a coupé top and cockpit heating – Whitney would turn comfort in the air to commercial gain in the years ahead – but eventually it was agreed that Parkhouse would sell his own Avian. Whitney was familiar with it, Parkhouse had owned it since new and at £480 it was more than a third cheaper than the Moth. The transaction was completed shortly before Dartington Hall School began its fourth year, and the family had returned from a summer break back at Applegreen. While away, Whitney 'added about 20 solo hours in his logbook, flying anything he could persuade anyone to let him try'.[33]

Considerably less money was spent on Whitney's first car. He acquired a battered old Model T Ford for £10, painted it yellow and called it the *Yellow Peril*. The car had only one seat, no roof, and there was no glass in the windscreen frame – just a large brass bell hanging from it. The *Yellow Peril* was not as fast as Whitney's motorbikes, but it was the most popular vehicle on the estate as far as the juniors were concerned. After games of hockey in a field down by the woods, all the players would clamber aboard for Whitney to drive them backwards at speed up the hill to the Hall. Reverse gear had more torque on the *Yellow Peril* than any of its forward gears, and Whitney driving backwards up hills became a common sight.

Polly Hunter was a recent arrival at Dartington, and in later life recalled that the Dart ran flat and shallow through the summer of 1929, presenting Whitney with a new way of taking the juniors swimming. Naked, they would pile on board the *Yellow Peril* for him to drive them at speed down the field and straight into the river. She also remembered an evening when she was woken by the sound of the car's bell, and she opened the window to see Whitney and his chums racing round a field. A scandalised matron came in and put Polly back to bed, 'but the memory of that whooping, swooping car in the growing dusk has never left me'.[34] A much younger Dartington resident may also have been woken by Whitney's antics. Bill Elmhirst, the youngest of Dorothy's five children, had been born in February.

One day that summer, in contravention of Wales' wish to bring only younger children into the school, a senior collected a 14-year-old boy from Totnes Station and asked Whitney to show him round. Whitney told him to climb aboard the *Yellow Peril* and off they set. In old age, the visitor retained a very clear memory of the tour:

> He went all over the place and we'd go down in the fields and then we'd go up the steep hills in reverse ... I was very impressed with this boy ... And I thought, 'God, I might be able to have a *car* here.' What a wonderful school it might be. So I said sort of 'Yes' immediately, as it were, when I was interviewed – of course I'd like to come there.[35]

The visitor was Michael Young. Upon joining the school, he was virtually adopted by Dorothy and Jerry and became Dartington's most famous son. The manifesto he drafted helped sweep the Labour Party into power in 1945, and he was the architect of the Consumers' Association, *Which?*

magazine and the Open University. When he was made a life peer in 1978, he took the title Lord Young of Dartington.

On 13 November, just a week after his 17th birthday, Whitney went up to Haldon Aerodrome to qualify for his Pilot's 'A' Licence. The Royal Aero Club issued him with certificate number 8892, and it can safely be assumed that at this point he was the youngest qualified pilot in the country. Within days, he very nearly became Britain's youngest dead pilot. He was flying back to Haldon from London, making slow progress as an Atlantic low drove strong crosswinds in from the south. Running out of daylight, he found a suitable field to put down in and landed well enough, but as he slowed the Avian he saw he was rapidly approaching a barbed wire fence. He opened the throttle and gained enough lift to hop over it, but now he had too little space in which to stop, and he collided heavily with the bank at the far end of the field. Mercifully, Whitney was uninjured. Parkhouse told him he had done well to land in such a spot at all, patched the Avian up and took it back in part-exchange for a new de Havilland Moth, complete with blue fuselage and gold wings. The Moth was just the first of Whitney's aircraft to bear a flamboyant colour scheme, but his 17th birthday present, a four-door Alvis Silver Eagle tourer, established a preference for black cars that would stretch throughout his racing career and beyond.

Whitney regularly gave aerobatic displays over Dartington, which his former sidecar passenger, Roy Bolt, recalled with affection decades later.

> When he appeared, the cry would go up, 'Whitney's over.' Everybody downed tools or pens and assembled on the lawn. All faces turned towards the sky, and watched the display for thirty minutes or so. One of his favourite stunts was to fly between the two trees near the summerhouse. It seemed impossible that a plane could pass between them.[36]

Another involved him identifying Dorothy on the ground and diving directly at her.

By the time Whitney collected his new aircraft, Dorothy and Jerry had left Dartington on a three-month tour of Europe, North Africa and India. The timing could hardly have been worse. Jerry's brother Vic was growing increasingly disenchanted, and Pop Wales was struggling to run the school. Had he been more ambitious he could undoubtedly have made a legitimate case to become its first proper headmaster. As it was, he simply insisted that Dorothy and Jerry appoint one, for in the absence of any real leadership the school was drifting.

On 1 March 1930, Wales sat down to record his thoughts. The school was losing money. He was perceived by many around him to be autocratic, yet there were so many questions about the school he could not answer. Only Dorothy and Jerry could, and they had been out of contact for two months. The estate departments increasingly wanted nothing to do with the school, which had 'sunk from the position of being the focus of the whole experiment to that of a poor and disreputable relation'.[37] Wales was tired of dealing with the perennial problem of behaviour in the dining room when he had more important things to focus on. The search for a headmaster had been under way for some time and Wales knew that the successful candidate would demand his own staff and complete independence from Dorothy, Jerry and the estate. Above all, therefore, he queried what the school meant to its founders, and whether they wanted it to continue.

Within days, Dorothy and Jerry finally surfaced in Venice, and Wales sent them a letter, not only about the school but about his concerns for Whitney:

> We are not doing nearly enough for him, and he has now no close friendship with, or confidence in, anyone here, senior or junior. I have a tremendous sympathy with his isolated position, and with many of his criticisms of conditions and people here. I hope he will be able to talk to you at length, Dorothy, when he gets out to you; he needs your counsel and companionship very badly ... He also reacts in his way of life on the others; he is not working any too steadily, and the car and the aeroplanes don't conduce to a very orderly existence. He is charming and reasonable when one talks to him, but he is not happy, and he has no assurance in himself at the moment that there is anything or anyone worthwhile in this place.[38]

Jerry's response to Wales did not address his concerns about Whitney, and was less than clear about the future of the school. He explained that if the right person was not found to lead it, then the load would be too great for him to manage. Equally, if a founding principle was sacrificed in appointing an outsider then the very basis for having the school might be lost.

'Perhaps,' he concluded, 'we have failed to make it clear in the past that the whole of Dartington is one social experiment in which out of the raw of present society we are trying to mould a social unity with the help of education.'[39]

It was hardly a ringing endorsement of the school, but another of those Dartington introductions via a personal contact was about to do a great deal more than simply save it. Dorothy interviewed Margaret Isherwood, a Cambridge graduate who would fill several roles at Dartington and become a close friend. She was teaching at Oak Lane Country Day School, a liberal establishment in Philadelphia where her brother-in-law was headmaster. Born, like Jerry, in the north-east of England and, like Jerry and Rawson, a graduate of Trinity College, he seemed the personification of everything that Dorothy and Jerry could wish for. His name was Bill Curry.

They visited him at Oak Lane and liked what they saw, and his reaction on first seeing Dartington was equally positive. They offered him the role of 'Director of Education to the Social and Educational Experiment now being carried out at Dartington Hall',[40] and once he had been assured that he would indeed have total independence from its founders and freedom to recruit his own staff, he accepted. He joined Dartington in September 1931, and set about making it one of the greatest liberal co-educational boarding schools the world has known. Pop Wales was one of many swept away by Curry's new broom, but retained his Dartington salary as he studied history at the London School of Economics. Upon graduating, he learned that one of Curry's hires had not worked out, and he was able to return to Dartington to teach History and Latin.

But all this came too late for Whitney. On Friday, 4 April 1930, he arrived at Cannes' Hotel Beau-Site, to join Dorothy, Biddy and Michael for a family holiday. In between tennis lessons and hanging out with the local jazz band, he and his mother discussed his future. He had changed his mind about a US university. Now he wanted to sit the London Matriculation exams with a view to going to Cambridge, where he could also work on his flying and music. This was not the only sensitive subject discussed on the holiday. Thirteen-year-old Michael was not happy with family life at Dartington. Like Whitney and Biddy, during school term he slept in the dormitory and was banned from parts of the Hall. Only during school holidays could they sleep 'at home', and even then Michael not infrequently found someone else in his bed. When Jerry learned from Dorothy of Michael's unhappiness, he was not amused. 'Will you discuss seriously with the Straights "Homemaking" and how it is I and Dartington symbolise obstruction. They must help you and I to do it – a little research, tell Michael.'[41] Yet by the time of this exchange, the Elmhirsts and Straights had been living together at Dartington for more than three years.

It was a problem for all of Dorothy's children. Whitney's stepsister Ruth would forever resent not eating supper with her parents until she was a teenager, and would raise her own children very differently. When her brother Bill visited Whitney in 1950, aged 22, Whitney found him 'incapable of doing anything except be psychoanalysed ... he is a really nice kid and has been so dreadfully neglected by Mother and Jerry – when I think of all this it makes me a little bitter over all the neglect I suffered in my early years.'[42] Richard Elmhirst, another of Jerry's brothers, summed it up best. Jerry 'was always perfectly at home with other people's children, not his own'.[43]

On 21 April, as 17-year-old Whitney left Cannes, he was in effect leaving home and school too. He had been deprived of a consistently warm family background and close relationships with those of his own age, yet he had very much enjoyed many other aspects of his unique upbringing. That initial bricklaying lesson in the value of money gave way to gifts of flying lessons, and first of one aircraft and then, on crashing that, a second. How many youngsters careered around an estate on a succession of motorbikes and cars, or rowed on a private stretch of river in a boat of their own construction? It was the very fact that Whitney was the son and stepson of Dartington's founders that made him more able than any other junior to fulfil its original goals – he really did embrace in himself 'all the elements necessary for adventurous living'.[44] For all its idiosyncrasies, Dartington Hall School taught Whitney some lessons in life. He learned how to manage his time, negotiate for the common good, weigh up an objective and work hard in successful pursuit of it. A dozen years later, that broad French vocabulary developed under Mr Gibbs would help save his life.

And just as Dartington, as a home and a school, allowed Whitney to indulge in his passion for wings, wheels and water, so it introduced him to the fourth great love of his life – women. More than a decade later, when he came to spend the Christmases of the late 1940s there, he would stay in his old room in the Hall. The experience prompted him to reminisce in his diaries, and to recall in particular the girl to whom he lost his virginity.

Her name was Leslie. There was no junior of that name through the early years of the school, and just the one teacher. This was the woman, just four years older than him, who had come to Dartington as a consequence of the Bonser Report to teach dance and organise folk activities. In her first school report on Whitney, she noted, 'he has good physique, and is naturally supple'.[45]

4

Cambridge or Racing?

When Jerry finally realised just how serious Whitney was about going to Cambridge, he arranged two meetings for his stepson. These took place on Tuesday, 29 April 1930, nine days after Whitney returned from Cannes. The first was with history lecturer J.R.M. 'Jim' Butler, an old Trinity College contemporary of Jerry's who was already something of a Cambridge institution. Actually born in Trinity, where his father had been Master, he had been president of the Cambridge Union and, briefly, member of parliament for the university. Butler listened sympathetically to the confident 17-year-old, but pointed out a problem. Latin was a compulsory subject in Trinity's entrance exam, but the boat-building, engine-stripping and flying lessons had left no room for it in Whitney's Dartington syllabus.

The other meeting was with Guy Donald of the university's Appointments Board. He was impressed by Whitney, but queried in a letter to Jerry whether Trinity was a realistic objective. Donald recommended Jesus College:

> They really are a good college and always seem to have a number of interesting fellows ... The Tutor quite thinks they might make room. There, too, there is an entrance examination but it is mostly an essay and a quite general paper, designed to bring a man's interests and promise to light.[1]

But Whitney was determined to attend Jerry's *alma mater*: it was to be Trinity or nothing. He rented an apartment in London's Cadogan Place and began working with a tutor, Mr Frazer, in a bid to acquire the necessary Latin. A handsome teenager with a generous allowance, Whitney encountered many more distractions in London than the Devon countryside, and Mr Frazer made little progress. In the meantime, Jerry approached other Cambridge colleges. In a particularly creative letter to St John's, he suggested that Whitney 'suffers from the usual difficulty of Americans in a lack of a knowledge of grammar',[2] conveniently ignoring the fact that the school he had founded had failed in three and half years to teach grammar to this most anglicised of Americans. By April 1931, a year after leaving Dartington, Whitney had made little progress, and a new tutor, W.H. Lawson, was appointed on 8 guineas a week.

Mr Lawson certainly earned his money, for Whitney had a new distraction. He had replaced the Alvis with a sleek Brooklands Riley Nine. The original Riley Nine had been launched at the London Motor Show of October 1926, and when world land speed record holder John Parry Thomas drove the prototype he was confident that it would make a good competition car. He was based at Britain's only racetrack, Brooklands. He had won races there, the development workshop he ran with partner Kenneth Thomson was located there and the pair even lived within the circuit. Parry Thomas' plans for the Riley Nine were extensive: twin carburettors; a lower, shorter chassis; a squat, two-seater racing body; and a smaller radiator. When he was killed in March 1927 trying to win back his land speed record, his protégé, Reid Railton, completed the work, creating one of the best-performing 1,100cc cars available, with a top speed of over 90mph.

Whitney's Riley was registered GJ18 and delivered to him in his trademark black. For the first time, he added a personal insignia to a car, just in front of the cockpit – a narrow, elongated 'W' in white, its base facing forward. Its similarity to the Speedbird insignia on the tailfins of generations of BOAC aircraft, and the eight years Whitney would later serve as a director of BOAC, have somehow fuelled the idea that he designed the Speedbird logo himself, but this is just one of several myths that have grown up around his racing. In fact, Theyre Lee Elliott was responsible for the Speedbird design, which first appeared in Imperial Airways' advertisements a year or so after Whitney added his 'flying W' insignia to the Riley.

In 1931, British-based drivers and cars were competing well on the international stage. In January, Donald Healey had won the Monte Carlo Rally.

Cambridge or Racing?

A month later, Captain Malcolm Campbell had been made Sir Malcom on his return from Daytona Beach, reward for pushing the world land speed record past 245mph. In June, an Alfa Romeo may have triumphed at Le Mans after four consecutive Bentley wins, but that had been driven by two of England's most respected drivers, Tim Birkin and Lord Howe. Yet domestic motor sport was a low-key affair, restricted to hill climbs and speed trials on private land or beaches, and to short-distance handicaps at Brooklands. True, the Tourist Trophy was a red-blooded, 5-hour, 400-mile challenge held on public roads in Northern Ireland, but in 1931 Britain had no road circuits and no Grand Prix.

Whitney decided he would introduce himself and the Riley to this world. First on his list was the hill climb taking place on 11 July at Shelsley Walsh, set in the rolling hills of the Teme Valley, some ten miles west of Worcester. *Autocar* magazine mused on what made Shelsley so special:

> It's curious how that historic climb attracts. It is at best a brief but exciting rush up a straight, a wiggle and a straight, yet one looks forward to it more, if possible, every year, and each of the two meetings is a sort of rendezvous to which every enthusiast in the country goes very much with the idea of meeting every other enthusiast.[3]

For Whitney, the years spent tearing along Dartington's drives would surely serve him well at Shelsley: leave the start line with a minimum of wheelspin; keep his foot down as much as possible through two open left-handers; brake hard and line up for the Esses; avoid sliding too much and stay off the banks through the quick left-right; then exit smoothly and accelerate up the straight to the finish line. From start to finish was precisely 1,000 yards, and a climb of 328ft – an average gradient of about one in ten, but under one in six at its steepest.

The record for the climb, 42.8 seconds, had been set twelve months previously by Hans Stuck of Germany, but few Continental drivers were expected to compete this time. The Belgian Grand Prix was taking place the next day, and there was a certain resentment towards Shelsley's organisers, the Midland Automobile Club, for refusing to pay appearance money, known as starting money in international motor sport. It was a concept unheard of in Britain, but, even before he had turned a wheel in anger, Whitney learned that a living could be made from motor racing.

His debut appearance in British motor sport lasted 60.4 seconds. Those last two-fifths of a second were costly, as only drivers who completed their first climbs in under a minute were allowed a second attempt. Whitney took a vantage point on the bank looking down on the course to watch the second runs. Ray Mays was favourite. His car, the *Villiers Supercharge*, had been developed over several years by his friend, Amherst Villiers. Both men had gone to Oundle School, and had enjoyed their time in the engineering workshops there. Later, they had both left Cambridge University without completing their degrees to focus on motor sport, and Mays had already set Fastest Time of the Day (FTD) at Shelsley Walsh twice before. Today, on his second run, he certainly looked fast through the Esses, and there was general surprise and dismay when it was announced that he had gone slower: his supercharger had given out just when it was needed most, on the flat-out sprint up to the finish line. FTD went to Dick Nash in his hill climb special, the Terror, in 43.3 seconds.

When the overall results were posted, Whitney learned that his 60.4 seconds had won him third in class – twice. By the simple expedient of entering the Riley for both the 1,100cc racing and sports classes, he appeared in the results for both categories. The sports class had been tightly contested by four Riley drivers, and Whitney had come within 3.8 seconds of the quickest of them, T. B. Wood. Even in the racing category, he may have fallen a long way short of Ron Horton's best-in-class 48.6 seconds, but he had still beaten two other entrants. It was a highly respectable debut, and Whitney wanted more. Next on his list was Brooklands.

The idea for the world's first dedicated motor racing circuit had come to Surrey landowner Hugh Locke King during a holiday in Italy in 1905. He had been disappointed to find no British cars competing in the Coppa Florio, held on a 100-mile course near Brescia. When he learned that this was because the low speed limits on Britain's roads left manufacturers with nowhere to test, Locke King instructed designer Henry Holden to create a speed bowl on land he owned next to the railway line running south-west out of London's Waterloo station.

The 2.77-mile circuit at Brooklands was originally envisaged as a roughly egg-shaped track, to be raced on in an anticlockwise direction (Fig. 1). The Members' Banking formed a relatively tight first bend and led out on to the Railway Straight. This ran into the wider Byfleet Banking, while the return straight incorporated a slight dog-leg right to take account of a

Cambridge or Racing?

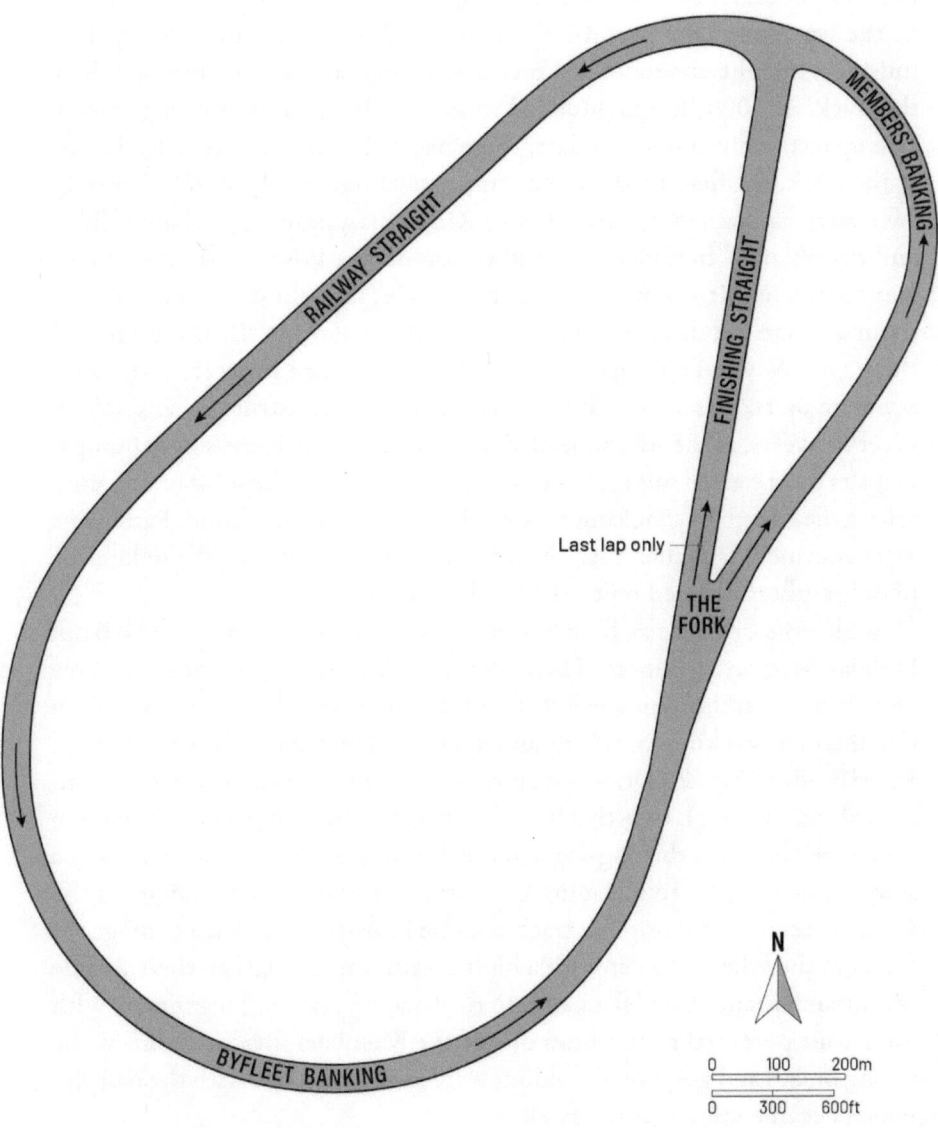

Fig. 1: Brooklands' standard Outer Circuit layout, as first encountered by Whitney in 1931. Races generally consisted of several laps, going right at the Fork, until the last lap, when drivers headed up the finishing straight.

factory built on land previously sold by Locke King. The finishing straight ran straight on from this kink, climbing at the far end to meet two-thirds of the way round the Members' Banking. This oval layout with separate finishing straight was modelled on horse racing, as was the great width of the track. At 100ft, it was intended to accommodate drivers racing side by side up to the finish line. To date, there had only ever been two dead heats at the track, the first during the opening meeting, in July 1907. That only two years had passed between Locke King's disappointing Italian holiday and Brooklands' first race is an indication of just how swiftly the circuit was completed. It was made of concrete slabs, laid out on a sandy subsoil to an average depth of 6in. Only where the Members' Banking crossed the River Wey, on a bridge made of steel-reinforced concrete resting on concrete piers, was a more substantial method of construction employed. Over the years, as the subsoil settled, Brooklands grew increasingly bumpy. Repairs were carried out each winter, but a solution to the substantial bump where the Members' Banking crossed the river was never found. Faster cars were routinely launched into the air at that point, much to the delight of photographers perched on the lip of the banking.

Whitney's first race at Brooklands took place on a sunny, windy Bank Holiday Monday, 3 August. There were ten races on the programme. Three were run over a shortened layout first used the year before. The Mountain Circuit, as it was known, was designed by the new Clerk of the Course, A. Percy Bradley (Fig. 2). Drivers sprinted up the traditional finishing straight, turned right through two-thirds of the Members' Banking, and raced down to the fork between the dog-leg and the finishing straight, which was now a sharp right-hand hairpin leading back on to the start–finish straight. If the Outer Circuit, as the original track became known, rewarded a courageous driver at the wheel of a car with a high maximum speed, then the 1.2-mile Mountain Circuit called for genuine road-racing craft and ingenuity, with numerous potential racing lines out of the Members' Bridge Bend, while strong brakes and good road holding were needed to cope with the hairpin, which became known as the Fork.

Whitney paid his 3 guineas entrance fee for the Third August Mountain Handicap, the eighth race on the card. This was open to 'motor cars in racing or touring trim propelled by means of internal combustion engines only'.[4] The only other stipulation was that 'cars must have, in working order, effective brakes on all four wheels'.[5] A broad-ranging field of fifteen cars lined up

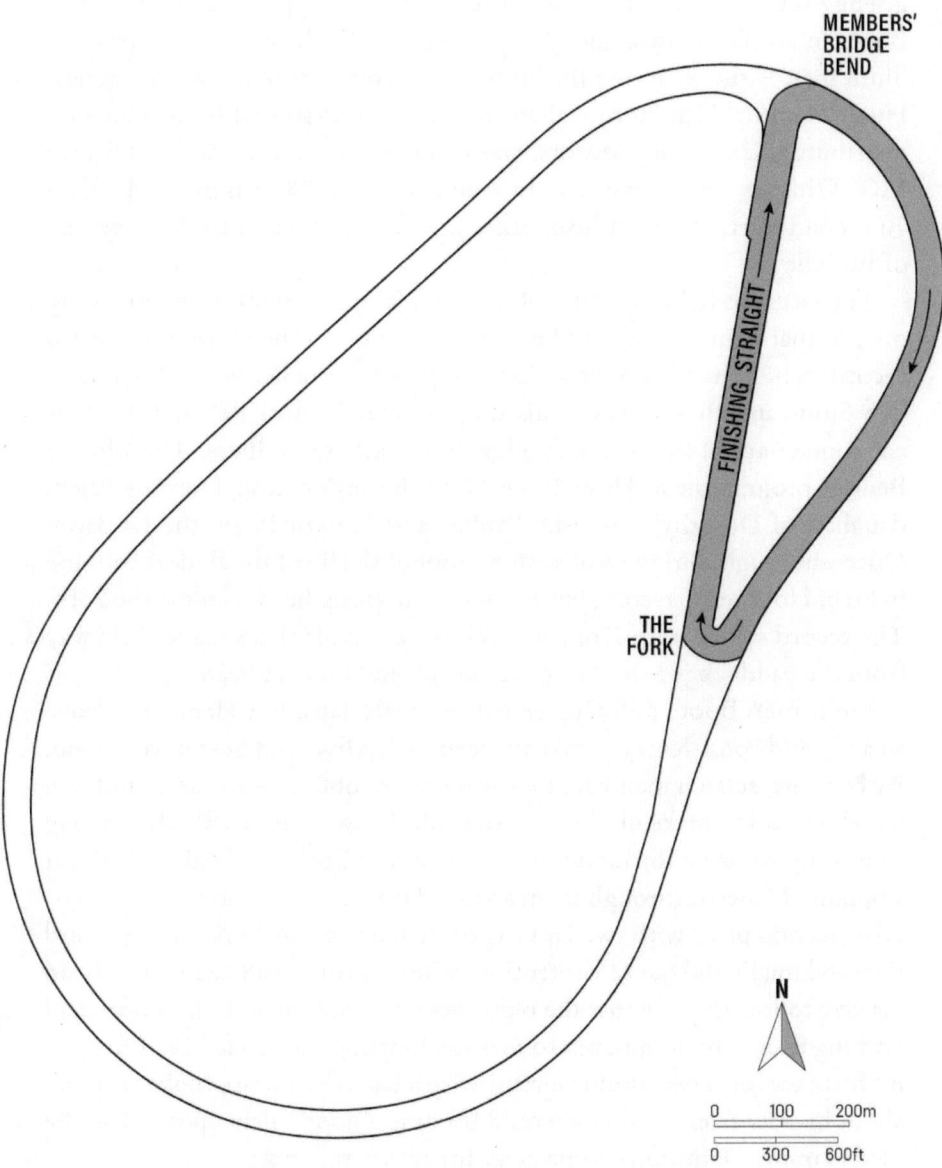

Fig. 2: Brooklands' Mountain Circuit, over which Whitney reigned supreme, winning numerous races and breaking the lap record even more frequently.

for the ten-lap, 12-mile race. W.K. Faulkner was 'scratch man' – the driver giving everyone else a start – in his supercharged Type 43 Bugatti. R.S.L. Boote in a 750cc Austin and C.L. Guiver in a 1.1-litre Salmson were the 'limit men' – those getting the biggest start from Faulkner, at 70 seconds. Hugh 'Hammy' Hamilton, a salesman and demonstrator with MG's London distributor, University Motors, was receiving 40 seconds in his 2.5-litre MG. Whitney, in his first-ever race and aged just 18, was granted only a 10-second start, along with six other drivers – testament to the potential of his Riley.

The race was held back until 4.50 p.m., 50 minutes after the preceding one, so that Tim Birkin could make an attempt on the Outer Circuit lap record, which had been set at 137.58mph the year before by Kaye Don in a Sunbeam. Birkin was in his single-seater Blower Bentley, another car supercharged by ex-Cambridge man Amherst Villiers. The Blower Bentley programme had been funded by Whitney's cousin, Dorothy Paget, daughter of Dorothy's late sister Pauline and Almeric Paget, the 1st Baron Queensborough. Birkin went within a foot of the lip of the Byfleet Banking in his bid for the lap record, but encountered strong head winds at the Fork. The record stayed with Don, and Whitney and his rivals made their way from the paddock for the Third August Mountain Handicap.

Limit men Boote and Guiver led the early laps, but Hamilton drove steadily and consistently to take the lead on lap five, and held it to the end. By contrast, scratch man Faulkner was erratic, oblivious to the 12 miles in which he had to make up those 70 seconds. He was up to fifth place on lap four, only to drive through the barriers at the Fork and resume without stopping. He went through them a second time two laps later, and had just taken second place with two laps to go when he got the Fork wrong a third time and finally slid out of contention. Whitney drove sufficiently neatly on his way to fourth place that the reporters from *Autocar* and *Motor Sport* had nothing to say about him, but to manage fourth place in a field of fifteen in his first race, on a demanding circuit with a harsh handicap, spoke volumes about his raw talent. And he would become a good talent spotter too: he filed Hammy Hamilton's name away for future reference.

Seven weeks later, Whitney experimented with another form of British motor sport, beach racing. The flat, 7-mile expanse of sand running from Southport to Formby, on the Lancashire coast of north-west England, had been the scene of Henry Segrave's 152.33mph world land

Cambridge or Racing?

speed record in March 1926, the mark beaten by Parry Thomas a month later. The Southport Motor Club began hosting races there the same year, and, six years on, their Championship Meeting of 19 September comprised two events – a sprint competition for cars and motorcycles over a flying kilometre, and a 20-mile race for cars. Under thick cloud, a light onshore breeze was unable to dry out the heavy sand. The meeting got off to a late start and took until dusk to finish. Whitney came third in the 1,100cc class of the sprint competition, and was one of nine to line up for the 20-mile race. This was something of a procession, Whitney finishing third behind a Bugatti and an Amilcar. The Southport MC were strongly recommended to make their events more interesting for drivers and spectators by introducing handicap races, and Whitney never went near sand racing again.

Back at Brooklands for the final meeting of the season, on a dry and chilly 17 October, he had a much more satisfying day, one that led to him wanting more motor racing even while cramming for Cambridge. He was entered for the first event on the seven-race programme, the Cumberland Junior Short Handicap, to be run over slightly more than two complete laps of the Outer Circuit and finishing on the Railway Straight, a distance of about 6½ miles. On handicap, Whitney sat towards the middle of the eighteen-car field. He was due to receive 39 seconds from E.L. Meeson's 4.2-litre Vauxhall, but this had suffered engine problems and never started. As everyone shunted up in the handicap, Philip Fotheringham Parker and Mike Couper were more on Whitney's mind. These experienced drivers, in a 2-litre Alvis and 2.5-litre Speed Model Rover respectively, were giving Whitney just 6 seconds.

Past the Fork for the first time, limit man G.E.W. Catchatoor still led in his 750cc Austin, but the handicaps unwound over the next lap and Fotheringham Parker was first past the Fork next time round, with half a lap to run. Couper was right behind him, with J.A. Robinson in an aging Brescia Bugatti third. Next up came Whitney, still reeling back the 8 seconds he had given Robinson. He caught the Bugatti on the Members' Banking and sprinted home third, 1.2 seconds behind Fotheringham Parker and just 0.4 seconds down on Couper – not bad for a young man a month short of his 19th birthday, driving a 1,100cc car.

He parked the Riley in the paddock and went off to find a good position from which to watch the third event on the card. This was a new race, the Mountain Championship, to be run over fifteen laps of the Mountain Course (some 18 miles), and, unusually for Brooklands, there would be no handicaps. The race attracted eight of the best road-racing drivers and cars in the country, including Birkin in his 2.5-litre Maserati, Campbell in a 7-litre Mercedes and Howe in his Grand Prix Delage. Howe got bogged down at the start, but the rest of the pack got away well and were still tightly bunched heading down to the Fork for the first time. Campbell was the early leader, but Birkin was putting on a most impressive display, drifting high on the Members' Bridge Turn, spinning his rear wheels at 60mph, flame shooting from his exhaust as he changed down for the Fork, tyres squealing as he exited it. He overtook Campbell for the lead on lap three and never eased up, matching the 75.21mph record he had set in August on his final lap and finishing 1,000 yards clear.

The day gave Whitney much to think about. Against more experienced drivers in bigger cars, he had acquitted himself well. Over the course of the last few months he had experienced the breadth of British motor sport and done reasonably well in four events. He clearly knew something about how to prepare a competition car – in the different environments of Shelsley, Southport and Brooklands, the Riley had never missed a beat. Now he wanted to test his prowess as a driver further, and for this he would need a faster car. Tim Birkin's flaming, squealing Maserati came to mind.

Alfieri Maserati had spent the early 1920s modifying and racing Diatto touring cars. He and some of his brothers established their own business in Bologna in 1926, and the city's trident symbol appeared over the radiator of the first Maserati racing car, the Tipo 26, in that year's Targo Florio, winning the 1,500cc class. In 1930, the brothers produced their most powerful car yet, the 26M 8C-2500. The first part of the car's designation reflected its evolution from its predecessors, but the second represented the expansion of Maserati's traditional 8-cylinder engine to 2.5 litres, giving the car a top speed of 140mph. Birkin had entered his 26M Maserati for the Monaco Grand Prix in April, but a faulty cylinder head gasket had prevented him from racing. In June, in the 10-hour French Grand Prix at Montlhéry, he and George Eyston shared the car on its way to fourth place, but a month later, Birkin had finished a distant tenth in the German Grand Prix. If he were to be successful in Continental grands prix in 1932, he would need something faster. For Whitney, who had just turned 19 and competed in only four events, the Maserati was a very considerable step up. A deal suited both men and Whitney bought the car, replacing Birkin's British racing green with his favoured black, but retaining the distinctive silver radiator.

With the purchase of his first purpose-built racing car secure, Whitney focused fully on cramming for Trinity's entrance exam. On Tuesday morning, 15 December, he walked through the College's Great Gate, no doubt glancing up at the statue of founder King Henry VIII, and into the Great Court, Europe's largest enclosed courtyard. Four years earlier, Lord Burghley had run the 405 yards of its perimeter path before the chapel clock had finished striking midnight – a feat rather inaccurately reproduced in the movie, *Chariots of Fire*. Whitney made his way to Corridor I and found his seat for the start of a day-and-a-half of papers. The results were published several days later: twenty months after leaving Dartington, Whitney had qualified to read Moral Sciences at Trinity College.

As Christmas approached, he weighed up where to make his debut in the Maserati. Brooklands' first meeting of the 1932 season was not until Easter Monday, 28 March, but a Swedish driver he had met at Brooklands, Henken Widengren, suggested he race a month earlier, in the Swedish Winter Grand Prix at Lake Rämen, about 100 miles north-west of Stockholm. Whitney was still virtually unknown to the British motoring press, and generated a single sentence in the 'slow news' 1 January edition of *Autocar*: 'W. Straight of Totnes has entered a Maserati for the Swedish Winter Grand Prix, and reports from Sweden show that the course ought to be particularly good this year.'[6]

It was a remarkable course, with a twisty, 1.2-mile section laid out on the lake's frozen surface followed by a further 27 miles of steep climbs and descents on narrow forest roads. Drivers had to complete eight laps, making for an overall race distance of more than 225 miles. Whitney, the only non-Scandinavian driver competing, arrived on the Monday evening before Sunday's race. Practice began on Wednesday, and Whitney got to grips with the course relatively easily. More problematic was the weather. Heavy snow on Thursday evening gave way to a huge temperature swing on Friday and rain on Saturday. Even the local drivers were unsure whether to use studded tyres. Whitney ordered some, but opted not to go with them in the race.

On race morning, 28 February, the twenty-four drivers were drawn up on Lake Rämen in eight rows of three, their starting positions decided by ballot. Widengren was lucky and lined up on the inside of the front row, while Whitney was allocated the inside of row four, effectively tenth. On the outside of the front row sat the Bugatti of Knut Gustav Sundstedt, one of only three drivers to fit studded tyres. The scheduled start time of 11 a.m. was observed precisely, and Sundstedt used his studded tyres to good effect, building a substantial lead over the lake section. As the field headed into the woods, Widengren lay second and Whitney was already up to sixth. He drove within himself over the course of that first lap, finding it difficult to run close behind Einar Lindberg in another Bugatti because of the stones thrown up from the Swede's studded tyres – by the time Whitney finally overtook him, the Maserati had lost both its windshields. Sundstedt crashed in the forest and Widengren slipped down the field, so that when the leaders re-emerged on the lake, almost 30 minutes after leaving it, Whitney was up to third, close behind two Finns, S.P.J. Keinänen in a Chrysler and the previous year's winner, Karl Ebb in an SSK Mercedes.

When Whitney made an attempt to snatch second, Ebb blocked him, the two cars touched and Whitney spun harmlessly across the ice. But when he engaged first gear to resume his pursuit, he discovered that his front wheels had been knocked out of alignment, and steering had become a problem. By the time he completed a much slower second lap he was down in seventeenth place, and he slid into an orchard near Lake Sällnäs on lap three, damaging his front axle further. His long trudge back through the mud and snow in racing plimsolls only added to the disappointment of his first retirement, but he impressed the Swedish press by telling them the race had been great fun, that the brush with Ebb had been his fault entirely and that he would be back.

Once home, he arranged for the Maserati to be repaired, and sent off his entry for a challenge even greater than the Swedish Winter Grand Prix: the German Grand Prix was taking place on 17 July, at the 172-corner, 14.3-mile Nürburgring. As Easter Monday drew near and repairs to the Maserati dragged on, so Whitney arranged to race at Brooklands in a borrowed Bugatti, an unblown, 2-litre Type 35. He was entered in the final race of the day, another of those ten-lap, 12-mile handicap sprints around the Mountain Course. This had a full, sixteen-car field. Supercharger problems forced Kaye Don to withdraw his new 4.9-litre Bugatti, and this let reserve driver Morris Goodall into the race, at the wheel of a TT Aston Martin. He would now be limit man, receiving 2 minutes 10 seconds from scratch man Clifton Penn Hughes in a supercharged, 2.3-litre Bugatti. Among several drivers receiving 90 seconds were Faulkner, the man who had modified the Fork barriers three times in ten laps the previous August, and jazz saxophonist and clarinettist Rupert 'Buddy' Featherstonhaugh. Whitney was one of six drivers receiving 1 minute.

The task of setting the handicaps at Brooklands had belonged to Albert 'Ebby' Ebblewhite ever since 1907, and it was harder than usual at the season opener, when drivers had had more than five months to develop their cars, and to promise themselves to drive more smoothly. Ebby had cause to react after just one race on this occasion. When L.P. Driscoll dominated proceedings in the opening sprint in a little Austin, Ebby immediately slapped an additional 15-second handicap on him for the equivalent long handicap race. Driscoll still managed to haul himself up to second in that race, setting a new 750cc lap record in the process. It was the second new record of the week: during practice, Birkin had finally beaten Don's Outer Circuit lap record, raising it to 137.96mph, and adding it to the Mountain Circuit record he had set in the Maserati now owned by Whitney.

After a capacity crowd had enjoyed a dry day and close racing throughout the meeting, Whitney and his rivals emerged from the paddock at 5.15 p.m. for the Norfolk Lightning Mountain Handicap. Morris Goodall enjoyed his moment in the limelight around the first lap but was soon engulfed by faster cars and the race developed into a duel between Faulkner, noticeably smoother than in August, and Whitney, who in his bid to catch the supercharged car with a larger engine ran wide at the Fork several times. Coming up the finishing straight for the tenth time, the two cars were inseparable, and they crossed the line as one to record only the third dead heat in Brooklands' history. Whitney may have had to share his win, but in only his sixth-ever meeting, it was still something for him to savour.

Seven weeks later, on 16 May, Brooklands hosted its Whit Monday Meeting. The day held enormous significance for Whitney, for it represented his first time on the Mountain Circuit with the 26M Maserati. Birkin, one of the greats of British motor racing, had used the car to first break and then match the Mountain Circuit lap record. What could the teenage Whitney do with it? Ebby clearly thought he was capable of great things: when the programme was published, Whitney learned he was joint scratch man for the Nottingham Lightning Mountain Handicap, alongside Lord Howe, driving the 2.3-litre Bugatti in which he had recently finished fourth in Monaco.

Intermittent heavy rain played havoc with the meeting, bringing a temporary halt to racing and a rejigging of the programme, but Whitney no doubt enjoyed the entertainment laid on while the organisers waited for track conditions to improve. Flight Lieutenant Gerry Sayer, the man who would make Britain's maiden jet flight eleven years later, went up in a Hawker Fury, and his 'inverted gliding at just on stalling speed was as neat as the terrific full power climbs were spectacular'.[7] A highlight of the meeting was Buddy Featherstonhaugh's performances in the first two mountain handicaps, at the wheel of a supercharged, 1.5-litre Alfa Romeo. He won the first convincingly from scratch, prompting Ebby to slap an additional 20-second handicap on him for the second race, but Buddy won that too. He promptly ran straight on at the Fork on his slowing down lap – a timely reminder to Whitney as he came out for his race of just how difficult track conditions remained.

After Ebby had flagged the drivers away for the Nottingham Lightning Mountain Handicap, limit man Victor Gillow in a Riley, receiving 95 seconds from Whitney and Howe, used his opportunity well. It was not until lap seven that he lost the lead to J.H. Bartlett's Salmson, receiving 65 seconds in the handicap. But all eyes were on Whitney and Howe from the moment they left the line. Howe made the better start and pulled a few yards clear. Each time round, Whitney went far higher on the Members' Bridge Bend and took more speed on to the back straight, but Howe was neater round the Fork and chalked off another lap in front. During his pursuit of Howe, Whitney broke Birkin's lap record, raising it to 75.75mph. In his defence of the lead, Howe matched Whitney's new mark. As he tore down from the Members' Bridge Bend for the last time, Whitney saw Bartlett up ahead, making his way down to the Fork. On the sprint to the finish line, first Howe and then Whitney shot past him, Howe beating Whitney by 8 yards. To Howe went the spoils, to Whitney went the *Daily Telegraph* Trophy for his new lap record – he had broken it, Howe had only matched it – and to Ebby went pride in another case of fine handicapping.

This was the day when Whitney Straight truly arrived in British motor racing. The 26M was not an easy car to race: gear changing in particular was difficult, which might explain, at least in part, Whitney's wildness exiting the Fork. But he had gone head-to-head with a fine, experienced driver over twelve laps of a challenging circuit, and beaten the lap record set by another in the same car. Ten days later, Brooklands hosted an open day, and Whitney took the Maserati back to see if he could perfect his line through the Fork and improve still further on his record. Over the course of ten laps he obliterated it, raising it to precisely 78mph. Focusing solely on his own driving and not racing rivals may have helped, but this was almost precisely a 3 per cent improvement over a 1.2-mile circuit – an outstanding performance.

But there was a twist in the way *Autocar* reported on Whitney's achievement:

> On Thursday last week Whitney Straight put a fine finish, I hope temporarily, to his racing career, by pushing the Mountain record at the track right up to 78mph on the Maserati after ten or eleven really magnificent rounds, full of smoke and flame and sensation. This was a really fine run, and it was interesting to see the unusual course followed at the Members' Bridge Turn ... Unfortunately, Straight has to give up motor racing for the moment, but I think his Mountain record will last some time.[8]

Incredibly, with a string of Brooklands events, two Shelsley Walsh climbs and the German Grand Prix to look forward to before going up to Cambridge in October, it was now that Whitney was asked by Dorothy and Jerry to stop racing. He must have been devastated. He had qualified for Trinity, something Guy Donald at the Cambridge University Appointments Board had considered beyond him, and he had demonstrated that he was a match for anyone racing in Britain. What more did they want from him, and what sort of return was he going to generate from Dorothy's investment in the Maserati if he drove it in anger only three times? Perhaps it was the sheer potency of the car that prompted their decision. Whatever the reason, and however abrupt and unfair Whitney must have found it, he accepted it. The Maserati had only one other outing during 1932: Norman Black, winner of the previous year's Tourist Trophy, drove it to fourth fastest time of the day at the June Shelsley Walsh meeting, 2 seconds slower than Earl Howe's FTD.

So it was that, on Saturday, 1 October 1932, former racing motorist Whitney Straight took rooms at 32 Trinity Street, 100 yards south of Trinity's Great Gate. He was one of 146 freshmen entering the college – women were not admitted until the 1970s. Eton provided twenty students, Harrow fifteen and Stowe and Winchester ten each. Only one had been educated at 'Lincoln School, New York and Dartington Hall, Totnes'.[9] There was one familiar face, however. Jim Butler, the man from whom, two-and-a-half years earlier, Whitney had sought advice about entering Trinity, would be his tutor. Whitney's Director of Studies was C.D. 'Charlie' Broad. The 44-year-old Broad had won a scholarship to Trinity in 1906, graduating with first-class honours with distinction. During stints lecturing at St Andrews and Bristol universities, his books *Scientific Thought* and *The Mind and Its Place in Nature* had made his reputation, and he had become a lecturer in Moral Sciences in Cambridge's Faculty of Philosophy in 1926.

But the chief benefit of Cambridge to Whitney was the stimulating company of young men his own age. At 12 years old, he had looked upon his tutor and his future stepfather as his closest friends, and as Dartington's eldest junior he had endured years of relative isolation. Now, at Trinity, his closest friend was Dick Seaman, just three months younger. Dick was entering his second year, and lodging across the road at 16 Trinity Street. He had been schooled at Rugby, and he too had struggled with Trinity's entrance exam, but his parents had packed him off to a private tutor in Kent. He faced precisely the same distractions as Whitney – he had been in the crowd at Shelsley when Whitney made his competitive debut, and competed on the hill at the next meeting there, also at the wheel of a Riley – but the residential approach was clearly effective, and Dick had gone up to Trinity in October 1931.

Another friend was Peter Masefield. He was sixteen months younger than Whitney, but was entering the university at the same time – as obsessed with flight as Whitney, he had nonetheless taken the trouble to learn by heart Livy Book 9 in Latin and English, and had passed his entrance exam first time. He was reading Engineering at Jesus College, and had rooms in Chapel Court overlooking Jesus Lane, some 10 minutes' walk from Whitney's lodgings. He regularly cycled the 20 minutes over to Marshall's Fen Ditton Aerodrome for flying lessons. David Marshall had begun his working life in Trinity's kitchens aged just 14, and set up a chauffeur-drive company in 1909. While the company expanded into car sales and servicing, David's son Arthur graduated in Engineering at Jesus and celebrated by learning to fly. It was he who suggested to his father that they should open an aerodrome on land next to the family home, and it was there that Masefield introduced himself to the young owner of two brightly coloured aircraft, a Gipsy Moth and a Moth Major. He and Whitney became good friends during their brief time together at Cambridge, and their careers would intertwine in the decades ahead.

Whitney also came to know a third-year Trinity undergraduate, an avid *Autocar* reader named Guy Burgess, well enough that, on a trade mission to Moscow in 1963, he would visit the exiled spy. But in the autumn of 1932, the politicisation of Cambridge still lay in the future, and in any event Whitney had no interest whatsoever in Marxism. Rather, he occupied himself over his first two terms with good company, membership of the University Camera Club and sufficient study to stay engaged with his course. Even as his third term began, on Easter Sunday, 16 April 1933, he was back in his rooms at 32 Trinity Street – but he had made alternative arrangements for Easter Monday.

5

A Brief, Busy Attempt at Both

Early on Easter Monday, Whitney met up with Peter Masefield, cycled over to Fen Ditton Aerodrome and climbed aboard his blue and gold Moth Major. Three-quarters of an hour later, after flying over Duxford, Hatfield, Hendon and Heston, they landed at Brooklands and went their separate ways. Masefield refuelled the plane and chatted with the test pilot of the new High-Speed Fury, which had just emerged from Hawker's assembly hangar. Whitney went off to the paddock to prepare for an afternoon of racing with the Maserati.

No record survives of how he persuaded Dorothy and Jerry that motor racing and university could make good bedfellows. Perhaps confining himself to Brooklands and Shelsley Walsh until he had sat his exams at the beginning of June, and only setting about a full programme of Continental events once Cambridge's Easter Term had concluded, was a reasonable basis for at least experimenting with simultaneous study and racing. How ever he talked them round, he was able to demonstrate over the course of the afternoon that two terms of dedicated study had done nothing to blunt his capabilities as a racing driver.

He had reacquainted himself with the Maserati at a practice session earlier in the week and, though eleven months had passed since he had last driven it, he had unofficially beaten his own Mountain Circuit record several times. Now, basking in unseasonably warm weather, a large crowd looked forward to seeing him race in a pair of mountain handicaps. Ebby certainly gave Whitney no allowance for his lengthy absence, making him scratch man for the First Addlestone Mountain Handicap. He would have just five laps, or 6 miles, to make up the 75 seconds he was giving half a dozen drivers. One of them, R.H. Eccles in a 1.5-litre Frazer Nash, established himself as the clear leader over the first couple of laps, while Bugatti drivers 'Taso' Mathieson and Tim Rose-Richards, receiving 20 seconds and 9 seconds respectively from Whitney, gained on the slower cars ahead of them. At the back, Whitney was demonstrating his latest approach to the Fork Hairpin, arriving way over to the left, standing on the brakes so hard that the Maserati fishtailed, then gathering it all up to take a wide arc across the turn and kick up the dust on the grass verge of the finishing straight. By lap four he had dispensed with Rose-Richards and Mathieson, but there was still a gaggle of six more drivers to overtake before he could go after Eccles.

Whitney caught them on the approach to the Fork on the last lap, and dealt with them all by taking a tight line up the inside. He spun his rear wheels as he accelerated up the finishing straight in pursuit of Eccles, but was still 300 yards behind the Frazer Nash as it crossed the line. His consolation for second place was a new lap record, at 78.29mph, which prompted Ebby to slap a further 5-second handicap on him for the Second Addlestone Mountain Handicap.

This was another five-lap sprint, against slightly weaker opposition. Three drivers put themselves out of contention approaching the Members' Bridge turn on lap two by slowing for one another, while Noel Carr, who had been highly competitive at Shelsley and Southport, found the Mountain Circuit a very different proposition. His pirouette at the Fork as Whitney went past him was the second of three spins. Whitney judged his race to perfection, catching Australian novice Jay Cumming at the Fork on the last lap and accelerating away to win by 70 yards. Then, with a race win and a lap record under his belt, he met up with Masefield and flew back to Cambridge.

It had been a triumphant return to racing. In *Motor Sport*, 'Boanerges' wrote:

I find difficulty in restraining my pen when writing about Whitney Straight's magnificent handling of the 2.5 litre Maserati. Certainly no such driving has been witnessed on the Mountain Circuit before, and his record is likely to remain unbeaten for a long time. In spite of being so fast, Straight inspires the utmost confidence in spectators, and has that elusive 'mastery of man over machine' air which distinguishes the first-class Continental driver. With many dashing drivers on the Mountain Circuit one feels that at any moment they may overdo things a bit, but Straight always looks safe, and in complete charge of his car.[1]

The increasing popularity of Brooklands with drivers had resulted in the halving of mountain handicaps to just five laps, so that more races could be squeezed on to the card, but Whitney's next visit to the circuit, on 6 May, was for the 262-mile International Trophy. It was organised by the Junior Car Club – today's British Automobile Racing Club – which had grown adept at creating innovative circuit layouts at Brooklands by exploiting the large expanse of track below the Fork. For the International Trophy, the JCC introduced an alternative to staggered-start handicapping, which was all very well for five-lap sprints – indeed, riveting – but less satisfactory for long-distance races. A handful of 750cc cars droning around the Outer Circuit made the early stages tedious for spectators. Worse, once the whole field was racing, a slide rule was needed to establish whether a faster car might overhaul a slower one.

The JCC introduced a new circuit layout, with a clockwise lap round the Byfleet Banking, up the Railway Straight and Members' Banking to a sharp turn down on to the traditional finishing straight. Below the Fork, sand banks were employed to create three lanes. The lowest-powered Group 1 cars raced straight on to their next lap; the intermediate Group 2 cars negotiated a gentle S-bend; and the fastest Group 3 cars, including Whitney's Maserati, had to deal with a much tighter chicane away to the left (Fig. 3). Fans were about to enjoy the wonderful sight and sound of all twenty-eight cars leaving the start line together, and to know throughout the race who was leading.

The handicap lanes demonstrated their effectiveness immediately. Whitney and another Group 3 car, Fothringham's 2.3-litre Bugatti, led the howling pack into the complex from Howe in a Group 2 MG Magnette, but beyond the lanes Howe led from Elwes in another Magnette, with the leading Group 1 car, Aldington's Frazer Nash, third. Over the course of that first lap, Group 3 cars reasserted themselves – Campbell in one of his Sunbeams leading from Brian Lewis in the new, 2.3-litre Alfa Monza, with Whitney third – but the organisers were content with this, as the bigger cars would have to pit more often for fuel and tyres.

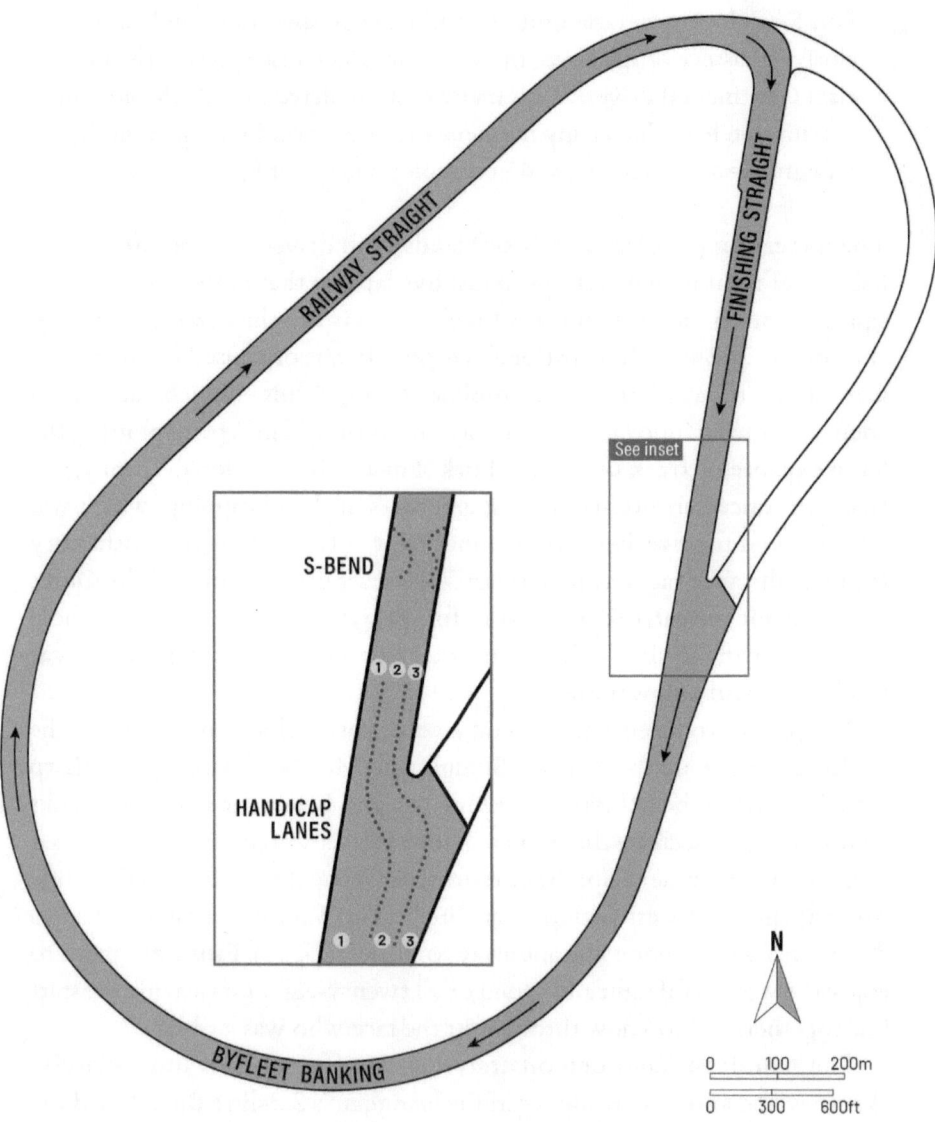

Fig. 3: Brooklands as laid out by the Junior Car Club, forerunner of today's British Automobile Racing Club, for the International Trophy races of 1933 and 1934. The lowest-powered Group 1 cars raced straight on at the handicap lanes to their next lap; the intermediate Group 2 cars negotiated a gentle S-bend; and the fastest Group 3 cars, including Whitney's Maseratis, had to deal with a much tighter chicane away to the left.

As they neared the end of the lap, it became apparent that, with this new circuit layout just as with the Mountain Circuit, Whitney would pursue his own line off the Members' Banking. While Lewis ran high up it and swooped down on to the finishing straight, Whitney swung in earlier, 'wrestling with the steering wheel, but maintaining perfect control'.[2] This put him second as they headed down to the handicap lanes, and he needed only two laps more to deal with Campbell, going round the outside of him to take the lead.

From that point, 'the much talked-of Cambridge undergraduate who had only that afternoon flown to the track'[3] pulled away swiftly, and within 45 minutes had lapped the entire field. But then he slowed suddenly. First Campbell and Lewis unlapped themselves, then they caught him again and started scrapping for the lead. A strange, thrashing noise was heard from the rear of Whitney's car, and he had fallen to fourth place by the time he pulled into his pit after thirty-two laps to post his first-ever mechanical retirement, his rear axle broken.

Campbell retired after eighty laps, leaving Lewis – otherwise known as the 2nd Baron Essendon – to run home a popular winner, leaving 'Casque' in *Autocar* to ask:

> ... what would have happened if Whitney Straight's control had kept him to better tactics, for, delightful as it must have been to drive faster and faster round that course, one cannot help thinking that the Maserati could have won and that there could hardly be the necessity to get as much as a lap lead before half the race was over.[4]

'Casque' was the pseudonym of former Le Mans winner Sammy Davis. He was an official observer that day and spoke directly in these tones to Whitney after the race. Whitney was unimpressed, replying, 'Look, this is what I am here to do. I haven't damaged anyone or myself, so therefore I will drive as fast as possible within those limitations.'[5]

But Davis would not let the matter rest, writing in September that Whitney:

> sprang to prominence by giving a good imitation of a hurricane when breaking the Brooklands Mountain record in a racing Maserati, and thereafter driving many hectic rounds until his car cracked up in the lead during the International Trophy Race ... As a rule his style has tended to fast laps and no finish, but when restraint is acquired he will be a really fine driver.[6]

It seems a harsh judgement. The fastest of Whitney's thirty-two laps – joint fastest with Campbell all afternoon – was completed in 1 minute 41.6 seconds, and the swiftest of the Group 3 pit stops took roughly a minute. If he had needed a late stop for tyres or fuel, a lap's lead would have been barely enough to keep him ahead. Of the twenty-eight starters, another nineteen retired in addition to Whitney, and none of them set anything like his pace. Three hours into the race, Kaye Don's 5-litre Bugatti was running a distant second to Lewis, three laps down and averaging 85mph to Lewis' 88mph, when he too retired with rear axle problems. It may be that Davis' stern view of Whitney's hurricane impressions lay in the premature end to his own most recent Brooklands race, a mountain handicap at the Easter 1931 meeting. The circuit was damp but, as scratch man in a 4.5-litre Invicta, he had felt confident of victory. He held a slide on the Members' Bridge Turn on the opening lap. Second time round, 'still cautious, I yet misjudged the thing'.[7] Drifting as he accelerated through the bend, the back of the car slid away from him. He suffered two severe leg breaks in the ensuing accident, and spent much of the following year in hospital. Perhaps 20-year-old Whitney's consistent ability to catch every drift and fishtail grated with him.

Whitney hoped to put the disappointment of Brooklands behind him three weeks later by making his second appearance at Shelsley Walsh. He took with him two cars and two drivers. His 'teammate', and indeed girlfriend, was Psyche 'Peggy' Altham. Nine months older than Whitney, her parents had separated when she was young and she and her brother had enjoyed the run of their great aunt's Shelford Hall, 4 miles south of Cambridge. Childhood summers were spent punting on the River Granta and swimming and diving at Shelford Mill. By the age of 18 she was a gifted choreographer, dancer and costumier, and had given a one-woman dance recital at the Cambridge Festival Theatre. Most recently, she had starred in cabaret at London's Grosvenor House Hotel. She was due to perform as Oscar Wilde's Salome at the Oxford Playhouse in the autumn, but she planned to spend her summer with Whitney, and enjoy a few competitive drives of her own.

She made her motor-sport debut in Whitney's latest road car, a 8-litre Bentley clad in a Gurney Nutting sedanca body – hardly the most appropriate hill climb car. A broken shock absorber, leaking radiator and soaked magneto interrupted her preparations, but she did a fine job keeping the heavy Bentley off Shelsley's banks and recorded a time of 59.4 seconds – a whole second faster than Whitney had managed in the sleek Riley on his Shelsley debut!

By the time Whitney drew up to the start line for his first run, rain had been falling for some time, ensuring that Stuck's three-year-old record of 42.8 seconds would remain intact. It also meant that the powerful Maserati was no more appropriate for the hill than the Bentley. Excessive wheelspin off the line and through the Esses contributed to an uncompetitive time of 48.2 seconds, and even this was struck off, for Whitney had jumped the start. His first outing in the Bentley went better: 53.8 seconds was the fastest run to date in the over-5-litre category.

During the lunch interval, Shelsley favourite Ray Mays finally arrived with his *Villiers Supercharge*, and was given special dispensation to have his first turn on the hill immediately before the sub-60-second competitors made their second runs. Amherst Villiers had come up with a solution to that great hill climb time-waster, wheelspin off the start line, by fitting distinctive twin rear wheels to the car. The greater contact patch between tyre and road surface provided more grip, and Mays exploited this to his advantage perfectly, setting the fastest time thus far, 45.6 seconds. His second run, in just 44.8 seconds, proved the point and gave him his fourth Shelsley FTD in eight meetings. When Whitney climbed back into the Maserati, he managed to slide his way up in 47.8 seconds, but this was only good enough for a share of fourth place in the 3-litre class. His disappointing Shelsley was complete when he failed to improve on his first run in the Bentley, and watched H.H. Stisted in a Mercedes S snatch first place from him in the over-5-litre category. More than forty years later, when the Midland Automobile Club invited Whitney to attend Shelsley's seventieth anniversary celebrations, he called the Bentley 'a slightly inappropriate chariot ... getting from first to second gear was almost bound to sound rather undignified'.[8]

He rushed back to Cambridge to cram for his Moral Sciences papers on the following Thursday and Friday, and sent the Maserati to the Thomson & Taylor workshop at Brooklands, for Reid Railton to address once and for all his gear-changing problems. Railton was a keen proponent of the Wilson pre-selector gearbox. It was used on Armstrong Siddeley and Daimler road cars, and Malcolm Campbell had benefitted from Railton fitting the device to the pair of 4-litre Sunbeams he raced at Brooklands.

The pre-selector gearbox was a complex set of epicyclic gears and bands, and running it required a lot of power. This reduced the car's top speed, but Whitney was focused on the benefits. The recalcitrant gear lever would be replaced with a plate within easy reach of the steering wheel, marked 'I' to 'IV'. Flying down the straight towards the Fork, he could turn the plate to 'II' and pre-select second gear. Then, after slamming on the brakes and on the point of turning in, he could engage second by depressing a foot pedal. He might lose ground to rivals down long straights, but benefit at Shelsley, the Mountain Circuit and Continental hill climbs. Above all, he could keep both his hands on the steering wheel, and that settled matters. When he flew into Brooklands on a warm Whit Monday, 5 June, the Maserati, complete with pre-selector gearbox, was ready for him.

Whitney's first race, the fourth of the day, was the First Cobham Mountain Handicap. As usual, he was scratch man, and as on Easter Monday he would have just five laps in which to catch limit man, Antony Powys-Lybbe, to whom he was giving 89 seconds. Unusually, Ebby got the handicaps all wrong. Powys-Lybbe finished a strong third, but Whitney managed to climb only to tenth place. The big race of the day, the Gold Star Handicap, brought further disappointment. Run over 20 miles of the Outer Circuit, only eleven of the eighteen entrants lined up. Limit man L.P. Driscoll in his 750cc Austin got away cleanly, chased by local garage owner Charles Brackenbury in his disc-wheeled, 1.5-litre Bugatti. Bizarrely, when Ebby went to flag the next few drivers away, they had not switched their engines on. This should have simplified Whitney's task of making up the 2 minutes 17 seconds he was giving Driscoll, and he was quickly past the car nearest to him in the handicap, Oliver Bertram's 10.7-litre Delage. But Whitney found conditions on the circuit unusual, and the Maserati was strangely skittish on the bankings. He was unable to take them flat, and Bertram re-passed him on the second lap. Bertram struggled too, almost losing control when he overtook other cars, but he was able to climb to second, 500 yards behind Brackenbury's winning Bugatti. Whitney trailed home a cautious fifth. The final pair of races, both five-lap mountain handicaps, saw little overtaking and were won by their limit men, again suggesting that Ebby had endured a bad day at the office with his handicaps. But Whitney's problem in the Fourth Cobham Mountain Handicap was that he could not start his engine. He got away late and completed only two laps, bringing the curtain down on the poorest Brooklands meeting of his career.

The next morning, he read in the *Cambridge University Recorder* that he had scraped a third in his exams – confirmation, if any were needed, that racing and university made poor bedfellows after all. Consolation came with the purchase of another car, an MG Magnette. The Magnette had made an outstanding debut in April, finishing first and second in class in the fearsome Mille Miglia, the 1,000-mile race run over every type of Italian road from narrow mountain pass to flat-out autostrada. Under the boxy, two-seater body on each of the Mille Miglia Magnettes was a light, ash timber frame. Sitting in it was a supercharged, 6-cylinder 1,086cc engine, mated to another Wilson pre-selector gearbox.

Whitney's plan was to ship the Maserati and Magnette to separate meetings across the Continent and fly between circuits, enabling him to compete in as many events as possible, against top-quality opposition – only then could he form an objective view of how good a racing driver he was. The Magnette would give him the opportunity to race in classic public-road races like the Tourist Trophy in Northern Ireland and Italy's Coppa Acerbo, and provide him with a fresh challenge at Brooklands, with less power than the Maserati but more favourable handicaps. It would also be a more appropriate chariot for Peggy than the Bentley. Whitney's Magnette was chassis K3011. Thomson & Taylor fitted it with a special pointed-tail body, decked out as usual in black.

With Cambridge's Easter term drawing to a close, Whitney entered the Maserati in his first Continental event of the year, the Kesselberg hill climb. This was a 3.1-mile climb away from the southern shore of Lake Kochelsee, almost 50 miles south of Munich. Strewn with sweeping bends and sharp hairpins, it made Shelsley Walsh look tame, and even regular competitors found it daunting. The climb was held on Sunday, 18 June, and the official practice session opened at 3 a.m. the day before, 2 hours before sunrise, so that drivers could make several ascents and familiarise themselves with the course. Even then, drivers asked for more time on the hill, and in the end the organisers permitted unofficial runs through the Friday.

None of this helped the first-ever British-based Kesselberg hill climb entrant. Whitney arrived late from Cambridge, and his recorded run up the hill was the first time he had ever seen it. In the circumstances, his performance was extraordinary. The over-2-litre category was won by Eugenio Siena, chief test driver to Enzo Ferrari, and winner of the previous year's Spa 24-hour race. He recorded a time of 4 minutes 4.0 seconds. Hill climb specialist Paul Pietsch, like Siena in an Alfa, was a tenth of a second slower. Whitney finished third in class, in 4 minutes 4.4 seconds. Even one practice run would surely have gained him the half-second that would have given him victory in the most closely contested category of the day. If he had practised on the hill from the Friday, he may well have beaten overall winner Manfred von Brauchitsch too.

As a new British-based driver came to Europe's attention, so, four days after Kesselberg, an established English great died. Over the course of the past twelve months, Tim Birkin's Blower Bentley programme had folded, a business partnership had failed, and the family fortune, generated in the lace industry, had all but been dissipated. Another former Le Mans winner, Bernard Rubin, had purchased a stable of cars for him to race on the Continent in 1933, and it was in one of these, a 3-litre Maserati, that he had taken third place in the Tripoli Grand Prix on 7 May. At some point over that weekend, he burned his forearms on the car's exhaust. His death in a London hospital seven weeks later is often attributed to septicaemia, brought on by the burns, but he only fell ill three weeks after the race. A return of the malaria he had first contracted while serving in Palestine in 1918 may have exacerbated his condition, but, as much as anything, Birkin was burned out rather than burned, dead at just 36.

Amid the outpourings of grief in the national and specialist press, 'Boanerges' offered a glimpse of the future to *Motor Sport* readers. With Birkin's death, he wrote, 'it looked as though Earl Howe would alone be left to represent England in Continental Grand Prix racing. Then that brilliant young driver, Whitney Straight, took his Maserati abroad and set about gaining some first-hand Grand Prix road-racing knowledge.'[9] The cause of this enthusiasm was Whitney's drive in the Marne Grand Prix on 2 July. It took place on the same road circuit 5 miles west of Reims that had hosted the previous year's French Grand Prix. At the time, Reims-Gueux was one of the fastest circuits in Europe, 4.8 miles in length and roughly triangular in plan. Away from the start line, drivers swept through open right–left curves before a right-angled right-hander led them through the outskirts of the village of Gueux and up through a wood. A second right-angled right-hander took them on to a flat-out, dead-straight section of the Route Nationale 31, down to a hairpin at Thillois, and back on to the start–finish straight. In contrast to Kesselberg, Whitney arrived a week before the race and set about learning the circuit, even before the roads had been closed to traffic.

The 26M was into its third season now, and Whitney found top gear on the new pre-selector gearbox was slipping. He did well to top 142mph down the back straight, but his fastest practice lap, in 3 minutes 30.8 seconds, was almost 29 seconds slower than Marcel Lehoux's in a 2.3-litre Bugatti. This was one of the first races where practice times determined grid positions, so, while Lehoux took up pole position, Whitney found himself at the back of the grid. The last time he had felt this much of a novice in a car, he had taken just over a minute to climb Shelsley Walsh. Today, he could expect to take the best part of 3 hours to cover the fifty-one laps under warm, sunny skies – almost 250 miles. Still, Whitney was, briefly, in the very best of company. Lined up beside him at the back of the grid was the 'Flying Mantuan', Tazio Nuvolari, in a 2.6-litre Alfa Romeo entered by Enzo Ferrari. Problems with the French customs authorities had caused Nuvolari to arrive late so he had not recorded a lap time. He was expected to tear through the sixteen-car field and do battle with Lehoux, Giuseppe Campari in the works 3-litre Maserati and Alfa privateers Philippe Etancelin and Jean-Pierre Wimille.

It took Nuvolari just a lap to take the lead, and two more to set the fastest lap. After twenty-two laps, with a lead of almost a minute over Etancelin, he came into the pits for fuel and fresh rubber, but the stop took nearly 3 minutes and he re-emerged in fourth place. He was back up to second place and closing on Etancelin when he pulled to a stop in Gueux with a broken rear axle. Enthusiasts noting the similarity of Nuvolari's drive with Whitney's in the International Trophy, and precisely the same reason for their retirements, would search in vain in the following week's *Autocar* for any criticism of the Italian. Nuvolari's retirement set up an extraordinarily tense finish, Etancelin beating Wimille to the line by just 0.2 seconds after 2¾ hours of racing. Meanwhile, Whitney had gone about his business professionally, managing that slipping top gear down the straights and climbing steadily through the field. He lost time restarting the car after his refuelling stop, and again after pitting for fresh plugs. Then, during a fight for third place with Raymond Sommer in another Alfa, he spun off into a wheatfield. It took him almost 10 minutes to push the car back out on to the road, by which time Sommer was long gone.

Only when Whitney pulled into his pit at the end of the race, the last of the four finishers and the only one not in an Alfa, did it emerge why he had taken so long to push his car out of the field. In this first full-length grand prix with the pre-selector gearbox, the Maserati's transmission tunnel had grown intensely hot, burning Whitney's feet and legs severely. He had shown an iron will to keep racing at all, but he was in very poor shape, and Birkin's death must have crossed his mind. Peggy helped get him back to England, where he had to spend several weeks in a London nursing home. His right foot would give him discomfort for the next year, and the nail on his big toe never grew back.

Whitney's burns were, mercifully, the only injury he ever incurred during his racing days, but they ruined his plans for July. Ten days after the Marne Grand Prix, he had been due to debut the Magnette in the Mannin Beg, a new race taking place on the streets of Douglas, on the Isle of Man. From there he had planned to fly straight to France, to race the Maserati in the Dieppe Grand Prix. As it was, more than a month would pass before he could resume racing, leaving him only eight weeks in which to cram as many events as possible before Cambridge's Michaelmas term began on 1 October.

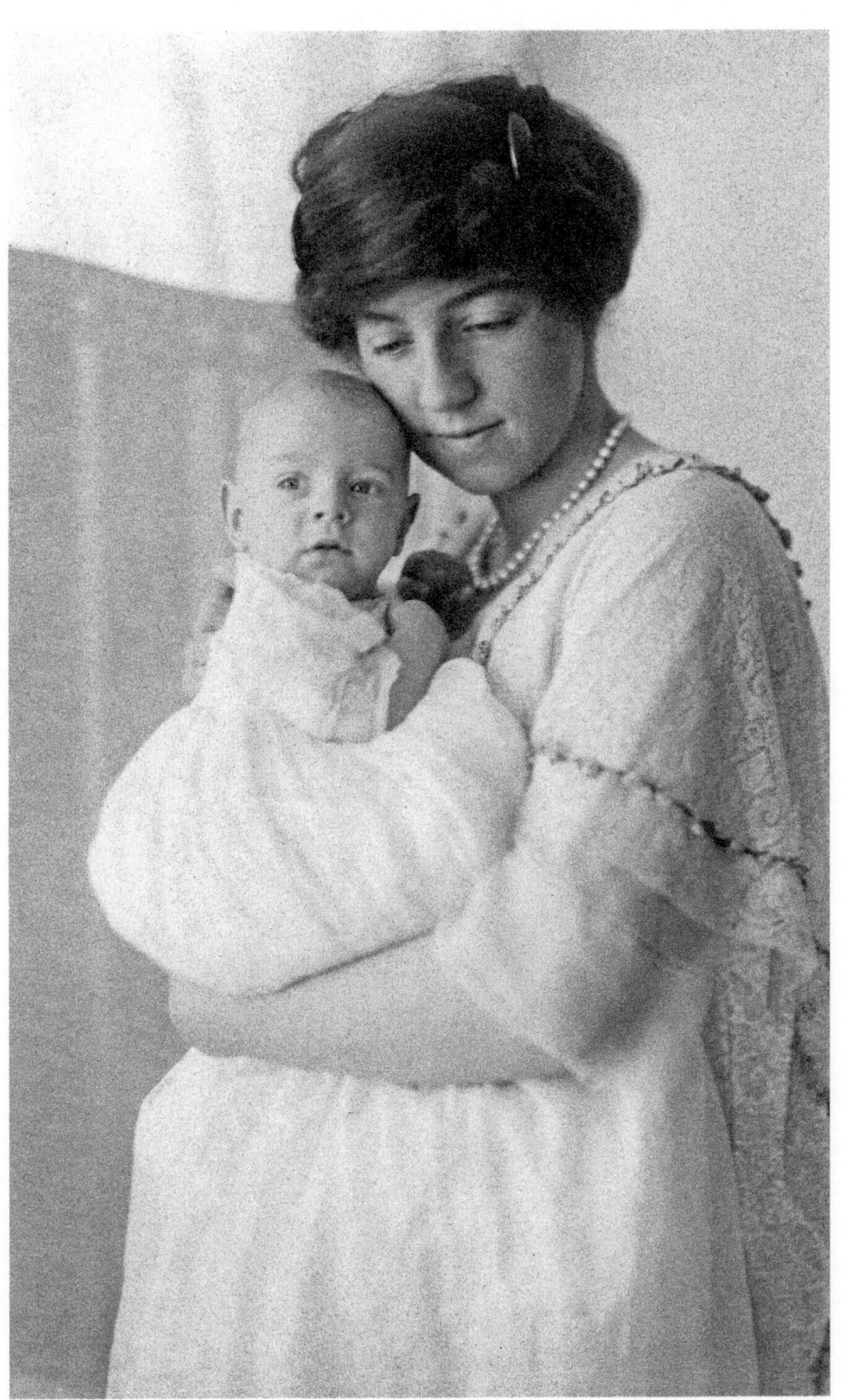

The infant Whitney with his mother Dorothy. (Dartington Trust/Elmgrant Trust)

With his father on the Applegreen lawn, the day before Willard sailed for France. (Dartington Trust/Elmgrant Trust)

At the controls of a 1-goatpower Studebaker, taking sister Biddy and brother Michael for a drive. (Dartington Trust/Elmgrant Trust)

Enjoying the aerobatics at Roosevelt Field with Michael. (Dartington Trust/ Elmgrant Trust)

Page boy at New York's first big social occasion since the war, the wedding of his aunt Flora Whitney to Roderick Tower, 19 April 1920. (Charlotte Fairchild)

His last US summer, 1924. Summer camp staff could not understand why such a sociable and confident boy wanted to spend every afternoon on his own in a boat. (Dartington Trust/Elmgrant Trust)

Next to Dorothy after her marriage to Leonard 'Jerry' Elmhirst, 3 April 1925. (Division of Rare and Manuscript Collections, Cornell University Library)

Dartington School's oldest 'junior' aboard his first motorbike, a 250cc Dunelt, purchased with the wages earned building a retaining wall in the old courtyard. (Dartington Trust/Elmgrant Trust)

The Avro Avian in which Whitney learned to fly, and in which he qualified for his pilot's licence just days after his 17th birthday. (Teignmouth and Shaldon Museum)

The initials of Whitney Willard Straight and his family, carved into a roof beam during renovations to Dartington. (Dartington Trust/Elmgrant Trust)

Leaning on his Brooklands Riley Nine, shortly before making his motor-sport debut at the Shelsley Walsh hill climb, 11 July 1931. (Kim and Mitch McCullough)

His first overseas race: the 1932 Swedish Winter Grand Prix. (Adam Ferrington)

Using Malcolm Campbell's stricken Sunbeam as a clipping point on his way to victory in Brooklands' chaotic Mountain Championship race, October 1933. (Autocar/Stringer/Getty Images)

Motor Sport marked Whitney's record-breaking ascent of Mont Ventoux by using as its cover image the photograph he took from the summit of his Maserati's cockpit. (Author's collection)

The Straight stable's first outing: Whitney in the Monaco Grand Prix, 2 April 1934. (Dean Butler)

Whitney's teammate Hugh 'Hammy' Hamilton lost his life in a last-lap accident in the 1934 Swiss Grand Prix. (Adam Ferrington)

Talking quietly with Dunlop Tyres' racing manager Norman Freeman (left) and John Cobb (centre), shortly before attempting to break Cobb's Outer Circuit lap record at Brooklands, 13 October 1934. (Dean Butler)

Whitney went for a tight line round the circuit in the bucking Duesenberg, but was still 2.59mph shy of Cobb's record when he wisely aborted his bid. (Chronicle/Alamy Stock Photo)

With trusted chief mechanic Giulio Ramponi, shortly before winning his last-ever race, South Africa's Border 100. (National Motor Museum, Beaulieu)

Whitney and Daphne leaving St Margaret's, Westminster, 17 July 1935. (Family collection)

Designer F.G. Miles and the man who gave him his brief, with the Miles Whitney Straight on press day, 22 January 1937. (Peter Amos)

The aircraft in flight the same day. (Peter Amos)

Ramsgate aerodrome's striking terminal building, designed by David Pleydell Bouverie. (T.G. Aviation)

The view from the dining room out on to Ramsgate aerodrome's apron, and two Straight Corporation aircraft in their distinctive livery. (T.G. Aviation)

6

Racing Wins Out

As his burns healed, Whitney took stock. Thomson & Taylor were working on the Maserati, attending to the overheating problem and slipping top gear, and preparing a twin-rear wheel arrangement for him to exploit on hill climbs. The Magnette was on its way to Pescara on Italy's Adriatic coast, where he would race on Tuesday, 15 August. He was confident that he would be well enough to compete in the Swedish Summer Grand Prix on 6 August, but he would need a car. He arranged to race the 2.3-litre Alfa Romeo Monza that Bernard Rubin had purchased for Tim Birkin.

Sweden's first Summer Grand Prix was being run over an 18½-mile circuit of narrow asphalt and gravel roads near Vram, 9 miles east of Helsingborg. Whitney was up against an unusual array of cars. Half the grid comprised Scandinavian drivers in road cars and one-off specials, some of them taking 'riding mechanics' with them. Whitney's nemesis of eighteen months earlier, Karl Ebb, was there in his SSK Mercedes, but the stiffest opposition would come from three 2.6-litre Alfas. Enzo Ferrari had entered a pair for Count Antonio Brivio and Mario Borzacchini, and Monaco's Louis Chiron would drive the third.

Practice opened early on the Wednesday morning. Rubin's car had not arrived, so Whitney set about learning the circuit in a road car. He became acquainted with the Alfa on the Thursday, and a rear axle problem was sorted in time for him to feel relatively confident as he took his place on the grid. He was almost as far back as in Reims, on the ninth row, but this time it was because grid positions had been allocated by ballot, not by practice times. Brivio was also unlucky: he had set fastest lap in practice, in a little under 14 minutes, but was starting on the eighth row, just ahead of Whitney. Some queried the wisdom of inexperienced drivers in standard cars leading the early stages of the race on narrow roads, but the organisers took the view that the faster drivers did not need the added advantage of occupying the front rows of the grid.

The folly of that decision emerged soon enough. Eugen Bjørnstad, in a 2.3-litre Alfa Monza like Whitney's, exploited his second-row grid position to build up a useful lead and, 2½ miles round the first lap, took a cautious line through a blind, adverse-camber right-hander. But second-placed Börje Dahlin slid wide under pressure from Olle Bennström's Ford and dropped the wheels of his Mercedes into a ditch. Apparently fearful that the car was going to roll, his riding mechanic, Erik Lafrenz, bailed out. Dahlin and the Mercedes cleared the ditch, ran through a hedge and ended up against a house, but Lafrenz was run over by Bennström, whose Ford came to rest upside down in the road, the contents of its ruptured fuel tank running across dry grass towards a second house. Next man on the scene, Henken Widengren's brother Per Victor, avoided Lafrenz but hit the Ford. Asser Wallenius ran into the ditch Dahlin had cleared, hit a culvert, somersaulted and severed a telegraph pole. Chiron hit Widengren's car, John Forsberg's Ford ended up next to Dahlin's Mercedes, and Oscar Wickberg was another to slide off into the ditch.

At that point, Lafrenz lay dead in the road, three others were injured, and Bennström's Ford and the house were alight. Fortunately, flags were now being waved ahead of the corner and the remaining drivers, Whitney among them, made their way through the mayhem at reduced speed before resuming their pursuit of Bjørnstad. There were still more than 220 miles to go, and now there were ambulances and fire engines to contend with too. Whitney ended that eventful opening lap in third place, 45 seconds adrift of Bjørnstad and 18 seconds down on Brivio. He had been more successful in overtaking Ebb this time, and lay more than 40 seconds ahead of him. Brivio took the lead on the second lap, and Whitney moved up to second on lap three. At that point, only getting updates on the gap to Brivio every quarter of an hour at the end of each lap, and with little hope of catching the Count in the larger-engine Alfa, he focused on his own race, difficult though that was. The image he retained of driving through the crash site each lap was of Lafrenz's shoe, left lying in the road. Eventually, after almost 3 hours of racing, he crossed the finish line second, 2 minutes 48 seconds after Brivio. Even by the standards of the time it had been a grim day. Börje Dahlin was blamed for the accident and never raced again. The Swedish Royal Automobile Club was criticised for its starting grid arrangements, and hosted only one other international race during the 1930s. The course at Vram was never used again.

By the time the grand prix circus gathered in Pescara a week later for the Coppa Acerbo, there had been widespread changes within the teams. These had been sparked by Nuvolari's disappointment with his broken axle at Reims-Gueux. It was his third such retirement of the season, and when Enzo Ferrari refused to give him a greater say in the running of the team, he switched to Maserati. His great friend Borzacchini joined him, while Campari and Luigi Fagioli joined Scuderia Ferrari, which was effectively Alfa Romeo's works team.

The Coppa Acerbo had been founded by Benito Mussolini's Agriculture Minister, Baron Giacomo Acerbo, in memory of his brother, Tito, who had been killed near Venice during the closing months of the First World War. Races were run over a roughly triangular course almost 16 miles in length. A long start–finish straight ran beside the railway hugging the shoreline on the way into Pescara. The course turned right on the outskirts of the city and embarked on a long, twisting climb through the foothills of the Abruzzo mountains until it wound round the village of Cappelle sul Tavo, then headed back towards the sea down a flat-out straight to the railway station in Montesilvano. There, a right-angled right-hander brought drivers back on to the start–finish straight.

Whitney was entered for two Coppa Acerbo events – a junior race over four laps for cars of up to 1,100cc, and a senior one three times as long for cars above that capacity. In the junior race, he and his Magnette would be up against a trio of Maseratis driven by Ferdinando Barbieri, Giuseppe Furmanik and Romano Malaguti. During practice, he found his gear ratios were not ideal for the combination of flat-out straights and long, winding climb, and he suffered persistent problems with oiling plugs. He was therefore pleased to be allocated a position on the front row of the grid, alongside Barbieri. For the senior race, Whitney would drive the 3-litre Maserati acquired by Rubin for Birkin, the car on which the unfortunate Englishman had burned his arm in Tripoli. Whitney would be up against a strong field of Alfas, Maseratis and Bugattis. He was less fortunate with his grid position this time, and would start from the outside of the fourth row, effectively twelfth on the sixteen-car grid.

The junior race started promptly at 8.40 a.m. Whitney and Barbieri got away side by side, but the Italian won the sprint down to the first corner, and gradually pulled away from Whitney as they climbed up towards Cappelle. Only when they headed back down towards the coastline did Whitney pick up ground and overtake Barbieri. His lead grew along the long home straight, and he ended the first lap 150 yards clear. A pattern emerged over the remaining three laps, Barbieri gaining on Whitney on the winding climb to Cappelle, but losing ground again on the straights. Whitney eased off over the last lap. Indeed, since his pit was situated just beyond the finish line, he took the chequered flag in neutral and pulled straight in. Even then, more than 10 seconds passed before Barbieri, still flat out, crossed the line. Whitney's well-judged win – his first on the Continent – was so dominant that it provoked several reactions. The authorities impounded the Magnette to ensure its engine capacity really was under 1,100cc. Raffaele Cecchini, who had trailed home fifth more than 6 minutes behind Whitney, tried to buy it. And Nuvolari, one of the favourites for the senior race, had now seen MG Magnettes take junior wins in both the Mille Miglia and the Coppa Acerbo, and wanted to race one. Whitney declined Cecchini's offer, but he would play a crucial role in satisfying Nuvolari's wish.

When the senior Coppa Acerbo was flagged away at 10 a.m., many drivers jumped the start and Whitney found himself dead last. He was up to eighth when he raced back along the home straight. Up ahead, Nuvolari was locked in a battle for the lead with Campari, while the more circumspect Fagioli was taking time getting used to his Alfa and lay fourth. Whitney started to encounter mechanical problems on lap three and finished it down in thirteenth place. He was lapped by Nuvolari and Campari shortly afterwards, and pulled off the road into retirement on his ninth lap. Campari had crashed by then, and Nuvolari had to pit late on, leaving Fagioli to inherit a lucky win.

There were now only five days until the Comminges Grand Prix, taking place in Saint-Gaudens, 55 miles south-west of Toulouse, and almost 900 miles from Pescara by road, so Coppa Acerbo drivers and teams had a challenge getting there in time. Indeed, Nuvolari and Borzacchini withdrew just the day before the race, infuriating the organisers, who had focused their publicity on the Flying Mantuan. As it was, Whitney and Fagioli only arrived in Saint-Gaudens after practice had concluded, and both men would have to start from the back of the grid. This was hardly a problem for Fagioli. The withdrawals had left him, in the latest Alfa, firm favourite. Indeed, he needed only a lap to take the lead and ran out a convincing winner by almost 2 minutes. Whitney's progress was steadier. He was up to sixth after ten laps, but then Rubin's Maserati let him down again. He had to pit on three successive laps, and retired at one-third distance with an engine problem.

But as his schedule of southern French events continued, so Whitney's fortunes improved. On arrival in Albi, some 110 miles north-east of Saint-Gaudens, he was reunited with his own Maserati. This had been towed down in the Bentley by Charles Brackenbury, the garage proprietor who had won June's Gold Star Handicap at Brooklands. The first-ever Albi Grand Prix was held on Sunday, 27 August, as at Reims-Gueux on a triangle of public roads. But rather than *routes nationales*, the Albi course was laid out on narrow, bumpy D-roads that twice crossed a railway line, and gave few opportunities for overtaking. More than twenty cars were entered, but some senior drivers, looking at the narrow, 5.7-mile circuit and reminded of the disaster in Vram, insisted that the event be split into two races, one for voiturettes under 1,500cc, and the other for more powerful cars.

Thus, after Pierre Veyron scored a home win in the junior race, Whitney lined up against only seven other cars for the twenty-two-lap Grand Prix. He was allocated pole position in the ballot, but squandered it by making a poor start and falling to third place behind Louis Braillard and Benoît Falchetto in a pair of Bugattis. Worse, Falchetto was slower than Braillard, and by sticking resolutely to the centre of the road was able to keep Whitney at bay while Braillard built up a considerable lead. It was not until the end of the ninth lap that Whitney was able to slip by on the short start–finish straight, much to the appreciation of the packed grandstand. During his relentless pursuit of Braillard, he set the fastest lap of the race, and at two-thirds distance was once more on the tail of a Bugatti. He made his move at the end of the sixteenth lap, but this time he spun and stalled, and just as at Reims he found the Maserati unresponsive to the starting handle. When the engine finally fired and Whitney leapt back aboard, he earned another cheer from the crowd but he had relinquished control of the race. Now, just as he had managed his gap to Barbieri in the Junior Coppa Acerbo, so Braillard did the same to him. The Swiss driver allowed Whitney to get within 6 seconds of him on the last lap, but no nearer. Whitney's poor start and spin had cost him the race, but the large crowd had loved every minute and the Albi Grand Prix became an annual fixture.

It was now that Whitney played his part in granting Tazio Nuvolari's wish to race a Magnette. He was effectively triple-booked for the forthcoming weekend. Committed to Sunday's hill climb on Mont Ventoux, almost 220 miles east of Albi, he knew full well that he would not use his entries for either the Maserati or the Magnette in the Tourist Trophy, taking place the day before in Northern Ireland. MG was thrilled at the idea of having Nuvolari race a Magnette in the UK's most important road race and, utilising Whitney's entry, rushed to prepare the car that had won the 1,100cc class in April's Mille Miglia. When Nuvolari scored a famous victory in it, Whitney was awarded the Tourist Trophy and £600 in prize money as the winning entrant!

At 7 a.m. the next morning, the D979 running east out of the village of Bédoin, 37 miles north-east of Avignon, was closed to local traffic, part of final preparations for the twenty-fourth Mont Ventoux hill climb. The 13.4-mile, loose gravel course rose gently away from vineyards through a beech wood to Saint-Estève. Here, a sharp left-hand hairpin marked the beginning of a steeper climb to Le Chalet-Reynard, the site of a wide concrete bowl of a hairpin, not unlike the Nürburgring's famous *Karussell*. From this point, 10 miles into the climb, vegetation petered out into a landscape of bleached limestone, and drivers met a brutal succession of hairpins on their way to the summit. Rudi Caracciola had won the last two climbs, and held the outright record, 15 minutes 12.4 seconds. French ace Phillipe Etancelin considered the time unbeatable.

Whitney gave himself the best possible chance of proving 'Phi Phi' wrong. This time, he arrived in plenty of time for practice and, upon finding several hairpins tricky on his first encounter with them, had a word with the start line officials ahead of his second practice run. He told them that the Maserati was proving difficult on the upper reaches of the mountain, so would they please leave a substantial gap before flagging away the next driver, to avoid any risk of a collision. This gave him time to drop back down sections of the course and make several runs through the most challenging corners.

The programme was straightforward. First came the motor cyclists, then the sports cars and finally the racing cars. In each group, competitors went up the mountain in the order of their engine capacity, smallest first. Thus it was that the final climb in the sports car group gave Whitney his second success of the weekend as an entrant. Charles Brackenbury had come to know Whitney's Bentley well after towing the Maserati behind it down almost 850 miles of French roads. The car now had a pre-selector gearbox, so that changing up to second gear was more 'dignified' than Whitney and Peggy had experienced at Shelsley. Brackenbury took the Bentley up the 'Giant of Provence' in 19 minutes 0.6 seconds. Victory in the over-5-litre sports category was somewhat hollow, as the Bentley was the only car in the group, but a win is a win and Whitney was happy to take it.

His competition in the racing class was stiff. A line-up of Etancelin, Moll, Siena and Sommer in Alfas and Braillard, Falchetto and Lehoux in Bugattis would, along with Whitney in the Maserati, have made for an impressive starting grid at any regional grand prix. Runs under 16 minutes were common through the afternoon. Lehoux got down to 15 minutes 8.4 seconds, beating Caracciola's 1932 record by 4 seconds, but he could do nothing whatsoever about Whitney. The Maserati's pre-selector gearbox and twin-rear wheels clearly helped, but Whitney looked exceedingly fast over the initial climb to Saint-Estève, and his cornering on the upper sections really marked him out.

The mechanism for timing each climb over such a challenging terrain and distance was as straightforward as the programme. Drivers were flagged away at precisely the time marked on the cards they carried with them to the summit. There, an official noted the time as each driver crossed the finish line, deducted the time on the card from it, and recorded the difference between the two. When Whitney handed the timekeeper his card, the official had to double-check his calculation. Whitney had climbed Mont Ventoux in 14 minutes 31.6 seconds, wiping more than 40 seconds off Caracciola's record – the record one of France's finest drivers thought could not be beaten.

In addition to his timing card, Whitney had also taken his Leica with him. In *parc fermé*, he climbed out, walked round to the back of the Maserati, and took a photograph of the car, the desolate limestone of Mont Ventoux's summit and the Rhône countryside below. It graced the December cover of *Motor Sport*. Inside the issue, Whitney spoke about the rumours that spread after his remarkable ascent up the loose gravel of Ventoux – surely this extraordinary young American must have cut his racing teeth on US dirt ovals. He patiently explained that he had moved to England when he was just 13, though he had tried Willard's old Chrysler on Applegreen's polo training ground ...

The final events of six hectic weeks of Continental competition for Whitney took place a week later at Monza, that cathedral of speed situated within Milan's royal park. The Monza Grand Prix was scheduled for the afternoon of Sunday, 10 September, and would comprise three heats run over fourteen laps of a narrow, 2.8-mile oval, slightly banked at each end. The first four finishers in each heat would qualify for the twenty-two-lap final. The Italian Grand Prix had been postponed from its original July date because of construction work, and would now take place on the morning of the Monza Grand Prix. This would be run over fifty laps of a 6.2-mile layout combining the oval and a 3.4-mile road circuit not unlike the modern-day track.

In the Italian Grand Prix, starting at 9.30 a.m., Whitney and his three-year-old, 2.5-litre Maserati were up against Europe's Grand Prix elite – Fagioli and Chiron in the latest Scuderia Ferrari Alfa Romeo P3s were expected to go head to head against Nuvolari and Taruffi in the 3-litre works Maseratis. Whitney could only soak up the experience of one of the biggest grands prix of the year, and hope to complete as many of the fifty laps as possible. In the end, after almost 3 hours of racing, he managed forty-three, two more than Lord Howe in his Bugatti, and finished eleventh.

Within 2 hours, Whitney was one of eight drivers lined up across the broad pit straight for the first heat of the Monza Grand Prix. The afternoon's opposition was very different from the morning's, and included two Counts. 'Didi' Trossi began racing, like Whitney, in 1931. At the end of that year, he invested money from the family-owned Banco Sella in Scuderia Ferrari and became the team's president. He was driving a narrow, 4.24-litre Duesenberg, designed for the ovals of US racing. Stanislas Czaykowski had won Brooklands' Empire Trophy in early July, and was racing a 4.9-litre Bugatti.

Whitney's pre-selector gearbox enabled him to make a good start in a slight drizzle, and he ran second round the first lap. The race developed into a fight for the lead between Czaykowski and Trossi, with Whitney content to maintain the top-four position that would qualify him for the final. The halfway mark, lap seven, saw Trossi coasting into the pits to retire, and Guy Moll spinning his Alfa through 720° exiting the South Curve. Somehow, he stayed on the narrow track and continued on his way to finish second, almost 12 seconds behind the victorious Czaykowski. Whitney also encountered problems on the South Curve but came home safely in fourth, 3.6 seconds down on Moll and just 0.6 seconds behind Felice Bonetto's third-placed Alfa. He went straight to the pit of Earl Howe, who was entered in the third heat, and advised caution on the South Curve. Moll went further and alerted race officials.

The second-heat drivers were left sitting in their cars, all lined up and ready to race, while marshals drove off with a broom and some sand to see what could be done about making the South Curve less slippery. When, after much delay and a word of caution from the race director, the race finally started, local heroes Campari and Borzacchini shot to the front. Campari was enjoying his last race meeting before switching to a career in opera, and wanted to leave the sport on a high. Borzacchini was keen to exploit the absence of his great friend Nuvolari, who had withdrawn from the afternoon's races. As they thundered down the back straight and entered the South Curve, all word of caution had left their heads. Accounts of what happened next vary, but the consequences are beyond dispute. Both men went over the banking. Campari's Alfa rolled several times, crushing him to death. Borzacchini was thrown clear of his Maserati but hit a tree and died shortly afterwards in hospital. Other drivers spun off to the inside and only three finished the first lap. All interest in the race ended and much time passed before news of Campari and Borzacchini's fates filtered through to a stunned crowd.

A further 2 hours went by while further efforts were made to sweep the South Curve and intense discussions took place between race officials and drivers. Eventually, the third heat was run, and Lehoux's Bugatti ran out a comfortable winner. Howe just missed out on fourth place and, therefore, the final. Only eleven drivers lined up for this, as only three had finished the tragic second heat. Whitney made another excellent start, leading round the first lap. Then Czaykowski and Lehoux broke clear and ran a close first and second. At the end of lap eight, Lehoux came by alone at reduced speed, signalling to his pit that another accident had occurred. A column of smoke rising from the far end of the straight confirmed this. Czaykowski had spun just beyond the South Curve and lay trapped beneath his burning Bugatti. He was already dead – his head had hit a stone. The race was flagged to a conclusion after fourteen of the scheduled twenty-two laps. Lehoux took a joyless win, and by strange coincidence Whitney was again a close fourth, again 0.6 seconds behind Bonetto.

Most magazines attributed the slippery nature of the South Curve to Trossi's Duesenberg. *Autocar* confidently stated that the car had 'burst its crank case and four gallons of oil were spilt on the track'.[1] Subsequent examinations of the Duesenberg proved conclusively that this was not true. The darkest day in a dark year for motor sport was more likely caused by a combination of the inappropriate nature of Monza's narrow oval, which was never used again in that form; by the drizzle that fell on and off throughout the day; and by the rubber and oil laid down by numerous cars racing through the South Curve over the course of the two events. Certainly, the Duesenberg's apparent connection with the tragedies did not trouble Whitney. Just as Trossi had thought that an Indy car might go well on Monza's oval, so Whitney thought it could be a contender for Brooklands' Outer Circuit record. Before heading home, he made arrangements with Scuderia Ferrari to acquire the car.

Just six days later, the British Racing Drivers Club hosted a 500-mile race at Brooklands. Whitney chose to race the Magnette, selecting Tim Rose-Richards as his co-driver. A stockbroker by profession, Rose-Richards had demonstrated his long-distance racing capabilities with three strong drives at Le Mans, and Whitney was looking forward to his first race on home soil in over three months. Regrettably, before a wheel had even turned, the day was marked by further tragedy. Early on race morning, a Vickers Virginia from RAF Manston on the Kent coast had overshot the Brooklands runway and run into the ditch inside the Byfleet Banking, killing the pilot. The aircraft lay where it came to rest, its back broken, for the duration of the race.

Adding to the macabre atmosphere, when the race began at 11 a.m., it involved just the one car. G.H.S. Balmain's MG Midget was the only un-supercharged car in the 750cc class, making him the sole limit man. He droned round for sixteen laps, quite literally in a race of his own, before a pack of supercharged 750cc and normally aspirated 1,100cc cars were flagged away in pursuit. Almost an hour passed before Rose-Richards, taking the first stint in the Magnette, finally started. He made steady progress and was running in the top six after three-quarters of an hour when he had to pit with ignition trouble. He handed over to Whitney at 2.10 p.m., but almost immediately the Magnette encountered a series of problems with the plugs and carburettor. Each time Whitney resumed racing, conscious that many cars were in trouble and that in such a long race on such a bumpy track, a good result was still achievable. But the next problem, a blown gasket, proved terminal and, only 40 minutes after taking the wheel, Whitney trailed into the pits to retire.

His frustrations were put into perspective when he saw a pall of black smoke rising from below the Fork. For the second time in a week, a car had overturned and caught fire. In July, when Whitney was winning plaudits for his brave drive at Reims-Gueux, M.B. Watson had come to prominence with a fine win in a fifty-lap Brooklands race in his MG Midget. Today, on just his second lap after taking over from his teammate, his car veered and flipped. Though he was thrown clear, the filler cap had been wrenched off and a tank full of fuel caught fire. The flames were so intense and the smoke so thick that officials only learned it was Watson by a process of elimination, after chalking off another lap against each of the other runners. He succumbed to his injuries 4 hours later in hospital, without regaining consciousness.

The run of dreadful news continued on the Monday morning, when the German press reported that Hammy Hamilton was dead. He had been performing wonders in the driving rain of the Czech Grand Prix, actually leading the 1,500cc class in his 750cc Midget, when his rain cape blew up in his face. He failed to take the next corner, hit a row of concrete posts and somersaulted into a field. Fortunately, reports of his demise were exaggerated. He had several cracked ribs and abdominal injuries, but he would live to race again. He convalesced over the winter on the Indian tea plantation managed by his brother and quit University Motors, intent on becoming a full-time, professional racing driver in 1934.

Whitney's antidote to all the tragedy was a weekend by the sea for himself and Peggy. Madeira Drive on Brighton's sea front was owned by the local council and was not, therefore, a public road, making it possible for the Brighton and Hove Motor Club to use a half-mile stretch of it for a speed trial. A year earlier, more than 100,000 people had watched Malcolm Campbell's Sunbeam race John Cobb's Delage from a standing start and take FTD in an average speed of more than 80mph. The decision to run the 1934 event with one entrant at a time was a wise one, for torrential rain would have made actual racing in such a confined space too hazardous. This made for a much longer meeting, but the B&HMC did an outstanding job of keeping to schedule, despite the appalling weather.

Peggy drove Whitney's Magnette to success in the 1,100cc racing category, in a time of 31.8 seconds, but the times started to tumble once Class 4D, for racing cars under 3 litres, got under way. Club president Earl Howe shot down the course in 25.6 seconds in his 2.3-litre Bugatti, an impressive time for the conditions. Whitney, with his pre-selector gearbox and the twin-rear wheel set-up he had used to such effect on Mont Ventoux, only managed to beat it by 0.2 seconds. But he had entered the Maserati in the unlimited racing category too. On his second run, armed with his knowledge of every puddle down the straight, he managed an average speed for the half mile from a standing start of over 74mph. Thus, 'Team Straight' emerged victorious from its day by the seaside, with Whitney setting FTD and Peggy best-in-class in the 1,100cc racing category.

A week later, on Sunday, 30 September, enthusiasts from all over the country descended on Shelsley Walsh in a state of great anticipation. The weather forecast promised a dry day, and if Whitney could take 40 seconds off Rudi Caracciola's Mont Ventoux record, then surely Hans Stuck's Shelsley mark, now more than three years old, was bound to fall. Arch-rival Ray Mays had entered two cars, in recognition that his big, heavy *Villiers Supercharge* had little potential left in it. He stood a better chance with a supercharged, 1,500cc Riley.

But first came the smaller cars. Peggy's initial run in Whitney's Magnette was ruined when the car came to a halt, popping and banging, between the Esses. She was obliged to coast backwards down the hill, but the Midland Automobile Club waived its sub-60 second rule and gave her a second run. In the afternoon she went up the hill in a poor 56.0 seconds, coming last-but-one in the 1,100cc sports category. The Magnette was clearly out of sorts.

Out came the 1,500cc cars, and Mays impressed in the Riley, catching the rear end swiftly as it stepped out in the Lower Ess. Moments later, the announcer, 'almost incoherent with excitement',[2] read out his time: 42.2 seconds. At his sixth attempt, he had taken 0.6 seconds off Stuck's record. It must have been a bittersweet moment for him. For a few minutes at least, he would be the outright record holder at Shelsley Walsh, but the most powerful cars were yet to make their first runs, and several were likely to be quicker than the *Villiers Supercharge*. First of the 3-litre class was Earl Howe in an Alfa, who went up in a disappointing 47.6 seconds. Lewis in a similar car managed 47.0 seconds, but 'the next entry on the programme was the reason for the migration of enthusiasts from obscure parts of England to

Shelsley Walsh that day'.³ Whitney drew up to the start line in the Maserati, wearing number 54. He was so focused as he pulled his black-lens goggles over his linen helmet that he did not notice Peggy standing beside the car.

'A perfect getaway,'⁴ called the commentator at the foot of the hill, Whitney's twin-rear wheels gripping the road almost instantaneously. It took a fraction longer for the Maserati's tail to snap back into line after the Lower Ess than Mays' Riley, but spectators clicking their stopwatches at the mid-point between the Esses reckoned that Whitney was 0.6 seconds up on Mays. Soon, hundreds of hats were being tossed in the air as the boy scouts operating the scoreboard hoisted up 41.4 seconds – Whitney had chipped a huge 1.4 seconds from Stuck's time, and lowered Mays' brief record by 0.8 seconds. Minutes later, Mays drew up in the *Villiers Supercharge*. 'One wished him luck now that his laurels had been snatched from him in the hour of triumph,'⁵ wrote *Autocar*, and Mays wrestled 42.4 seconds out of the old car, under Stuck's time but a second away from Whitney's. As the drivers trundled back down the hill for a spot of lunch and to prepare for their second runs, Leslie Wilson, Secretary of the Midlands Automobile Club, jumped down into the road and slapped Whitney on the back.

A curious feature of the afternoon was that few drivers improved on their first runs. Whitney was one of them, chipping a further 0.2 seconds from his time to leave the new record at 41.2 seconds. Still sat in the Maserati at the top of the hill, he gave a magnanimous interview to British Movietone. 'Well, I'm very pleased to have broken this record, but I'm only sorry that it hasn't gone to a British driver in a British car. I think actually the laurels of the day go to Mr Raymond Mays, who put up a time nearly as good in a car half the size.'⁶ Later, down in the paddock, the two men stood before a Pathé News camera. Mays spoke haltingly, looking down at his feet. 'I'm very glad indeed to have broken von Stuck's marvellous record for the hill of three years ago, and I'm also extremely glad that my friend Whitney Straight's done so marvellously on the Maserati.'⁷ He turned to Whitney, shook his hand and offered, 'Many congrats, marvellous show',⁸ but it was a beaming Whitney who made the handshake so vigorous.

The next day, Monday, 1 October, was the first of Cambridge's 1933–34 academic year. Whitney was still, formally, an undergraduate of Trinity College, but he quit within weeks. In the end, the decision was an easy one. All the pull was in one direction. Decades later, he admitted, 'I was fed up with my Moral Sciences course. I should have done Engineering.'[9] He had ignored the suggestion of Guy Donald on Cambridge's Appointments Board that he should go to Jesus College, where young men like Peter Masefield and Arthur Marshall had demonstrated that the college did indeed 'have a number of interesting fellows',[10] but even Engineering at Jesus would not have withstood the lure of racing.

Those extraordinarily intense eleven weeks between the mayhem of the Swedish Summer Grand Prix and Whitney's record-breaking Shelsley Walsh had proved to him that he could be successful among the very finest of European drivers. His nine races, two hill climbs and a sprint had delivered four wins, two seconds and two fourths. Only one of his three retirements had been in his own car. The four occasions on which he had also acted, in some capacity or other, as an entrant had generated three more overall or class wins and more prize money and trophies. Though he had also witnessed six deaths at close hand, he knew exactly how to go about the 1934 season. He would need his mother's capital to set him up, but thereafter he planned to earn a living from motor racing.

But he still had one more 1933 meeting, and Dorothy and Jerry were at Brooklands to see how he fared. It was due to be run on 14 October, giving Whitney his first weekend off since leaving for Sweden, but torrential rain forced it to be pushed back a week. The delay created a mouth-watering prospect. The highlight of the meeting was to be the Mountain Championship, an invitational, non-handicap race for eight leading Brooklands drivers over ten laps of the Mountain Circuit. Two years earlier, Tim Birkin's impressive win in this race had prompted Whitney to buy his Maserati. Current champion Malcolm Campbell was back in his Sunbeam, aiming to retain the Countess of Drogheda's trophy, and Whitney was also due to race against Lord Howe, Ray Mays, Brian Lewis, Tim Rose-Richards, 'Taso' Mathieson and A.H.L. Eccles. But Howe was recuperating from a shoulder operation, and he arranged for his Bugatti to be driven by Tazio Nuvolari, who was in England attending a dinner being held in his honour. So it would be Whitney *versus* Nuvolari, over ten laps of the Mountain Circuit.

Nuvolari arrived at Brooklands on the Thursday before the race. Mays was uncharitable, and indeed inaccurate, in his assessment of his performance: 'Being accustomed to road racing, the Italian found those great prairies of concrete a bit tricky and rather ill-suited to his own inimitable technique.'[12] In fact, the fans watching at the Fork thoroughly enjoyed the show put on by Nuvolari. Each time round, as he worked his way to within half a second of Whitney's lap record, he shaved a little more sand off the bank marking the outside of the hairpin. 'Once,' recorded 'Boanerges' in *Motor Sport*, 'he waved his hand, threw the car into a series of broadsides, perfectly controlled, and laughed delightedly.'[13] Sadly, Nuvolari was called to Paris that evening for a meeting about his 1934 options, and compatriot Piero Taruffi stepped in to defend Italian honour.

Race day dawned overcast but dry, and Whitney's exceptionally busy meeting began as early as the second race of the day, the Woking Senior Long Handicap, held over three laps of the Outer Circuit. He got away well in the Magnette and led Freddie Dixon's Riley down the Railway Straight, but the misfire that had so disrupted Peggy's performance at Shelsley returned and he finished well down the field. He may just have caught sight of Jack Duller getting crossed up on the Members' Banking, careering across the track, scything down a telegraph pole and being thrown from his Bugatti. Duller had the previous weekend's deluge to thank for saving his life – he landed in thick mud below the banking, and survived to do some business with Whitney the following year.

Whitney pulled into the paddock and jumped from the Magnette into the Maserati, still sporting its twin-rear wheels, for the Mountain Championship. Soon he was roaring away from the start line with six of Brooklands' finest, all intent on beating Taruffi to the Members' Bridge Turn. They failed. Mathieson was out immediately, a victim of fuel starvation, while Taruffi took a tight line into the turn and emerged in the lead. Rose-Richards spun wildly trying to track him and was hit broadside by Campbell, whose rear axle was damaged, locking his wheels and leaving the Sunbeam stuck fast in the road. Whitney avoided the melee by taking his usual high line, but at the Fork Taruffi was 80 yards clear of Lewis and Mays, with Whitney further back in fourth.

Bizarrely, when Taruffi arrived at the Members' Bridge Turn on lap two, he was confronted by a dozen or so spectators who had taken it upon themselves to leap down on to the track to help the marshals shift Campbell's car. At least one was facing Taruffi with his arms raised. Officials were waving blue flags, which at the time signified 'danger – drive with caution', but in the circumstances Taruffi could hardly be blamed for screeching to a halt. Lewis was next on the scene, followed by Whitney, who had already overtaken Mays. All three drove round the outside and continued racing, so Taruffi set off in pursuit, only to have to slam his brakes on a second time when he rounded the Fork and found Mays' Riley broadside across the track, stalled.

Only then, at the outset of lap three, did the 1933 Mountain Championship began in earnest, with Whitney chasing Lewis, and Taruffi 12 seconds back in third place. At least those last eight laps were thrilling. Whitney snatched the lead and used the tail of Campbell's stricken Sunbeam as a clipping point while each lap Taruffi hunted him down, demoting Lewis to third in the process. Whitney hung on to win by 2 seconds, something of a hollow win in the circumstances, but Taruffi put the whole thing down to experience and sportingly declined to lodge a protest.

Whitney was back in the Magnette for race five, the Oxford and Cambridge Mountain Handicap. This first-ever Brooklands inter-varsity race was a strange affair, for Oxford University prohibited its students from racing during term time. The five-car teams therefore consisted largely of former students and, in the case of Cambridge, included two men who had not completed their degrees. They duly came home first and second, Mays beating Whitney. The Magnette was still misfiring, but Whitney nonetheless managed to set a new 1,100cc lap record, at 69.74mph. Completing a 1-2-3-4 sweep for Cambridge was Whitney's Trinity friend, Dick Seaman, in his first Brooklands race.

In race six, the Woking Senior Mountain Handicap, the Magnette finally performed for Whitney. Over the course of five laps he overtook sixteen cars and broke the 1,100cc record again, raising it to 70.67mph. Only Dixon, the beneficiary of a very lenient handicap from Ebby, eluded him. At race's end, Dixon moved over into the passenger seat of his Riley, and Kaye Don's sister, Rita, climbed in behind the wheel for the five-lap Women's Mountain Handicap. It is claimed that, during practice and the race, he resorted to thumping her leg or even prodding her with a pin, if he felt she could go quicker on the banking and at the Fork. There was, apparently, money riding on her beating Brooklands' finest women driver, Kay Petre.

As in race six, the handicap favoured the Riley driver. Don was limit woman, receiving 20 seconds from Petre. Another woman joined Petre on scratch, even though she was competing in her first-ever race. It was Peggy – Ebby had clearly focused on her class win in Brighton more than her misfiring efforts at Shelsley. She would prove worthy of his respect. Don duly took off into the lead. After a lap, Petre's race craft had taken her from the back of the ten-car field to fifth, while Peggy was up to eighth. Over the remaining four laps, Petre climbed to second and got within 150 yards of Don, while Peggy finished a fine third, losing only 75 yards to Petre over the course of the 6-mile race. It was a highly creditable performance, in the last of her four competitive outings.

Whitney was already in the Maserati when she brought the Magnette into the paddock, scratch man in the last race of the day, but he was out after a lap with a mechanical problem. It was his last-ever race in the car. A light drizzle started falling, bringing down the curtain on a busy day, at the end of a long season.

Jerry had rather enjoyed it. Contradicting Brooklands' dubious slogan, 'the right crowd and no crowding', he told Whitney that he found motor racing 'a non-class affair: I have never seen such a mixture of types mingling in the paddock. Where in any other sport there is a definite segregation into peers and paupers, gentlemen and players.'[14] And he captured, simply but effectively, that cocktail of pride and anxiety felt by generations of racing drivers' parents:

> Don't think Mother is really against you racing as a sport – she really is not, and has a great admiration for the way in which you have gone into it and proved yourself. At the same time, owing to the nature of the sport, you will realise that it is with a sense of relief that we both learn of the safe conclusion of any meeting.[15]

Another conclusion was in the air. Over the winter, Whitney and Peggy went their separate ways, each to enter enduring marriages during 1935. He retained a sufficiently soft spot for her that her obituaries were pasted into the final pages of his racing clippings album. A fine driver to the end, she served during the Second World War as a senior commandant in the Mechanised Transport Corps. She was running an MTC training school in London when she fell ill, and she died in January 1945 of sepsis, contracted after an operation. She was just 32.

7

The Straight Stable

Even at that final Brooklands meeting of 1933, Whitney's plans for the following season were well advanced. Influenced by the experience he had gained racing the Maserati and the Magnette, the prize money he had generated as an entrant with Nuvolari, Peggy and Brackenbury and his exposure to the success enjoyed by Scuderia Ferrari, he made a bold decision. He would drive for and manage a team of cars competing across Europe and North Africa. The operation would be run as a limited company, and generate sufficient trade sponsorship, appearance fees and prize money to deliver a profit. To the Italians it was a *scuderia* and to the French an *equipe*, but in another reference to horse racing's influence over British motor racing, Whitney's team was generally referred to at home as 'the Straight stable'.

On 27 October, less than a week after Brooklands, Whitney wrote his last letter on Trinity College paper to Jerry, setting out his intentions. He had placed a provisional order with Maserati for three of its 8CM cars – '8C' for the latest 8-cylinder engine, now extended to 3 litres and delivering 250hp, and 'M' for *monoposto*, or single-seater. He had received offers of sponsorship and free fuel and oil, and was negotiating similar arrangements with spark plug and brake manufacturers. And he had chosen Bill Lambert as the operation's administrator. He had previously worked for Tim Birkin, and had kept Whitney's cousin, Dorothy Paget, informed of progress with the Blower Bentleys she had funded.

Whitney Straight Ltd was incorporated during December. In addition to Whitney, three other directors were appointed. Jerry was there to ensure that the £10,000 injected into the business by Dorothy was spent wisely, while Reid Railton had been engaged to make so many modifications to the Maseratis that it was entirely appropriate for him to have an executive role. The fourth director was John Pratt. Born in 1899 and educated at Eton and Sandhurst, his formal title was Lord Brecknock. In racing circles he was known as 'Breckie'. He had raced Sunbeams in his youth and supported Sir Henry Segrave in his world land and water record-breaking ventures. Since Segrave's death on Lake Windermere in 1930, he had acted as a senior marshal at Brooklands, the Tourist Trophy and at the Brighton speed trials, and he became a valuable source of advice to Whitney. Fred Gwatkin was another. He was the partner at the London firm of solicitors, McKenna & Co., who managed Dorothy's legal affairs in Britain. Whitney found it easier to take counsel from him, especially on financial matters, than he did from either his mother or stepfather.

Between them, Lambert and Gwatkin did their best to contain Whitney's ambitions. Lambert advised him not to extend the order with Maserati to four cars, as he doubted that three other drivers of sufficient quality could be recruited to race them – Count Antonio Brivio, the man who had beaten Whitney into second place amid the chaos in Vram, had already rejected an approach. But Whitney got his way, and the order for four cars was confirmed with Maserati during November. He met with some criticism in the letters pages of *The Motor* for buying foreign cars, and rebutted it with three columns of detailed argument in the magazine two weeks later. He concluded, 'I would like to say that from purely sentimental reasons, all other things being equal, I would far rather drive a British car than a foreign one. But the lamentable fact is that all other things are very far from equal.'[1]

Whitney Straight Ltd's administrative headquarters was established in Bush House, in London's Aldwych district. The building is perhaps most associated with the BBC's World Service and is today part of King's College, but it was originally set up as an international trade centre – the ideal base for an ambitious team racing across two continents. Whitney and Lambert played host there to the press, and proudly showed them a wall map of Europe and North Africa, pointing out the many races in which the Straight stable planned to compete.

Fig. 4: The locations of each motor-sport event entered by Whitney and/or the Straight stable, 1931–34.

The Straight Stable

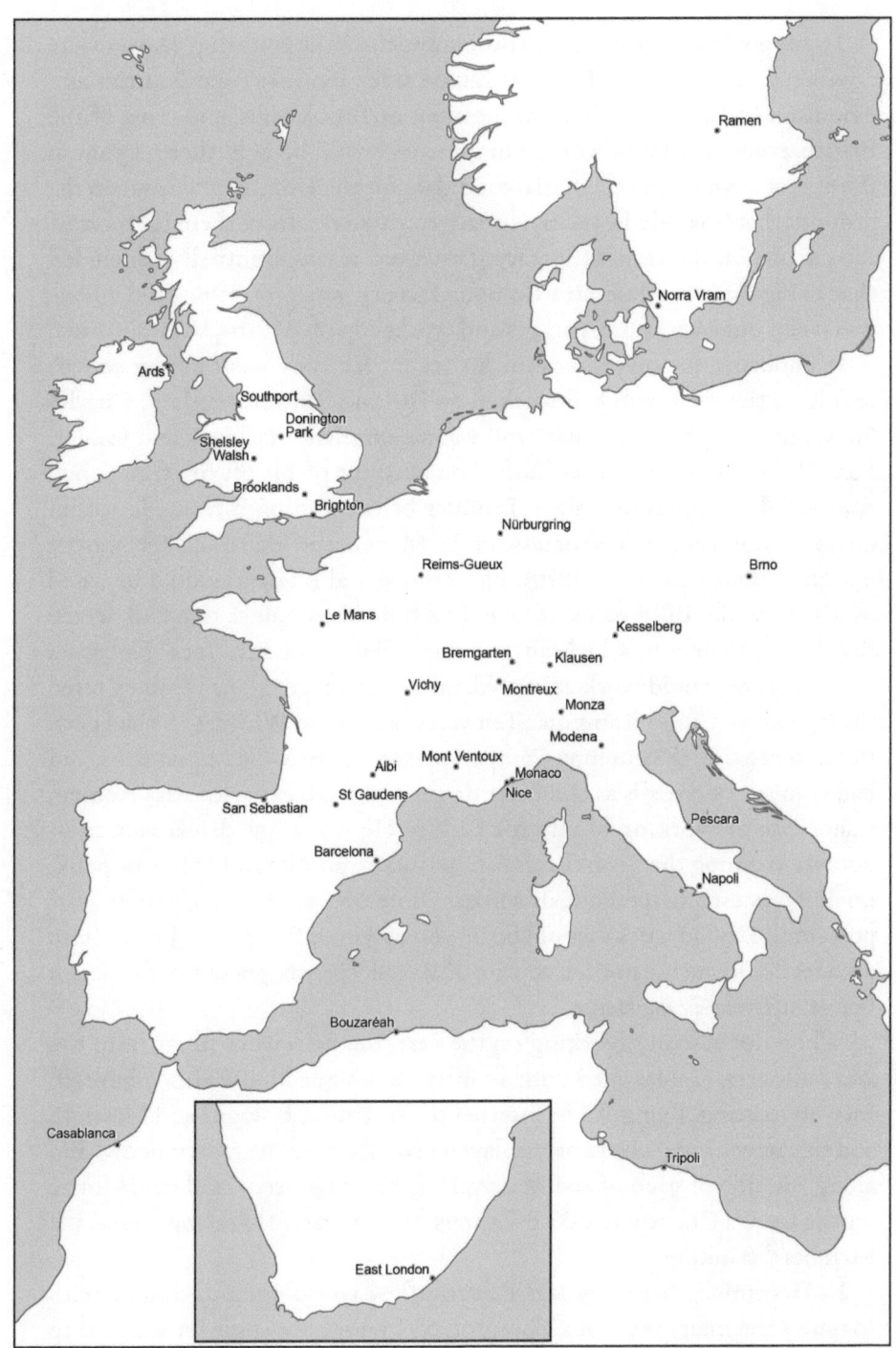

To support such an ambitious programme, two engineering centres were envisaged. The choice of a British base was obvious: Reid Railton and Thomson & Taylor ran their business out of Brooklands, and most of the British events the team would compete in would be held there. Lyon, in the east of France, was the initial candidate for the Continental base, on the grounds that it would be relatively easy to strike out from there for most of the circuits on the team's itinerary. However, it was eventually concluded that being near to Maserati's Bologna factory was preferable, and a lease was taken out on a house, garages and workshop on Milan's Via California.

In choosing the mechanics for his team, Whitney went a long way to reuniting the men who had worked on Birkin's Blower Bentleys. Charles Newcombe had been foreman, and was an excellent machinist and welder. F.R.W. England, known as 'Lofty' on account of his 6ft 5in frame, had completed an apprenticeship at Daimler before joining Birkin. He would go on to engineer Jaguar's successes at Le Mans in the 1950s, and become the marque's chairman in the 1970s. Newcombe and England would be based in Milan, while Billy Rockell, who had built the engines that had driven Bentleys to their run of Le Mans victories a decade earlier, 'Jock' Finlayson and Les Stone would work at Brooklands. To manage them, Whitney hired the legendary Giulio Ramponi. Ten years older than Whitney, he had been riding mechanic to Giuseppe Campari on successive Mille Miglia wins, and had enjoyed two spells as chief test driver and engineer with Alfa Romeo, either side of working briefly for Birkin. He was a fine driver too, most notably winning the Brooklands 6-hour race in an Alfa in 1928. Ramponi's uncle Francesco helped out in Milan, while one of the team's three purpose-built Dodge trucks would be driven by James Robertson Justice, two decades before he became a favourite of British cinema-goers as Sir Lancelot Spratt in *Doctor in the House*.

When not actually working on the cars, the men wore smart team ties and pullovers, emblazoned with an insignia designed by Whitney himself. Into his existing 'flying W' he inserted the trident of Bologna and Maserati, and this new badge would be displayed proudly over the radiator cowl and along the side of each of the Maseratis. It first appeared, in abstract form, on the team's Christmas 1933 greetings card, apparently racing round the Members' Banking.

In December, Whitney and Railton flew to Bologna to discuss with Maserati the many revisions Thomson & Taylor's ace engineer was due to make to the cars. A Wilson pre-selector gearbox was a given. Maserati's blunt, rectangular radiator cowling would give way to a slanted, heart-shaped arrangement, fronting a new radiator and cooling system. Revised rear suspension and shock absorbers were to be fitted. A 40-gallon fuel tank, constructed from a single, baffled piece of 22-gauge sheet steel, would be 20 per cent lighter than Maserati's standard, 24-gallon unit. A new oil tank would be almost half the weight of Maserati's, but hold as much lubricant. Bespoke bodywork would be fitted by coachbuilders Gurney Nutting, architects of the sedanca body on Whitney's old 8-litre Bentley – now replaced with a lower-mileage, 3-litre model. Maserati agreed to the modifications, and Whitney and Railton flew back to await delivery of the first car.

It did not show up until mid-February. This was because Alfa Romeo had delivered a blow to Whitney months ahead of meeting him on the racetrack. Ordered by the Italian government not to sell its cars to foreigners, it rescinded numerous orders, and as a result Maserati found itself inundated with requests for 8CMs. It tried to satisfy them all, and delivery times slipped alarmingly. Three years earlier, Birkin's crewman Clive Gallop had driven the 26M all the way from Bologna to Brooklands in full racing trim, devoid of lights or mudguards. In marked contrast, when the first of Whitney's 8CMs finally showed up, on 13 February, it sat snugly in the back of a Dodge lorry driven into the Brooklands paddock by Robertson Justice. By complete coincidence, it had precisely the same chassis number as the Magnette that Whitney was about to sell: 3011.

It was actually a late 1933 car in design, with the chassis rails and cockpit sides 620mm apart. As such, it did not conform with one of two stipulations motor racing's governing body, the Association Internationale des Automobiles Clubs Reconnus (AIACR), had introduced for its 1934 Grand Prix formula: cars were to be at least 850mm wide at the cockpit, and weigh at least 750kg. However, Whitney was not troubled by this: Brooklands' events, hill climbs and sufficient Continental races on the team's schedule were not run under AIACR regulations, and 3011 was assured of a busy season. Another AIACR regulation, that cars should run in the national racing colours of their entrants, meant that when Whitney, still an American citizen at this time, tested 3011 on the Mountain Circuit two days later, it was painted in US racing white and blue colours. It was yet to undergo Railton's modifications, so he was pleased to get within 0.4 seconds of the lap record he had set in the 26M. The second Straight stable Maserati, the wide-bodied 3012, left Bologna for Brooklands on 27 February, and that same week Ramponi reported for duty. As it was unclear when the other cars would arrive, Whitney decided for now to retain the 26M, but he sold the Magnette for £650 to his Cambridge friend, Dick Seaman, just in time for Dick to practise in the car in advance of Brooklands' first meeting of the year, on 3 March.

Whitney went along to watch Dick in action. He wore a smart, three-piece suit, striped shirt and team tie, quite unlike the Dartington country tweeds in which he had first appeared in the Brooklands paddock. On his arm was Lady Bridget Poulett, a favourite model of society photographers Cecil Beaton and Norman Hartnell. Dick was unplaced in all three of his races, but Whitney wrote to him afterwards, commiserating with him and inviting him to Bush House to discuss how Team Straight could best help him during the coming season. He concluded, 'Certainly if you were going in for racing seriously it would be advisable to leave Cambridge. But of course that is a personal matter for you to decide.'[2] Within weeks, Dick arrived at his parents' home with rather more luggage than a few weeks' break over Easter might require, and announced that he had quit university. His parents were appalled, but could not sway him from committing full-time to racing. His season would include the occasional race in which the Magnette would be entered as part of the Straight stable.

Whitney's primary choice as a full-time teammate was Hugh 'Hammy' Hamilton, who had returned to England, fully recovered from his Czech Grand Prix injuries, after a restorative six months in India. Whitney had been aware of Hammy since August 1931, when he had won that first Brooklands race Whitney had participated in. He was seven years older, and had first experienced Continental road-racing at Reims-Gueux in 1931, when Earl Howe paid him the compliment of having him take over his Bugatti for the latter stages of the French Grand Prix. A fortnight later, he performed wonders at the Nürburgring, not only winning the German Grand Prix's 750cc class in a little MG Midget, but running ahead of most of the 1,500cc cars too.

Since then, Hammy had consolidated his reputation as a fine road-racer, but there was a question over his temperament: the reason why Nuvolari had won the 1933 TT in the Magnette ostensibly entered by Whitney was because Hammy had so intimidated his riding mechanic during a pit stop that the poor man had spilt fuel, set fire to his gloves and overalls and struggled to buckle the bonnet strap. The stop took more than 7 minutes, while Nuvolari beat Hammy by only 40 seconds. Driving for the Straight stable would give Hammy the opportunity to demonstrate not only that he was fully recovered from his injuries, but that he could stay cool under pressure.

Whitney's choice of a third driver only confirmed Lambert's concern that the team might struggle to find sufficient driving talent to justify the purchase of four cars. He was Rupert 'Buddy' Featherstonhaugh. Better known for his jazz band than his driving, he had done little of note behind the wheel since his impressive, Ebby-defying brace of mountain handicap wins in May 1932, and Whitney actually gave him a trial in the 26M at Brooklands before confirming the offer of a drive. When Team Straight contested its first events, on Easter Monday, 2 April 1934, Whitney raced 3012, the wide-bodied 8CM, in the Monaco Grand Prix, while Buddy drove the 26M at Brooklands. Hammy sat the weekend out, and there was no question at this point of recruiting a fourth driver – in early April, there was still no indication of when Maserati would supply even a third car to the team.

To be one of only sixteen drivers invited by the Automobile Club de Monaco to participate in the first grand prix meeting of the new formula was a considerable compliment to Whitney, who was after all entering only his second full season of racing. His rivals included no fewer than five Scuderia Ferrari P3 Alfa Romeos, along with three works Bugattis, a fourth entered privately by Nuvolari and the 8CM Maserati ordered hastily by Earl Howe in the wake of losing out on his Alfa. Two further threats were still some months away from appearing on the track. Adolf Hitler had become Chancellor of Germany in January 1933, and announced at the following month's Berlin Motor Show a grant of 500,000 Reichsmarks to the German manufacturer building a car to compete under the 1934 grand prix formula. In fact, the funding had been split between two firms: Daimler-Benz was hard at work on its 8-cylinder, 3.4-litre W25 Mercedes, and Auto Union, the company created recently by the merger of Audi, DKW, Horch and Wanderer, was putting the finishing touches to its revolutionary rear-engine, 4.4-litre P-wagen. Both cars had been designed from scratch with the 750kg formula in mind, rather than the latest evolutions from Alfa, Bugatti and Maserati. If the Straight stable was to enjoy a successful season, it was likely that Whitney, Hammy and Buddy would need to get their winning in early.

The 1934 Monaco Grand Prix was held on Easter Monday, 2 April, over 100 laps of a 2-mile circuit that would in many respects appear familiar to a modern-day enthusiast. It was preceded by three days of practice, when each driver's fastest lap time would determine his grid position. Pace-setter throughout was Count Trossi in one of the Alfas, setting a pole position time of 1 minute 58 seconds. Whitney's best time on the Friday was 2 minutes 5 seconds, but he had already shaved 3 seconds off this – some 6 seconds better than Howe in a similar car – when he decided in the closing stages of the final practice session to take the tunnel flat out. After all, the Alfa drivers had been doing this as a matter of routine, and he felt it was here that he could improve further on his lap time. Regrettably, he learned the hard way that his car was less stable than the Alfas, pirouetting out of the tunnel and wrecking his rear axle against a kerb. If he was to race, he urgently needed a replacement.

A call to Thomson & Taylor revealed that they had an axle, and Birkett Air Services pilot L.H. Stace flew directly to Brooklands to collect it. His itinerary must have caused Giuseppe Ramponi palpitations. After clearing customs at Lympne on the Kent coast, some 70 miles from Brooklands, Stace planned to refuel at Lyon, 500 miles to the south, and hoped to make Marseille, 150 miles from Monaco, by midnight. Whitney needed another option, and started contacting 8CM owners who were not racing that weekend. He found Raymond Sommer at home in Paris, and the Frenchman kindly had the rear axle disconnected from his Maserati and driven out to Orly airport, from where the famous aviator Hélène Boucher flew it down to Nice, only a dozen or so miles from Monaco. As the *Daily Telegraph* correspondent drove into Monte Carlo from the airport that evening to cover the following afternoon's race, he was astonished to see Whitney weaving in and out of the traffic in the opposite direction. Plan B had comfortably beaten Plan A, and Ramponi and his crew may even have got some sleep in ahead of the race.

Rain on the morning of race day gave way to bright sunshine, and Whitney lined up eleventh on the grid. Trossi failed to convert his pole position and local ace Louis Chiron came through from the second row to seize the lead. Over 3 hours later, he was almost a lap ahead of second-place Guy Moll, making his debut for Scuderia Ferrari, when, just three laps from home, he ran wide at the Station Hairpin and buried the front of his Alfa deep in a sand bank. By the time Chiron extricated himself, Moll was long gone, and he had to content himself with second place. Whitney ran steadily to finish seventh, four laps down. Over 100 laps, this was roughly on a par with the 4 seconds he had ceded to Trossi over a single lap in practice. He could not, therefore, blame his race performance on his practice accident or on the replacement axle. It was a sobering moment. The P-wagen Auto Union was not yet race-ready, yet Hans Stuck had recently driven one to several world speed records. Mercedes was coming too, and if the latest Alfa really was that much faster than the 8CM Maserati, then it was going to be a long season for the Straight stable. The £64 18s starting money Whitney generated in Monte Carlo, and the £10 prize money Buddy earned for finishing second in a Brooklands mountain handicap the same day, were of little consolation.

Whitney's Monaco adventure included an interesting diversion. The track at Montlhéry, 20 miles south of Paris, comprised a banked oval with a far smoother surface than Brooklands and a twisty road circuit. It had hosted the French Grand Prix in recent years. Whitney dropped in there to meet Prince Nicholas of Romania. The estranged brother of King Carol II had competed in the Le Mans 24-hour meeting the previous year in a 7-litre Duesenberg SJ, only to be disqualified while the car ran fifth when his teammate made a pit stop sooner than regulations permitted. Whitney spent the day testing the Duesenberg, and concluded that he would co-drive it with Prince Nicholas at Le Mans over the weekend of 16–17 June.

On Saturday morning, 28 April, Reid Railton stood in the Brooklands paddock next to 3012, the Maserati Whitney had raced in Monaco. With him was Rodney Walkerley, the sports editor of *The Motor*, who wrote as 'Grand Vitesse'. Walkerley was gently prodding the top of Railton's new fuel tank, watching the 22-gauge sheet steel give 'as if it were an air cushion'.[3] He wondered whether it was robust enough to withstand 100 laps – more than 260 miles – of Brooklands' bumps. It was actually about to play a key role in the most closely fought of Whitney's victories.

All three Straight drivers were racing in the JCC International Trophy – Whitney's 8CM and Buddy's 26M Maseratis were in Group 3, and would be using the most severe of the Junior Car Club's handicap lanes, while Hammy's Magnette (K3009, entered by his friend Robin Mere) was in Group 2 and would be using the middle lane. The starting grid ballot was kind to all three of them, as they were each allocated places on the front row.

The weather had been appalling throughout practice, and more rain was forecast for race day, so the operators of the Tecalemit tyre-slicing machine – a device that cut thin, transverse grooves into the rubber to create a rudimentary form of rain tyre – had worked into the small hours of race morning. This was just as well, as a heavy downpour an hour before the 2.30 p.m. start time led to all thirty-seven drivers switching to wet-weather rubber. Then, as hooters counted down the final minutes and a Union Flag waved the field away, the sun broke through. The combination of bright sunshine and heavy spray made for an unnerving opening lap and rendered the handicap lanes 'a medley of hurdles, tubs, arrows and flags without exact definition'.[4] Yet there was something familiar about the leading pair as the field headed back down to the lanes at the start of lap two: Whitney was four lengths up on Brian Lewis, who was driving the 3-litre Maserati that Whitney had raced in Pescara and Comminges the previous summer, and which poor Birkin had burned his arm on in Tripoli.

After fifteen laps, Whitney took the first prize money of the day – £10 for leading at that stage – but two laps later he was obliged to change his rear wheels after a tyre tread gave trouble. Walkerley reported that he was stationary for only 37 seconds, yet the handicap lanes were working so well that when he resumed he was down in tenth place, and Freddie Dixon in his little 1.6-litre Riley – a Group 1 car – was out in front, pocketing the next £10 bonus for leading at thirty laps.

Whitney was soon tearing back through the field, up to eighth within four laps, and fourth in another nine, while Dixon made a series of pit stops and fell out of contention. At fifty laps, Whitney was back in front, the recipient of the last of the £10 bonuses. He was pulling clear of Lewis, while Hammy was disputing third place with another Magnette driver, W.L. Handley. At three-quarters distance, the track had finally dried out, the drivers could make out their handicap lanes more easily and the repair gangs were no longer attending to broken fencing and ruptured sandbags. Whitney was well clear of Lewis, while Hammy, delayed by a pit stop to solve a radiator problem, still seemed assured of a top-five finish.

Then it all seemed to go wrong for the Straight drivers. Hammy retired with a blown gasket, Buddy earned his one mention in the following week's magazines – 'Featherstonehaugh, with the elder Maserati, seemed just to fade out at the end'[5] – and, with just ten laps left, a white warning strip appeared on Whitney's right front tyre, a sign that the tread was wearing out. There was too little time left for him to stop for a fresh tyre and regain the lead, so he faced a dilemma – sacrifice the win but do the sensible thing and finish the race in one piece, or pursue victory but risk a high-speed accident should the tyre blow. He chose the latter option. At the end of lap ninety-four, with six to go, he led Lewis by 32 seconds. On successive laps the gap fell to 23 seconds, then 9, then 4 ... and there, tantalisingly, it stabilised, Whitney managing the lead by monitoring Lewis in his mirror as keenly as he watched the distressed rubber in front of him. The tyre finally threw what little was left of its tread just beyond the finish line, with Whitney still holding that 4-second lead, after almost 3 hours of absorbing racing.

It was one of Whitney's finest drives, but Railton's pliant fuel tank had played its part too. Lewis' car was fitted with a standard-issue tank, and he pitted for fuel twice. His first stop took 54 seconds, and his second, when he also changed two wheels, took 1 minute 27 seconds – a total duration in the pits of 2 minutes 21 seconds. Whitney's early stop for fresh rubber cost him 37 seconds, while his scheduled stop for fuel and tyres took 1 minute 10 seconds – a total of 1 minute 47 seconds. Thus, Lewis spent 34 seconds longer in the pits, and lost the race by only 4. If Whitney had not had Railton's new tank, Lewis would have won by half a minute, and probably much more, since Whitney would have been more inclined to change the tyre if he was already running second, with plenty of time in hand to still finish clear of third-place Tim Rose-Richards.

The 1934 JCC International gave the Straight stable one of its biggest pay days of the season. In addition to the £20 bonuses for leading at fifteen and fifty laps, Whitney earned £500 as the winning entrant and £25 as the winning driver, plus bonuses from sponsors of £327 10*s* – a total of £872 10*s*. But post-race festivities were kept to a minimum, as Whitney and Hammy had an appointment in North Africa. They would be racing the following weekend in the Tripoli Grand Prix, and practice was scheduled to begin on the Friday.

8

From Brooklands to Bremgarten

Whitney and Hammy took turns at the wheel of the Bentley, making short shrift of the 1,300-mile journey across France, over the Alps and down to Naples for the sea crossing to Tripoli. Three trucks were also making their way to the port. Aboard one of two Team Straight lorries was Whitney's car for Tripoli, 3011. The other was empty, in expectation of receiving its cargo in Naples. A transporter from the Maserati works carried a new 8CM, painted in Italian red. Chassis number 3016 had been allocated to Tazio Nuvolari, but he had broken his leg in a racing accident. Maserati, desperate to work through its backlog of orders, decided that, since he was not able to race the car, it would go to the Straight stable. Repainted in US racing colours, it became Hammy's primary car for the next four months, but the team's schedule was so busy that it never made it back to Brooklands to receive Reid Railton's modifications.

The Tripoli Grand Prix was run on 6 May over forty laps of an exceedingly fast, roughly rectangular, 8.2-mile circuit with gently banked bends. Hammy, as new to the circuit as he was to his car, impressed early in practice when he averaged 115mph in posting a lap time of 4 minutes 9 seconds, almost 19 seconds under the previous year's lap record. Soon, however, Varzi and Chiron were lapping their Alfas in under 4 minutes, and the 8CMs of both Whitney and Hammy were among several Maseratis to encounter piston problems, curtailing their practice sessions. It made no odds to their grid positions, which were determined by race number.

Hammy had the advantage of starting from the front row of the twenty-six-car grid, while Whitney lined up near the back.

Whitney's engine was still not running well come race day, and though he climbed to fifteenth place over the first lap, he managed only eleven laps before retiring. Hammy gave a much better account of himself, running third behind Varzi and Chiron until a magneto problem forced him into retirement at three-quarters distance. Moll came through to second, so that Alfas romped home first, second and third. Etancelin was fourth in another independently entered 8CM, almost 7 minutes behind the victorious Varzi, yet Bill Lambert was in relatively bullish mood when he updated Jerry ahead of the team's next race, in Casablanca, on Morocco's Atlantic coast: 'On the Tripoli showing I think our cars stand a good chance of being in the first three.'[1]

But first, the team had to negotiate the 1,500-mile journey from Tripoli to Casablanca. Whitney and Hammy once more took turns driving the Bentley, 'going through country which had hardly been opened'.[2] By Sunday, 20 May, a full week ahead of race day, they were safely ensconced in Casablanca's Hotel Transatlantique. James Robertson Justice had a more eventful trip at the wheel of the truck carrying Hammy's car. He was 20 miles outside Algiers, the halfway point in the trek along the North African coast, when his right front wheel hub sheered. Fortunately, the truck remained upright on three wheels and 3016 was undamaged. Robertson Justice hired a replacement truck in Algiers and reached the circuit on the Thursday, too late for that morning's practice. Still, Whitney and Hammy put in strong performances during the Friday and Saturday sessions and lined up fourth and fifth on the grid, behind only Lehoux and Chiron in Alfas and Etancelin in his Maserati.

Race day was sunny, but the drivers had a strong Atlantic breeze to contend with as they set off on the first of sixty laps of the 4-mile circuit. Through the early stages, Hammy ran fourth and Whitney fifth, but Hammy had to pit to replace a tyre, dropping to eighth. His was the first of many punctures that marred the race – the circuit had recently been widened, and perhaps debris had been left on the track surface. He was back up to sixth by one-third distance, but was obliged to retire after forty-two laps with a leaking fuel tank. Whitney had a long fight for fourth place with the third of the Scuderia Ferrari drivers, Gianfranco Comotti, and this became third when Lehoux suffered a puncture. By lap fifty-five, Whitney was within 20 seconds of second-place Etancelin, who was nursing fading brakes, but, with just three laps to go, it was Whitney's turn to pick up a flat tyre, and at a stroke a likely second became a frustrating fourth – all the more so because Etancelin continued to slow in the closing stages, while Lehoux spent his final lap contending with another puncture. Only Chiron seemed free of tyre problems, and made up for his Monaco disappointment with a comfortable win.

The Straight stable dusted itself down, pocketed £441 10s in starting money and fourth-place prize money, and headed for Europe. One truck took 3011 back to Brooklands, so that it could be fitted with a different rear axle and twin-rear wheels in preparation for the first Shelsley Walsh meeting of the year, on 9 June. Whitney, Hammy and the truck carrying Hammy's 3016 made for Lake Geneva, where the Montreux Grand Prix was to be held over ninety laps of a 2-mile, 'round-the-houses' circuit on 3 June. The race was being run under AIACR regulations, so Whitney was driving the wide-bodied car in which he had won the JCC International, 3012.

The race clashed with the Eifelrennen meeting at the Nürburgring, where Auto Union and Mercedes were racing each other for the first time, so Scuderia Ferrari sent Chiron to Germany and entered Alfas for Trossi, Varzi and Moll in Switzerland. Interestingly, the 8CMs seemed more competitive on this street circuit than at Monaco, and the three practice sessions, marred by intermittent, heavy rain, became a battle for pole position between Etancelin and Whitney. 'Phi-Phi' won out with a fastest lap of 1 minute 54 seconds, 3 seconds faster than Whitney, while Hammy lined up fifth.

A hailstorm on race morning gave way to bright sunshine. Etancelin made a strong start and gradually pulled clear. Moll briefly demoted Whitney to third but had to pit with oil feed problems, and thereafter Whitney used the tight nature of the circuit to good effect, holding Varzi and Trossi at bay. Hammy ran in a secure fifth. Whitney slowed slightly at about one-third distance, apparently to wipe oil from his goggles, and that was all the opportunity the Alfa drivers needed. They slipped by and were able to increase their pace immediately. Trossi took up the chase of Etancelin when Varzi also encountered oil feed problems, and managed his race to perfection, overtaking the Frenchman with just two laps to go. Whitney came home fourth, one lap behind, and Hammy fifth, two laps down.

Whitney Straight

The pair's performances were good enough to generate another £387 in starting fees and prize money, but their frustrations were mounting. The Maserati 8CM was clearly no match for the P3 Alfa Romeo, and yet the Alfa was now only the third best racing car in Europe. At the Nürburgring, Chiron had finished a distant third to Manfred von Brauchitsch's Mercedes and Hans Stuck's Auto Union, and the most striking thing about the German cars was not their speed *per se*, but that they could exit corners so much faster, without wheelspin. The Straight stable cars were not even the fastest of the Maseratis — Etancelin's privately entered 8CM had started from the front row in Monaco, and outperformed Whitney and Hammy in Tripoli, Casablanca and now Montreux. Most disconcertingly, Montreux was the first time, after Tripoli and Casablanca, that Whitney had consistently run better through a race weekend than Hammy, whose car, bar a coat of paint, was the same as it had left the Maserati factory. It was evident that Whitney's preference for the pre-selector gearbox was costing him dearly on faster circuits.

They headed home, Hammy for a weekend off and Whitney to see if he could post the first sub-40-second run up Shelsley Walsh. He was odds-on favourite to retain his Shelsley crown. Ray Mays and his associates had put so much effort into making their own car, the ERA (English Racing Automobile), ready for the big day — which they failed at — that their Riley, which had briefly held the hill record at the previous meeting, was not well-prepared either. Mays could manage no better than 42.8 seconds — slower than in September. So Whitney's main concern as he pulled up to the line in 3011 was Shelsley's new starting system. It comprised a series of lights counting down from five to one, before a green light signifying 'Go!' The problem was that the countdown lights were not set at regular intervals, so some drivers (most notably Mays on his first run) anticipated the green light and jump-started, while others (most notably Whitney on his) were surprised by it and were late away. It made little difference to the outcome. In spite of his front wheels leaving the track surface when he finally leapt away from the start line, and again as he accelerated out of the Lower Ess, Whitney set a time of 40.0 seconds dead, 1.2 seconds under the record he had set in September. There had been no trace of a slide or a drift through the Esses, and this, combined with his tardy start, had made his run look deceptively slow to many spectators. They were, wrote Sammy Davis in *Autocar*, 'only gradually becoming accustomed to the fact that bank bumping and forty-five-degree skids are not good technique'.³

Another Shelsley win for Whitney added £226 in prize money and sponsors' bonuses to the stable's coffers, but Whitney went home unclear if he would follow a 40-second drive one weekend with the world's most iconic 24-hour race the next. That morning's *Daily Telegraph* had quoted his Le Mans co-driver, Prince Nicholas of Romania, describing Whitney as 'a brainy and courageous driver who handles a car the way I like to see them handled, besides being a thorough gentleman'.⁴ Yet, though exiled and living in Munich, Prince Nicholas was under pressure from his family not to race. Eventually, he drove to Paris on the Wednesday before the big race, and Whitney flew over to Le Mans.

This gave him a maximum of five practice sessions in which to acquaint himself with the 8.3-mile circuit and its famous Mulsanne Straight, and to see how the 7-litre Duesenberg would fare against the favourites, four privately entered, 2.3-litre Alfa Romeos. Two of the sessions took place in daylight, and three overnight, between 10 p.m. and 6 a.m. It was during the last of these, in the early hours of race morning, that a piston seized on the Duesenberg, putting Whitney and Prince Nicholas out of the race before it had begun. At 4 p.m. the next afternoon, the sole-surviving Alfa, driven by Luigi Chinetti and – that man again – Phi-Phi Etancelin, won the twelfth Le Mans 24-hour race, thirteen laps clear of a little 1.5-litre Riley. Whitney was left to wonder, 'What if?'

Hammy fared little better that weekend. He raced 3016 in the Penya Rhin Grand Prix, on Barcelona's Montjuïc circuit, but he was unable to exploit another front-row grid slot, trailing into the pits after a lap to investigate an oil leak. The problem worsened and he retired after eleven of the seventy laps, powerless to stop Varzi, Chiron and Lehoux cruising to another one-two-three for Scuderia Ferrari, three laps clear of the rest of the field.

The following Saturday, 23 June, Whitney was back at Brooklands for the Empire Trophy. He was in his Shelsley-winning Maserati, 3011, while Dick Seaman was an official Whitney Straight Ltd entry for the first time, driving Whitney's old Magnette, K3011. The race was a handicap over 100 laps of a specially designed, 3-mile circuit (Fig. 5). It involved a clockwise lap of the Outer Circuit, starting below the Fork, with several additional features designed to lower overall speeds. On the Railway Straight, a double-ess bend called the Railway Snake was set out in straw bales and barrels, while halfway round the Members' Banking more straw bales funnelled the drivers down to a short straight at the bottom of the track, then fanned back out to allow faster drivers to exploit the rest of the banking before turning down the back straight. Here, the Fork Hairpin was in operation, but on a tighter line than on the Mountain Circuit, since drivers could only use half the width of the traditional finishing straight. They quickly faced an equally tight left-hand hairpin to come back down the straight and complete the lap.

None of these additions were handicap turns, as with the JCC International. The whole field had to negotiate them, and the handicapping was carried out in the traditional Brooklands fashion, with each driver given set start times according to the size of their engine. The opening stages of the race therefore saw the supercharged 750cc and unblown 1,100cc and 1.500cc cars set off at 2 p.m. precisely, Freddie Dixon setting the pace in his 1.5-litre Riley. At 2.06 Dick was among the next group flagged away, along with a Brooklands debutante, John Houldsworth in a 2-litre Bugatti. Only at 2.20 did the 3-litre cars leave the start line, and yet it took Whitney, visibly quicker than anyone else through the Railway Snake, just 10 minutes to seize the lead.

An hour into the race, he led comfortably, but his pace slowed suddenly and Dixon was able to re-pass him. Even at reduced speed, Whitney was running a strong second when, at around 3.30, he came up to lap Houldsworth. Unable to overtake him before reaching the Members' Bridge Snake, Whitney waved him on. Houldsworth acknowledged the signal and led into the complex, but he moved so far to the right so as to stay out of Whitney's way that he placed himself on the top end of the traditional finishing straight, giving himself a steep adverse camber to negotiate as he went to exit the Snake. The back end of his Bugatti slewed round, the car shot into the straw bales and was launched into a sickening series of barrel rolls, flinging Houldsworth out. Whitney did well to avert a collision, and raced on in pursuit of Dixon.

Eric Gardner, Brooklands' medical officer, was observing the race as usual from the paddock tower, looking out at the cars on the Byfleet Banking. On hearing the noise behind him, he turned round and saw Houldsworth lying motionless next to the Bugatti, well above the straw bales. As he ran down the tower steps, he signalled to the ambulance driver to pick him up, and within a minute he was with the stricken driver. He knew instantly

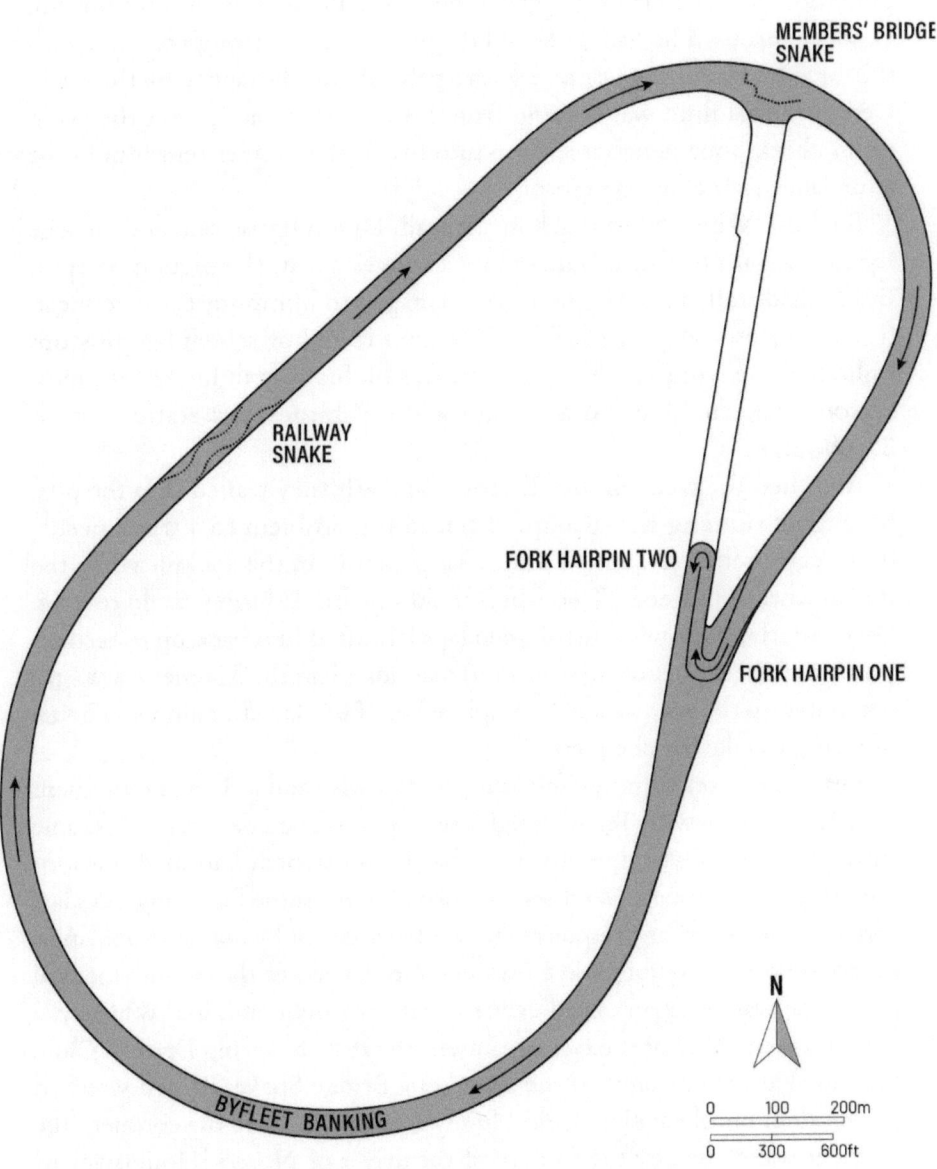

Fig. 5: The most creative Brooklands layout Whitney raced on, for the 1934 Empire Trophy race.

there was nothing he could do. Houldsworth was unconscious, with a deep puncture wound to his right cheek bone, about the size of a thumb tip. Gardner surmised he had sustained the injury either through contact with the car as he was thrown out, or with a pebble when he landed on the track. Cerebrospinal fluid was seeping from his nose, indicating that the crack to his cheek bone penetrated deep into his skull. Gardner sent him in the ambulance to Weybridge Hospital.

By 4.30, Whitney was back in the lead, Dixon lay second and George Eyston was up to third. Baulked by a slower car in the second hairpin, Eyston had stalled his Magnette yet managed to bump start it – no mean feat with a pre-selector gearbox. The next round of scheduled pit stops tightened the front three up: Eyston was on his way in just 29 seconds, Dixon's stop took almost a minute while Whitney was stationary for 2½ minutes.

And then the race fell into Eyston's lap. Whitney trailed into the pits, his engine running flat. Ramponi traced the problem to a stuck needle in the carburettor jet, and Whitney sat patiently in the cockpit while the Italian worked to free it. Two laps were lost before Whitney could resume. Dixon's retirement with just sixteen laps left lifted him back up to second, yet though he closed on Eyston at 20 seconds a lap, the Magnette was still 2 minutes up the road when it completed its 100th lap after almost 4 hours of racing to take the chequered flag.

Any frustration Whitney felt at losing the win, and at Dick's retirement from his first race with Team Straight, were put to one side when news came through from Weybridge Hospital that Houldsworth had died without regaining consciousness. Whitney attended his inquest the following Tuesday, and was absolved of any responsibility for the accident by one of Brooklands' official observers, Major Goldie Gardner. No relation of the circuit's medical officer, he was an experienced driver in his own right and, like Whitney, a committee member of the race organisers, the British Racing Drivers' Club. Stationed at the entrance to the Members' Bridge Snake, he had watched the accident unfold at close hand. 'In my opinion,' he told the coroner, 'the accident was caused by the anxiety of the driver of No. 39 [Houldsworth] not to obstruct the faster car [Whitney's] which was following.'[5]

Whitney was back at Brooklands three days later, for an attempt on the world flying kilometre and flying mile records for Class D cars. These both stood at 131.22mph, and had been set more than two years earlier at Montlhéry, by Albert Divo in a Bugatti. Brooklands had become an inappropriate location for speed record attempts. It was far bumpier than Montlhéry, and it was ill-suited to the AIACR's stipulation that, for a record to be set, it must be based on the average time set over two runs of the measured distance, made in opposite directions. Whitney mitigated this by working out with the Brooklands officials precisely how far the fastest mile and kilometre stretches lay beyond each end of the Railway Straight. Even then, he ran complete laps of the Outer Circuit in each direction to maximise his speed, raising the kilometre record to 136.98mph, and the mile record to 135.49mph. The latter was rendered slower by Whitney needing to use more of the bankings to achieve it.

After a weekend's relaxation, Whitney and Hammy resumed their Continental racing programme at Reims-Gueux, scene of the Marne Grand Prix on 8 July. By now, Nuvolari, who had returned to racing with his broken leg still in plaster, had fully recovered from his accident, and he was able to set the fastest practice time of any 8CM, in 2 minutes 56.0 seconds, but this was still more than 7 seconds slower than Varzi, the quickest of the Alfa drivers. Over a race distance of sixty laps, the gulf remained as big as ever. Whitney was using Hammy's regular mount, 3016, and so might have been expected to be faster down the long straights of Reims-Gueux than usual, since he was not incurring the loss of top-end speed caused by the pre-selector gearbox he used normally. Even so, his fastest practice lap, in 3 minutes 2.3 seconds, was good enough only for sixth place on the grid.

Hammy lined up eighth, more than 7 seconds slower than Whitney, but then he was giving the team's old 26M Maserati its first overseas outing of the season. As it was, retirements ahead of him enabled him to take fourth place, first Maserati driver home behind yet another Scuderia Ferrari one-two-three. Whitney was among the retirees, two melted pistons bringing him to a halt after just three laps. In spite of another relatively poor Continental performance, the Straight stable continued to rack up impressive starting fees, simply because race organisers were keen to have such well turned-out cars, clad in US racing colours, on their starting grids, at least giving the impression of opposition to the all-conquering Alfas. Adding in the prize money from Hammy's fourth place, the Marne Grand Prix generated another £350 for the team.

Hammy was unlikely to fare so well the following weekend. Reunited with 3016, he was racing in the German Grand Prix at the daunting, 14.2-mile Nürburgring, up against not only the Scuderia Ferrari Alfas but Auto Union and Mercedes too. Just as at Reims-Gueux, the car continued to suffer piston failures – two during practice alone – and, though he received a favourable grid slot on the middle of the front row in the pre-race ballot, he was out after just two laps.

Whitney spent the weekend in the central French spa town of Vichy, which was running a grand prix for the first time on a narrow, 1½-mile street circuit. It featured a preponderance of right-angled bends around street corners, and the restricted nature of the circuit led the organisers to arrange two, thirty-lap heats, with the top four in each race, plus the faster of the fifth-place drivers, qualifying for a sixty-lap final. After Count Trossi had won the first heat comfortably in his Alfa, Whitney, back in 3012, lined up on the outside of the front row for the second heat, next to Marcel Lehoux's Alfa. A sudden rainstorm made for trickier, slower conditions than in the first heat, but Whitney made an excellent start and over the course of the first lap built up a healthy lead over the cautious Lehoux. He could even afford a 360-degree spin on the front straight and stay in front. He was still 1.1 seconds clear of Lehoux when he took the chequered flag for his first win on foreign soil since Mont Ventoux, more than nine months earlier.

Grid positions for the final were determined by practice times. Whitney sat on the outside of row two, next to the first heat winner, Trossi. Ahead of them, Etancelin's Maserati occupied pole position, with Lehoux alongside him. The four men served up a most entertaining race. Etancelin shot into the lead, while Lehoux, in his keenness to stay with his countryman, ran wide on a corner, clouted a kerb and had to change a rear wheel, dropping him to last place. He spent the rest of the race hauling himself back up to fifth. Etancelin completed the opening lap with a huge lead over Trossi, while Whitney struggled to maintain third place under pressure from René Dreyfus in a Bugatti. Indeed, Dreyfus was up to second by lap four, but Whitney hunted Trossi down and overtook him for third on the thirteenth lap. Perhaps for the first time all season, and for just a few laps, not a single Alfa driver was placed in the top three, but Whitney could pull no more than 8 seconds clear of Trossi, and on lap twenty-three the Italian slipped back into third. By thirty laps, halfway, Etancelin was having trouble with his brakes again, Trossi had overtaken Dreyfus and the top four were separated by just over half a minute. Over the next few laps, Whitney overtook Dreyfus and set off after the hamstrung Maserati of Etancelin, who had lost the lead to Trossi. Whitney caught him on lap forty-eight, causing Phi-Phi to throw his arms in the air in frustration as he passed the pits. With ten laps left, Whitney lay almost 18 seconds behind Trossi. It proved too big a handicap, and Trossi still had 5 seconds in hand as they took the chequered flag after almost 90 minutes of racing.

Even on a tight circuit that narrowed the performance deficit to the P3 Alfa, and in a race where one of the Alfa drivers put himself out of contention on the first lap, Whitney had only managed second place, but he had already shaken up the team's forthcoming schedule. He sent in entries to more minor races, deliberately avoiding the German teams at a minimum, and preferably Scuderia Ferrari too. The weekend after the German and Vichy Grands Prix provided the first test of the new approach. Enzo Ferrari had entered five cars for the Coppa Ciano in Livorno, and two in the Dieppe Grand Prix, where Whitney and Hammy had been due to race. Instead, Hammy went to Albi, scene of Louis Braillard's narrow win over Whitney the year before, to race one of Whitney's usual cars, 3012. He was joined there by Buddy, enjoying his first overseas race in the 26M, and by Dick, whose Magnette was entered by the Straight stable in the junior 1,500cc race. Whitney would not race at all, but prepare instead for his first meeting with Mercedes and Auto Union a week later, in Switzerland's premier mountain climb, Klausen. It was time for some cost-saving measures too. When Robertson-Justice quit the team abruptly to join the League of Nations police force in the Saar, Whitney chose not to replace him, and became part-time truck driver to his own team.

Mixed though the team's performance in the pair of Albi races proved to be, it certainly justified Whitney's action. In the voiturette race, Dick lost the benefits of pole position by stalling with an overheated engine. Onlookers rushed forward to give him a push start, which earned him a 100 franc fine, he pitted at the end of the opening lap and retired at one-third distance. The main race was a very different affair. Hammy got a better return on his pole position and leaped into a lead that grew with each lap, while Buddy started from fourth on the grid and worked his way up to second within a dozen laps. Hammy visited the pits on lap fourteen to investigate why his engine had dropped on to seven cylinders, but, once it was established that there was no simple solution to the problem, he resumed at slightly reduced pace. The paucity of the opposition was such that not only did Buddy win in his four-year-old 26M, but Hammy came home second, 2½ minutes down on his teammate, but a lap clear of the rest of the field. Buddy's victory was the first by an Englishman in a Continental grand prix since Breckie's old friend Henry Segrave had triumphed in the French Grand Prix of 1923, and Team Straight's one-two generated £743 12s in starting fees and prize money, its biggest haul in European racing.

A week later, on Sunday, 5 August, Whitney and Hammy competed in the daunting Klausen hill climb, and Dick came along to soak up the atmosphere. The course matched Mont Ventoux's 13.3 miles precisely, but was very different in nature, with a pair of steep, hairpin-strewn sections either end of a long, relatively straight stretch of road running beneath the crest of Urnerboden, Switzerland's largest alp. Conditions were made still more difficult by three days of heavy rain, which finally relented only an hour before timed runs began. Many drivers had not even practised, as the last section of the climb had been shrouded in snowstorms. Even when the rain finally stopped, drivers had to contend with drifting mist, and rivulets of rain water running across the straight section.

Hammy performed mightily in Robin Mere's Magnette, winning the 1,100cc category in a time of 17 minutes 53.6 seconds, a new class record. His average speed of almost 45mph, dealing with the toughest of courses and conditions in such a small car, demonstrated what a fine driver he had become. Whitney was back in the twin-rear-wheel 3011, and was up against two of Europe's greatest mountain climbers – Hans Stuck in an Auto Union and, at the wheel of a Mercedes, Rudi Caracciola, who delighted the hordes of German fans who braved the weather to watch him take 28 seconds off the Klausen record he had set two years earlier to leave it at 15 minutes 22.2 seconds. Stuck ran him very close indeed, setting a time only 3.2 seconds slower, while Whitney came third overall, in 16 minutes 20.6 seconds. To lose by under a minute over 13 miles to two far more powerful cars, driven by acknowledged mountain climb aces, was a highly creditable performance, and burnished Whitney's own reputation as a mountain climber further.

Whitney, Hammy and Dick then made for Pescara, to compete in the Coppa Acerbo races ten days later. In the junior race – the four-lap race for cars up to 1,100cc – Hammy was down to drive Robin Mere's Magnette, while the stable entered Dick in K3011, the car Whitney had won the race in twelve months earlier. Raffaele Cecchini, the man who had been so impressed by Whitney's drive that day that he tried to buy the car, had acquired a Magnette of his own, and was intent on preventing another win for K3011. Whitney and Hammy would be racing Maseratis in the main event.

The starting grid ballot for the junior race was kinder to Dick, who lined up fifth, than to Hammy – ninth and last – and Hammy made things harder for himself by stalling and needing a push start to get away. The Italian officials took no action against Hammy for receiving outside assistance. He soon made up for his error, and was third by the end of the opening lap, 15 seconds down on Cecchini in the lead, and a similar distance ahead of fourth-place Dick. At the top of the climb to Capelle on lap two, Hammy seized second, and he overtook Cecchini for the lead on lap three, while Dick moved up to third. By the end of the fourth and final lap, Hammy was a minute clear of Cecchini and over 2 minutes ahead of Dick. As he pulled into his pit, he found Whitney ready with a glass of champagne.

The main race was the first time that Mercedes and Auto Union had raced on Italian soil, and the starting grid ballot made for an intriguing front row, with Stuck's Auto Union alongside Varzi's Alfa Romeo and Caracciola's Mercedes. Whitney lined up sixth, while Hammy again drew the short straw, starting from the back row. Rain fell in the interval between the junior and senior races, and made the winding, uphill stretch to Capelle and the flat-out straight back down to the shoreline treacherous. Whitney finished lap one already over a minute behind the leader Caracciola, and yet he considered these opening laps on a slippery circuit among his finest of the season. He spent them disputing sixth place with Nuvolari, and he found that he was quicker than the great man in the wet, even though the Italian's 8CM had a standard transmission and, therefore, a higher top speed. It was Whitney's only fond memory of a difficult day. He retired after six laps with an engine problem, and mechanical problems forced Hammy out too, while Nuvolari benefitted from the misfortune of others to finish second. Worse, the young Algerian Guy Moll, who had raced so well in his first season with Scuderia Ferrari after that fortunate win in Monaco, was killed in an enormous accident on the run down to Montesilvano.

Whitney Straight

The Maseratis were sent back to Milan in preparation for a busy end to August, while Whitney flew straight to France, where the team's third 8CM, 3012, was waiting for him to drive in the Nice Grand Prix. This was run over 100 laps of a simple, 2-mile circuit, comprising a pair of straights up and down the quayside connected by hairpins, interrupted on the back leg by a detour round the local park. Whitney drove more laps than anyone in practice and his best was within 2 seconds of the pole time. This only earned him seventh on the grid, but suggested, with the German teams absent, that this might be a day when Maseratis might be able to compete with Alfas. In the early stages, Nuvolari was the primary Maserati driver taking the fight to the Alfas of Varzi, Trossi and Chiron, but Whitney ran in a strong fifth place, 9 seconds ahead of Etancelin after ten laps. Regrettably, three laps later he missed his braking point for the hairpin at the end of the front straight and bent his front axle against the straw bales. As at Pescara, there would be many retirements, and Etancelin ended up finishing second to Varzi. For the second time in five days, Whitney had retired while running ahead of the driver who would finish runner-up.

Sunday, 26 August saw the Straight stable out in strength. Hammy and Dick were in Bern, where the inaugural Swiss Grand Prix meeting was being held at a 4½-mile circuit laid out in the forest of Bremgarten, to the north of the city. The Straight stable had entered Magnettes for them both in the voiturette race for cars up to 1,500cc. Hammy was also racing his usual 8CM, 3016, in the seventy-lap Swiss Grand Prix, up against the might of Mercedes and Auto Union, as well as three Scuderia Ferrari Alfas. Whitney, meanwhile, had stayed in the south of France to drive 3011 in the Comminges Grand Prix, alongside Buddy in the 26M. Their opposition would be weaker, but Enzo Ferrari still sent two Alfas for Lehoux and the man brought in to replace Moll, Gianfranco Comotti, while Phi-Phi Etancelin would as usual represent the most challenging of the independent drivers.

Whitney lined up on the front row of the grid, slower only than Etancelin and Lehoux, while Buddy was on the middle of the third row. Whitney made an excellent start, completing the first of the thirty-five laps 6 seconds clear of Lehoux and Comotti, but first the Alfas caught and passed him, then Etancelin. His luck changed almost an hour into the race, when Phi-Phi retired with an engine problem and Lehoux's Alfa threw a valve. Approaching half-distance, Whitney lay in a secure second place, with Buddy fifth, but the team's prospects unravelled during the stops. The starting handle on Buddy's car broke as he went to restart his engine and, rather than incur a 500 franc fine for a push start, he retired, passing up on the opportunity to win the 6,000 francs prize money for fifth place. His employer is most unlikely to have agreed with his logic, and this proved to be Buddy's last drive for the stable. Whitney's stop was extended when he needed to replace a tyre as well as take on fuel. Billy Rockell was given a special award that evening for the speed with which he changed the wheel, but when Whitney resumed he had slipped to third behind Goffredo Zehender's Maserati. Worse, he had to give up his chase of the Italian when an oil leak developed in the cockpit. 'My overalls and my feet were soaked. I simply couldn't keep my feet on the slippery pedals, and the wheel was too slippery to hold.'[6] When the chequered flag fell after 239 miles of racing, he was almost 3 minutes down on Comotti and 1 minute 40 seconds behind Zehender.

That evening, another trying day for the team grew far worse. News came through from Bremgarten that Hammy had crashed during the closing stages of the Swiss Grand Prix. This time there was no mistake and there would be no reprieve. He was dead.

9

Facing Facts

In that morning's Bern Grand Prix, Hammy and Dick had again drawn short straws in the starting grid ballot, Hammy lining up seventeenth of the twenty-three starters, and Dick on the back row. To compound matters, Hammy had, just as in Pescara, stalled and got away dead last after another push start. Yet by lap five he was up to third, just 4 seconds down on race leader Romano Malaguti, while Dick lay fourth, a further 13 seconds back. Engine problems forced Hammy out two laps later, but Dick kept coming, climbing to second when local favourite Hans Rüesche retired, and taking the lead when Malaguti's magneto packed up. He came under pressure in the closing stages from Veyron, but held on to record his first-ever race win. That it should come in an 1,100cc car, in a prestigious international race against a large field of cars of up to 1.5 litres, was still more impressive. Elated, he sat back to see how Hammy would fare in the afternoon's Swiss Grand Prix.

The answer, it seemed, was reasonably well. After more than 3½ hours of racing and just a single, scheduled pit stop, Hammy lay seventh, ahead of one of the Alfas and only five laps down on the man who had led all the way in his Auto Union, Hans Stuck. Tragically, as Stuck was completing his seventieth lap to claim victory, Hammy, just a mile from the finish line himself, left the circuit, hit one tree and then slammed into another. He was killed instantly. *Autocar*'s obituary concluded, 'British and international motor racing has lost a fearless driver – and a man of the best type.'[1]

Dick sent Whitney an eyewitness account of the accident:

Chiron tells me that he was fairly close behind Hammy when it happened. It was a left-hand bend through a wood, which was rather bumpy and could be taken at about 110mph. Apparently Hammy got a wheel into the loose stuff on the right-hand side of the road, the car skidded and hit the trees on the other side of the road. Chiron says he nearly did the same thing several times on that bend.[2]

Hammy was buried in the Bremgarten cemetery, and Dick, who had liaised with the local authorities and the British consul over the funeral arrangements, completed his responsibilities to his fallen teammate by towing Hammy's Magnette home, whereupon Robin Mere, wanting nothing more to do with the car, sold it.

Whitney took stock. He had lost both his main drivers. Maserati had neither delivered the fourth car and spare engine on order, nor repaid his deposits on them. Bill Lambert was scathing: 'Although the Maserati Company has never enjoyed a high reputation for punctiliousness in its commercial dealings, it could hardly have been anticipated that they would behave as badly as they have done.'[3] The stable's finances were in poor shape. By the end of August, a little over £5,800 had been generated in starting fees, prize money and bonuses, and Lambert budgeted that a further £4,000 in starting fees would come from the remaining races on the team's calendar. Even then, after allowing for the scrap sale of Hammy's wrecked Maserati and depreciation on the other cars and trucks, he estimated that more than £11,000 in prize money and bonuses would be needed simply to break even.

Before leaving for the Italian Grand Prix, taking place at Monza on 9 September, Whitney took several decisions. He would give Dick more drives, and entered him and the Magnette in the 1,100cc class at Mont Ventoux on 16 September. Marcel Lehoux's contract with Scuderia Ferrari had expired after the Comminges Grand Prix, and Whitney snapped up the Frenchman to race 3012 in the Spanish Grand Prix a week later. And while he sought to run more drivers in the remaining races of 1934, he decided to disband the stable at the end of the season – the surviving Maseratis and the Dodge trucks were put up for sale.

The Italian Grand Prix organisers had taken note of the previous year's tragedies and made radical changes, incorporating elements of Monza's road circuit and oval within a twisty, 2.7-mile course, including a tight hairpin, two right-angled corners and two chicanes. The exhausting nature of the circuit and the unseasonably hot weather combined to make the 116-lap race an endurance event. Five of the nine finishers needed co-drivers just to complete it. Not so Whitney, who displayed immense stamina over 4¾ hours of racing to come home eighth, just four laps down on the winning Mercedes shared by Caracciola and Fagioli.

A week later, and a year on from Whitney's heroics on Mont Ventoux, the new-look Straight stable met with further success on the mountain. Dick's Magnette was fitted with twin-rear wheels and he used them to good effect, completing the 13.4-mile climb in just over 16 minutes. He won the 1,100cc class by almost 3 minutes, and was faster than anyone in the 1,500cc and 2-litre categories too. Whitney was driving 3011, which sported horizontal plates behind its front wheels to stop stones on the loose road surface from dashing his face. He went up in 13 minutes 58.4 seconds, over half a minute quicker than his record climb of the previous year. But this time he was up against an Auto Union, and Hans Stuck secured victory with a time of 13 minutes 38.3. Still, losing only 20 seconds to the more powerful German car over more than 13 miles was another superb effort.

At this point, Whitney had only one more overseas race on his programme, the Algerian Grand Prix at the end of October. Almost three months had passed since he had last raced in Britain, but now came four domestic events – two Brooklands meetings book-ending the autumn Shelsley Walsh and his first trip to Donington Park, the 2½-mile circuit laid out on estate roads around Donington Hall in the East Midlands. His participation in Brooklands' BRDC 500 on 22 September was eagerly anticipated, for he was finally going to race the Duesenberg that he had acquired from Count Trossi – indeed Trossi was to be his co-driver. Sadly, the Italian never made the trip, while Whitney felt unwell and withdrew. Still, the weekend produced some welcome revenue for the team.

In San Sebastian, on Spain's north coast, Lehoux raced 3012 to eighth place in the Spanish Grand Prix, and it seems he had a teammate that day. The Maserati 8CM driven by another ex-Scuderia Ferrari driver, Luigi Soffietti, went through three colour schemes over the course of the meeting, and since the last of these was US racing white and blue, it appears that a last-minute deal was negotiated for the Italian to drive for the Straight stable. He finished tenth, two laps down on Lehoux and three behind

Fagioli, who won again for Mercedes. Whitney's new recruits won no prize money, but at least they generated a pair of starting fees.

Whitney's own season resumed the following weekend at Shelsley Walsh. The fine weather of practice gave way to heavy rain on the morning of the climb, but an expectant crowd looked forward to another duel between Whitney and Mays. Whitney was driving 3011, which had been repainted in his favoured black now that the car was no longer appearing in AIACR-sanctioned meetings. Mays was in his latest 2-litre ERA. Whitney made the best of the bad conditions through the first runs, posting 44.6 seconds to Mays' 45.2. The rain ceased during the lunch break, and Mays put together a tidy second run in 44.0 seconds, but Whitney spoiled his chances by spinning his rear wheels off the start line. Thereafter, he was inch perfect, but the damage was done and he could only get within 0.2 seconds of Mays. He had to settle for second place overall, and a win in the 3-litre racing category.

The next day, Soffietti and Dick were in action for the team. The Italian was unplaced in the Montreux-Caux hill climb in Switzerland, but Dick fared better in the 1,500cc category of the Masaryk Grand Prix in Brno. In an arrangement not unlike Nuvolari's participation in the previous year's Tourist Trophy, Dick was driving a works MG Magnette, K3020, but under the banner of Whitney Straight Ltd. After 272 miles and 4 hours of racing, he came home fifth, just 10 seconds behind the much more experienced George Eyston in another Magnette. The three drivers ahead of them were all in 1.5-litre cars – Dick's driving had matured rapidly since leaving Cambridge.

On the Wednesday after Shelsley, Whitney dropped in at Brooklands and broke the Mountain Circuit lap record yet again, raising it to 79.18mph. Then he was off up to Donington. Before 3011 had even turned a wheel, the Derby & District Motor Club had nominated it the best turned out car in the paddock. It was less well turned out by the end of the Donington Park Trophy, for the race began in a steady drizzle. Whitney dominated proceedings, leading throughout and setting fastest lap on his way to beating Clifton Penn-Hughes by almost 50 seconds. The rain was even heavier during the 100-mile Nuffield Trophy, but Dick acquitted himself well again, bringing his Magnette home second to Mays' ERA.

A week later, on 13 October, Brooklands hosted its traditional season closer. Whitney had 3011 and the Duesenberg with him. A break had been inserted five races into the programme, so that he could take the American car out for an attempt on the Outer Circuit lap record. John Cobb had raised it to 140.93mph during the August Bank Holiday meeting. His car was another creation of Reid Railton's, the Napier Railton. Powered by a 24-litre Napier Lion aero engine, it had a wheelbase of almost 11ft, a track of 5ft and weighed 30cwt. The Duesenberg, by contrast, was fitted with a 4.4-litre engine, had a wheelbase of 8ft 3.5in, a track of 4ft 9in and weighed under 20cwt. It seemed far less suited to Brooklands' bumps. Perhaps this is why Cobb and Dunlop Tyres' racing manager, Norman Freeman, appeared so serious as they talked quietly with Whitney while he waited in the car to be called out on to the track.

At around 2.40 p.m. he left the paddock and drew up in front of Ebby at the start line. Flagged away, he worked his way up to full speed as quickly as possible, completing his standing lap at an average speed of 123.38mph. He took a low line round the Members' Banking, the Duesenberg still leaping clear of the track on the pronounced bump over the River Wey, and bucking so much that the photographers gathered at the lip of the track had difficulty snapping a clear image of the attempt. The Byfleet Banking was taken in one long drift, Whitney's rear wheels noticeably higher than his front ones, then he pulled down early on to the Home Straight. In marked contrast to his normal cornering style at Brooklands, he was taking the lighter, smaller Duesenberg on as short a route round the Outer Circuit as possible. Recording 137.58mph on his first flying lap, his next circuit looked even more alarming. He completed it in 138.34mph, but then he eased off and pulled into the paddock. On learning that he had fallen short of Cobb's mark, he muttered, 'Sorry, but the car wouldn't go any quicker.'[4] Artist Roy Nockolds made a better job than the photographers of recording the attempt, capturing Whitney coming off the Byfleet Banking with the wide expanse of the Front Straight and the Fork ahead of him. When Nockolds asked his subject what he thought of the painting, Whitney replied, 'It's not right, you have shown the car pointing straight ahead – it was never straight, it was sideways all the time!'[5]

At least the Duesenberg was nicely warmed up for race six on the card. The Second Kingston Long Handicap was run over three-and-a-half laps of the Outer Circuit. Whitney was scratch man in a mixed field of thirteen cars, giving over a minute to the limit man. He made every one of the

9 miles count: still sixth as he entered the Members' Banking for the last time, he caught two cars at its exit and swept below them to finish fourth. His only race in the Duesenberg was over. He had it packed up and shipped down to Montlhéry for an assault on Stuck's 1-hour record. Next up came the Mountain Championship, run over ten laps. Whitney had won it in comical fashion from Piero Taruffi twelve months previously, but this time he and 3011 won the Kathleen Drogheda Trophy on merit. In the opening laps, Mays gave chase in his ERA, but Whitney was noticeably smoother round the Fork and eased clear to win by 6 seconds. On the way, he broke the Mountain Circuit lap record one last time, leaving it at 81.00mph. In the eighteen months he had routinely been racing on the little circuit quicker than anyone else, he had improved on Birkin's old record by almost 5.8mph, or more than 7 per cent.

Race nine on the card was the Record Holders' Mountain Handicap, a five-lap race open to drivers and cars who had held a category lap record on the circuit during the year. As such, Whitney should have been up against Malcolm Campbell in one of his Sunbeams, a pair of ERAs – Mays in the 1.5-litre version and Cook in the original 1-litre car – and two 750cc runners, Driscoll in an Austin and Everitt in an MG. As it was, Campbell withdrew, a supercharger problem prevented Cook from starting and Mays retired after a lap. From such unpromising circumstances, Whitney, Driscoll and Everitt served up the race of the day, Whitney reeling in his 26-second handicap to the pair while Driscoll eked out a slender lead over Everitt. Whitney was still third as he started the last lap, but climbed high above Everitt on the Members' Bridge Turn to take second. Exiting the Fork for the final time, he was still 100 yards down on Driscoll, but the grand prix Maserati ate up the gap to the little Austin so quickly that Whitney was 10 yards in front by the time he crossed the line. In contrast to much of the previous three months, in the space of a fortnight in England he had run up three wins, a second, a fourth, two lap records and a fastest lap.

Dick's afternoon was less successful. Whitney had entered him and the Magnette in the final pair of mountain handicaps. These were Dick's last races in the car – Whitney advertised it for sale in the following week's *The Motor* – and he was unplaced in both, though he did manage to set a new 1,100cc lap record. The other Straight stable entry of the weekend saw Luigi Soffietti finish seventh in the Modena Grand Prix, three laps down on victor Tazio Nuvolari. Mercedes and Auto Union had already wrapped up their seasons to focus on 1935, but Enzo Ferrari had entered no fewer than six Alfa Romeos in his home-town race, so Nuvolari's win – his first of the year – was on merit. His Maserati was powered by a new, 3.7-litre engine. If only this had been available in March, rather than October.

A week later, the team had a representative in each heat of the final event of the European season. The Coppa Principessa di Piedmont took place on a twisty, hilly 2.6-mile circuit overlooking the Bay of Naples. Soffietti was in his own 8CM again, and this time 3012 was driven by Giovanni Minozzi. Nephew of the great Antonio Ascari, he had been racing in minor grands prix across the Continent for a decade. Each man finished third in his heat and qualified for the forty-lap final, in which Soffietti came home sixth, 8.6 seconds clear of Minozzi. They finished three laps down on Nuvolari, who won for the second time in eight days with Maserati's new engine.

Yet another Straight stable line-up assembled the following weekend at Bouzaréah, a hill outside Algiers, for what was due to be its final event of the year, the Algerian Grand Prix. Whitney was racing 3011, and the local fans were delighted to see Marcel Lehoux aboard 3012 – in the absence of their young hero Guy Moll, killed at Pescara, at least they could support a Frenchman who lived and ran a business in Algeria. Luigi Soffietti completed the line-up. The trio's chances of ending the season on a high seemed reasonable – the German teams and Nuvolari were absent, and only Chiron and Brivio were driving for Scuderia Ferrari. The event was to be run over two heats of fifteen laps of a twisty, hilly 5-mile circuit. Drivers' aggregate times over the two heats would determine the result. The starting grid for the first race would be decided on the basis of practice times, while the drivers would line up for the second heat in the order in which they had finished the first. Practice threw up a surprise, Jean-Pierre Wimille's Type 59 Bugatti comfortably taking pole position by more than 5 seconds from Chiron. Whitney lined up fourth on the two-by-two grid, alongside Brivio. Lehoux was on the inside of row three, fifth fastest, and Soffietti was immediately behind him, seventh.

After a minute's silence for Moll, Chiron made the best start to the first heat but brake trouble dropped him behind Wimille and Brivio, forcing him into the pits and promoting Whitney, Lehoux and Soffietti into third, fourth and fifth. Lehoux disappointed the large crowd by skidding on loose sand two laps from home and sliding into a ditch. He was able to get the car back to the pits, but it was too damaged and he was forced to retire.

Whitney came home third, just over a minute behind Wimille and some 40 seconds down on Brivio. Soffietti finished fifth, behind a recovering Chiron. In the half-hour before the second heat, Brivio was taken ill and pulled out, promoting Whitney to the front row of the grid alongside Wimille, and prompting Chiron, mistrustful of his Alfa's brakes, to switch to Brivio's car. In the early laps of the second heat, Chiron grew frustrated as he struggled to pass Whitney, but once he was through he was soon in the lead, only for a broken shock absorber bracket to slow him. Wimille regained the lead, while Whitney overtook Chiron for second with two laps to go. Frustratingly, his gearbox broke on the final lap, and he coasted to a halt fewer than 5 miles from the finish. Soffietti cushioned the blow by finishing third, his best result during his brief time with the team.

And that should have brought the curtain down on the Straight stable. Whitney flew up to Montlhéry for some acclimatisation runs in the Duesenberg, but before he could make an attempt on Stuck's 1-hour record, an offer for the team to race one more time proved irresistible. Edward 'Brud' Bishop, motoring editor of South Africa's *East London Daily Despatch*, had looked round the Marine Drive, a scenic, 15.2-mile route bounded by the Indian Ocean and the Buffalo River, and concluded that it would make a wonderful motor racing circuit. The Border 100, a handicap race over six laps of the circuit, was due to take place on 27 December. Bishop was keen for the Straight stable to be involved, but Whitney told Dick on his return from Algeria, 'I've been thinking over the question of the South African race and on the whole I think it is quite impossible for me to go there personally.'[6] In the end, he 'thought of a starting money figure, quadrupled it'[7] and Bishop agreed, passing the cost on to the beachfront hotel, whom he promised would benefit handsomely from the crowds flocking to see Europe's finest independent racing driver.

The Straight stable's final line-up ranged from the familiar to the unique. Whitney would drive 3011. MG would lend Dick the Magnette he had raced in Brno, K3020, and even pay for it to be shipped to South Africa, on condition that Dick sold the car after the race. He would have to pay for it to be brought back to England if he could not find a buyer. The third driver, making his only appearance in a race, was Whitney's brother, Michael. He had spent the year between leaving Dartington and going up to Trinity at the London School of Economics, sharing with Whitney the house they had rented from P.G. Wodehouse on Norfolk

Street, a short walk from Whitney's Bush House headquarters. Whitney had since bought a house for himself at 10 Woods Mews, just off Park Lane, but he persuaded his 18-year-old brother that joining him in South Africa was a more interesting way to spend his first Christmas down from Cambridge than going back to Dartington. Michael would race his road car, a Railton Terraplane. Based on an American Hudson chassis and engine and clad in a lightweight two-door sports body, Reid Railton had little to do with the Terraplane's design, but leant his name to it in return for a royalty on each car sold.

Ramponi accompanied all three cars down to South Africa on the mail boat, arriving in East London on 15 December, twelve days ahead of the race. The next day, he went out on the circuit and pronounced it 'very, very fast'.[8] He altered 3011's rear axle ratio, and reckoned the car would be capable of 150mph on the straights. This was just as well, as Whitney would be up against as broad a range of road and racing cars as he had faced in his Swedish races, and he had no way of knowing how tough the handicaps were. He was giving over 22 minutes to the limit man, almost 7 to Dick and nearly 8 to Michael. The five drivers with the most favourable handicaps would be on their second lap before he was even flagged away. But for now, Ramponi's work was done. With all three cars fully prepared and housed in their garages, he sat back and awaited the arrival of his drivers on Tuesday, 18 December. But there was a problem – they were stuck in Salisbury (now Harare), more than 1,200 miles to the north.

Whitney had hired a de Havilland Rapide from Brian Lewis, the man who had run him so close in April's JCC International and who, when not racing, ran a flourishing aircraft dealership. The Rapide had ample space for the three drivers, their luggage and some spares for the Maserati. Whitney's 'devoted slave',[9] Percy Dewdney would also be on board. Part butler, part chauffeur, his support of Whitney's racing had included bringing the Bentley to Brooklands on days when Whitney had flown there, and standing discreetly behind the Maserati on the Shelsley Walsh start line with plug spanner in hand. Perhaps it was his prowess at mixing pink gins that made him an indispensable member of the party taking off from Heston early on Sunday, 9 December.

They landed in Marseille after 9 hours 40 minutes in the air, and made for Cairo the next day. The leg to Khartoum took almost 11 hours. A week later, they endured their earliest take-off, from Harare at 3.45 a.m.

They were due to reach East London that same afternoon, but the flight lasted only seconds. In the dark, Whitney did not spot a barbed wire fence beyond the runway, and snagged his wings on it, ripping the canvass and damaging the wing struts. Repairs took four days to complete. On Saturday, 22 December, they set out again for East London, taking on fuel at Bulawayo and Johannesburg, but when they made their final refuelling stop at Pietermaritzburg, they encountered a fresh problem. There were no fuel pumps, no staff and no telephone. Fortunately, Captain J.S. Shephard, an Imperial Airways pilot, was tending to his Puss Moth after flying up from Cape Town for a pre-Christmas break, and he recognised Whitney as he clambered out of the Rapide. He knew the nearest phone was at a local brickyard, and Whitney was able to call a garage and arrange for fuel to be brought out to the airfield. Thanks to Shephard, only 30 minutes were lost, and 12 hours 45 minutes after leaving Salisbury, Whitney landed safely at East London. Over the past thirteen days, he had spent almost 83 hours at the joystick.

The lengthy repairs in Salisbury and Christmas festivities left Whitney, Dick and Michael little time to learn the circuit, but the race proved more straightforward than the trip. Retirements over the course of the opening lap meant that Whitney was already placed thirteenth of the eighteen starters before he turned a wheel, and he was cutting through the field by lap four, cheerfully waving at Michael as he went by. As he began his final lap, he was still winding in the 11 minutes 45 seconds he had given Herbert Case in a home-built, alloy-bodied Ford V8, but by the time he took the chequered flag to win his final race he was 2 minutes clear. Michael finished third and Dick, delayed by a faulty fuel pressure feed, fifth. The race, now considered to be the inaugural South African Grand Prix, was watched by more than 40,000, at a time when East London's entire population was only 30,000, and judged a great success. Whitney was considered integral to that success, and Whitney Straight trophies were still being won in races all over southern Africa decades later.

He flew back into Heston on 13 January after another eventful trip, and found that even the lucrative arrangement he had made with Brud Bishop had failed to balance the team's books. Playwright and screenplay writer Alfred Edgar, who wrote about 1930s motor racing under the pseudonym Barré Lyndon, was given access to the stable's accounts and recorded that a total income of £10,325 had been generated through starting fees, prize money, sponsorship and bonuses. Of course, had the Maseratis been faster and more reliable, this figure could have been much higher. Lambert calculated that the 5 seconds by which Trossi beat Whitney in July's Vichy Grand Prix had cost £500 in prize money and bonuses, and that the puncture and oil leak in Comminges had lost the team £773. Buddy's bizarre decision to withdraw from the same race cost a further 5,500 French francs. Then there was the carburettor needle that denied Whitney victory in the British Empire Trophy, the puncture that turned second place into fourth in Casablanca and the last-lap gearbox failure in Algeria that lost Whitney another runner-up slot.

Yet, even with better fortune, it is unlikely the stable's income would have exceeded the 'total direct racing expenditure'[10] of £13,100 recorded by Lyndon. This covered salaries, travel, spares and equipment, insurance, entry fees, customs dues and garaging, and excluded the loss on disposal of the team's cars, which was not accomplished until well into 1935 – most buyers were more interested in the P3 Alfa Romeos and Type 59 Bugattis coming on to the market than in Whitney's Maseratis and the unproven Duesenberg. In the end, Harry Rose, scion of the family that had founded Great Universal Stores, acquired 3011, while Buddy initially borrowed the old 26M he knew so well and eventually bought it. The Duesenberg was rescued from its lock-up garage at Montlhéry by Jack Duller, the man saved by the mud inside Brooklands' Members' Banking the previous year, while the remains of poor Hammy's car, 3016, was sold for scrap.

Whitney decided to keep the remaining Maserati, 3012, and convert it into a twin-seater road car. Ramponi and Rockell undertook the intricate work of shifting the steering column and pedals to the right, and Gurney Nutting designed an attractive body with long running boards. The car – black, of course – looked fabulous, but Whitney admitted later, 'It was not, in fact, very successful as a touring car, as it heated up in traffic and although it would do over 120 miles an hour between the lights on the Great West Road, it was not always useful in practice.'[11] The conversion costs on 3012 were not included in Lyndon's figures, and, since Ron Horton had to put the car back into single-seater mode before he could race it, he is unlikely to have paid Whitney much for it. Thus, all in all, the actual loss incurred by Whitney Straight Ltd after its single season of racing is likely to have been far higher than the £2,775 deficit recorded by Lyndon.

If Whitney failed to meet his financial objectives, how should the stable's 1934 season be viewed from a sporting perspective? Overall, including heats, hill climbs and junior categories, it scored ten wins, seven seconds and eight thirds. Five of the victories were secured by Whitney and 3011 at home, and two more domestic wins were denied only by the recalcitrant carburettor needle in the Empire Trophy and excessive wheelspin off the start line in the autumn Shelsley Walsh meeting. His only other domestic race was in the untried Duesenberg, and even then he managed fourth place. The team scored two further runner-up spots at home – Buddy in a mountain handicap at the start of the season and Dick in October's Nuffield Trophy.

It was abroad where Team Straight's season suffered. Whitney managed only two wins from sixteen starts, in his heat at the Vichy Grand Prix and in South Africa, where his only real competition came from the handicapper rather than the opposition. Buddy had his moment in the spotlight in Albi, leading Hammy home in a 1-2 win for the stable, while Dick won on two of the occasions Whitney Straight Ltd entered his Magnette, in the Bern Grand Prix and in the 1,100cc category on Mont Ventoux. Hammy's 3016 suffered from particularly poor reliability, and part of the tragedy of his untimely death is that his results with Team Straight do not reflect what a very fine driver he had become.

Of course, the die was cast from the first meeting of the year, when Whitney spun off trying to emulate the Alfa drivers in taking Monaco's tunnel flat out. It was immediately clear that the Maserati 8CM was no match for the Alfa Romeo P3. Nor was it as reliable: a third of the team's overseas starts ended in retirement. Nor, in spite of Dorothy's capital, the workshops at Brooklands and in Milan and personnel of the quality of Ramponi and Rockell, was the Straight stable a match for Scuderia Ferrari, with its Banco Sella funding and, estimated Whitney, 'about sixteen cars and about thirty mechanics'.[12] When Mercedes and Auto Union entered the fray, and the 8CM was relegated to fourth fastest car on the grid, Whitney had to change the team's programme and deliberately enter races where the competition was less intense. None of this is to criticise him: it was simply unfortunate that the best car available to him was slower and less reliable than three others he could not acquire.

Bill Lambert was probably right in thinking Whitney too ambitious. Ordering a fourth car from Maserati was manifestly a waste of money since it was never delivered, while Buddy was largely restricted to the four-year-old 26M, incapable of doing justice to an 8CM. As to the extensive modifications Whitney specified for the cars, Reid Railton's 40-gallon fuel tank may have won him the JCC International, but there is a question over the pre-selector gearbox fitted to 3011 and 3012. Whitney exploited its advantages to good effect on hill and mountain climbs and on the tight confines of Brooklands' Mountain Circuit, but most Continental races were run on open road circuits that placed a premium on speed, and on these Whitney often found it difficult to match Etancelin's 8CM. He admitted that Hammy's 3016, which by virtue of its late delivery was never fitted with a pre-selector gearbox, was the fastest of the team's Maseratis. The Coppa Acerbo speed trap, on the downhill stretch to the Adriatic shoreline, highlighted the weakness. Nuvolari was fastest of the Maserati drivers, at 155.3mph, while Whitney recorded only 143.4mph. Perhaps better results would have been obtained by fitting the pre-selector gearbox to just the one car, using that for Brooklands, Shelsley and mountain climbs, and employing two manual cars for Continental road races.

Whitney no doubt considered each of these points in deciding in the weeks following Hammy's death to disband the stable at season's end and sell the Maseratis, but his mind was positively febrile when it came to what he should do in 1935. He ordered a stunning 11.3-litre Hispano-Suiza and considered racing it at Le Mans. He and Ramponi drew up plans for a specialist engineering and tuning workshop in Byfleet, next door to Brooklands. Within weeks, he talked of sharing the premises he was planning to house the business in with the former protégé of supercharging guru Amherst Villiers, Tom Murray Jamieson. Yet another idea involved the construction of a car. Whitney had not yet turned 22, and legal advisor Fred Gwatkin found him impetuous. Gwatkin told Jerry, 'I think it has been very fortunate that Whitney has not had the command of a large amount of capital. If he had, my impression is that he would have jumped into a number of ventures which would have absorbed that capital without any corresponding return to him.'[13] Yet even while Whitney weighed up a dizzying array of business opportunities – at least as many were aeronautic as automotive – he told Bill Lambert that he still wanted to race in 1935, 'in a set number of events, chiefly for the purpose of maintaining his international reputation to the benefit of his commercial future'.[14] But he would not continue racing for the sake of it. He wanted to win. He wanted an Auto Union.

Most retrospective articles on Whitney's racing claim variously that he tested for Auto Union, that he was offered a drive but turned it down, or that he signed for the team but rescinded the contract. Whitney appears to have prompted these stories himself, in interviews he gave during the 1970s to journalists like Dennis May and Eoin Young. Sadly, he was prone to unnecessary exaggeration in his final years, and there is no contemporaneous evidence to support the claims. There is no mention of Auto Union in the many letters that passed between Jerry, Gwatkin and Lambert, updating each other on Whitney's plans for 1935. The extensive Auto Union archives in the Saxon State Chancellery in Dresden and in the Audi Heritage collection in Potsdam contain no record of him. He certainly played no part in the famous trials that Auto Union conducted at the Nürburgring in late October, which led to Bernd Rosemeyer forging an immensely successful career with the team.

The only references in the British motoring press of the time to any dialogue between Whitney and Auto Union relate to enquiries he made about running a car independently. Before leaving for the Algerian Grand Prix in late October, he discussed the matter with the journalist who was perhaps closest to him, *Motor Sport*'s Boanerges, who wrote, 'If the cars are to be sold outside the team he has been promised the first one, and [he] is naturally waiting anxiously to hear whether the Leader's decree is favourable.'[15]

Since Benito Mussolini had forbidden foreign drivers from acquiring the latest Alfa Romeos, it seemed unlikely that Adolf Hitler would permit a British-based American to compete on equal terms with a team his government had funded. Sure enough, even before the December issue of *Motor Sport* containing Whitney's exchange with Boanerges reached the newsstands, Rodney Walkerley recorded bad news for Whitney in the weekly periodical, *The Motor*. Paraphrasing Thomas Carlyle, he wrote:

> It seems there is going to be a little Hitlerising of motoring sport next year. If all accounts be true, the fiat hath gone forth that none but true Aryan Germans may drive German Grand Prix cars in 1935. This sounds the knell of the hopes of those who in other countries wanted to buy Auto Unions or Mercedes to be raced independently.[16]

And so, unable to compete at the highest level, Whitney walked away from racing, after a meteoric career lasting just two full seasons.

Strangely, for a man who had been so happy to talk to the motoring press, he made no announcement about his decision, and it took months for journalists and enthusiasts to comprehend that he really had quit. *The Motor* of 15 January reported, 'It looks as if Whitney Straight will not be in the field quite so often this season, which is a pity, for this brilliant young driver was making tremendous strides towards fame.'[17] By 29 March *Autocar* was clearly concerned: 'Whitney Straight's motor racing plans still remain doubtful. Is he deserting cars for aeroplanes?'[18] As late as 16 April, *The Motor* remained hopeful: 'the fact that he is invited to compete (and hopes to drive) in the Monaco GP again this year speaks for the Continent's respect for this young driver.'[19] While May's *Motor Sport* clearly left no room for doubt, reporting, 'Unable to get the Auto Union he wanted, Straight has gone in wholeheartedly for aviation',[20] fans gathered for the spring Shelsley Walsh meeting that month were still shocked by his absence. He had entered 3011 months earlier, and Harry Rose had acquired the entry when he bought the car. When it drew up on the start line, it was still in Whitney's favourite black, and still displayed the No. 18 on its radiator with which he had raced in South Africa – but he was no longer behind the wheel.

Two questions remain: how good a driver was he, and how good could he have been, had he raced on? He arrived with a bang on the domestic racing scene when he first drove the ex-Birkin 26M Maserati at Brooklands, in May 1932. At the time, Tim Birkin was still a genuinely fine driver, perhaps just past his prime, Lord Howe was about to win at Shelsley Walsh, and the pair had been victorious at Le Mans the previous summer. Yet 19-year-old Whitney broke the Mountain Circuit lap record in the same car in which Birkin had set it, and came within 8 yards of beating Howe over ten laps of the challenging circuit. He had already developed his uniquely high line through the Members' Bridge Turn and, ten days later, when he returned to Brooklands and broke his own lap record, he was close to perfecting his path round the Fork, 'full of smoke and flame and sensation'.[21] Over the eighteen months between next winning on the Mountain Circuit and his valedictory tour of Shelsley Walsh, Donington Park and Brooklands in the autumn of the following year, he was widely acknowledged as the man to beat in British motor racing.

His arrival on the European mountain climbing scene was equally stunning. Experienced mountain climbers demanded an extra day's practice to familiarise themselves with the 3.1-mile climb up Kesselberg, yet a 20-year-old undergraduate, encountering each braking point and apex for the first time, came within 0.4 seconds of winning his category. Slashing 40 seconds off Caracciola's record on Mont Ventoux was an outstanding achievement. A year later, in appalling conditions on the 13.4 miles up Klausen, he lost under a minute to Caracciola and Stuck in much more powerful cars, and only 20 seconds to Stuck on his return to Ventoux. In Germany, Stuck was widely known as *Bergkönig*, or 'King of the Mountains', but his crown would surely have been in jeopardy had Whitney competed with him on equal terms in 1935.

The precision, co-ordination and courage needed to excel at mountain climbing came naturally to him, but the reason why Whitney was so keen to *race* abroad was because he wanted to hone his craft against the Continental greats on the most challenging road circuits in Europe and Africa. Overtaking scores of slower cars at Brooklands enjoying a start from Ebby was one thing: they were relatively easy to pass on the track's 'great prairies of concrete'.[22] Disputing third place with Ebb in Ramen in May 1932, and with Sommer at Reims-Gueux two months later, or trying to pass Braillard for the lead in Albi in August 1933, was a different matter, and on each occasion he spun off. But during his final season, his slide into the straw bales in Nice was his only error. Few drivers could have maintained that 4-second gap to Brian Lewis over the closing laps of the JCC International, on only three good tyres. And when the opportunity arose on tighter circuits, where the Alfas had less of an advantage, he was able to overtake and pull away from Trossi at Vichy, keep Varzi at bay at Montreux and frustrate Chiron in Bouzaréah. Even Sammy Davis would have been impressed by his win in the Donington drizzle, pulling clear in the early laps, then throttling back yet still winning by almost a minute.

Consider, too, the iron will he displayed when racing on at Reims-Gueux while the burns to his feet and legs grew worse, and the extraordinary stamina he showed over almost 5 hours round the twists and turns of Monza's new layout, and there is little doubt that Whitney became Europe's finest independent driver. In its 1934 review, *Motor Sport* called him 'a first-class driver of natural ability and exceptional endurance powers ... he drives with a cool, precise style which is always good to watch'.[23]

Whitney judged his own prowess against two drivers. He was proud to be quicker than Tazio Nuvolari in the wet, while accepting that the

Flying Mantuan remained faster in the dry. And he observed a weakness in Hans Stuck. 'I think the new German cars are magnificent,' he told *The Motor*, 'but I don't think their drivers are capable of getting the best out of them. At Pescara, in the Acerbo race, Stuck was going quite slowly on the corners, and then simply streaking away on the straights.'[24] In 1934, Stuck was European Mountain Champion, and won the German, Swiss and Czech Grands Prix. The following year, he retained his Mountain Championship and won the Italian Grand Prix, while teammates won the Czech and Tunis Grands Prix. After all the lessons learned through two intensive years racing at home and abroad, and still aged only 22, Whitney would surely have gone on to become one of the pre-war greats, alongside Nuvolari, Caracciola and Rosemeyer.

Then again, it could all have ended abruptly. Of the eight men who drove for Team Straight, three lost their lives in racing accidents. As Whitney himself said, 'I don't think the prospect held much in the way of life expectancy. The Auto Union was a tricky car to handle, a 16-cylinder car with 600 horsepower that weighed 12cwt and spun its wheels up to 160 …'[25]

10

Daphne

Two weeks before the 1935 Monaco Grand Prix took place without him, another reason emerged for Whitney's departure from motor racing. The 'Forthcoming Marriages' column in *The Times* of 11 April recorded: 'The engagement is announced between Mr Whitney Willard Straight, elder son of the late Mr Willard Straight and Mrs L.K. Elmhirst, and Lady Daphne Margarita Finch-Hatton, elder daughter of the Earl and Countess of Winchilsea and Nottingham.'[1]

Daphne Finch Hatton was born on Sunday, 13 July 1913, in the family home, The Links House in West Byfleet, a short walk from Brooklands' Byfleet Banking. At the time, her father Guy was Viscount Maidstone, a financier by profession and long-term treasurer of St George's Hospital. During the First World War, he had served as a lieutenant commander in the RNVR and later as a lieutenant colonel in the RAF, winning the DSC and OBE. He was married to Margaretta Drexel of the Philadelphia banking family. Her grandfather Anthony had founded a finance house with J.P. Morgan in the 1870s, but when he died, Anthony Jr, Margaretta's father, preferred a life of philanthropy to banking and settled in London's Grosvenor Square, where Guy and Margaretta's wedding reception was held. Guy became 14th Earl of Winchilsea and 9th Earl of Nottingham upon the death of his father in 1927.

Daphne was educated at home, and then in London's Sloane Square at Francis Holland School, founded by the Chaplain to Queen Victoria. Most recently, she had studied ballet under Marie Rambert in Notting Hill Gate. In August 1934, while Whitney was racing in Italy and Spain, her boyfriend had driven her up to north Wales in his Buick, for a holiday at the home of her friend Caroline Paget, eldest daughter of the Marquess and Marchioness of Anglesey. Daphne found him 'a complete schizophrenic. He was tough and quite cruel, but at the same time he could be very sentimental.'[2] By the end of the holiday, Daphne could tolerate Ian Fleming no longer. Her parting gift was a sampler which read, *'Elle a passé comme une ombre charmante dans ma vie'* (She has passed through my life like a charming shadow).[3]

Daphne spent forty-five years in the next man's life she entered. She and Whitney met at a party at Leeds Castle in Kent, which had been transformed into one of England's great country homes by a cousin of his, Olive Baillie. There was an instant attraction between them, and their relationship began after they met again at a party at Ditchley, the Oxfordshire country home of another Anglo-American, Ronnie Tree, a Conservative member of parliament. According to Dick Seaman's mother, Lillian, Whitney's retirement from motor racing was Guy Finch Hatton's 'wise proviso'[4] in return for his daughter's hand in marriage.

The wedding took place on Wednesday afternoon, 17 July, at St Margaret's, Westminster. Situated next to Westminster Abbey and opposite the Palace of Westminster, it had served as the unofficial parish church of the House of Commons for centuries, and hosted many grand weddings. Daphne's parents had married there in 1910, as had Winston Churchill and Clementine Hozier before them, and Lord Louis Mountbatten and Edwina Ashley after them. The Bishop of Winchester, Cyril Garbett, and St Margaret's curate, Frederick Rowbotham, officiated.

The decidedly mixed nature of the congregation meant that the wedding was not only one of the society events of the year, but also entered Dartington folklore. Dukes and duchesses were invited, along with marquesses and marchionesses, earls and countesses (including Kathleen, Countess of Drogheda, whose Mountain Championship Trophy Whitney still retained), viscounts and viscountesses and barons and baronesses. The Belgian and German ambassadors to Britain attended, as did Air Vice Marshal Frederick Halahan and Brigadier General Sir Charles Gunning. The world of motor racing was represented by Dick Seaman (one of Whitney's ushers), Lord Howe and Oliver Betram. Ian Fleming accompanied his mother, Evelyn.

And then there were the Finch Hatton and Elmhirst estate workers. When the number of 'primary' guests was deducted from St Margaret's capacity and divided by two, it was determined that about seventy Dartington employees would be able to attend. In the end, invitations were given to those who had worked for Dorothy and Jerry for at least eight years, and just after midnight on the morning of the wedding, seventy-three men and women set off in several buses and cars. They had only reached Chudleigh, 16 miles away, when the headlights on one of the cars went out. The vehicle was tucked into the middle of the convoy, and fortunately it was already light at 5 a.m. when the group pulled into Salisbury, 100 miles further east, an hour ahead of schedule. A small stall served refreshments, and the party was on its way again at 7 a.m., reaching its next port of call, Basingstoke, 90 minutes later. Since no hotel could serve the whole group, they split into two for breakfast, and after a wash and a shave they set off on the final, 50-mile leg into Westminster, parking near the House of Commons. They were settled in their pews 40 minutes before the service began, so that the echoes of hobnail boots had faded by the time the opening bars of the Overture in D from Handel's *Water Music* sounded.

Daphne walked up the aisle on the arm of her father, wearing a striking dress of heavy silver lamé with a long train, and a headdress that hugged her face and neck, made of silver net sewn with orange blossom, and fashioned in the shape of a crusader's chain mail camail. Whitney's half-brother and sister, Bill and Ruth Elmhirst, were two of her four child attendants, along with two young Drexel cousins. Bill, just 6 years old, spent the entire ceremony repeating to himself: 'Don't step on the train, don't step on the train.'[5] Ten older bridesmaids, including Whitney's sister Biddy and Daphne's sister Diana, completed the procession, clad in pale blue dresses and matching Juliet caps.

Waiting at the chancel stood Whitney and his best man, his brother Michael, in matching black frock coats, grey trousers, pale waistcoats, wing collars and cravats. Given Whitney's voting record in the opening week of Dartington Hall School – no church attendance whatsoever – it is unlikely that he played a part in drawing up the order of service, which appeared as one long profession of the Christian faith. The choir sang an arrangement of Psalm 21, *Levavi oculos* (*I will lift up my eyes*), the Russian imperial composer Dmitry Bortniansky's setting of the Lord's Prayer and John Stainer's *Sevenfold Amen*. During the signing of the register, *God Be in My Head* was sung. It had been composed only recently by Sir Henry Walford Davies, Master of the King's Music. The congregation joined in on *Praise My Soul the King of Heaven* and *O Worship the King*.

At the end of the service, the Overture from Wagner's *Die Meistersinger* played as Whitney and Daphne led their attendants and bridesmaids out of the church, past a large crowd of onlookers and into Parliament Square, before leaving for the reception at a packed Dudley House on Park Lane. Separate arrangements were made for the Dartington contingent. They checked into their hotel on Russell Square, then enjoyed a tour of the capital and an evening of Cole Porter songs in *Anything Goes* at the Palace Theatre. After a late-night supper back at the hotel, one member of the party, encountering electricity for the first time, struggled to blow out the 'candle' in his room – 'I can't, it's in a bottle!'[6] – while another, on learning that his bedside phone connected directly to room service, enjoyed a breakfast of two brandies while chatting happily to the maid who had delivered them.

The next morning, Whitney and Daphne flew to Paris, on their way down to the château de l'Horizon, overlooking the Golfe-Juan between Cannes and Antibes. Designed by architect Barry Dierks for the American actress and socialite Maxine Elliot, Whitney had been drawn to its rocky shoreline location and natural port. Dick also flew to France that morning – his latest racing car, one of Ray Mays' ERAs, would let him down in the weekend's Dieppe Grand Prix – while the Dartington guests were taken to Dudley House to see the couple's wedding presents, laid out on a 50ft table in the Picture Gallery.

Some of the most valuable items, like the rope of pearls Whitney had given his bride, and the aquamarine and diamond tiara she had received from her parents, were locked away, but there was plenty more to see: the gold cigarette case Whitney had received from Daphne, the round silver tray and matching cocktail glasses her parents had given him, the brandy goblets from Biddy and a Ben Nicholson painting from Michael – the brothers had collected Nicholson's work while living together on Norfolk Street. The Dartington visitors were particularly proud to see their own present, a silver salver, on display. Then it was time for them to climb back into their buses and cars and head for home. Lunch was taken in Basingstoke and tea in Yeovil, while a final stop was made at an inn outside Ashburton, 6 miles north of Dartington. Amid the step dancing and drinking, 'a few kind words and general appreciation of Mr Straight's kindness was demonstrated in a time-honoured manner'.[7]

After several days of sunbathing and swimming at the château de l'Horizon, the newly-weds made the short trip east to Villefranche and boarded SS *Rex*, en route from her home port of Genoa for New York. She had recently lost her Blue Riband record for the westbound Atlantic crossing to SS *Normandie*, but within five days of pulling anchor after a brief stop in Gibraltar, she sailed into New York, where Whitney and Daphne stayed on Park Avenue. After a few days in the city and a visit to Applegreen, they made for the old family holiday home by Raquette Lake in the Adirondacks, where Whitney had first learned to fish. Here, they joined Dorothy, Jerry, Biddy, Ruth and Bill, who had sailed over from England. Only Whitney's best man was missing: Michael was one of six Cambridge students on a group tour of the Soviet Union, in the company of an art historian named Anthony Blunt. Next came a stay in Saratoga Springs, the horse racing and spa town in which Whitney's grandfather William had invested heavily. The couple returned to New York at the end of August and sailed home aboard SS *Bremen*, docking at Southampton on 5 September. Percy Dewdney drove them back to their first marital home, an apartment at 11, Hyde Park Gardens Mews.

And so began a very special marriage that, despite the many challenges Whitney put in its way, survived until his death forty-four years later. He and Daphne loved each other deeply, and were each other's best friend, yet he was a very physical man and frequently had a mistress, to whom he was no more faithful than he was to Daphne. She was stoic and tolerant of this side of her husband and rarely intruded. Indeed, when a woman to whom Whitney grew particularly close lost her life in an accident, Daphne comforted him in his grief, while he drove himself through it by focusing on the love and responsibility he felt for Daphne and their family. She even found a way of coping with the longest-running of Whitney's relationships, with a woman who bore him a son.

One reason for the success of the marriage is that they were entirely open with each other, and kept no secrets. Whitney's personal code of conduct helped too. Discretion was essential. He only took his girlfriends to certain nightclubs, only dined with them at certain tables in certain restaurants and entertained them at Woods Mews, never the marital home. And there was a line beyond which lovers could not cross. He tolerated no interference in his marriage, and invariably broke off with any woman who wanted more than an affair.

A consecutive pair of entries in his diary from January 1950, almost fifteen years into Whitney and Daphne's marriage, demonstrates where they jointly felt the line lay. Over lunch one Sunday, Esmond Harmsworth, 2nd Viscount Rothermere, told them how upset he was that his wife Ann had resumed her affair with Ian Fleming. Whitney called it a 'pretty disgraceful show – and Esmond is unhappy and obviously does not like being *le marie cocu*'.[8] The next day, he noted, almost in passing, that Daphne had become aware he was having an affair. The distinction may not seem obvious, but the Rothermeres divorced and Ann married Fleming, whereas Daphne retained total confidence in the claim Whitney often made to friends and family: he could never imagine being married to anyone else.

11

High Flyer

The Straight stable's 1934 season had barely begun when Whitney demonstrated how much of an attraction flying still held for him. He had just completed the last leg of his trip home from the Monaco Grand Prix, flying into Croydon from Paris aboard Imperial Airways' *Horatius*, when he shared some surprising news with an *Evening News* reporter: 'I have decided to add flying to my racing activities and I have entered a fast single-engined machine for the King's Cup race.'[1] This was an annual, two-day, cross-country competition, and the 1934 event was to be held over the weekend of 13 and 14 July.

Days later, Commander Harold Perrin, secretary to the Royal Aero Club, made it clear that Whitney's entry would not be accepted, on the grounds that only British citizens could participate. It seems odd that Whitney, who had just raced in Monaco in US colours, should be unaware of this regulation, and even then he remained an American citizen for another two years. It was not until July 1936 that he finally adopted British citizenship, obliged to by the administrative burden of relying on Britons to be the registered owners of aircraft he was purchasing for his aviation business.

Regardless of his King's Cup disappointment, Whitney pressed ahead with his 'fast, single-engined machine'. The Hendy Heck was a sleek monoplane designed by Basil Henderson and powered by a de Havilland Gipsy VI engine to give a top speed of 190mph. The bodywork was clad in a stunning black and gold colour scheme designed by another British-based American, Edward McKnight Kauffer, who had become well known for his poster artwork for Shell. Other refinements specified by Whitney included armchairs in check upholstery, a Marconi wireless with remote controls and a pair of quick-release parachutes. He finally took receipt of the aircraft in March 1935, but after just a few flights in it, he sent it to the Air Ministry for testing. It was found to be unstable at low speed, and when concerns over its ailerons led to its Certificate of Airworthiness being withdrawn, Whitney walked away from the project altogether.

By then he had founded Straight Corporation Ltd to act as the holding company for his civil aviation interests. Bill Lambert joined him in the move from racing to become secretary of the new company. Its first operating subsidiary was Ramsgate Airport Limited, set up to operate a municipal airport on the north-western tip of Kent on behalf of the local town council. Dick Seaman was Whitney's partner in the venture, joining him and Fred Gwatkin on the board. Whitney and Dick also took stakes in, and became directors of, Air Commerce Ltd, which offered charter flights out of Heston, to the west of London.

In Dick, Whitney had, for the first time in his life, formed a genuine friendship with someone of his own age. The 'Dear Seaman' as they negotiated over the sale of the Magnette had become 'My dear Dick'. Little more than a year after advising Dick to quit university if he was serious about motor sport, now Whitney encouraged him to follow him into business: 'You must give up motor racing soon, as it does not really lead anywhere ... and I think you ought to concentrate your ability on something more constructive.'[2]

The agreement with Ramsgate Town Council came to serve as the model for Straight Corporation as it expanded. Whitney was given exclusive use of a 90-acre site just outside the town on which to operate a flying club and daily services, along with a restaurant and bar. In return, the council received an annual rent and a small proportion of the aerodrome's revenue, and enjoyed a boost in tourism through the summer flying season. Leasing sites from local councils made Whitney's new business feasible, as it avoided excessive capital outlay on land, and this made Dorothy and Jerry – already delighted to see him walk away from racing unscathed – all the keener to support him in his new venture.

Actually, flying was if anything more dangerous than motor sport. Daphne's uncle, Denys Finch Hatton, immortalised by his lover Karen Blixen in her book *Out of Africa*, had been killed in Kenya in 1931 when his aircraft crashed in flames shortly after take-off. Just eight months after Hélène Boucher's express delivery of a spare axle enabled Whitney to race in Monaco, she lost her life when the plane she was testing came down in woods near Versailles. The day before Whitney and Daphne's wedding, a de Havilland Dragon crashed on take-off from Heston, killing two and injuring five, and prompting questions in the House of Commons. This accident briefly had an adverse effect on Whitney's nascent business. Dick addressed a letter to him on New York's Park Avenue, the first stop on the US leg of Whitney's honeymoon, reporting that adverse publicity about the Heston incident had caused Air Commerce's passenger volumes to fall, while protesters carrying anti-flying placards had demonstrated at Ramsgate.

Otherwise, Dick's news was entirely positive. He was writing from Straight Corporation's new offices in Brettenham House, an imposing building at the northern end of London's Waterloo Bridge. He had been at Ramsgate for the inauguration of the scheduled service to Ostend operated by Hillman's Airways, the airline that would shortly be merged with several others to form the first iteration of British Airways. He and Ramsgate's mayor, in full ceremonial dress, had made speeches, then flown to Ostend, where they were treated to a civic lunch and champagne. He confidently expected the number of passengers joining Hillman's flights at Ramsgate to increase once an on-site customs office opened, and he had negotiated revenue shares from pleasure flights at the airfield and two 'air circuses' that would visit in August. His only concern was Whitney's fertile brain: 'I hope you have a marvellous time in America, but don't come back with too many completely revolutionary ideas on airport design.'[3]

As it was, Whitney was distracted by everything aeronautical except airport design. In Chicago, he flew the Vultee V-1 and found it fast and comfortable, but concluded that passengers may not wish to fly in a single-engine plane. In Denver, he tried out two new light aircraft, the Hammond Y-1 and the Gyro AG-4 Crusader. He considered the Hammond very slow, but was so impressed with the Crusader that he wanted to acquire European rights to it. He also spoke with numerous airline executives, pilots and mechanics, and rated American Airlines highly, though he noted that even with capital of $15 million and a fleet of around 100 aircraft, it had only just generated its first monthly profit.

Shortly before the *Bremen* set sail for Southampton, Whitney invited Osmer Gorton, manager of Dorothy's New York office, on board to talk about his business plans. His first passage across the Atlantic, when he moved to Dartington as a 13-year-old, had been arranged by Gorton, and Whitney found it easy to turn to him for advice. Straight Corporation needed more working capital, but in trying to avoid further assistance from Dorothy, Whitney had become overdrawn at his bank, the London branch of New York finance house Guaranty Trust. Gorton feared Whitney was using his facility at the bank's Paris branch too, but when Whitney asked him to become a director of Straight Corporation and provide financial advice he felt obliged to decline – he was too far away and knew nothing of British business practices. Gorton could readily see what Whitney required: 'He needs someone in whom he has explicit confidence, and I fully believe that he would be guided by the person and not rush into enterprises through his present inexperience and the lack of someone in whom he may fully confide.'[4] It would take a year for the right person to emerge.

Upon his return from honeymoon, Whitney was obliged to confront the pressing issue of his personal finances. He enjoyed a considerable regular income from the yield on shares in US family trusts, but he had been living beyond his means for several years and making inappropriate investments – most notably a stake of more than £5,000 in a chain of dairies that would need writing off. He still owed money on the Hispano Suiza, and had not yet paid Cartier for the pearls he had given Daphne on their wedding day. Gwatkin was in such despair, saying of Whitney, 'He is always wanting to put money into this or that',[5] that he was considering his future as a director of Straight Corporation. In early October, a meeting was held at Brettenham House, at which Dorothy, Jerry, Gwatkin and a representative of Guaranty Trust sat down with Whitney to establish a way forward.

Humiliating though it must have been for Whitney, it proved to be a most productive meeting. He undertook to make no more investments without the approval of Jerry and Gwatkin, to hold regular board meetings for Straight Corporation and the subsidiaries being set up under it, and to live within his means. In return, Gorton would release a tranche of US capital to settle Whitney's personal and business debts, and Dorothy would finance the next phase of Straight Corporation's growth. 'I think he has learned his lesson,' thought Gwatkin. 'His financial position worried him terribly, and this is always a good sign.'[6] Whitney sent his thanks in a handwritten letter to Jerry: 'I'm most terribly grateful for the way in which you have come to the rescue, and I feel very ashamed that I have had to fall back on you in this way.'[7] Even then, it took four months for Whitney to clear his debts. In early February, he sent a more formal letter to Jerry, enclosing a cheque to clear a personal loan and a statement of account demonstrating that he had paid off all his creditors. Jerry thanked him for the update and the repayment, 'which I am very happy to have, chiefly because it represents a sign-post that you are turning the corner into the straight, and I see no reason why you should not go from strength to strength'.[8]

Jerry was quite right. In the first quarter of 1936, Whitney took on the management of three further aerodromes. Some 30 miles north-east of Dartington, Exeter Council had been considering a municipal airport for years, but it took Whitney to galvanise it into action, and he acquired the rights to operate an aerodrome at Clyst Honiton, the site of Exeter Airport to this day. He took over the management of Plymouth's Roborough Airfield, a little over 20 miles west of his former home. In Ipswich, some 80 miles north-east of London, his old racing rival Brian Lewis felt he had taken the local aerodrome as far as he could, and paid Whitney to take it over from him. In each case, Whitney set up three entities: a limited company to manage the aerodrome, a flying club to help generate revenue from it and a separate limited company to operate the flying club. The same structure had already been put in place at Ramsgate, where Thanet Aero Club and Thanet Aero Club Limited operated at the airfield managed by Ramsgate Airport Limited. There was a pragmatic reason for this plethora of limited companies. In the event of a fatal accident, the potential for litigation would be restricted to a single aerodrome.

Straight Corporation's rapid expansion brought it to the attention of Sir Harold Hartley. Born in London in 1878, he had won a scholarship to Balliol College, Oxford, emerging with first-class honours in natural science. He returned to Oxford after an eventful First World War, in which his expert analysis of German chemical weapons led to him attaining the rank of brigadier general. In 1930, he left academia to explore the application of science in industry with the London, Midland & Scottish Railway Company, and four years later he was chosen to head up a new company, Railway Air Services. This was formed by LMS, three other major railway corporations and Imperial Airways to exploit the best of rail and air travel across the UK. The rail companies provided their marketing and administrative capabilities, while Imperial Airways' pilots and aircraft drastically shortened travel times on longer routes – the 11½-hour train and ferry trip from London to Belfast became a 4-hour flight. By the end of 1935, Railway Air Services had a fleet of eight de Havilland aircraft.

Hartley requested that enquiries be made at the Air Ministry about its views on the growing number of municipal aerodromes coming under Whitney's management. Major R.H.S. Mealing, the Air Ministry official responsible for licensing civil aerodromes, was quietly sounded out, and Hartley was advised that 'as far as the Ministry is concerned they will assist Mr Whitney Straight in any way which will contribute towards the improvement of aerodromes and aerodrome management'.[9] In principle, Railway Air Services stood to gain from more aerodromes being run on commercial lines by experts, but with only eight aircraft, it was suffering from 'dead mileage' – flying an empty plane to pick up passengers elsewhere. Since Whitney was planning to have his own planes stationed at each of his aerodromes, Hartley's concern was that Straight Corporation would not face this problem, and would be able to offer more competitive rates if it moved into the airline business. The two men would see a great deal of each other in the years ahead.

From the outset, Whitney strove to extend his customer base beyond pilots and passengers. He wanted everyone – flyers or not – to enjoy visiting his aerodromes, and to come again. He played up the 'club' aspect of his flying clubs by adding swimming pools and squash or tennis courts. He made plans for modern terminal buildings with restaurants and bars. Visitors were encouraged to experience the thrill of flying on brief pleasure flights. Once smitten, they could take flying lessons at his aerodromes. But he saw an obstacle to his bid to bring flying to the masses. His aerodromes were dominated by slow biplanes with cold, open cockpits. A pilot could yell to a passenger or student down a tube, but conversation was impossible. What was needed was a simple, affordable monoplane, with an enclosed, heated cockpit and side-by-side seating, easy handling, a good cruising speed and low landing speed. After his unhappy experience with Brian Henderson and the Hendy Heck, Whitney chose to give this brief to F.G. Miles.

Born in 1903, Miles had left school as a young teenager to run a motorcycle repair business and a delivery van, and maintain the projector equipment in his local cinema. This generated sufficient income for him to explore flying as a pastime. He was taught to fly at Shoreham Airport on the Sussex coast, and he went into business there with his tutor, operating a flying school and giving pleasure flights. One day, he delivered a plane to the school run by Jack Phillips and Charles Powis at Woodley Aerodrome, near Reading in Berkshire. Within three years, their company was still called Phillips & Powis, but Phillips had moved on, Miles had become a director and the business was producing an attractive series of low-wing monoplanes.

The Hawk, with its pair of cockpits still open to the elements like the biplanes Whitney despaired of, was swiftly followed by the Falcon, with a three-seat cabin, and the Merlin, in which pilot and four passengers could cruise at 145mph. Phillips & Powis went public in March 1935. Six months later, Tommy Rose won the King's Cup in a Miles Falcon, and was followed home in second, third and fifth places by other Miles aircraft. In seeking a designer who could fulfil his brief for a comfortable, affordable monoplane, and a company that could oversee its mass production, Whitney felt confident about F.G. Miles and Phillips & Powis.

The plane was formally designated the M.11, and the prototype, first flown by Miles on 3 May 1936, called the Miles Whitney Straight Special. It was built of Port Orford plywood to ensure a rigid structure and easy maintenance. The cabin contained dual controls and two wide seats, and was accessed by a large door on the starboard side. Fitted with a 130hp de Havilland Gipsy Major engine, it could cruise at 130mph, twice as fast as the biplanes of the day, yet extendible flaps fitted to the trailing edge of its wings enabled it to take off steeply at just 50mph, and touch down almost vertically in a headwind. No less a pilot than Charles Lindbergh, the first man to fly solo across the Atlantic, tested the prototype and was so impressed that he flew it on a tour of Germany, Poland, the USSR, Czechoslovakia, France and Holland.

The conspicuous success of the prototype led to an initial production run of twenty-five aircraft, called the Miles Whitney Straight and selling for £985. On these, the cabin door was switched to the port side and a single sheet of Perspex fitted as the windscreen. The unimpeded view this afforded pilot and passenger became a strong selling feature, and was commented upon when Whitney and Miles hosted a press day at a damp, blustery Heston on 22 January 1937. Three planes were present. One, designated the M.11B because of its unique engine, had flown in on its maiden flight. Its engine was designed and built by the man who ran Straight Corporation's

Technical Development section. He was Amherst Villiers, in whose *Villiers Supercharge* Ray Mays had contested several Shelsley Walsh hill climbs with Whitney. Villiers' engine was lighter and more powerful than the Gipsy Major, but he could not possibly compete with the economies of scale enjoyed by de Havilland, and the Maya engine and the M.11B remained one-offs.

The highly successful press day was followed by a sales tour, conducted by F.G. Miles' brother George, who was joined on parts of it by Whitney. By the time M.11s finished September's King's Cup in second and fourth places, further production runs of ten and then fifteen aircraft had been ordered. Some thirty Miles Whitney Straights had been sold in the UK to private owners and flying clubs, and in Australia, Belgium, Egypt, France, Germany, Italy, New Zealand, Romania and Switzerland. Production only ended at fifty aircraft in September 1938, the same month as the Munich Agreement, because Phillips & Powis was already committed to supplying trainer aircraft to the RAF. Ironically, it is perhaps the wartime record of the Miles Whitney Straight that best demonstrates what a successful aircraft it was. Roughly half of the fifty were requisitioned by air forces. The RAF employed twenty, the Royal New Zealand Air Force three and the Free French Air Force and Malayan Volunteers' Air Force one each. Even the Luftwaffe may have used an M.11.

Shortly after F.G. Miles and Charles Lindbergh had first flown the prototype Miles Whitney Straight Special, Whitney finally met the perfect candidate for the role of mentor that Osmer Gorton had identified. His name was Louis Strange. Born in 1891, he was 22 when he took a break from his father's farm after a sheep kicked him in the face, and spent the summer taking flying lessons at Hendon, winning his pilot's licence after flying solo for just 3½ hours. He joined the Royal Flying Corps in May 1914, and though he spent much of the First World War training pilots at Gosport, he saw sufficient action to be awarded the MC, DSO and DFC. He already knew Ramsgate Aerodrome, after winning the Thanet Air Race there in 1932, and he had most recently been chief test pilot and a director of Spartan Aircraft. The Air Ministry wanted him to join the Austin Motor Company to oversee an aircraft construction programme, but Strange preferred to join Whitney.

When interviewed by Gwatkin, Strange said he thought a lot of his time would be spent saying 'no', and asked how Whitney might respond.

Gwatkin was delighted: 'As I have had to adopt for some time past the role of the wet blanket in many of Whitney's projects ... I should personally be very glad to know that this role had been passed onto someone else who could speak from actual experience.'[10] Charles Gray, founding editor of the weekly magazine, *The Aeroplane*, was still more pleased at Strange's appointment to Straight Corporation's board. He told Whitney:

> What he does not know about aeroplanes and about flying is not worth knowing, and he ought to be able to run about from one aerodrome to another and talk sympathetically and find out just what everybody has to grouse about and either put them in a good temper or else come back to you and tell you really what does want doing.[11]

Whitney brought other experienced people into the business. In January 1937, he acquired Haldon Aerodrome, where he had learned to fly. He hired his old tutor, Bill Parkhouse, as part of the deal and put him in charge of Exeter Airport too. Upon taking control of Ipswich Airport, he made Noah Creasy, trainer at the Eastern Counties Aeroplane Club, manager of the aerodrome and chief instructor of the newly formed Ipswich Aero Club. Like Strange, Creasy had forsaken the family farm for flying, and had spent five years with the RAF. In July 1937, when the Duke of Kent flew into Ipswich on his way to a prize-giving at a nearby school, he enjoyed Creasy's tour of the airfield. Creasy's great prowess at pilot instruction led to him moving to Whitney's head office to oversee training across the group, and to him becoming one of the first fifty airmen to be awarded the Master Flying Instructor's Diploma.

There were exits too, and two of these severed Whitney's final links with racing. Bill Lambert left the business, to be replaced by Stanley Cox, whose membership of the Chartered Institute of Secretaries and experience working for the White Star shipping line, particularly after its merger with Cunard, served him well in dealing with Straight Corporation's increasing complexity. And Dick ignored Whitney's wishes for him to come full-time into the business, selling his shares in Air Commerce and resigning as a director of the Ramsgate companies to focus exclusively on racing. He was still happy to help Whitney circumvent the restrictions of his US citizenship by having aircraft registered in his name, but by the time Whitney finally became a British national, Dick was enjoying such success in a Delage maintained by Giulio Ramponi and Billy Rockell that he was invited to join Mercedes for 1937.

The finances of Whitney's business remained precarious. Whitney Straight Ltd, originally set up to run the Straight stable, had become a hybrid automotive/aeronautic vehicle, its balance sheet swollen by some £19,000 of aircraft ordered but not yet received and a similar amount relating to aircraft sold but not yet delivered. The sum seems so close to the combined sales value of the original production run of twenty Miles Whitney Straights that it appears Whitney was not making a margin on the aircraft that bore his name. The company's cumulative losses to December 1936 had grown to almost £4,000, and this was before the £500 still owed by Maserati was written off.

Straight Corporation's figures were still more troubling. Just months after joining the company, Strange thought the loss for the year to September 1937 was likely to be in the region of £15,000, and that commitments under existing leases would drive cumulative losses for the following period to £25,000. He insisted that capital expenditure be restricted to aircraft, airport terminals and hangars, and that there should be no outright purchases of airfields – only leasing of municipal sites, as at Ramsgate. Even then, the prescient Strange was concerned by increasing tensions across Europe. Gwatkin reported to Whitney that, 'as Colonel Strange has pointed out, the progress of civil aviation has been retarded by the Armament Programme, and this programme will probably continue over a period of three or four years'.[12] Precisely three years later, Britain was at war with Germany.

But Whitney chose to focus on making his many companies the best possible organisations to work for, even if this did little to help their profitability. He made flight training free for staff members, and gave any of them who had qualified for an 'A' pilot's licence 20 hours of free flying a year. In the spring of 1937, he unveiled a pension and life assurance scheme for his employees, assured by Legal & General, and launched *Straightaway*, an in-house monthly magazine. Each heavily illustrated edition featured introductions to key head office and aerodrome employees; lists of happy customers at each airfield who had gone solo or achieved their 'A' licence; and an opinion piece from Whitney – one might highlight progress across the group, the next might summarise the negotiations he was conducting on behalf of the Aerodrome Owners' Association with the Air Ministry on government funding.

Straightaway, and the striking colour brochures promoting Whitney's air training schools and his highly successful county air days, were edited by Mary de Bunsen. A woman with a great passion for flying, she had learned to fly at Phillips & Powis' school, and had most recently been in charge of publicity at Heston Airport. She resigned when the government acquired it, fearing that a state-run airport would not give a woman the same opportunities she currently enjoyed. Just three weeks later, Whitney put her in charge of marketing at Straight Corporation. In search of material for the first edition of *Straightaway*, she made a tour of the aerodromes by motorcycle. The 800-mile round trip took her six days, so she hired an aircraft from her old employers at Heston to complete her next circuit in a third of the time. She only claimed her mileage by road for this, but when Whitney learned of her ingenuity, he reimbursed her in full and thereafter she exploited Straight Corporation's staff benefit of 20 hours' free flight to ferret out the best stories at each aerodrome. She was eighteen months older than Whitney, and 'tremendously impressed by the ease and efficiency with which he ran the firm and handled his staff, many of whom were hard-headed war veterans and a great deal older than himself'.[13]

King George VI's coronation, on 12 May 1937, marked the beginning of a particularly busy period for Whitney. Exeter Airport was not due to open officially until the end of the month, but it received its first incoming flight that day, when Stuart Scott, chief pilot of Air Dispatch, arrived with photographs of the day for the local newspapers. His namesake, Charles Scott, flew to Plymouth carrying film of the proceedings, enabling Teignmouth's Riviera cinema to show footage of the coronation that same evening. On 31 May, Exeter's mayor, Alfred Anstey, hosted the airport's official opening, and was flown over the city by Jersey Airlines, which commenced four flights a week into the airport. The next day, Whitney and Daphne rejoiced at the birth of their first child, a daughter named Camilla.

Whitney attended the Exeter opening in the company of one of the architects he had commissioned to design the terminal buildings there and at Ipswich. Anthony Chitty had co-founded the famous Tecton firm of architects that had designed the enclosures at London Zoo, and had recently gone into partnership with Robert Hening, resident architect at Dartington. David Pleydell Bouverie, nephew of the 6th Earl of Radnor, had done a splendid job of designing Ramsgate's art deco terminal, with a roof profiled like an aircraft's wing, but Whitney was attracted to Hening and Chitty's modular approach to their designs. This focused on a terminal building that could cater for the needs of both customers and Whitney's staff, from flying club, restaurant and recreation facilities on the one hand to offices and training rooms on the other. After considering the inevitable need for future expansion, the pair designed a steel framework of standardised bays that could be extended easily. The effectiveness of the design was demonstrated even before Exeter's terminal was completed. Additional modules were incorporated beside and over the core construction to satisfy the Air Ministry's request for offices and accommodation quarters for a meteorological signals unit.

On 3 July, Ramsgate Municipal Airport, as it was now called, was officially opened when the Director-General of Civil Aviation, Sir Francis Shelmerdine, activated the airport siren. The sun shone, the band from nearby RAF Manston played *God Save the King* and Pleydell Bouverie's terminal building was so busy that visitors carried deckchairs on to its roof to enjoy the day. The aerodrome's Holiday Aviation Camp was already flourishing. Whitney may not have invented glamping, but he put aspiring pilots up in comfortable tents with a raised wooden floor, a proper bed and an armchair, and offered extensive breakfast, lunch and dinner menus in the restaurant, and Dartington cider in the bar. Dancing, fishing, tennis, boating and swimming featured, and 5 guineas a week gave campers a free flying lesson, cross-country flights in a variety of aircraft and talks on aircraft design, map reading and meteorology. A fortnight's stay at the camp gave holidaymakers a genuine chance to gain their 'A' licence for as little as £15, and, by the beginning of August, 300 had stayed at Ramsgate Holiday Aviation Camp. Four Auxiliary Air Force squadrons joined in, holding their own summer camp at the airfield and taking part in gunnery exercises on the nearby Isle of Sheppey.

Aviation journalist Lewis Selby rated Ramsgate the best municipal airport in the country, praising its proximity to the centre of town, the smoothness of the airfield surface, the design of the terminal building and the quality of food on offer in the restaurant. 'It seems strange,' he wrote, 'that all this should come from a young man who, until quite recently, stood in our minds as a millionaire undergraduate racing motorist, and nothing else. If only everybody with a fortune would make something so constructive out of their lives the world would be a better place.'[14]

Whitney's cluster of aerodromes in the west hosted a highly successful Devon Air Day on 24 July. He provided a typically bullish foreword to Mary de Bunsen's twelve-page programme:

> The corporations of Plymouth and Exeter have been wise and far-sighted and have provided fine airports which will bring trade and commerce in the future as sea harbours have done in the past. We have been entrusted with the management of three airports and we do not bear our responsibilities lightly. We are determined that the faith that has been placed in us will be well placed and that Devon's Airports will be second to none in efficiency. Devon Air Day is the first step forward.[15]

The main attraction of the day was an air race laid out over a triangular course, starting and finishing at Plymouth, with the first turn at Haldon and the second at Exeter. The surprise winner was Captain P. Phillips, who squeezed an average speed of more than 103mph from his old Avro 504N biplane. A complex programme for each of the three airports contained the same highlights, but at different times of the day. Three large RAF Saro London flying boats lumbered out of Mount Batten in Plymouth Sound and flew over Plymouth Airport before dropping special messages from the Lord Mayor of Plymouth over Haldon and Exeter. All three aerodromes were treated to acrobatic displays by a team of Gloster Gladiators from 54 Squadron. In all, more than 45,000 watched proceedings, and almost 900 enjoyed pleasure flights. Dorothy and Jerry could have watched it all from Dartington, but they were holidaying at Applegreen. Upon their return to England, Dorothy rushed straight to Woods Mews, where she was 'thrilled to the marrow over her granddaughter',[16] while Jerry revelled in Whitney's success:

> I was delighted to get the full report of the Devon Air Day and to see what a first rate job you and your staff must have put up. I have now read the press accounts and you certainly had a good press. I also think it was a remarkable feat to pull off anything of that kind in such good order.[17]

It was just as well that Whitney's mother and stepfather were so impressed with him, because his next move would require Dorothy's biggest capital injection yet: he decided to add another municipal airport to his chain, in

Weston-super-Mare on the north Somerset coast, and the transaction came with an airline, aero club and engineering facilities. Weston officials had first been attracted by the commercial benefits of flight in 1910, when an airship flew over Cardiff. The Welsh capital lay just a dozen miles across the Bristol Channel, and since the principality had been 'dry' on a Sunday since the 1880s, Weston's hotels and pubs stood to gain by making the crossing as swift as possible. When civilian flying resumed after the First World War, pleasure flights taking off from Weston's beach became a common sight, and soon Sands Aerodrome was a popular destination for pilots. In 1932, Norman Edgar began running regular flights out of Bristol, and Weston's councillors were as excited as their predecessors by his proposal for a 12-mile flight between Weston and Cardiff replacing the 60-mile road trip. They purchased 52 acres of land to the south-west of the town and began construction in early 1936 on Weston Airport. Edgar moved his business, Western Airways, there and carried the majority of the 25,000 passengers who used the airport in its first year.

In addition to the regular ferry service to and from Cardiff, Western Airways began scheduled flights linking Weston with Birmingham in England's West Midlands and with Le Touquet on the French coast. Edgar appeared to be running a highly successful business, but Western Airways was poorly managed and heavily loss-making. In January 1938, Whitney agreed to inject £15,000 into the business in return for a controlling interest, and simultaneously negotiated with Weston council a revised twenty-one-year lease on the airport and the removal of any landing fees there for Western Airways aircraft. But when Gwatkin saw the company's books, he insisted that Whitney renegotiate the heads of agreement he had signed with Edgar: 'The Weston organisation appear to have failed to comply with so many different provisions of the Companies Act that the liabilities of these companies and the directors for penalties under the Companies Act must now be considerable.'[18] The deal went ahead, but Edgar left Straight Corporation before the end of the year.

By the time the 1938 flying season began in earnest over the Easter weekend, Whitney had acquired the rights to three more municipal airports. Two were to be satellites of Ipswich – Clacton lay 40 miles to the south on the Essex coast, and Bury St Edmunds, 25 miles north-west – and their acquisition prompted the creation of another airline, Southern Airways, to run ferry services between the three sites. The other acquisition was very much an outlier. The council in Inverness, in the north of Scotland, invited Straight Corporation to develop its existing aerodrome, overlooking the Moray Firth.

The developments gave Whitney such prominence in the British civil aviation sector that he came to adopt a position of influence. He was part of a fifteen-strong deputation from the Aerodrome Owners' Association who joined with representatives from Denmark, Finland, Italy, Norway and Sweden on a trip to Germany, as guests of the Reich Association of German Airports. Ostensibly, the trip was designed to establish if airport charges could be standardised across the Continent, but Whitney was most struck by the sheer scale of Berlin's vast new airport, Tempelhof. He considered it five times too large for current demand, and that, by the time it reached full utilisation, aircraft design might have changed so much that the entire site might be obsolete. Then again, he recognised that Tempelhof was not to be judged on commercial or practical grounds: 'Herr Hitler's ambition is to make Tempelhof the air focus of Europe ... a symbol of Germany's development, and a centre for Berlin.'[19]

Whitney gave evidence to Lord Cadman's Committee of Inquiry into Civil Aviation, but failed in his bid to win government funding for aerodrome lighting that would better support night flying across the country. He was more influential in talks with the Air Ministry and the Treasury about the creation of a Civil Air Guard scheme. Its objective, given the increasing threat of war, was to create a large pool of qualified pilots, and it provided aerodromes with a much-needed additional income stream. By the summer, Straight Corporation had already received 800 applications to join the scheme, and Whitney planned to launch Civil Air Guard training across the group from 1 October.

Another benefit to the company of the government's increased focus on national security came when it won one of the largest 'army co-operation flying' contracts to be awarded to a civilian enterprise. Straight Corporation racked up more than 1,500 flying hours supporting army units on exercise. The most concentrated day involved nine of Whitney's aircraft – almost a quarter of his fleet – ferrying personnel to areas of operation. The company was congratulated 'on the accuracy of the courses flown in a difficult district and under adverse weather conditions'.[20] Increasing volumes across the core aerodrome and airline business, combined with these new revenue streams, more than doubled Straight Corporation's revenue in the year to September

1938. 'We look forward to the new financial year with greatly increased confidence,'[21] wrote Whitney.

And so he grew the business further. He agreed terms with Lord Jersey for a landing ground in Swansea at Jersey Marine, and added a Cardiff–Swansea leg to Western Airways' ferry services with Weston. By the following summer he had increased the opportunity for seaside holidays for thousands of people, with a regular service from Manchester in the north-west of England to three destinations along the north Devon and Cornish coast, and another from Ilford on the eastern outskirts of London to Ramsgate.

Straight Corporation moved its headquarters from Brettenham House to 17, Manchester Square, half-a-mile west of Oxford Circus. W.A. Street, a member of the Chartered Insurance Institute, was hired to take overall responsibility for the numerous county air days now running each summer across Whitney's 'estate'. W. Lancaster joined from the recently formed British Airways after completing servicing courses in the US with Lockheed and Pratt & Whitney. He took on the new engine overhaul shop at Ipswich. Within months of it opening, it had to be expanded to three times the size. Another key hire was Owen Roberts, who took charge of flying training and the Civil Air Guard scheme. Educated at Eton and Sandhurst, he had quit the Scots Guards after two years to focus on aviation, but it was only after writing off two aircraft in careless accidents that he grew serious about his flying. Now he had a string of qualifications under his belt, including pilot's 'B', wireless telegraphy and radio telephony licences. Upon joining Straight Corporation, he teamed up with Chief Wireless Instructor J. McGillivray to invent a device that tracked a plane in flight on a cockpit map.

Even when one notable champion of the group quit, he continued to support Whitney. Ramsgate's local member of parliament, Harold Balfour, was obliged to resign as president of Thanet Aero Club when he was appointed Under Secretary of State for Air, but one of his first tasks in his new role was to officially open Ipswich's striking new terminal building. The same duty was performed at Exeter by Balfour's new boss, Sir Kingsley Wood, watched by a crowd of 30,000.

The business was becoming so sophisticated that the traditional 'flying season', from April to September, ceased to be of significance. The Weston–Cardiff–Jersey Marine service, normally suspended in mid-September, ran right through the winter. A Weston–Cardiff flight on the evening of Sunday, 2 October, was the first British night-time civilian passenger flight, and was marked by a BBC broadcast. Bad weather caused radio contact with the aircraft to be lost on take-off, but the BBC's redoubtable Wynford Vaughan Thomas, commentating from Cardiff, filled the void eloquently, spotted the approaching plane's lights and gave a graphic description of its landing. A paint shop was opened at Weston, and Freddy Froome head-hunted from Phillips & Powis to run it. Fitted with an air-conditioned spray booth, it was kept busy throughout the winter, ensuring that each of Straight Corporation's forty aircraft maintained its crisp appearance, with dark metallic blue/grey fuselage and wings, and crimson and white-striped rudder.

A memorable landmark was achieved over the Whitsun weekend of 1939. Western Airways carried more than 2,500 passengers, enabling Whitney to claim 'a world's record for passengers carried in so short a period by any airline company'.[22] The 'Congratulations' column of the previous month's *Straightaway* was the longest yet, with seventy aspiring aviators gaining their 'A' pilot's licences at Straight Corporation training schools, and a similar number of pilots renewing their licences under the Civil Air Guard scheme. Yet in the same edition of the magazine, Whitney felt obliged to strike a cautious tone. He concluded an article entitled 'Hard Thinking', 'The winter's planning has been directed towards participation in the universal process of preparing for national emergency, to the fullest extent compatible with the maintenance and development of essential civil flying activity.'[23]

As the storm clouds gathered across Europe, Whitney faced losing his staff, his aircraft and his airfields. Western Airways' longest-serving pilot, A.L. Mortimer, had more than 5,000 Weston–Cardiff crossings under his belt and had recently been appointed chief instructor at Weston, but when the Air Ministry learned he was one of the few instructors capable of providing flying boat training at Hamble, he was called up. In the context of what was rapidly escalating into another world war, the threats to an independently wealthy man's business may not appear important, but it was a profoundly troubling time for Whitney. While he wrestled with the implications for Straight Corporation, he found it easier to decide his own future. His father may have considered it 'a bad business, this airman game',[24] but more than twenty years later Whitney had no hesitation in choosing how he would defend the country he had adopted: he accepted a commission to join 601 Squadron as a pilot officer.

Dick Seaman was another young man with some hard thinking to do. A patriotic Englishman, he was nonetheless racing for a German team, and had recently married a young German woman, Erica, daughter of BMW's general director, Franz Josef Popp. Most observers believe he would have returned home and, like Whitney, served as an airman in the forthcoming war, but fate intervened. On 25 June, he was comfortably leading the Belgian Grand Prix, held in teeming rain on the fearsome Spa-Francorchamps circuit. He was thirteen laps from home when, just like Hammy, he lost control of his car, glanced off one tree and smashed into another. Unlike Hammy, his only injury was a broken arm, but the impact knocked him out and, before he could be dragged clear, he was engulfed in flames. Eight hours later, he was dead.

At the end of July, Whitney was appointed trustee of a fund set up to finance the creation of a memorial to his great friend, but events rapidly overtook the plan. Though no one knew it at the time, Brooklands hosted its last-ever race meeting a week later, on 7 August, and within a month prime minister Neville Chamberlain was obliged to tell the nation: 'This country is at war with Germany.'[25]

Baby Whitney. (Dartington Trust/Elmgrant Trust)

Willard sent illustrated parables to young Whitney from France. One drew a parallel between the Gauls fighting the Romans and the Allies fighting the Germans. Here, Gallic leader Sabinus hunts a sanglier (wild boar). (Division of Rare and Manuscript Collections, Cornell University Library)

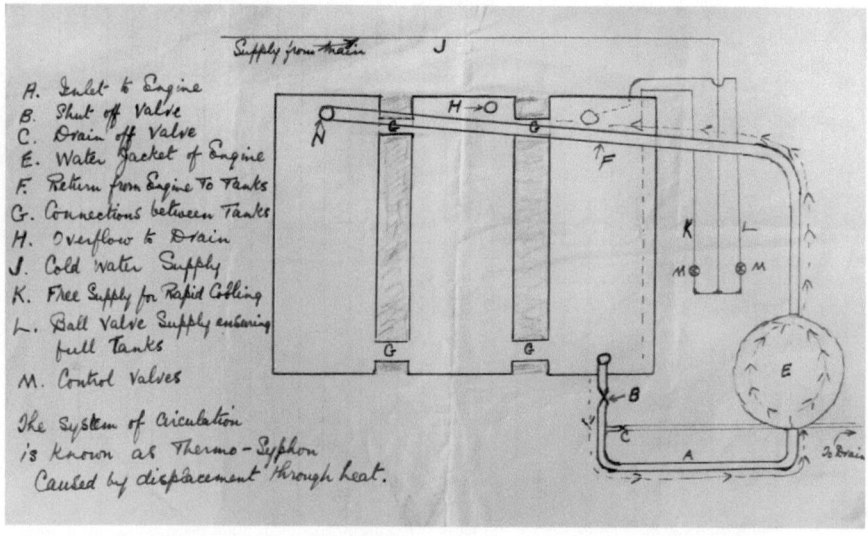

One item on Whitney's school curriculum was the maintenance of the generator providing electricity to Dartington Hall. (Dartington Trust/Elmgrant Trust)

Roy Nockolds' depictions of Whitney's record-breaking ascent of Mont Ventoux ... (National Motor Museum, Beaulieu)

… and of his abortive attempt on Brooklands' Outer Circuit lap record. (Family collection)

The Straight stable's 1933 Christmas card featured its logo – a fusion of Whitney's original 'flying W' insignia and the trident of Maserati and Bologna – on the Brooklands banking. (Dartington Trust/Elmgrant Trust)

Nockolds painted the Miles Whitney Straight too. (Author's collection)

Promotion of the aircraft focused on the comfort of its cockpit. (Author's collection)

Sir William Rothenstein's sketch of Squadron Leader Straight, 242 Squadron. (Family collection)

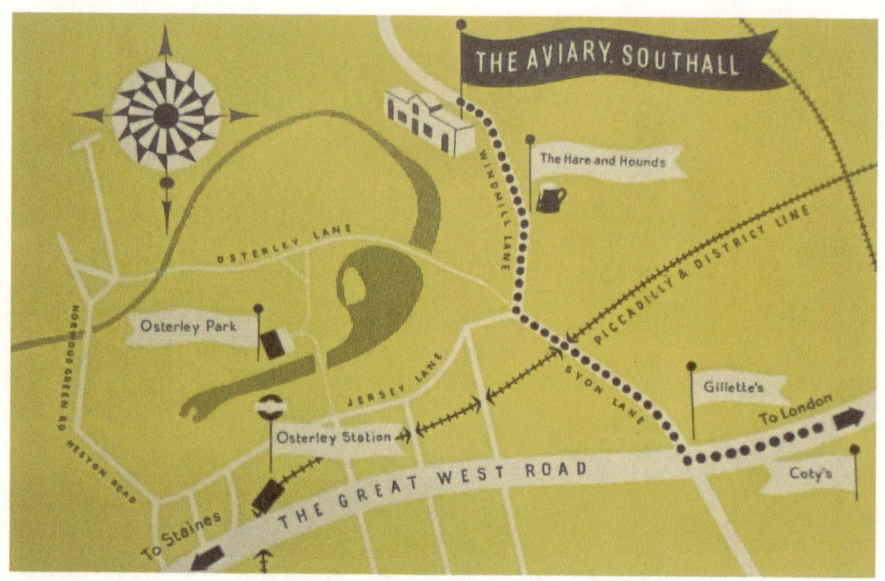

Directions to The Aviary in 1950, long before the M4 came through Whitney's property. (Author's collection)

Whitney at BOAC. (Author's collection)

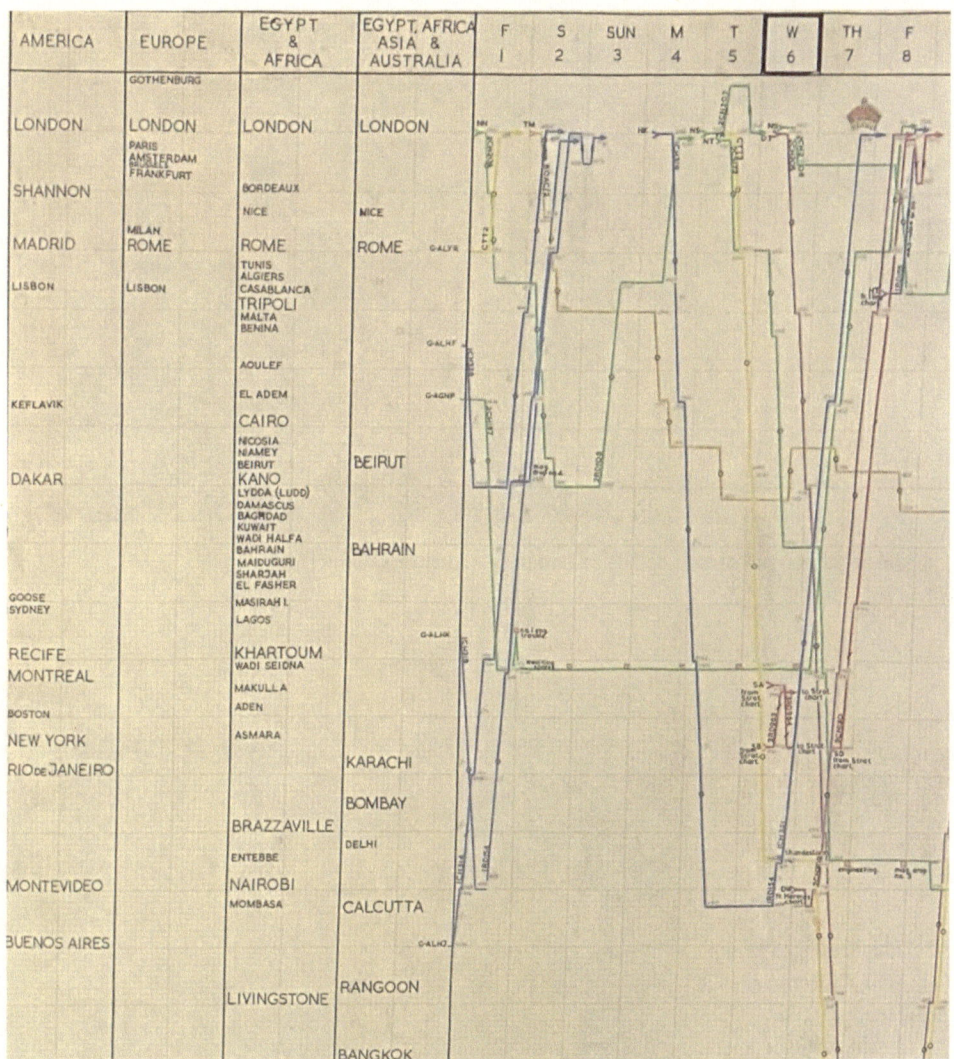

BOAC's February 1952 slip chart. The long, steep blue line leaving Heathrow on 4 February represents the Argonaut carrying Princess Elizabeth and Prince Philip to Nairobi. The black edge around 6 February marks the death of the King, prompting another long, steep blue line: the return flight of the royal couple. The crown under 7 February captures the arrival at Heathrow of Queen Elizabeth. (British Airways Heritage Collection)

An architectural sketch of Villa Camanda. (Author's collection)

The Straights' 1961 Christmas card, painted by the famous cartoonist Giles. Whitney and Daphne have become grandparents, and, as Daphne and Amanda watch on, the Bowaters parachute down on a snow-bound Aviary from Whitney's Cessna. (Family collection)

The 'double-line alphabet' created by Banks and Miles, the design consultants selected by Whitney's Design Advisory Council to develop a clear corporate identity across the Post Office's disparate businesses. (John Chenery)

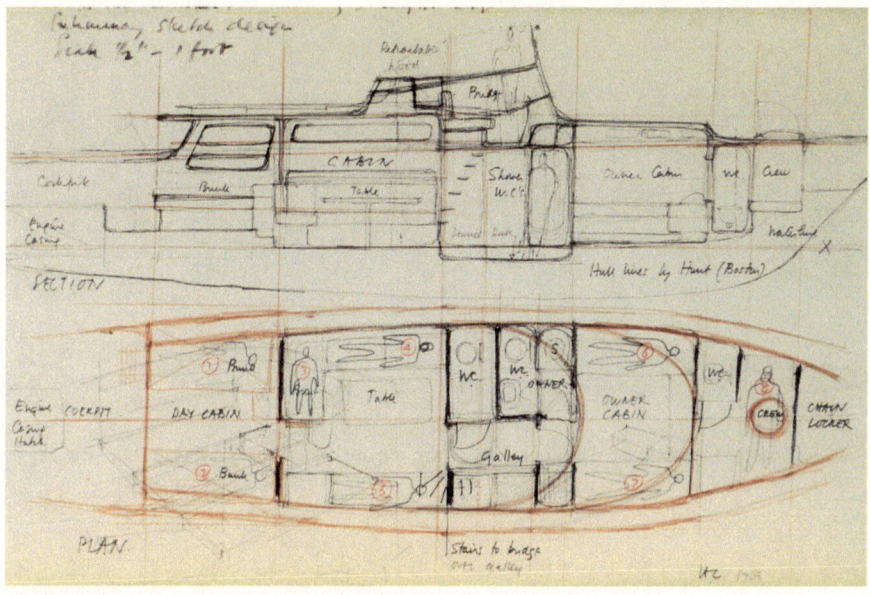

Hugh Casson's preliminary sketch design for *Camanda IV*. (Author's collection)

Casson was an inveterate sketcher – here are eight scenes from a day in the life of Villa Camanda. (Family collection)

12

War

601 Squadron, formally known as County of London, was one of the first Auxiliary Air Force squadrons to be formed, in October 1925. The concept of an auxiliary air force had been a feature of Lord Trenchard's initial development of an RAF independent of army and navy. He envisaged the airborne equivalent of the mounted yeomanry of earlier times, and 601's founder, Lord Grosvenor, had himself long harboured dreams of a territorial air force. Informally, 601 was called 'the Millionaires' Mob', the perfect environment for Whitney, packed full of strong, well-heeled personalities like himself, including Loel Guinness of the brewing family and the future press baron Max Aitken. The man given the unenviable task of 'instructing' Whitney was Squadron Leader John Peel, later credited with firing the first shots in the Battle of Britain, while Flight Lieutenant Roger Bushell, the real-life 'Big X' on whom Richard Attenborough's Roger Bartlett was based in the movie *The Great Escape*, signed Whitney's log book after his first month of flying with the unit.

The squadron had been based at Hendon, immediately to the north of London, for a dozen years, and was equipped with Blenheims, a light bomber that also served as a night fighter. Whitney first flew one on 9 June, and needed fewer than 2 hours in the air for Peel to judge him ready to fly solo, which he duly accomplished with a 35-minute flight three days later. At the end of August, Squadron Leader Brian Thynne judged him 'above the average'.[1] 601 moved to Biggin Hill in Kent on 2 September, and Britain went to war with Germany the next day. Pilot Officer Whitney Straight's first wartime action came the following evening, with some night flying practice. A regular schedule of exercises and night-time interception work continued through to the end of the year without Whitney so much as seeing an enemy aircraft, and he grew frustrated and bored. At least the turn of the year brought some welcome diversions from the 'Phoney War', that lull in hostilities in western Europe after the fall of Poland. 601 moved to a new home at Tangmere, near Chichester in Sussex, and on New Year's Day 1940, Whitney logged his first 15 minutes at the controls of a Hurricane. He swiftly came to love flying the plane on his own, 'upside down, half rolls coming out at terrific speed, pulling out with the blood running from one's nose, eyes driven back into their sockets',[2] and he took great satisfaction in 601's formation flying too: 'a team spirit greater than in any game'.[3]

On the ground, two responsibilities preoccupied him: his family and Straight Corporation. Young Camilla, almost 3 years old now, had been whisked out of harm's way and was living with her aunt Biddy in New York. Daphne was in New York too, working for the British philosopher and political thinker, Isaiah Berlin, helping him prepare reports and analysis for the British Press Service. Almost five years into their marriage, she and Whitney had grown distant emotionally as well as physically, and she was having an affair with a man well known to Whitney, who wrestled with the implications. He wondered might Daphne be more suited to a life with her lover. 'I have a great responsibility for her happiness, which I must honour.'[4] He himself was involved with several women, and giving a lift to one of them and her Pekinese dog in a Blenheim landed him in trouble. Increasingly frustrated with the lack of action, he asked his contacts at the Air Ministry for 'a nasty job somewhere'.[5]

Whitney was soon granted his wish, but his negotiations with the Ministry over the future of his business were proving less successful. In the opening months of the war, Straight Corporation's larger aircraft had been employed under government contract to ferry military personnel and supplies around England and France, while the smaller planes had been used as targets in searchlight exercises. With Whitney at 601 and Owen Roberts now serving with the Coldstream Guards, it had fallen to Louis Strange to run the company. Wheedling money out of the Treasury to pay the wages of colleagues not already called up, and extending Exeter's runways to accommodate the aircraft of Experimental Flight, moved there at a day's notice, taxed even his ingenuity. In time, as a member of the RAF

Volunteer Reserve, the 48-year-old Strange was called up too, and Stanley Cox was left in charge of Straight Corporation.

Whitney argued that his business, and other airlines and charter companies, should serve as the airborne equivalent of the Merchant Navy, but by December many of his staff had been conscripted, and Straight Corporation effectively reduced to a small servicing and repair facility at Weston-super-Mare. The only assurance he received was that no one else could fly the company's routes – it was free to operate any aircraft it could find that had not already been pressed into military service. This was of little consolation to Whitney, as it was the seizing of his aircraft that most grated with him. His frustration burst forth in a strongly worded letter that he drafted but found prudent to ask someone else to sign. It was published on 11 April in *Flight* magazine, apparently sent by Lord Apsley, a former chairman of Western Airways. It concluded:

> The company cannot help reflecting that if the Government at the present stage of the war already requires aircraft so badly that they cannot do without the four or five veteran machines needed by Western Airways' services, then surely there should be an immediate and searching enquiry into the true facts of our aircraft position.[6]

By then, a nasty job had been found for Whitney. Germany was importing the bulk of the high-grade iron ore needed for its war effort from Sweden, and shipping it out of the Norwegian port of Narvik. Despite Norway's neutrality, Britain decided to mine her territorial waters in a bid to cripple German industry, but Hitler reacted to this threat far more quickly than Britain did in executing it. By the time that mining operations commenced, the Germans already held Norway's capital, Oslo, and its major ports as far north as Narvik. In considering how to put in place the air cover essential to removing them, the Air Ministry turned to the man expert in the setting up and maintenance of aerodromes. On 2 April, Whitney received a telegram, ordering him to join the invasion force being assembled at Barnard Castle, in County Durham in the north-east of England.

The plan was as weak as most aspects of Britain's disastrous Norwegian campaign. How were airfields to be created and maintained in hostile territory when the enemy already had mastery of the skies? Whitney requested 200 skilled workmen, first-class anti-aircraft defences and heavy plant and equipment, but was granted none of it. Keeping his reservations to himself, he rang Daphne's mother, Margaretta, explaining that he would be away for a time, and asking her to discourage Daphne from returning from New York as planned. He left instructions at Tangmere for his Hurricane, about to have its 180-hour inspection, to have his 'flying W' insignia added to its fuselage, then, at 7.50 a.m. the next morning, he left for Barnard Castle. Barring a swift refuelling stop with the cans he was carrying, he drove non-stop and completed the 300-mile journey inside 4 hours.

Whitney was given the acting rank of squadron leader and sent to Rosyth, on Scotland's Firth of Forth, to join a group of some thirty officers and 670 Royal Marines and seamen being assembled for Project *Primrose*, a small-scale landing in advance of a major assault on Trondheim, in central Norway. They boarded four Royal Navy sloops and, on the morning of Monday, 15 April, set sail. The vessels sat low in the water because of the great weight of equipment they carried, and the rough sea conditions forced the party to lay up overnight in Invergordon, further up the Scottish coast.

There, the group was instructed to make for Åandalsnes, a small port some 40 miles up the fiord of Romsdalsfjorden, almost 125 miles south-west of Trondheim. They crossed the North Sea in calmer conditions the next day, and at 10 p.m. arrived off Åandalsnes. The jetty there could only accommodate two vessels at a time, but by morning all four had been unloaded, and Whitney set about his task. On Sunday, 21 April, he teamed up with the man who had been placed in charge of what remained of the Norwegian Air Force, Captain Bjorn Øen. His face bearing the signs of the burns he had suffered in a recent crash, Øen confirmed to Whitney that all aerodromes were now in enemy hands, and that the only option was to go up in an open-cockpit Tiger Moth fitted with skis to search for a site on which one could be constructed from scratch.

Whitney had neither helmet nor flying suit and had never encountered such cold, but evading the attack of a Heinkel He 111 warmed him up, and he and Øen found what they were looking for some 30 miles to the south-east – a frozen lake at Lesjaskog, lying under 3ft of snow. They contacted the local mayor, and a 200-strong workforce cheerfully set about clearing a runway on the lake. The pair returned to Åandalsnes to find that continuous bombing of the town had begun, but the phone exchange was still functioning on Wednesday, 24 April, when Whitney cabled the Air Ministry to advise that the lake would be ready to receive a group of Gloster Gladiators that afternoon. Bang on schedule, Squadron Leader J.W. 'Baldy' Donaldson of 263 Squadron led eighteen Gladiators from an aircraft carrier through a snowstorm to land safely on Whitney's makeshift airstrip. So far everything had gone according to plan, but the developments on the lake had been monitored by German reconnaissance aircraft, and bombers moved in early the next morning.

By lunchtime, twelve of the Gladiators had been destroyed on the ground, and, by evening, the lake had been rendered useless as an aerodrome by more than 130 bomb craters. Donaldson led the surviving planes to a new landing ground to the north, but his pilots were obliged to destroy them when they ran out of fuel. His unit had fought bravely, shooting down six German aircraft in the face of overwhelming odds and losing none of its own in aerial combat, yet all eighteen of its planes were out of action. The situation was even bleaker back at Åandalsnes, where barely a building still stood.

Wherever Whitney went – the RAF HQ outside Åandalsnes, the Navy HQ 50 miles to the north-west in Molde or another option for an aerodrome he investigated, across the estuary at Vestnes – he found himself subjected to bombing. When the order finally came to evacuate, the bombardment remained so intense that HMS *Fleetwood*, tasked with putting in at Åandalsnes to rescue the evacuees, could not reach them. Starving, suffering from a heavy cold and demented from the near-continuous bombing, Whitney spent the night sheltering in a nearby village. The next morning, he was a passenger in a truck heading back to the rendezvous point when he heard what he had come to regard as inevitable – the direct approach of a bomb. It missed the truck, but landed sufficiently close that he was thrown from it, knocking him unconscious, ripping a jagged wound in his back and severely perforating his eardrums. He came round to find himself lying face down in mud, and 10 minutes passed before he felt able to stand, whereupon he became aware of the warmth of the blood running down the side of his head. When he finally made it into Åandalsnes, he was asked if he had seen Squadron Leader Straight, and for a moment he feared that his face had been disfigured beyond recognition, but then he recalled the mud he had been thrown into.

Whitney was patched up by an overworked Norwegian doctor in the only functioning dressing station, then stretchered on to a waiting whaler. One of the lucky ones, he was taken to a hospital ship, HMS *Sikh*, which arrived in the naval base at Scapa Flow in the Orkney Islands on Thursday, 2 May. Five weeks later, Baldy Donaldson and the courageous men of 263 Squadron were among more than 1,500 killed when the aircraft carrier on which they were returning, HMS *Glorious*, was sunk, along with its escort vessels, *Acasta* and *Ardent*.

Whitney had served with great courage, and would be awarded the Military Cross – a rare distinction for an airman – and the Norwegian War Cross for his valour. Yet Project *Primrose* serves as an example of everything that was wrong about Britain's Norwegian campaign in the spring of 1940. Poor planning, late decision-making and inadequate supplies gave Whitney and his comrades little chance of success. He was left bitter by the experience: 'It was maddening to hear the report of Chamberlain's platitudinous speech, i.e., enemy losses greater than ours, our losses small, withdrawal from Åandalsnes without loss of a single man. The official figures must show things up and there is bound to be the hell of a row.'[7] Indeed there was: a frank, two-day debate in the House of Commons led to Neville Chamberlain's resignation as prime minister on 10 May, and Winston Churchill's appointment in his place.

By this time, Whitney was recovering in the military hospital at Davyhulme in Manchester. Park Hospital had recently been converted for military use, and those injured in Norway were among the first to be treated there. He felt well enough by 17 May to write a frank report to the Air Ministry. In it, he highlighted two points: first, the damage to morale caused by continuous bombing, and second, the utter futility of planning an invasion without parity or preferably superiority in the air. It seems so obvious, yet it took ignominious defeat and unnecessary losses for the lesson to be learned. 'We said we would help Norway,' Whitney noted in his diary, 'but all that has happened is that her countryside has been razed to the ground and she has been conquered anyway.'[8]

After a month in hospital, he felt wretched. The back wound was healing slowly, but he wondered what his continued deafness, headaches and dizzy spells meant for his future: 'I want to avoid a hamster desk job.'[9] News of the war upset him further. During May, 601 pilot Charles Lee Steere lost his life over Dieppe; Roger Bushell, who had moved to 92 Squadron, was shot down over the French coast; and Mike Peacock, another former 601 man who had taken over 85 Squadron, was killed when the fuel tank he attacked blew up, taking him and his Hurricane with it. So much frustration was vented in a letter that Whitney scribbled to Jerry that he slipped back into the American vernacular he had lost at Dartington. 'I'm a fairly lucky guy to have got off so lightly. Getting too near a 500 pounder is something I would not recommend to a friend of mine. I should be outa this joint in about ten days good as new plus a coupla cute scars and a personal antipathy for them god damn bastards.'[10]

But one story from the fall of France brought a smile to his face. Louis Strange, now 48 years old, had been posted to 24 Squadron to perform an extension of the transport role he had played in his final months with Straight Corporation. On 21 May, he helped deliver rations and anti-tank ordnance to the airfield at Merville, fewer than 40 miles south of Dunkirk. Looking at the damaged Hurricanes around the base, he decided to stay and help patch up as many as possible. Two RAF pilots who had parachuted from their damaged fighters and shown up on foot were the first to benefit, when Strange sent them home in repaired aircraft. Then, as German tanks and infantry advanced on the airfield, and Merville's ground crew and the handful of troops defending them left for the coast in a lorry, he climbed into the next most-airworthy Hurricane. Soon, he was flying far faster than he had ever known, skimming treetops to escape the attention of German aircraft, then low across the Channel to land at Manston, 3 miles from Ramsgate, where he and Whitney had enjoyed such success before the war. Strange received a bar to his DFC, and a letter of congratulations from Whitney: 'It all goes to show that there is a great deal of life left in the old dog yet!'[11]

Whitney's spirits rose further when Daphne returned from New York and began visiting him. Once he was well enough, they dined together in the evenings at Manchester's Midland Hotel. He was finally released on 2 June, and sent to the RAF's Central Medical Establishment in London to undergo tests. His back wound – 'like a packet of raw meat'[12] – was healing well, and his hearing had recovered, but his perforated ears were not yet up to the rigours of flying a fighter. He was kept on sick leave and told to report back in four weeks. With Daphne due to return to New York the following week to resume her British Press Service work, Whitney treated his extended leave of absence as an opportunity to take her away for a short break on the Thames, near Wallingford in Oxfordshire. They toured up and down the river in a small boat, he fished and she knitted, and for a few short days they were closer than they had been since before the war.

Nevertheless, when she returned to New York, Daphne resumed her affair, while Whitney's love life grew even more complicated. He remained deeply fond of the Pekinese owner but, just as she began to press him about a more permanent relationship, so, during a restorative break at Dartington, he met a young woman in the dance school there named Nellie van der Brink. He found her 'the loveliest creature I have ever seen – perfect figure – wonderful skin – a beauty which is second only to Garbo – I am profoundly disturbed by her'.[13] She provided a welcome distraction from the country's dire predicament.

On Monday, 24 June, Whitney joined the Directorate of Plans at the Air Ministry, co-ordinating sources of intelligence ahead of the anticipated German invasion. Within days he was attending meetings with Sir Frederick Handley Page about the desperate need to increase aircraft production, and with the new Secretary of State for War, Anthony Eden, whom he found bitter about the state of affairs he had inherited: insufficient men, guns and tanks. Whitney was struck by the sense of foreboding hanging over London. 'People are waiting – two vast armed camps with powers of destruction beyond the imagination of man sitting 20 miles apart with the Channel between them. Six minutes by air, that is the incredible thought.'[14]

Yet he had the presence of mind that summer to secure a deal that would prove of great significance to him and his family. His mother-in-law, Margaretta, learned over dinner one evening that Lady Jersey, owner of an estate to the west of London called Osterley Park, was willing to let off part of the property. Whitney had enjoyed doing business with her husband over the Jersey Marine airfield in Cardiff and, without so much as seeing the house and its 48 acres of grounds, he took a furnished lease on the property. It was called The Aviary, and he so fell in love with it that in due course he bought it outright. Osterley Park had developed around a manor house built by Sir Thomas Gresham in the late sixteenth century. During the 1760s, the renowned architect Robert Adam extensively redesigned the house, under the patronage first of Sir Francis Child and then his brother, Robert. The chief feature of the estate were three stretches of water forming a semicircle around the house, with the Garden Lake to the south, and the Middle Lake curving round the east until it met the North Lake. The Aviary lay beyond the North Lake, in parkland and woods of its own. It had once literally been a bird house, built to house the exotic bird collection of Robert Child's wife.

In August, Whitney's maps at the Air Ministry took on a radically different hue: '600+ approaching Portsmouth – Looked as though the Blitz had really begun.'[15] The day before, 601 had lost four pilots in close combat over the Channel. Now it played a vital role in defending the naval base at Portland. Whitney, who had just been grounded for a further month, went down to Tangmere at the end of the week to see how his comrades were coping. He was particularly struck by the change in Flight Lieutenant Willie Rhodes Moorhouse. The son of the first airman to win the Victoria Cross, he had been something of a *bon viveur* before the war, but now, Whitney felt, he had found his destiny. He had recently been awarded the DFC, and had destroyed two Messerschmitts during the week. Whitney was gripped by Willie's vivid descriptions of a sky 'black with aircraft'[16] but feared he would not survive long. Indeed, just three weeks later, and only six days after receiving his DFC at Buckingham Palace, Rhodes Moorhouse was killed, leaving Whitney genuinely conflicted about being grounded.

He was also torn in his private life. He remained committed to Daphne provided she was committed to him, his affair with Nellie had been consummated with a moonlit liaison in the loggia at Dartington and he was still sufficiently close to the Pekinese owner to consider the question of a permanent relationship with her once the war was over. But she wanted marriage now, and grew increasingly unhappy with the situation. She was staying in the Regent's Park home of Audrey Pleydell Bouverie, cousin by marriage of the man who had designed the terminal building at Ramsgate aerodrome. Whitney had a great regard for Audrey. He found her conversation a joy, and he was impressed that her great wealth and close connections with the Royal Family and senior politicians had not spoilt her. She did her best to comfort Whitney's friend, and did him a further favour on Sunday, 18 August, when she took him to Coppins, the large former farmhouse near the village of Iver in Buckinghamshire that had for the last four years been home to the Duke and Duchess of Kent. 'They were out on the lawn', recorded Whitney, 'he looking very brown and fit – she cool and beautiful.'[17] The youngest surviving brother of King George VI was an enthusiastic airman in his own right, qualifying as a pilot in 1929. At this point, the Duke held the rank of group captain and was attached to RAF Flying Training Command. He had formed a favourable impression of Whitney's organisational skills after his visit to Ipswich aerodrome three years earlier and, aware that Whitney was grounded, had a proposal for him. He wanted him to become his aide-de-camp.

Whitney was at least a month away from returning to active service, and frustrated by his planning role at the Air Ministry. He therefore agreed to raise the Duke's idea with Air Marshal Leslie Gossage, the RAF's Air Member for Personnel, and matters moved quickly over the following week. On the Monday, he and the dog-lover met for lunch at Claridge's and agreed to go their separate ways. Two days later, Gossage gave Whitney permission to accept the Duke's offer, but advised him to expect to return to active duty as soon as his injuries permitted. On the Friday, Whitney went over to the War Room for the last time to hand over his maps, and on the Saturday, still less than a week after meeting the Duke, he was formally posted to HQ Flying Training Command.

An eventful first day in the role left him under no illusions as to its challenges. At Command HQ, Shinfield Park, near Reading in Berkshire, Whitney was told that the Duke had not been near the place, and that he was extending his activity well beyond Training Command. Gossage rang Whitney while he was there to inform him that the King's private secretary, Sir Alexander Hardinge, wanted to see him, and an appointment was arranged for that same afternoon. There was just time for a light lunch at Coppins, where the main topic of conversation concerned finding the Duke a more appropriate role, then Whitney drove up into London through an air raid, and encountered great difficulty gaining access to Buckingham Palace. The meeting did little to raise his spirits. Hardinge explained that he would be grateful if the Duke – something of a *bon viveur* himself – could be kept out of London as much as possible, and Whitney left the Palace wondering how he was going to explain this to the Duke. In the end, he set about scheduling an itinerary that neither focused on Flying Training Command, nor kept the Duke out of town.

Indeed, the partnership began on London's Bond Street, with a visit to an exhibition of photographs hosted by the RAF's Director of Public Relations, Air Commodore Sir Harald Peake. They drew up a list of those 601 pilots killed since Whitney had last flown with the squadron, a conversation that upset him deeply. Peake proposed that he should move to the US and represent the RAF there, but Whitney declined the offer, saying he needed more operational experience first. At the end of that first week as the Duke's ADC, Whitney wrote to Hardinge enclosing an itemised list of visits and meetings, highlighting those at which the press had taken photographs. Hardinge thanked him, noting that, 'These visits evidently went very well, but I hope that His Royal Highness will have soon got some definitive job, which he will find of greater interest than the last.'[18]

Whitney did his best to create an interesting itinerary for the Duke, arranging a dinner for them both with senior RAF and US Army Air Corps officers at the Orleans Club on London's Pall Mall, and taking him to Manchester to visit the hospital where he had been treated. Whitney considered the visit particularly successful: 'The men were delighted to have him talk to them, and he gives a definite impression of a personal interest in each man.'[19] A bond grew between them. They dined together at Coppins and at The Aviary, and the Duke did as much of the driving as Whitney: 'He drives fast and fairly well but is inclined to cut in a bit.'[20] Whitney's role broadened in ways that Air Marshal Gossage can never have envisaged. He was with Nellie at The Aviary one evening when Audrey rang and explained that the Duke and Duchess were with her, there were no other men there, and would he please join them? His final task at the end of an unusual night was to make up beds for the party in a downstairs alcove when they refused to use an air raid shelter.

But the extra month's leave of absence was all Whitney's ears needed to finally heal, and on 23 September, he was passed fit to fly. He made his apologies to the Duke, formally applied to Gossage to return to 601 and was posted back to the unit with the rank of flying officer. In the seven months he had been away, he and the squadron had met with contrasting fortunes. At the end of May, as he lay wounded in Davyhulme, nine 601 pilots had enjoyed a night out in the doomed city of Paris after escorting Churchill across the Channel for one of the final meetings of the Anglo-French Supreme War Council. But the squadron had suffered heavy casualties providing air cover above the Allied troops trapped at Dieppe and Dunkirk, and through the early weeks of the Battle of Britain. On 19 August, 601 was offered apparent respite when it was pulled out of Tangmere and posted to Debden, north of the inner ring of fighter aerodromes surrounding London. Cruelly, the very next day, the Luftwaffe turned its attention on the capital and 601 remained in the thick of the action until it was sent to Straight Corporation's old aerodrome at Exeter on 7 September. The squadron's Intelligence Officer, Tom Waterlow, was particularly grateful. 'I don't enjoy my work when it entails rushing around the countryside looking at crashed aircraft and identifying my friends by the numbers on their machine guns.'[21] All told, a dozen 601 pilots had been killed in the time Whitney had been away. He may have been back on familiar ground at Exeter, but the Straight Corporation caterer serving the officers' mess was one of the few people he recognised.

He spent more than 4 hours in the air on his first day back in a Hurricane and suffered no ill effects. Within a week he had engaged with a Messerschmitt Bf 110 and a Dornier Do 17, without success, and had assumed command of the squadron's A Flight. The Battle of Britain drew to a close at the end of October, and Whitney and his flight switched to a pattern of regular patrols. The morning of 12 December began like many others over the preceding six weeks, but this time he spotted a Heinkel He 111 some 500 yards away to his left, and a little in front of him. Ordering his section into line astern, Whitney chased after it and saw it take evasive action, diving steeply towards the sea. He dived after it, closing to within 300 yards and firing at it in short bursts. He pulled out of his dive at 1,000ft, but the Heinkel was unable to and ploughed straight into the sea. There were no survivors. This was the first time Whitney had taken human life, but the evident enthusiasm with which he recounted the engagement to his mother suggests he felt no remorse. By this point in the war, Dorothy had lost her pacifism, and would in due course become a keen student of military strategy. She ended a detailed account of Whitney's first 'kill' to Jerry thus: 'It's wonderful and terrible, isn't it?'[22]

601 was on the move again before Christmas, relocating this time to Northolt. Into the new year, it was confined to formation flying and weather tests, but it was given a more offensive role in February 1941, by which time Whitney had been promoted to flight lieutenant. On 2 February, he was put in charge of B Flight, and led it as part of a raid on Boulogne. 601 was providing cover to the bombers of 139 Squadron, and Whitney's section was detailed to weave behind them. The group had set out on the return leg and was flying at 15,000ft when he spotted a lone, yellow-nosed Messerschmitt Bf 109, flying in the opposite direction, 3,000ft beneath him. He peeled round after it and adopted the ideal position – the sun was above and behind him, and he was above and behind the 109. Its pilot was oblivious to the peril he was in, and banked into a gentle left-hand curve. He was not even aware when Whitney opened fire on him from 300 yards,

for his pursuer was on too gentle an arc and aiming behind him. Whitney tightened his turn and continued firing as he closed to within 150 yards. The 109 suddenly dived and burst into flames.

Whitney was not only making up for lost time in the theatre of aerial combat, but was proving equally adept at low-level 'Rhubarb' attacks on enemy installations. The raid on the Belgian town of Ghent on 30 March was notable less for the damage done to German facilities there, but what Whitney got up to on the return leg of the sortie. Having circled the town at roof height, and flown up the main street to the acclaim of the locals, he attacked a German flak ship in the Channel. Whitney's all-round prowess brought him to the attention of the Deputy Chief of the Air Staff, Air Vice Marshal Sholto Douglas.

Douglas was looking for a new squadron leader for 242 Squadron. Disbanded after the First World War, it had been reformed in October 1939 as an all-Canadian unit. This suited a broad range of Allied agendas. Canada wanted to demonstrate participation in the war as early as possible, Britain wanted Germany to realise she was up against the full might of the Empire, and it was hoped that French morale might benefit from some native French-speakers flying overhead. 242 had fought with distinction through 1940, first during the fall of France and then in the Battle of Britain. It was while regrouping after the return from France in June that the famous English ace Douglas Bader became squadron leader. When he left in March 1941 to take command of the Tangmere wing, he was replaced by W.P.F. 'Treacle' Treacy, but only a month later Treacy and two of his pilots were killed in a mid-air collision. A total of six 242 pilots lost their lives that April. 'I realised,' wrote Douglas, 'that as a CO the squadron needed somebody who was quite out of the ordinary if the spirit fostered by Bader was to be maintained, so I had Straight take over 242.'[23] Whitney arrived at the squadron's new base, Stapleford Tawney in Essex, on 23 April, and considered 242 'a bloody marvellous outfit'.[24]

For the next two months, 242's workload comprised night patrols over London, bomber escort work and offensive sweeps against enemy installations. On 14 May, for example, Whitney led a party of four in an early morning attack on Ostend aerodrome. His Hurricane was now armed with four cannon, and a short blast from them was enough to cause an explosion in a hangar. All four men were back in time for breakfast, but a similar raid on Saint-Omer the following week was more costly. Pilot Officer David

Oak Rhind, who had flown number two to Whitney in Ostend, was shot down over the Channel. A month later, Whitney embarked on a lone, late-night raid on the airfield at Merville, in German hands since Louis Strange had been the last Briton to leave twelve months before. He descended out of cloud at 4,000ft to find the aerodrome brightly lit, and a Bf 110 flying nearby with its navigation lights on. The Germans, evidently, felt under no threat, and even when Whitney destroyed the aircraft with a short, single burst of cannon-fire, the aerodrome remained illuminated until he attacked its control hut. He used his combat report to pass on the lessons of a strange night. The flash from the Hurricane's cannon was very bright, 2 to 3ft long and 1ft wide. It was not disruptive to the pilot's night vision when he was looking through his reflector sight at an enemy aircraft, but it made aiming at ground targets more difficult in night-time conditions. And the blackout in occupied France seemed much less rigorously enforced than at home!

A week later, a group from 242 joined with fighters from 56 and 306 Squadrons, escorting two dozen Blenheims on a larger, more conventional raid on a chemical works in Chocques, not far south of Merville. They were met by approximately sixty enemy aircraft, and a vicious dogfight ensued for half an hour. Whitney and his men were subjected to repeated beam attacks by the enemy, who swept down from one side, broke away and climbed, then dived in again from the other. Whitney turned towards each attack and fired on almost a dozen German fighters, hitting two. He was thus able to claim one 'probable' and one damaged enemy aircraft, but it had been another costly day for 242, with three more men lost.

On 18 July, Whitney was advised that the squadron was to move to Manston, to perform 'Roadstead' sorties, escorting light bombers in attacks on enemy shipping in the Channel. As Sholto Douglas explained:

> Since Whitney Straight was already known to us as the man for difficult jobs we arranged for his squadron to be one of two that were to specialise in this type of fighter escort for the bombers. The enemy shipping had their own fighters escorting them, and they were also protected by heavily armed flak ships.[25]

Whitney was unimpressed when he arrived the next day and found that the outgoing 222 Squadron had not yet left the base, but his spirits rose when the two squadrons were instructed to team up as escorts to a group of Blenheims targeting a 6,000-ton tanker that was accompanied by a flak ship. 'I went down first and gave it all, breaking away at 50ft. As I left I heard a ping and smelled powder.'[26] Whitney had established his *modus operandi* – he would literally take the flak.

Each day followed the last, 242 Hurricanes diving in and strafing the decks of flak ships, attempting to keep their gunners occupied while Blenheims aimed their bombs on the target vessel, at great risk and with limited success. The mission of 23 July proved particularly galling. A large tanker was protected by no fewer than four flak ships, which reserved their fire for the bombers. All the 242 pilots made it back, but only two of six Blenheims returned. That evening, Whitney invited the crews of 21 Squadron back to the 242 mess. 'We got the furtive stock of beer out – I spent the rest of the evening filling up tankards. Those boys have a really rough time and no wonder they are really scared … Every trip offers little prospect of return.'[27]

Whitney enjoyed some well-deserved leave over the following weekend. On Friday, 25 July, he flew to Heston, picked Nellie up from The Aviary and took her to the cinema. He had grown very close to her, attracted by a heady combination of good looks, *joie de vivre*, speed in the swimming pool and a relaxed approach to air raids. On the Saturday, he learned that he was to receive the DFC. 'At last,' he recorded, 'I am clearly, officially and undeniably not a stooge.'[28] Further evidence of this came when he opened a letter from Anthony Eden's principal private secretary, Jim Thomas, proposing that he should enter Parliament after the war. Whitney sent Thomas 'a non-committal negative',[29] but Eden and indeed Churchill would try again.

Back at Manston on the Sunday, Whitney led a 242 escort operation intended to support a motor torpedo boat attack on a German destroyer in the Channel. The naval force never appeared, and though Whitney was able to claim two more 'probables', 242 lost one of the last Canadians on its roster when Sergeant George Prosser crashed into the sea.

The weather closed in, grounding 242 for the next two days, and Whitney was in reflective mood on the Tuesday night:

> On the whole I feel the war is going well. But of course one's judgement in these sorts of things is most influenced by personal consideration and

I am very happy at the moment. I like my boys and they like me and the AOC [Air Officer Commanding] thinks a lot of me and so on. The only thing is that things are going just a bit too well and I must be very careful not to put up any sort of black ... WS, be very careful, the spirit of my grandfather says to me this evening. I am now going to have a bath and go to bed. It is exactly 2300 hours – still raining. Tomorrow a Channel sweep for shipping. I want to sink a ship.[30]

It was to be the last entry in his 1941 diary.

13

Captivity

At 2.30 the next afternoon, Wednesday, 31 July, Whitney led a group of eleven Hurricanes out of Manston on another bomber escort mission. They failed to locate the enemy vessels reported to lie off Dieppe and the Blenheims turned back. The words of caution Whitney had written just the night before went out of his head, and he instructed his men to follow him down the Channel in search of a ship to sink – an unlikely objective, without bombers. They found a particularly challenging target between Fécamp and Le Havre, a destroyer with the usual escort vessels. Whitney led his group in on the attack, but he had taken the flak once too often, and this time the concentrated 20mm fire he faced found its target. With his engine and propeller damaged, he pulled out of his dive and levelled out. 'I have been hit,' he radioed. 'Am going to force-land in France. I order the squadron to return to base.'[1]

Whitney had little height to work with and found his undercarriage would not drop, but he was able to force-land in a wheat field near the village of Gerville, about 3 miles south-east of Fécamp. Apart from minor cuts and bruising to his forehead and a knee, he was in one piece and able to climb from his aircraft. Farm workers appeared, and Whitney took a box of matches from one of them in a bid to destroy his plane, but he had done such a capable job of force-landing without his undercarriage that the fuel tanks had survived the impact intact, and the Hurricane obstinately refused to catch fire. He was wearing RAF trousers, a leather flying jacket and a pair of ankle boots. He had no option but to flee the area as swiftly as possible.

After running for 2 miles, Whitney was able to dispose of his jacket at a farmhouse and acquire a beret. Now more suitably attired, he walked by road until he came across a railway station, and hid in the last carriage of a train waiting there. When the train moved out he found that the carriage he lay in was not coupled to it, so he resumed walking. By nightfall, he was 2 miles south of the small town of Bolbec, already some 18 miles from Fécamp, and exhausted. He asked a farmer for shelter, but German troops were billeted on the property and Whitney was told to move on. Too tired to find alternative accommodation, he chose to sleep under straw in the man's barn, sharing it with the very soldiers looking for him.

He cleared out before dawn the next morning and reviewed his options. He needed to get out of occupied France as quickly as possible – if captured there, he would be sent straight to an *oflag* deep in Germany. Even in unoccupied Vichy France he would be incarcerated. He had to reach neutral Spain, where he might expect a short period in custody, but diplomatic wheels would turn and he would be home soon enough (Fig. 6). But first he would make a brief visit to Paris, where he felt assured of a welcome at both the US Embassy and at the branch of the Guaranty Trust Company of New York where he had run an overdraft in the early days of Straight Corporation. He carried enough French Franc notes to last a day or two, he had some less useful British coins in his pockets and he retained the broad French vocabulary he had learned at Dartington. His confidence was high.

He had no idea that the Air Ministry had made his task considerably harder. It had announced that he was missing, and that his 242 comrades had seen his plane 'gliding over the French coast, towards the land'.[2] The British press ran with the story, *The Times* recording that Whitney was 'believed by his fellow pilots to have force-landed in France'.[3] The Germans therefore knew that the fugitive RAF pilot they were searching for in Normandy was Whitney Straight, the millionaire racing motorist. It would be a considerable coup if they could capture him.

Whitney made his way to a small railway station near Bolbec, and purchased a ticket for Paris via Rouen. While waiting for his connection in Rouen, he found a use for his loose change. He walked up and down residential streets, dropping British coins through the letter boxes of houses requisitioned by the Germans. He reached Paris by evening, and made straight for the US Embassy, at the north-west corner of the Place de la Concorde. Now, the spirit of his father may have been on his mind.

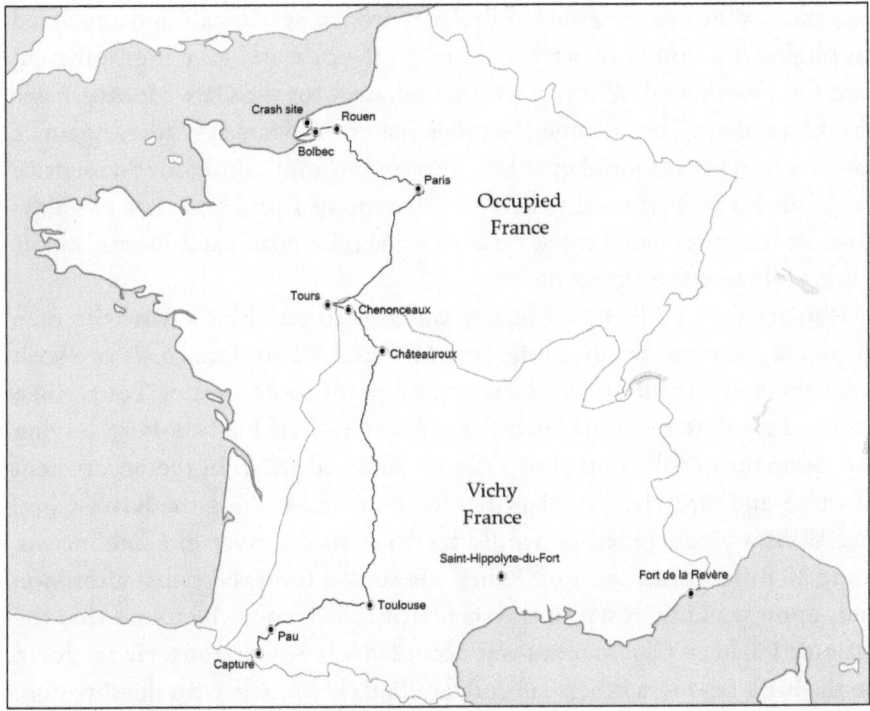

Fig. 6: The route taken by Whitney in his bid to reach neutral Spain after being shot down in Normandy on 31 July 1941. He was captured a week later, just inside Vichy France's border with Spain, and spent the next year as a prisoner of war, first at Saint-Hippolyte and then Fort de la Revère.

Next door was the Hotel de Crillon, where Willard had died more than twenty-two years before. His grave lay just a few miles to the west. The Embassy was shut, and nor was there any answer when Whitney phoned. He toured a number of hotels until he found one, the Hotel de Moscou in Montparnasse, which would give him a room without demanding papers.

The next morning, 2 August, he returned to the Embassy. This time the main door was open, but a notice inside read, 'All enquiries should be directed to the American Embassy, Berlin.'[4] An official came out to offer assistance but, on learning his identity, told Whitney that he could not help him and that he should leave immediately, as the building was being watched. Disappointed, Whitney went over to his bank, where the manager recognised him but also refused to help. Short of money and increasingly desperate, Whitney rang the US Embassy from a nearby café and explained his plight. A member of staff met him in the café and gave him sufficient cash for a week, and Whitney left immediately for the Gare Montparnasse to take a train to Tours, some 150 miles nearer the Spanish border. Again he found a hotel that would give him a room without asking for an identity card, but his lack of food tickets was becoming a problem. For two days now, he had sustained himself on coffee, beer, ice cream and sweets, and he could feel the effect on his heart.

Remarkably, in Tours, Whitney was able to purchase a Michelin map displaying the border dividing occupied and Vichy France. It ran west from the Swiss frontier near Geneva to a point south-east of Tours, then dropped south to meet the Spanish border at St-Jean-Pied-de-Port, leaving the Germans in full control of France's Atlantic coast. In the department of Indre-et-Loire, the boundary ran for some miles along the River Cher, and Whitney concluded he would try to cross the river in Chenonceau, some 20 miles to the west of Tours. He took a train there that afternoon and, upon walking down to the river from the station, he found that the majestic Château Chenonceau was occupied by the Germans. He sat down on the bank next to a fisherman and familiarised himself with the situation. A German foot patrol came by him every 15 minutes, and on the far bank, downstream of him, was a small wood. He waited for the guard to pass him and slipped into the river. Swimming underwater as much as possible, he made good use of the current and was able to slip into the wood unseen. There, he stripped off to let his clothes dry and breathed in free French air. A double-bonus awaited him in a nearby village. He found a hotel that not only turned a blind eye to his lack of an identity card, but also fed him.

On the morning of Sunday, 4 August, Whitney travelled the 50 miles or so to Châteauroux by bus. From here, he made the longest leg of his journey – a train took him 250 miles due south to Toulouse. There, he bought a more detailed map of the south-west of France and considered how best to cross into Spain. He chose the 58-mile, single-track railway line running from Pau through the Aspe Valley and the Somport tunnel to Canfranc, fewer than 5 miles beyond the border. He reached Pau, almost 120 miles west of Toulouse, the next day.

On Tuesday morning, 6 August, Whitney set off on what he planned would be the last leg of his week-long trek to freedom. The first two-thirds of the journey proved uneventful, but at Bedous, just 20 miles from

Canfranc, a policeman boarded the train and asked passengers for their papers. Whitney had to claim that he had left his identity card in Pau, and that he would return to collect it. Once the train pulled away without him, he set out on foot for the border. By nightfall he was tired and hungry and, after three days of walking in flying boots soaked in the River Cher, his feet were in poor condition. He came to a small village, found a room for the night and, in the only café, admitted that he had no food tickets but would pay double for a meal. Regrettably, upon leaving the café, he discovered that the man who had earlier vacated the table next to his, and whom he had taken to be a civilian, was actually a policeman and was now waiting for him, armed and in uniform. Whitney again put on a show of not having his papers with him, but this time the policeman escorted him back to the house where he had taken a room. He tried to escape via an upstairs window, but the policeman was waiting for him, revolver drawn. After a week on the run, and travelling more than 750 miles from the Channel coast to the Spanish border, the game was up. Whitney was marched away and locked in a cell for the night.

Precisely eleven years later, on a holiday with Daphne and Camilla, Whitney retraced the path he had taken though France during the first week of August 1941. It was a bittersweet experience. Upon finding the farm where he had spent his first night, he and his family were treated to 'a vin d'honneur amid much handshaking'.[5] He met with less success in locating the field in which he had force-landed, and found that many of the locals he approached could recall the day but were reluctant to help. He eventually left with a bitter taste in the mouth. More than a decade on, he had inadvertently rekindled the conflicting emotions of allies and collaborators still living as neighbours. Whitney and his family drove south and visited the Château Chenonceau, looking down on the river he had swum across. Eventually, south of Pau, they wound their way up into the Pyrenees and Whitney swiftly located the café where he had been apprehended. He found the owner '*malade*'[6] as she recounted the night and tried to excuse her reluctance to get involved on the grounds that she thought he was a German. Whitney also took Daphne and Camilla to the gendarmerie where he was locked up: 'It was terribly grim.'[7]

On the morning of 7 August 1941, Whitney sat in that grim gendarmerie and concluded that, since he had no means of escape, he would admit to being a British serviceman. He took more precaution over his identity than the Air Ministry had a week earlier, and claimed that he was Captain Willard Whitney of the Royal Army Service Corps, thinking that in this way he would attract less attention to himself. The attitude of the police relaxed immediately, and Whitney found the ensuing interrogation a courteous affair. He was given ration tickets and a hotel room – the very things that would have facilitated his escape the night before – and an officer apologised for placing any restrictions on him at all.

On 9 August, Whitney was taken to an internment camp that had been established at the beginning of the year in the seventeenth-century fort at Saint-Hippolyte, some 30 miles west of Nîmes. He was one of a growing number of RAF personnel joining British troops who had been captured as France fell. In all, some 220 prisoners were held under armed guard in a twin-storey barrack block, situated in a courtyard within the fort. Whitney recognised Saint-Hippolyte's Senior British Officer (SBO) immediately. Pat Gibbs had been squadron leader of 616 Squadron when he force-landed his Spitfire near Le Touquet in early June, and had also been arrested by a French policeman near the Spanish border, this after a six-week trek through France. Whitney learned from Gibbs that while escape from the camp was possible, the odds of reaching Spain undetected were greatly enhanced by working in co-operation with the local escape organisation. It was led by two men based in Marseille, Ian Garrow and Albert-Marie Guérisse.

Garrow, a captain in the Seaforth Highlanders, had avoided capture after the surrender at Saint-Valery on the Channel coast in June 1940, and reached Marseille in October. Dismayed by the growing number of British refugees and evaders in the city, he concluded that he would stay and help them rather than seek escape for himself. Guérisse had been a doctor in the Belgian army who had escaped from Dunkirk, but returned to France as a Special Operations Executive (SOE) agent under the pseudonym of Patrick O'Leary. Captured and sent to Saint-Hippolyte, he escaped and made his way to Marseille, where, trained in underground work and a native French speaker, he became the ideal partner for Garrow.

A series of measures introduced earlier in the year to reduce the number of escapes from Saint-Hippolyte had effectively changed the status of its inmates from internees in a neutral country to genuine prisoners of war, yet Whitney was still able to leave the camp temporarily, just three days after arriving. He travelled with Gibbs to Marseille to attend the monthly meeting of the Mixed Medical Board, which ruled on cases put before it of prisoners considered medically unfit for further military service, and therefore eligible for repatriation. It comprised three men: a French army medical officer and two civilian doctors, one appointed by Swedish diplomats representing German interests in Vichy France and the other chosen by the US consular officials responsible for British interests. This last man, a British-born, French citizen of Greek heritage named Georges Rodocanachi, could be relied on to fabricate medical evidence in support of prisoners' claims. Moreover, the upstairs apartment on Marseille's rue Roux de Brignoles in which he lived served not only as his surgery. It was also home to Garrow and O'Leary, and the base for their escape line.

After the Medical Board session, Whitney and Gibbs were also able to meet Garrow, who gave Gibbs the address of a safe house in Nîmes. Within the week, Gibbs had cause to use it, and to benefit from Garrow and O'Leary's escape line. On 18 August, he rushed the front gates of Saint-Hippolyte and escaped on a bicycle hidden for his use. He made his way to the safe house and, after Garrow had provided him with an identity card, was guided over the border into Spain. Whitney actually tried to escape with Gibbs, but was apprehended at gunpoint outside the camp gates. 'I did not receive any punishment,' he reported, 'as I bluffed and bullied the Camp Commandant into believing that I had not tried to get out at all.'[8]

Just nine days after being sent to Saint-Hippolyte, Whitney found himself SBO. In addition to becoming the main point of contact with prison and Vichy officials, the US Consulate and the Mixed Medical Board, he also assumed responsibility for the orderly conduct of the men under his command, with his own powers of arrest. Working effectively across this very broad constituency, with all its potential for conflict, Whitney developed communication and management skills that would serve him well for the rest of his life.

At the next Medical Board meeting, on 9 September, he and Rodocanachi were able to exploit his Norwegian wounds to argue successfully for him to be passed unfit. It was after this that frustrations set in. Whitney found that the prisoners given dispensation at both the August and September Medical Board meetings, many of them RAF men like himself, had not been granted exit visas. Then the new Commandant of the camp, Captain Digoine, ended the practice of the SBO attending the monthly meetings, thereby denying Whitney the opportunity to meet regularly with Garrow and O'Leary. Pressure was being applied by the Vichy authorities – unless the escapes from Saint-Hippolyte stopped, the exit visas would.

This was a wretchedly difficult situation for Whitney to manage. He himself was on the list of Medical Board men awaiting exit visas, but if this group was to get away, he had to order other men with escape plans to defer them. Into the new year of 1942, a further source of tension was the growing realisation within the camp that escaped pilots were of more value to the Allied war effort than escaped troops. Whitney in turn was frustrated by those soldiers who wanted to escape simply so that they might return to women they had met in the north of France. 'This I regard as desertion,' he wrote. 'The thing that weighs on my mind is my RAF personnel. I shall have failed badly if I don't get them away.'[9] And even while a prisoner in the south of France, far from Nellie and much further from Daphne, Whitney's love life remained complicated. Daphne's cables and letters from New York indicated that her affair remained serious, and that decisions needed to be taken. Whitney even resorted to wiring her lover, effectively asking him about his intentions. A cable from Nellie, still living at The Aviary, troubled Whitney further. She was over-spending, and his bank had intervened. He wired Fred Gwatkin, requesting him for more information about this.

Happier news reached him early on Saturday, 24 January, when he was called to a meeting with Colonel Tavernier, a representative of the Vichy authorities in Nîmes. Exit visas were finally to be granted to the Medical Board group, now numbering forty-three men. Tavernier even volunteered to bid farewell to Whitney in person on the day the men passed through Nîmes on their way to Barcelona. But the administration around the repatriation became a new source of frustration, and Whitney had to maintain frequent contact with Tavernier, the US Consulate in Marseille and the British Embassy in Madrid to push matters along. More than three weeks passed before he learned that exit visas had been made out for the group. Once signed by the Prefect in Nîmes, they would be issued and departure for Spain could be expected within ten days. When weeks passed with no further development, Whitney wrote a strongly worded letter to the Consul, demanding departure by the end of the following week. He was franker still in his diary: 'Six months as CO of this place without a day's respite is more than flesh can bear.'[10]

On Tuesday, 3 March, just four days before the visas were due to expire, Whitney was informed of the final travel arrangements. The Medical

Board group would leave Saint-Hippolyte early on the Thursday morning, board a train at Nîmes, and reach Spain by nightfall. Repatriation home via Gibraltar would follow. By the cruellest of coincidences, the night of 3 March also witnessed the largest Allied bombing raid of the war to date. More than 200 aircraft attacked the Renault factory in the Paris suburb of Boulogne-Billancourt. It was considered a legitimate target because it was estimated to be manufacturing 18,000 trucks a year for the German war effort. Every attempt was made to minimise civilian casualties, with a low approach and the massed use of flares, but the proximity of workers' apartment blocks to the factory left almost 400 civilians dead and more than 550 injured.

Whitney woke to news of the raid, and became concerned about its potential repercussions when he learned that the meeting scheduled with Tavernier in Nîmes had been cancelled. Nevertheless, US Vice-Consul Donaldson still arrived at Saint-Hippolyte from Marseille and the scheduled drinks party with the French officers went ahead. Whitney rose early on Thursday morning in good spirits: '4.30, damp but happy now. Gone with the wind, six months' prison – Barcelona tonight.'[11] Whitney, Donaldson and the rest of the party left the camp on schedule and, in spite of a missed connection in Nîmes, where the newsstands were full of stark headlines about Billancourt, they boarded the next train and left for Spain. But when it drew into the station in Perpignan, just a dozen miles from the border, Whitney found it 'full of troops, tin hats and fixed bayonets, like a regal reception'.[12] He and the rest of the party were instructed to disembark, so that they could be sent back to Saint-Hippolyte. For the second time in seven months, his bid for freedom had been thwarted within a few miles of success.

In direct retaliation for the Billancourt raid, the Vichy authorities had rescinded the exit visas of the Medical Board men. Whitney's immediate thought was to try to escape but he knew the odds were stacked against him – he had no papers or contacts. He also felt a responsibility to quell any trouble. There was little likelihood of that, with eighty armed troops escorting the men back to Saint-Hippolyte, and twenty extra gendarmes and the guard doubled when they arrived. But if both Whitney and the French expected trouble, there was none. 'Gave the men a talk. They took it well.'[13]

The next day, Whitney was remarkably phlegmatic. 'My principles are deeply affected. Why should these civilians die ... England now runs Germany a pretty close second in French expectations. We are so consistently ham-fisted in our dealings with Vichy France.'[14] Then, after writing to both the British Embassy in Barcelona and to the US Consul, the least helpful thought of all occurred to him: 'If only they had been 24 hours quicker.'[15]

With the growing realisation that the mass release of more than forty prisoners through the auspices of the Mixed Medical Board was now much less likely, discipline in the camp began to slip. Upon discovering that twelve internees had been selling blankets provided by the Red Cross, Whitney dealt with them severely, sentencing them to three weeks in detention. He did the same with three more men the next day, and when the original dozen refused to go back to their cells after an exercise break, he paroled them and marched them back to their cells, nipping any insurrection in the bud.

Just days later, worse news came. The prisoners were to be moved to the more secure Fort de la Revère, one of a chain of strongholds built in the late nineteenth century to protect the south of France against Italian invasion, and situated on a narrow ridge to the west of Monaco. To Whitney, the view from the fort was the only good thing about it. He complained about the poor beds and the lack of exercise space, and introduced a policy of passive resistance: 'If we are to be treated as criminals we will act like it.'[16] Several parades collapsed in farce and only when Digoine agreed to consider a list of Whitney's demands did the camp return to normal. More comfortable beds arrived the next day, a radio and the old maps and flags from Saint-Hippolyte were installed in the mess, and even Whitney privately conceded, 'There is no doubt, we are the best fed in Europe at this moment.'[17]

He took further comfort from frequent correspondence with Daphne. Her New York affair was over, and through the spring they became first reconciled and then recommitted to each other. This might not necessarily have meant the end of his relationship with Nellie, who as part of an economy drive had recently moved to a flat just north of London's Hyde Park, so that The Aviary could be let out to tenants. Unfortunately, it was now that she chose to write to Whitney about marriage. This was rarely a wise move by his girlfriends, and in a string of increasingly frank letters and cables, he made it clear to her that not only was it out of the question, but that the relationship must end. There was a war on and he was imprisoned in a foreign country, but even so it was a brutal way for him to break from the woman he had once considered the loveliest creature he had ever seen. He castigated himself for being unable to 'separate copulation from affection. This has landed me in much trouble in the past and has more in store.'[18]

By May, the number of men given dispensation by the Mixed Medical Board stood at fifty-seven, but Whitney's sense of responsibility towards them began to waiver when he learned that the Vichy authorities were now linking their repatriation to that of French pilots interned in England. Attempts to escape from the fort – some authorised by him, others not – were on the increase, and it became difficult for him to deter the men under his command from fleeing when the same thought was on his mind. His expectations of an impending Allied invasion of occupied France would prove wildly optimistic – D-Day was still more than two years away – but he was concerned that it might cause the Italians to take over control of the camp. He felt he had no option but to escape. The US Consular team asked him to stay, but they recognised he had committed to his decision when, late that month, he sent them his private papers for safe keeping.

Fortunately, he would not need to rely on a train journey to Spain this time. Ian Garrow had been a prisoner himself for the last eight months, but Patrick O'Leary now had scores of people working for him, including a reliable wireless operator who could keep him in better touch with his contact at MI9. This was the War Office section responsible for the support of Allied personnel on the run in enemy-occupied territories. O'Leary's contact there was Agent Sunday, Donald Darling, who had recently moved from his distant base in the Portuguese capital of Lisbon to Gibraltar, where he could assist in the evacuation by sea of larger numbers of escapers and evaders.

Whitney recognised that the chances of escape from the fort were slim, so with the support of Dr Rodocanachi, he had himself referred to the Pasteur Hospital in Nice, on apparent account of headaches and ear trouble. He arrived on 6 June, and found no fewer than four fellow prisoners. Sergeant Stefan Miniakowski of 300 Squadron had injured his arm after baling out of his aircraft on a raid over Cologne in April, and had been sent to the Pasteur shortly after arriving at the Fort. Private Charles Knight of the Dorset Regiment had exploited the numerous wounds he had suffered during the fall of France, while Private Sydney Fullager of the Queen's Royals had contracted a skin complaint after lying in crude oil while evading capture. Lance Corporal Prady of the Royal Northumbrian Fusiliers had been admitted by feigning madness.

Fullager and Prady made a bolt from the hospital within days of Whitney's arrival. They reached Marseille by train and were led on foot across the Pyrenees by three guides working for O'Leary. Their escape had two implications for Whitney, one positive, one not. O'Leary now knew exactly where the man most wanted home by MI9 was, and he gave one of his best agents, Francis Blanchain, the task of ensuring Whitney's safe passage into the escape line. But that required Whitney to get out of the hospital undetected, and he, Miniakowski and Knight were now under much closer surveillance. Two armed guards monitored them, and their rooms had bars on the windows and were locked at night. Even though four policemen patrolled the outside of the hospital, escape during daylight hours was the only viable option.

In the end, the solution was a simple one. On 22 June, the day before Whitney was due to be sent back to the fort, the three men quietly followed one of the guards down a flight of stairs, and when he turned one way at the bottom, they turned the other and ran for an exit. They never saw the second guard, nor the policemen. Blanchain was waiting for them and led them to a safe house. This is how Whitney related his escape from the Pasteur Hospital to MI9 after returning to England. A more colourful account was provided by Vincent Brome in his 1957 book on O'Leary, *The Way Back*. In this version of events, a nurse passed some sleeping tablets to Whitney, who slipped them into the drinks of the guards during a lunchtime game of cards. He and an accomplice escaped across a flat roof, where they were met by Blanchain, who escorted them by bus to the home 'of a certain Dr Levy',[19] whom Brome implied was the source of the sleeping tablets. It is known that the Antibes villa of gynaecologist Louis Lévy was used as a safe house by SOE agents arriving in the south of France, but he is not normally associated with escapers. Moreover, Brome's account is riddled with errors, claiming that Whitney was asked for his papers by a policeman on a train to Châteauroux rather than Bedous, almost 400 miles nearer the Spanish border; that he was arrested by three gendarmes rather than one; that his alias upon capture was Squadron Leader Smyth rather than Captain Whitney; that only eight Medical Board repatriates were turned back at Perpignan rather than forty-three; that Whitney left the hospital with one accomplice rather than two; and that he escaped from France in September, when in fact he returned to England on 24 July. Repeated requests were made to Frome's literary executor for access to his papers, but this was not granted and, in the circumstances, the only conclusion is to discount his tale of the nurse, the sleeping tablets and Dr Lévy, and to rely upon Whitney's own account of his escape.

MI9 left nothing to chance. If Whitney were to be stopped again and asked for his identity card, this time he would have one. He became Jean Fournier, born like Whitney on 6 November 1912, but in Lille, near France's border with Belgium, and living on the rue Dominique in nearby Roubaix. The card had apparently been issued in Roubaix on 7 November 1939, two months after the outbreak of war, and referenced M Fournier's 1.78m height, straight nose, oval face, grey eyes and absence of moustache or distinguishing features.

Five days after their escape from the hospital, Whitney, Miniakowski and Knight were taken to a fifth-floor apartment on the Quai de Rive Neuve, overlooking Marseille's old port. One of the most important safe houses on O'Leary's escape line, it was home to businessman Louis Nouveau and his wife Renée, and O'Leary himself was there to greet the men and brief them. As the days passed, other escapers and evaders arrived. SOE agent André Simon was followed by Sergeants Beecroft and Hanwell of 301 Squadron. Members of the same bomber crew who had crash-landed near Mannheim in Germany, they had made it over the border into Switzerland, from where the British Legation in Bern had sent them by train to Marseille. Lieutenant Anthony Deane-Drummond had taken the same train journey. Part of an SAS unit captured in Calabria in the south of Italy in February 1941, he had also escaped to Switzerland.

On Sunday, 12 July, the men left Nouveau's apartment in small groups, each with a guide, and travelled by train to Béziers, more than 140 miles west of Marseille. They reassembled in woods behind the long beach running by the village of Saint-Pierre-la-Mer, about 15 miles to the south, and rested up. During this stage of the operation, they were joined by Sergeant T.G. Johnson of 102 Squadron, who had bailed out of his aircraft near Dunkirk eleven weeks earlier. At 11 p.m. that night, the group walked down on to the beach and spread out, waiting for two flashes of a red light out at sea. The signal was due from HMS *Tarana*. It had been one of the 'little ships' that two years earlier had helped in the evacuation from Dunkirk of more than 300,000 Allied troops. Now, it had been converted to support the landing of agents and the collection of escapers and evaders along the Mediterranean coast.

The holds had been replaced with quarters designed to comfortably house 100 people, and the ship was fitted with a 12-pounder gun disguised to resemble a winch. *Tarana* had left Gibraltar in the traditional grey of the Royal Navy and flying the White Ensign, but once at sea the crew had repainted the ship a dirty brown, festooned the decks with fishing tackle and run up a Portuguese flag. The skipper was Lieutenant Commander 'Nobby' Clark of the Royal Navy Reserve, who had made his living before the war on the Liverpool–Belfast run. On seeing the corresponding flashes of a blue light from the shore, he ordered two of his crew into a dinghy to pick up their special cargo.

The quiet, still figures strung out along the beach waited patiently for the welcome sound of oars gently splashing against water, but the anticipated 10- or 15-minute wait after the exchange of signals became 30 minutes and then an hour. It was the crew on the deck of the *Tarana* who were the first to hear the dinghy, and then see to their consternation just their two colleagues aboard it. The ebbing tide and an offshore breeze had proved too strong for them, and they had returned to pick up an extra oarsman. Ron Stephens, a crew member who would be awarded the Croix de Guerre for his service on the *Tarana*, recalled, 'We thought we were tense, but it didn't take much imagination to realise the state that the escapees [sic] must be in, waiting like sitting ducks on the shoreline.'[20]

More than 90 minutes had passed now. Deane-Drummond tried to cheer himself up by assuring Whitney that all would be well, because it was now 13 July, and 13 was his lucky number. No sooner had Whitney muttered, 'Well I hope you are right'[21] than another red flash was spotted, much closer to shore this time, and the dinghy emerged from the dark. Whitney and his comrades bade farewell to their guides and clambered aboard. Now the current and the breeze were in their favour, and soon they were shinning up scaling nets on to the deck of the *Tarana*, where they were given the most British of greetings – jam sandwiches and cocoa.

Come daylight, normal procedure aboard *Tarana* was to go about the business of being a trawler. Its guests had to stay out of sight, but Whitney, MI9's prized 'parcel', was given preferential treatment and allowed up on deck to sunbathe. The vessel had a top speed of 12 knots, but throughout that day it pottered about giving such a good impression of a Portuguese fishing boat that Whitney asked Clark how long the 700-mile voyage to Gibraltar might take. Clark explained that he had one further task on his itinerary, and this had been delayed a day by a violent storm. He rendezvoused with a smaller vessel, the *Seawolf*, and exchanged the six SOE agents he had brought with him for more than fifty Polish operatives who had been smuggled away from a creek east of Marseille.

After more than a week at sea, and still some 36 hours from their destination, Whitney, along with everyone else on board, was handed a paint brush and instructed to restore *Tarana* to its Royal Navy grey before it could sail back into Gibraltar. They finally arrived on the morning of Thursday, 23 July. Donald Darling was there to greet them, and instruct them to remain silent about their voyage: they were to give the impression that they had arrived via Spain. Seven of the men taken off the beach at Saint-Pierre-la-Mer were back at sea the next day, sailing home aboard RMS *Llanstephan Castle*. Whitney was again given preferential treatment, and flown out of Gibraltar that same night. His plane landed at Heston early the next morning, a year to the week since he had last taken off from Manston.

He was driven straight to London, for the first of two debriefs with MI9. His host was Agent Saturday, Airey Neave. The two men had much in common. Seven months earlier, Neave had been the first British officer to escape from the notorious prisoner-of-war camp at Colditz. He too had stayed at Louis Nouveau's apartment in Marseille, and benefitted from the local knowledge of Francis Blanchain during his trek through the Pyrenees. Neave found that Whitney related his account of the last year with 'restrained amusement and valuable detail'.[22] After his escape from Colditz, he had himself been forced to kill time while waiting for a train, and had chosen the relative safety of a cinema. He was, therefore, astonished by the use to which Whitney had put his loose change in Rouen.

Next, Whitney cabled Daphne in her New York hotel. She was literally packing for her flight back to England when the page boy knocked on her door, and she was thrilled by the news. Whitney was at the airport to greet her when her plane landed, and his only frustration was that 5-year-old Camilla had not returned too – he had yet to hear her speak. Unlike the unfortunate news of his forced-landing in France a year earlier, no publicity was given to Whitney's return, and he and Daphne enjoyed the look of surprise on friends' faces when they visited some of their favourite London restaurants and clubs. On 31 July, a year to the day since being shot down,

Whitney drove to Northolt and spent 90 minutes in the air – his first flight in a Spitfire. Before recording the details in the log book that had been returned to him, he flipped back a page to learn how his last sortie had been recorded. A 242 administrator had written, 'Failed to return'. Whitney took out his pen and wrote alongside, '(sez you)'.[23]

Officially a 'supernumerary pending posting'[24] he was able to take Daphne away to Dartington. Dorothy told them about her recent speaking engagements in the US, and his sister Biddy's marriage to French exile Louis Dolivet the previous February. Whitney had now missed both his siblings' weddings – Michael had married in America a week after Britain had declared war on Germany. Whitney and Daphne enjoyed the sun and country air, cycling along Devon's quiet lanes, but their rural idyll was brought to an abrupt end when a motorcycle patrolman from the Automobile Association approached them. He had a telegram from the Air Ministry, requesting Whitney's presence back in London.

It was time for him to return to duty.

14

Expanding Horizons

When Whitney learned what Air Chief Marshal Wilfrid Freeman, the RAF's Vice-Chief of Air Staff, had in mind for him, he was only too pleased that his leave had been curtailed. As the war progressed, so the flow of reinforcement aircraft from Britain and the US had increased and the volume of military air transport had grown. It had now been decided to bring ferry and transport operations under a single authority, headquartered in Cairo. 216 (Air Transport and Ferry) Group would initially operate across much of North Africa and the Middle East. In due course, the south of France, Italy, the Balkans, Greece and even India would fall within its remit. The group would control all transport, ferry and communications aircraft under RAF Middle East Command, the routes on which they flew and the signalling systems they used. It would also operate and maintain the staging posts used for stopovers and refuelling, and manage the personnel in the Air Delivery Units (ADUs) who crewed the ferry aircraft.

The man in charge of Middle East Command, Air Chief Marshal Arthur Tedder, thought Whitney the ideal man to command the expanded group. Sholto Douglas, who was due to succeed Tedder at the turn of the year, and who had put Whitney in charge of 242 Squadron, agreed. The role would give Whitney vastly more responsibility than he had known at Straight Corporation, but the year of managing the difficult environment at Saint-Hippolyte and Fort de la Revère had made him a more thoughtful, more measured leader, and he felt ready. Promoted to air commodore, six rungs up the air force ladder since beginning the war as a humble pilot officer, he prepared to move out to Cairo in early September.

Daphne would be staying in London. She still reported to Isaiah Berlin in New York, but she had joined the American Division of the Ministry of Information, based at Senate House, at the heart of London University. Her reports to New York were well-received from the outset. Hamilton Fish Armstrong, the first American to interview Hitler, and the man whose 1933 book, *Hitler's Reich: The First Phase*, opened with the ominous words, 'A people has disappeared', rated Daphne so highly after receiving a single letter from her that Berlin told her, 'Your future as a political commentator is genuinely bright.'[1]

At the outset of the war, Whitney had made few arrangements about how his personal and business affairs were to be conducted if he were incapacitated. While he languished in Saint-Hippolyte, for example, it had fallen to Fred Gwatkin to find Nellie somewhere to live after she had been obliged to leave The Aviary. This time, as he prepared for life in Cairo, Whitney gave power of attorney to Frederick Handley Page. The man whose company had developed the O/400 'bloody paralyser' heavy bomber in the First World War and whose Halifax bombers were playing their part in turning round Britain's fortunes in the current conflict had been so impressed with Straight Corporation that he had considered investing in it. Now, he was prepared to carve time out from his Halifax production commitments to watch over Whitney's affairs. An early task was to approve the sub-letting of The Aviary to the Duke of Westminster. Quite why one of Britain's biggest landowners spent eighteen months in Whitney's home is an intriguing question – perhaps he found The Aviary close enough to London to be convenient, but far enough out of town to avoid being bombed.

The main beneficiary of Handley Page's involvement was Stanley Cox. The chartered company secretary had done a very effective job of guiding Straight Corporation through the war to date, but now he was only too pleased to take the counsel of one of British aviation's greats. All the company's aircraft had been requisitioned, along with all but of one of its aerodromes, and the catering contract at Exeter had just ended – the officers' mess there had concluded that it should pocket the profit Cox had been generating – but the 45,000 sq ft of facilities at Weston Airport were fully utilised in Civilian Repair Organisation (CRO) work. A workforce of almost 400 men, women and boys was employed in assembling, overhauling and repairing Curtiss Tomahawks and modifying Avro Ansons, and the annual profit generated by CRO work was approaching £4,000.

Whitney's preparations for Cairo were interrupted on the morning of Wednesday, 26 August with the most tragic of news – the Duke of Kent was dead. He had been on board an RAF Sunderland flying boat that had taken off the previous afternoon from Invergordon, on Scotland's Cromarty Firth, bound for the RAF station in Reykjavik, Iceland. Forty minutes later, the plane flew into a hillside and exploded. All on board perished except the tail gunner, whose turret was flung clear on impact. Among the dead was the Duke's latest equerry, Pilot Officer Michael Strutt. Had Whitney's ears not healed, and had he continued to serve the Duke, he would have been on the flight.

The following Saturday, he found the Duke's funeral, in Windsor Castle's St George's Chapel, a profoundly moving affair:

The Duchess a tragic, heavily veiled figure, the Queen Mother unflinching. Later the procession, the pure sexless voices of the choir, followed by the King, D of Glos, Kings of Norway, Greece, Yugoslavia, all the great company of State. The ceremony was regal yet friendly somehow. The King, deeply wrapped in emotion, scattered soil from Coppins as the coffin was lowered into the vaults below. Tears came to us all. The Duchess knelt, overcome. Later the last post by RAF trumpeters. Then the procession left slowly in funeral time. With it a great loss to us all.[2]

At 8 a.m. on 10 September 1942, Whitney took off from RAF Lyneham in Wiltshire, bound for Cairo. He was flying a Liberator, a four-engine bomber equipped for transport use. In addition to six passengers, he carried 3,500lb of Cairo freight, and a further 1,500lb to drop off in Gibraltar. The fall of France, and Spanish and Portuguese neutrality, meant that the trip had to be made in two legs: 9 hours round the Iberian Peninsula to a stopover in Gibraltar, then a further 11 hours across North Africa to Cairo, staying well south of the Desert War battle zone. Whitney's Gibraltar payload included pheasants and cigars for the officers of *Tarana*. He was only one of two *Tarana* 'parcels' able to return to Gibraltar during the war and thank its crew in person.

Given how cumbersome the Liberator could be at low speed, and how many critical eyes must have been watching his arrival at Heliopolis, Whitney was pleased with his landing. He was whisked away by car to the famous Cairo hotel, Shepheard's, where he met with Tedder, who told him,

'You are going to have a difficult job and you will find much opposition and many long faces.'[3] Whitney recalled later, 'Those first few days I felt very alone – very conscious that this was the big test of my life.'[4]

It was an intriguing moment to have arrived. Erwin Rommel had seized Tobruk on 21 June, earning promotion to field marshal, and his Axis forces had crossed into Egypt on 1 July, causing consternation in Cairo. Thousands watching the smoke rising from the chimneys of British military buildings as sensitive files were destroyed assumed the worst and headed for the railway station. But the opening skirmishes of the First Battle of El Alamein were as close as Rommel ever got to the city. Lieutenant General Bernard Montgomery took over the 8th Army on 13 August and, with each passing week, reinforcements of troops, tanks and aircraft increased the advantage he held over Rommel.

Within three weeks of arriving, Whitney demonstrated that his was not to be a desk job (Fig. 7). Over the course of ten days, he used one of 216's great workhorses, a Douglas Dakota, and a pair of Lockheed Hudsons to rack up 54 flying hours as he began the process of learning about his 'estate' and its condition. These tours were a constant feature of Whitney's years in Cairo, as he strove to increase productivity, and improve the safety and well-being of the people serving under him. When building work fell behind schedule at one staging post he demanded a bulldozer. When he saw that sickness rates among British personnel at another was treble those of the US station on the same airfield, he asked to be shown round the USAAF installation and identified the need for a dedicated RAF chef, and air conditioning and fly-proofing in the kitchens. Cold storage units were installed at more stations so that freshly killed meat could be hung properly. Whitney arranged for fruit juices and soda stream installations at 216's Persian Gulf stations.

Busy though he was from the outset, he soon found himself in a relationship. At a party on 19 October he met a woman named Marcelle Matossian. Some seven years older than him, she was married to a successful tobacco manufacturer of Armenian descent, Joseph Matossian. He lived in a fine house in Alexandria, while she preferred Cairo. The arrangement suited Whitney perfectly. His immediate reaction was 'marvellously excited'[5] and within a month he and Marcelle were lovers.

The Second Battle of El Alamein had been raging for two weeks when 216 Group delivered the supplies that helped bring about its conclusion.

On Friday, 6 November, Whitney's 30th birthday, he took the only aircraft available to him, an old Audax biplane, and flew 180 miles north-west of Cairo to the airfield at El Amiriya. There, he inspected the thirty-seven Hudsons and seven assorted bombers converted to transport specification that were loaded with supplies for the front, and spoke with their crews. Satisfied that they were 'all well and raring to go',[6] he swapped the Audax for a Hurricane and flew on to El Dabaa. There, the scene that confronted him was so shocking that he overshot the runway and had to go round again. Even then, he had to strain his eyes for bomb craters as he landed. He climbed out to see 'a scene of havoc and desolation. The Huns had only been gone twelve hours, prisoners mostly Luftwaffe were still being taken out of holes and caves. The ground was covered with dead, stinking already. Profoundly moving. Victory and rout. Death and dehydration. There was little cheer.'[7]

Four days later, with the second El Alamein effectively won, the Deputy Quarter-Master General at GHQ Middle East, Major General George Surtees, requested a meeting with Whitney so that he could thank him in person for the role 216 had played in securing the victory. Rommel was in flight, and Operation Torch, the Anglo-US invasion of Morocco and Algieria, was progressing smoothly. With the Allies making such significant progress across North Africa, Whitney looked forward to 216's theatre of operations expanding in 1943.

He would also have more aircraft to call upon when required. On his return from the battle front, he was advised that BOAC's North African fleet could be placed at his disposal as and when necessary. This effectively added more than sixty aircraft to Whitney's roster and delighted him, but it did little to impress BOAC's executives. British Overseas Airways Corporation had been born out of a government-sponsored merger of Imperial Airways, a long-range airline operating since 1924, and British Airways, the corporation that had acquired a number of short-haul airlines competing with Straight Corporation, like Jersey and Hillman's. All these companies had been private enterprises, but BOAC was government-owned and, with a war on, was instructed to prioritise the transport requirements of the RAF. In North Africa, this led to an uneasy relationship with 216 – little wonder that the company acquired a new acronym: 'Better on a Camel'.

216's cargoes took on a festive nature as 1942 drew to a close. Montgomery required 10½ tons of rum for the 8th Army, while eleven of 216's Hudsons

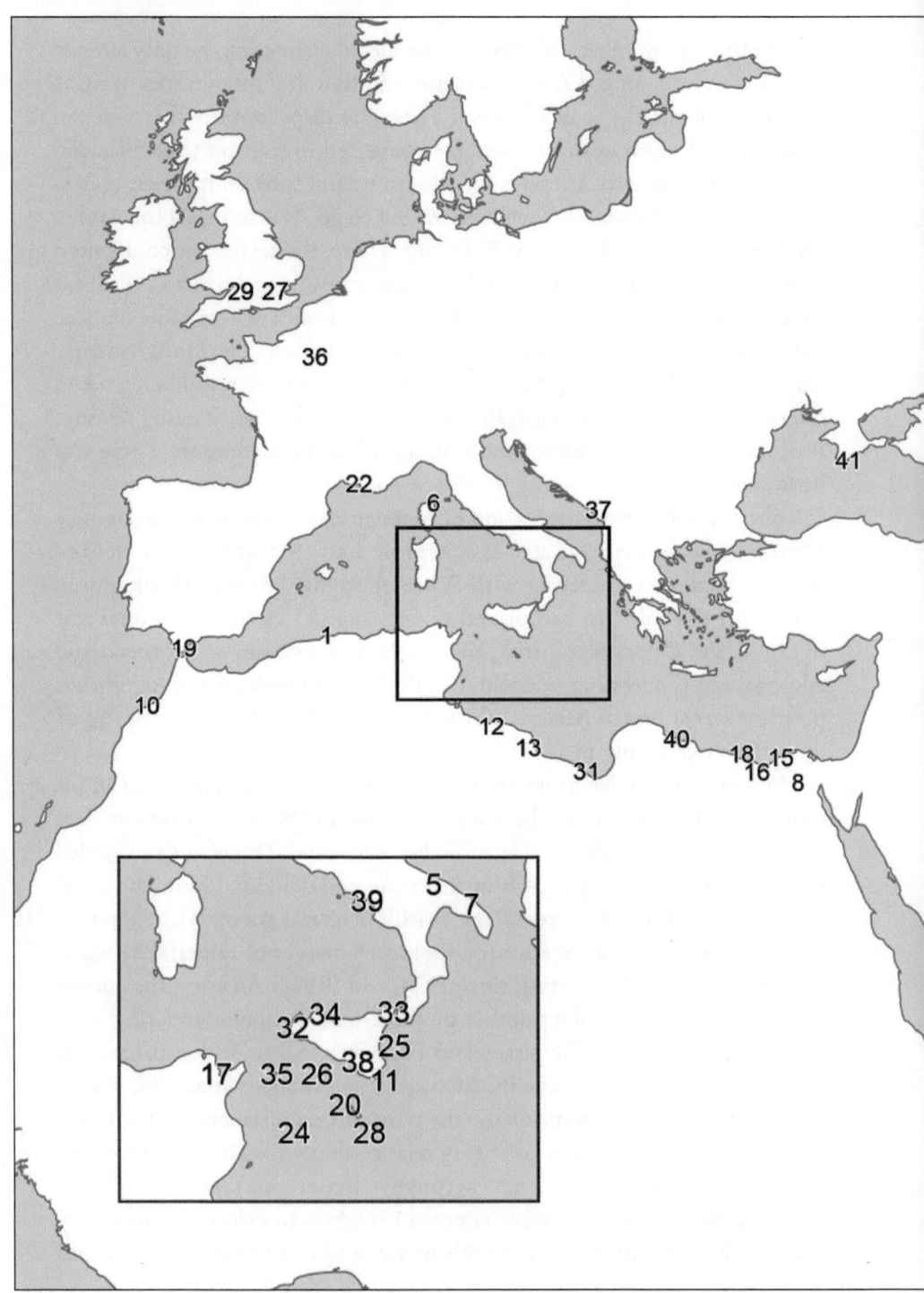

Fig. 7: The locations visited by Whitney during his time in charge of 216 (Air Transport and Ferry) Group.

1	Algiers	22	Istres
2	Assam	23	Kohima
3	Baghdad	24	Lampedusa
4	Bahrain	25	Lentini
5	Bari	26	Licata
6	Bevinco	27	London
7	Brindisi	28	Luga
8	Cairo	29	Lyneham
9	Calcutta	30	Manipar
10	Casablanca	31	Marble Arch
11	Cassibile	32	Marsala
12	Castel Benito	33	Messina
13	Darragh	34	Palermo
14	Delhi	35	Pantelleria
15	El Alamein	36	Paris
16	El Amiriya	37	Petrovac
17	El Aouina	38	Ponte Olivio
18	El Dabaa	39	Salerno
19	Gibraltar	40	Tobruk
20	Gozo	41	Yalta
21	Imphal		

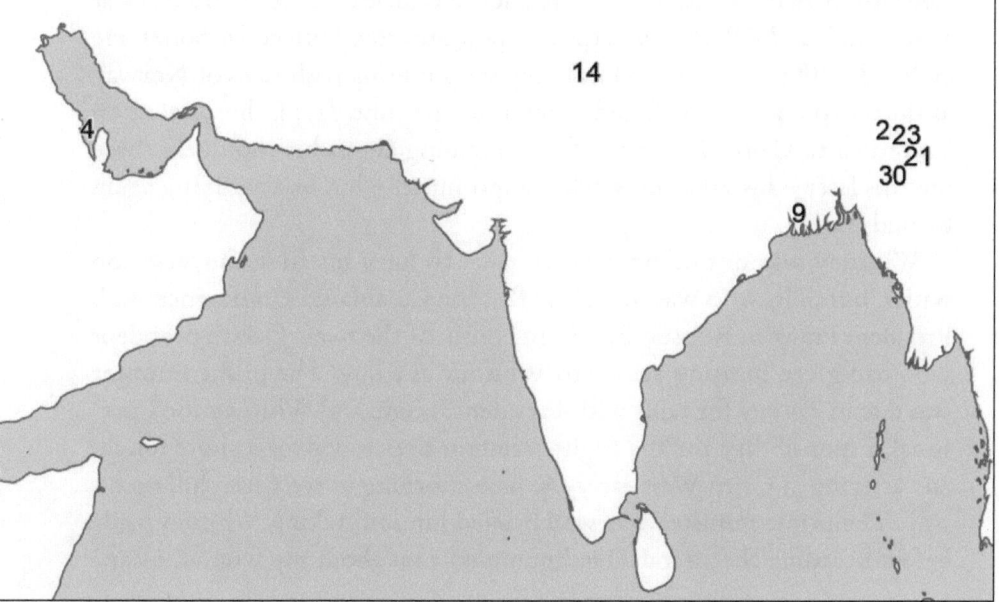

spent Christmas Eve delivering turkeys. On New Year's Eve, Whitney himself ferried 1,000 eggs and four cases of whiskey to the local staging post at Cairo West. He chose not to celebrate the new year, preferring to take to his camp bed and reflect on how much his fortunes had changed since seeing in 1942 in Saint-Hippolyte.

Developments came thick and fast in the new year. A new staging post was to be built in Tripoli at what the Allies called Marble Arch, the ceremonial structure built in 1937 by the Italians as the Arco dei Fileni. The new station would house eight permanent officers and provide transit accommodation for 100 more, with 1,000 ferry aircraft passing through each month. Revised documentation was implemented, with loading diagrams for each type of transport aircraft, so that freight and fuel loads could be optimised. Procedures were laid down for the reporting and investigation of accidents and forced landings. This may have been in reaction to the accident on 4 January that befell a Lodestar on approach to Heliopolis. It burst into flames, killing all eleven passengers and crew on board.

Whitney was involved in an accident himself shortly afterwards, but this was on the ground. Over the course of four days, he had flown a Hurricane in a series of short hops west, taking in the construction work at Marble Arch. His final stop on the afternoon of 20 January was at the USAAF airbase at Darragh, some 120 miles west of Tripoli. He hitched a ride into town on the back of a jeep, but the vehicle collided with a truck at a crossroads and Whitney was thrown out, breaking both collar bones. He endured a difficult night in a local hospital, suffering flashbacks of Norway as the morphine wore off, and spent a further nine days in hospital upon his return to Cairo. He was still complaining about his shoulders three months later – his swimming felt compromised – but he was flying again by mid-March.

Whitney was out of hospital in time to have his first conversation with Churchill, who was in Cairo after the Casablanca Conference with President Franklin Roosevelt, distant cousin of the twenty-sixth president who had given hunting knives to Whitney as a boy. The prime minister was due in Turkey for talks with President İnönü, and Whitney took personal responsibility for the flight, briefing the crew over a short lunch, and arriving at Cairo West early the next morning to see Churchill on his way. The prime minister was well briefed himself, taking Whitney aside before boarding the aircraft. He 'mumbled a lot about my wound, escape and Anglo-American relatives – a brilliant, flowing brain. All aboard and to my relief away.'⁸ It was a significant moment. Whitney had taken on a role he would perform for many years to come – seeing dignitaries off from airports – while Churchill had joined in Anthony Eden's attempts to charm Whitney into politics.

Ironically, at the end of March, Whitney learned that he was wanted back in London for talks about a different role altogether: Director-General of BOAC. When the airline's directors learned that the formation of RAF Transport Command still left it without a clearly defined role, all but one of them resigned, and Harold Balfour, the Under Secretary of State for Air who had once been Thanet Aero Club's president, thought Whitney could re-establish some order. Marcelle wept bitterly when she heard the news, but his new boss, Sholto Douglas, thought it might be a good career move.

Whitney's shoulders were not up to the task of manhandling a Liberator for 20 hours over two days, so this flight home from Cairo was the only one he made as a passenger. This time, the stopover in Gibraltar gave him the opportunity to reminisce over drinks with Agent Sunday, Donald Darling, about his escape. The next day, after landing at Lyneham and catching the train from Swindon to Paddington, he and Daphne enjoyed an emotional reunion at Claridge's. There followed 2 hours of detailed talks about BOAC with Arthur Street, Permanent Secretary to the Air Ministry, and several more over the next few days.

Whitney came to the conclusion that taking on BOAC was at best premature. 216 Group now comprised four squadrons, three air delivery units and six ferry controls, operating a total of thirty-four staging posts. His leadership of it over the previous seven months had brought him nothing but plaudits. Why suffer frustration and compromise at BOAC? Then there was the longer-term problem, neatly articulated by Daphne in one of her missives to Isaiah Berlin:

> Sir Stafford [Cripps, Minister of Aircraft Production at the time] continues to insist that facilities cannot possibly be detracted from the making of warplanes and put on to civil construction; nor does it seem possible to provide for research workers in this field. We are presumably relying almost entirely on the conversion of bombers or on our American friends for immediate postwar civil planes.⁹

A month after Whitney turned down the role of BOAC's Director-General, Air Commodore Arthur Critchley, then in charge of RAF Training Command, accepted the position, while Lord Knollys, Governor of Bermuda, became chairman. Soon, Whitney was so focused on a significant new operation that all thought of BOAC went from his head – it was time to prepare for Operation Husky, the Allied invasion of Sicily.

This, the largest amphibious invasion of the war, would involve two large land forces, under Montgomery and Lieutenant General George Patton, supported by naval barrage and by the type of aerial support that Whitney had cogently argued for after Norway. 216 would play a far greater role than it had at El Alamein. It would have primary responsibility for the provision of personnel and supplies to the invading forces on the island, and in the evacuation of casualties from it. In principle, the unit would be operating under Air HQ, Desert Air Force, based on Malta, but Whitney was 'vested with overriding priority to be exercised if necessary'.[10] To ensure the relationship worked smoothly under what would be exceedingly trying conditions, he sent a liaison officer to Malta.

On 28 June, Whitney made an advanced HQ on the airfield at El Aouina in Tunis, just 140 miles south-west of Marsala, on the western tip of Sicily. He based ten Dakotas there, and a further ten Dakotas and twenty Hudsons at Castel Benito in Tripoli. Concerns over the likely congestion of the airfields on Malta led to six Sunderland flying boats being stationed on the coast, while a similar number of air ambulance aircraft of the Royal Australian Air Force were also made available. A far greater expansion of Whitney's resources came some days into the invasion. As soon as US Troop Carrier Command (USTCC) had completed its primary task of conveying troops to Sicily, its aircraft were handed to 216.

The invasion was launched on the night of 9–10 July. In the weeks leading up to it, 216 dealt with a plethora of requests to move essential army personnel, USAAF ground staff, pilots, jeeps, trailers and equipment to forward positions in Tunisia, Malta and the tiny island of Pantelleria, situated some 40 miles east of Tunis. One man impressed with Whitney's planning was his step-uncle – two years younger than Jerry, Air Vice Marshal Tommy Elmhirst was at the time in overall charge of administration for the Desert Air Force. Decades later, when Dartington held a memorial service for Whitney, he sent a handsome tribute: 'Twice in the war, just prior to El Alamein and just prior to the invasion of Sicily, he visited me

Expanding Horizons

in my caravan and within an hour we had "tied in" the staff arrangements for the air support he could give. So easy with someone of his ability and cheerfulness. I always admired him.'[11]

During that first night of operations, a 216 Dakota was lost, running out of fuel on the return trip over the Strait of Sicily. The pilot was picked up after 11 hours in the water, but his fellow crew members went down with the plane. By contrast, the nightly courier service between El Aouina and the Maltese airfield at Luqa worked well from the outset. The modifications carried out in May and June to the stretcher racks on the group's entire fleet of Dakotas, so that they could accommodate both British and American stretchers, helped with the rapid loading of casualties and the short turnarounds at Luqa. The group's only other fatalities of the campaign came on 11 July, and incensed Whitney. 216 was asked to provide four Dakotas to drop incendiary flares and dummy parachutes over Marsala, in a bid to distract German forces from moving south to counter the actual invasion. The mission succeeded in its aim, but one of the planes burst into flames shortly after take-off and crashed, killing everyone on board. Examination of the wreckage revealed that a flare had ignited in flight, setting off the other incendiary devices on board. Whitney attended the burial of six colleagues the next day and was deeply troubled by the unnecessary loss of life.

On 13 July, he entered the campaign himself, leading eight Dakotas on a two-legged mission to move the ground echelon of a squadron attached to the American 31st Fighter Group to Sicily. A second group of 216 Dakotas, loaded with seventy-five USAAF personnel and 1,700lb of baggage and equipment, carried the servicing echelon for the entire group. The first leg entailed a 45-minute flight to the Maltese island of Gozo, where a precarious airstrip had been laid out for Whitney's planes among vineyards. The next morning, all fifteen aircraft set off again, scurrying low across the water, watched from above by a pair of escort Spitfires. They landed on another brand-new airstrip at Licata, on the central southern coast of Sicily. There followed a 25-mile hop east to Ponte Olivio, to pick up more casualties. Whitney's aircraft were the first transport planes of the campaign to land on Sicily, and the first aircraft of any type to fly out from the island. On the final leg of the mission, from Gozo to Tunis, he carried a unique payload: sixteen wounded Americans, Germans and Italians, and a USAAF crew who had survived the loss of their bomber.

Within days, 216 was operating a direct, daily service between El Aouina and Ponte Olivio, which was swiftly extended to Cassibile, on Sicily's east coast. On 20 July, the first of 216's Air Delivery & Reception Units (ADRUs) arrived on the island, a signals and cypher party from 25 ADRU joining the increasingly sophisticated set-up at Cassibile. A day later, three Dakotas flew a party from 26 ADRU into Ponte Olivio, complete with light equipment, tents and jeeps, to provide support to Patton's 7th Army as it advanced on Palermo. Finally, at month end, six 216 Dakotas brought an advance party from 24 ADRU into Lentini, some 35 miles north of Cassibile, and just 8 miles from the front line. They carried forty-eight personnel and 30,000lb of freight, including more jeeps and trailers. These interventions helped with the shortage of military transport on the island, caused by the loss of naval vessels in the early days of the invasion. Whitney had hand-picked the three ADRUs as the best-equipped to switch from static, routine situations to the more mobile work required on Sicily. 'They are working under difficult conditions,' wrote Whitney's colleague, Squadron Leader A.R.H. Downing, 'required to improvise continually, use unceasing tact, particularly in dealing with VIPs and self-considered VIPs, and, of course, are on duty round the clock always.'[12]

On 25 July, the day Benito Mussolini was ousted from power and large-scale defections from the Italian military began, Whitney handed back to USTCC the aircraft it had entrusted to him, to focus solely on the remaining requirements of the 8th Army and Desert Air Force, along with the regular courier flights to and from Sicily and Malta. The potential for Anglo-US friction over the arrangement had, according to Downing, been eliminated by Whitney's 'efficient, natural, friendly and open method of working'.[13] For example, Whitney invited USAAF officers to eat at 216 Advanced HQ whenever they wished. In return, they gave Whitney a key to the Sicilian villa they had procured, so that he and his colleagues could enjoy a shower.

Sicily finally fell on 17 August, when first Patton and then Montgomery entered Messina, too late to prevent the evacuation to the Italian mainland of 60,000 Germans. Over the course of the five-week operation, aircraft under Whitney's command had clocked up 1,400 flying hours, carried over 2,300 passengers and more than 760,000lb of freight, and evacuated 2,500 casualties. The Allied invasion of Italy began less well. The Italian state may have surrendered, Whitney may have been due to add almost fifty of its aircraft to his group's ever-expanding fleet, but three German divisions had the US 5th Army bogged down at Salerno, and 216 had to land vital supplies on makeshift airstrips laid out on the beaches. Whitney was concerned: 'There is a great lack of control. No one knows who is running the battle. There is duplication and chances are being lost. The air support on which all our past victories were based is being brought up too slowly.'[14] A few days' leave, spent with Marcelle high up in the Cypriot hills, restored his humour. They had grown very close, and he could also reflect with pride on his first year in charge of 216: 'A phase forward in my life. Another battle won. I feel strong and ready for whatever may come – it may be disappointment and reverse – but my will to fight has been reborn.'[15]

That renewed will was put to the test during a largely frustrating visit home in November. In meetings with his friend and mentor Frederick Handley Page and with Joseph 'Mutt' Summers of Vickers, Whitney was disappointed at the lack of progress being made on new civil airliner designs. He harangued Lord Beaverbrook, Stafford Cripps' predecessor as Minister of Aircraft Production, over plans to convert the Avro York, the transport aircraft based on the Lancaster bomber, into a passenger plane. A meeting at the Air Ministry to settle his demands for compensation over Straight Corporation's commandeered assets broke up without resolution. On the other hand, Harold Balfour talked about 'huge jobs'[16] for Whitney when peace came, and in spite of his passion for Marcelle, he enjoyed spending time with Daphne: 'She has been sweet and tolerant and I do feel deeply fond of her.'[17]

As 1944 unfolded, so 216's war broadened even further. The group's Advanced HQ was relocated to Bari, on Italy's Adriatic coast, from where it could better serve the Partisan army in Yugoslavia. Whitney made one of 216's earliest Balkan sorties himself, on 19 March. He made the short hop south from Bari to Brindisi in his Dakota to collect a jeep, then flew out north-east across the Adriatic for Petrovac. After 2 hours and 40 minutes, right on schedule, Whitney and his crew gave a cheer of relief as the airfield loomed up out of the dark, and he landed well in the snow. He shook hands with Marshal Josip Tito, leader of the Partisans and the man destined to become Yugoslavia's first president, gave him the jeep, picked up eleven passengers and set off straight back to Bari. By the summer, droppings and landings in Yugoslavia and the evacuation of casualties had become a regular feature of 216's work. But as the fighting in the Balkans intensified, so it became impossible for aircrews who had bailed out or force-landed to be rescued by air. They faced a march of several weeks under Partisan escort to the Adriatic coast for evacuation by sea. An instruction to 216 crews was issued, to 'take sturdy footwear with them on all sorties to Yugoslavia ... such footwear [to be] readily available in the event of bailing out'.[18] The memo was written by Squadron Leader W. Townson, 216's Senior Air Staff Officer, but the input of Whitney, and his memories of hobbling towards the Spanish border in his flying boots, is clear.

Just as 216's provision of supplies to the Partisans in Yugoslavia began, so the unit was abruptly called upon to support the fight against the Japanese 15th Army in the north-east of India. The British bases at Imphal and Kohima, near the border with Burma, were surrounded and in urgent need of airborne provisions. The signal for 216 to send fifteen Dakotas to Manipur was received on the night of 29 March. Preparations began the next morning, and by 2 April the first flight of five aircraft had arrived, to be joined the next day by the remaining ten. The crews had to supply isolated pockets of Allied troops, making daylight drops from low altitude in the face of enemy aircraft and anti-aircraft fire. Nine weeks later, only thirteen Dakotas returned to Cairo, and Whitney gave their crews a week's leave. They had carried over 7,000 personnel, 200 mules and 4.8 million pounds of freight, and rescued 500 evacuees. Together with several other RAF units, they enabled the British garrisons to hold out until reinforcements arrived, and the Relief of Imphal became the catalyst to drive the Japanese not only out of India, but Burma too. When Lord Louis Mountbatten, Commander-in-Chief of South East Asia Command (SEAC), came to Cairo later in the year, he made a point of visiting 216, and left a message in the visitors' book: 'I am glad to have this opportunity of saying thank you to 216 Squadron for saving the day at Imphal.'[19]

On 12 April, within two weeks of his aircraft leaving for Imphal, Whitney himself flew out of Cairo, bound for the sub-continent. The development of the war effort against Japan, and the far greater volume of aircraft being sent to India, called for the air trunk route there from Britain to be strengthened, and Whitney needed to see for himself what was required. He inspected 216 Group staging posts in Baghdad and Bahrain on his way out, then, once in India, established the requirements for the new trunk route in a series of high-level meetings – in Delhi with Air Chief

Marshal Sir Richard Peirse, Commander-in-Chief of Air Command, South East Asia; in Calcutta with Major General Thomas Hardin, the former executive of American Airlines and TWA, who was now head of the US Army Transportation Corps in Indo-China; and in Assam with General William Old, commanding officer of the region's US Air Carrier Command, who held responsibility for both USAAF and RAF troop carrier units. By the time he touched back down in Cairo, twelve days after setting off, Whitney had racked up another 47 flying hours.

Further Allied progress over the course of the year would in due course mean that the new trunk route could be diverted to run across France, far shorter that the initial path along the North African coast. Whitney celebrated D-Day, 6 June, with Marcelle and a bottle of champagne, listening to the King on the radio: 'This time, the challenge is not to fight to survive but to fight to win the final victory for the good cause.'[20] 216's preparations for Operation Dragoon, the invasion of southern France, began a month later, when a detachment of Dakotas was despatched to Bevinco, on the north-east coast of Corsica. They were used on the first day of the landings, 15 August, to carry out a decoy attack, using radar-jamming devices. Thereafter, they performed their usual transport and carrier roles, moving the ground echelons of RAF fighter wings, USAAF fighter groups and French squadrons up to liberated airfields. By the end of their involvement in the operation, 216 had carried more than 1,700 passengers and almost 2 million pounds of freight into France.

Whitney's preparations for Operation Dragoon were dogged by disappointment and ill health. He learned on 8 June that he had been awarded a CBE (Commander of the British Empire) in the King's Birthday Honours list, when he had been hoping for a CB (Companion of the Order of the Bath) – one rung higher, and second only to a knighthood. In fact, he had been nominated for the higher award in the most glowing of terms, as 'a commander of outstanding ability, organisation, power and determination',[21] and his name had only been included on the list of CBE nominees in case he was not selected for the CB. As it was, he considered his award a 'horrid little pink gong which is given to stooge group captains'.[22] He looked more favourably upon another honour bestowed a few months later, when he was appointed Air ADC to the King, but it took Marcelle to remind him that he was young, he had a great future ahead of him, and he should not be too impatient.

On 3 July, Whitney was taken into hospital with abdominal pains and rectal bleeding. This seems to have had no link to the similar maladies he had suffered as a baby – an enema and internal examination suggested he had amoebic dysentery – but four days into his stay, he was struck down with malaria and became gravely ill. His temperature soared, his head hurt to the touch and he could only speak in monosyllables. He was put on a course of quinine, and then a second. His symptoms began to fade after a week, but even then he was not well enough to be discharged until 23 July.

The liberation of Paris a month later landed Whitney with another special assignment. Charles de Gaulle wanted the members of the Algiers Consultative Assembly – effectively his Free France cabinet in exile – flown home, and Whitney was instructed to lead a fleet of Dakotas from Cairo to Algiers to collect a group of 100 generals, deputies, ministers, officials and staff. Early on the morning of Sunday, 3 September, the planes departed in rough, wet conditions, but entered clear skies over the Mediterranean, so that their passengers broke into cheers when Marseille came into view. Whitney himself became emotional as he led the party over Chenonceau and recalled swimming from occupied France into Vichy France. After almost 8 hours in the air, Paris' devastated marshalling yards hove into view, and Whitney and his colleagues deposited their special cargo at Le Bourget, which seemed much smaller to his eyes than when he had visited it before the war. He flew on to Northolt for an evening at Claridge's with Daphne, and by lunchtime the next day he was back in the air, en route for Casablanca.

Whitney was back in London a little over a week later, but the trip weakened his resolve to serve in Britain's post-war civil aviation industry. Meetings with Air Chief Marshal Sir Frederick Bowhill at Transport Command, dinner with Frederick Handley Page and lunch with Harold Balfour all proved inconclusive. He was left with the impression that no decisions would be made until BOAC's future as 'a socialist set up or private enterprise'[23] was determined. Perhaps it was because this decision could only be taken by the political party that formed the first post-war British government that Whitney began to think more seriously about entering Parliament. At least Churchill and Eden were clear in wanting him. Back in Cairo, he wrote to Eden declaring that he wanted to be a candidate for the Conservatives at the next election. When Daphne learned of this development, and in particular the constituency which Whitney wanted to represent, she was stunned:

Whitney has suddenly and out of the blue decided to run for a Conservative seat, but in deciding that his home-town Totnes is the place, has omitted consideration of the fact that this seat is already firmly held by a Conservative who is well dug-in, is quite well-thought of by the Party, and who has no intention of moving ... I think he [Whitney] would be very ill-advised to establish himself in such close proximity to his family, who can always be counted on to support the Labour point of view however crassly stupid or inept, who already speak of the Totnes member as 'that dreadful man' although he is quite harmless and fairly competent, and with whom Whitney would be bound to find himself in very awkward disagreement.[24]

In November, at the conclusion of a series of 216 meetings in Italy, Whitney was able to make an entirely personal flight, from Rome to the airfield at Istres, north-west of Marseille, which had been liberated by the Americans in late August. He borrowed a jeep and set off east for the Château de l'Horizon, where he and Daphne had honeymooned nine years earlier. It had been occupied by the Germans but Whitney was pleased to find that it had escaped damage, and that Fanny, the old maid, was still there. He drove on up the coast to visit the US Consulate in Nice. There, he was addressed as 'Captain Whitney' for the first time in almost two-and-a-half years, and reunited with the diary he had kept in Saint-Hippolyte and Fort de la Revère, and had deposited with the Consulate as he planned his escape. His final destination lay just a few miles further up into the hills. The Fort de la Revère was now occupied by US troops and, for the first time, Whitney was able to walk in and out of the place freely, and to fully appreciate the extraordinary view it afforded of the Mediterranean.

At the end of the month, he was back in hospital. With the malaria behind him, it was time to establish the reason for his abdominal pains and rectal bleeding. He was kept in for two weeks and subjected to numerous tests, including a barium scan, yet nothing definitive emerged. Nor, when he was discharged, had anything definitive been decided about his future. There was now the possibility of remaining in Cairo, with promotion to Air Vice Marshal, though Marcelle still feared losing Whitney at war's end. 'She accused me of avoiding the issue by going home,' wrote Whitney. 'This is so wrong because I would love to stay here. The brave thing is to leave.'[25] Even in his diary, he could separate the convenient from the truth when it came to women. Of course he would return to London when peace came: the only question was, would it be for politics or civil aviation?

Whitney was able, at least for a time, to bury his personal deliberations beneath preparations to fly the senior Allied delegates to Yalta, on the Crimean coast, for the final major conference of the war. He was even more fastidious about this than usual after news came through of the loss of an Avro York aircraft carrying Foreign Office delegates from Britain to Malta, on their way out to the conference. The aircraft had circled the Sicilian island of Lampedusa in the dark for an hour before running out of fuel and crashing with the loss of all fifteen people on board. It seems possible that the crew had thought they were over Malta, and had simply been unable to locate the airfield at Luqa.

A fleet of sixteen C-54 Douglas Skymasters had been assembled at Luqa to take Churchill, Roosevelt and a host of politicians, senior officers and diplomats to Yalta in the early hours of Saturday, 3 February. Leaving nothing to chance, Whitney had two aircraft – one for Churchill, Eden and their senior advisors, the other for Roosevelt and his – taxied to a corner of the airfield the morning before departure, 'aloof and exclusive'.[26] Then he met with senior US Air Transport Command officers and the pilots of the two planes, going over the route and weather reports. Night fell and instructions issued to take a few hours' sleep – even Whitney lay down but continued to receive updates on the weather. Then the airfield became a flurry of activity, and he performed his usual duty of escorting his VIPs aboard their plane. After watching the ailing Roosevelt, who had just two months to live, being lifted into his aircraft, Churchill and Whitney shared a brief word: 'The Old Man said I must go into the House and that he wanted me. His words were all beautifully put and phrased.'[27]

It was much the same when Whitney planned the prime minister's flight home after the conference. He had frequent conversations with the Met Office about the fog in England, which eventually led to Churchill's aircraft being diverted from Northolt to Lyneham, but late on Sunday, 18 February, it was agreed that the direct flight from Cairo could proceed the next day. Shortly before departure, Whitney enjoyed a whisky and soda with Churchill and Eden. 'The PM made me sit down and we talked about Parliament. Anthony came up and put his arm round me – said loyalty was already fixed.'[28]

The prime minister and his foreign secretary clearly thought they had their man, but Whitney cannot have been open with them. He was due back in London at the end of the month, and the only meetings he was scheduling were focused either on BOAC or on compensation for Straight Corporation. The one person he was frank with was Marcelle. At war's end, he would return to London, and the relationship must end. 'I'm afraid she will be unhappy. Looking back, I have loved her a great deal – more than anyone else. There has been great physical closeness.'[29] But it would end, there was no doubt of that.

Whitney landed at Lyneham at lunchtime on Wednesday, 28 February and was driven straight to Transport Command to meet its new commanding officer, Air Marshal Sir Ralph Cochrane. He advised Whitney that his service days were numbered, and that Lord Swinton, Minister of Civil Aviation, was keen to meet him. Whitney moved on to Claridge's to see Daphne, then spent much of the next day being updated on Straight Corporation by Stanley Cox. On Friday, Whitney visited Ariel House on the Strand, home of the Ministry of Civil Aviation, where Lord Swinton told him he had two directorships in mind for Whitney, at BOAC and a new company focused on shorter-haul routes around Britain and Europe. Swinton was less positive about compensation for Straight Corporation, but agreed to further discussions on the matter over dinner. After a conversation with his mother and with Fred Gwatkin, both of whom recommended BOAC over politics, Whitney rejoined Swinton for dinner at the Dorchester, and learned that he had little or no hope of compensation.

The meetings continued through the weekend. On Saturday, he met with Lord Knollys, BOAC's chairman, but was perturbed to learn that Knollys expected to be both chairman and managing director of the post-war company. 'These are two separate jobs,' reflected Whitney, 'and I should be managing director. There is no doubt in my mind this is right and in the best interests of the show.'[30] Today, it is generally considered best practice for the roles of chair and chief executive to be separate, and institutional investors will rail against any executive holding both positions, but it was a more common practice in the early post-war period, and would come to haunt Whitney during his time with the company.

Cochrane had much better news for him on the Sunday. He proposed giving Whitney command of 46 Group. This was effectively the northwest Europe equivalent of 216, and had been formed during preparations for D-Day to provide freight in support of Allied troops fighting in France and to evacuate casualties. Just as 216 had played an important role in the invasions of Sicily, Italy and southern France, so 46 had been heavily involved in D-Day and at Arnhem. Whitney was delighted. Here was a clear route back to London, where further negotiations about his precise role at BOAC could take place without undue pressure.

That evening, Whitney and Daphne dined quietly, and agreed upon his next steps. Early the next morning, he wrote to Churchill:

> Lord Swinton has asked me to join the board of BOAC and one of the new corporations which he is proposing should be formed. Unfortunately for statutory reasons it would be impossible to do this and at the same time occupy a seat in the House of Commons. I want to make the greatest contribution I can, both now and in the post-war period, and after careful and searching consideration, I feel I should be best employed in British aviation. This note is to thank you for your kind personal interest and to assure you of my deepest loyalty and devotion.[31]

There was still time for one more meeting. If the Air Ministry could not or would not pay damages to Straight Corporation for its requisitioned aircraft, then he would appeal to the company that had used many of them during the conflict. Railway Air Services had spent the war flying government ministers and mail between Liverpool, Belfast and Glasgow. The company was still run by Sir Harold Hartley, the man who, nine years earlier, had asked for discreet enquiries to be made about Whitney, and had been advised 'to watch his progress'.[32] Whitney met with Hartley and a colleague of his to argue his case for compensation, but made little progress: 'They admitted I was owed some money but said they didn't see how they could find an accountable means of paying.'[33]

Whitney was back in Cairo when Churchill's terse response reached him: 'I am disappointed that you will not stand for Parliament. I think you are making a mistake, but of course the matter is for you to settle.'[34] For the next two months, Whitney did his best to stay focused on 216's operations spreading ever northward through Italy. Finally, on Sunday, 6 May, he took the bumpy road out to Cairo West in advance of making his last wartime flight back to Lyneham. He was astonished to find that one of his passengers was Brigadier H.E.F. Smyth, who had suffered severe shrapnel wounds in

Norway and had come to know Whitney on their journey back to Scapa Flow aboard their hospital ship. On the first leg of the flight, to Malta, Whitney encountered heavy rain and violent winds, but the weather the next day across France was much better. He made good time, and Daphne was waiting for him at Woods Mews.

He woke the next morning, Tuesday 8 May, VE Day, thinking he would meet with Cochrane at Transport Command and Knollys at BOAC, but he found that 'the holiday atmosphere had confused all'[35] and concluded that it was time for him and Daphne to join the celebrations. They lunched with Dorothy, dined at the Dorchester and then headed into the East End, where 'people crowded us with beer and were incredibly friendly. I was very moved. Then there was a bonfire outside. Later we walked the streets. Piccadilly Circus was incredible, a sight I shall never forget ... a thrilling and memorable day.'[36]

Thus ended Whitney's war. It had on balance been a good one. He had begun it as a carefree buccaneer, so bored with the Phoney War that he deliberately sought danger elsewhere. Even his time in Norway, enduring day after day of low-level bombing and then serious injury, did nothing to curtail his exuberance, for fifteen months later he was shot down risking not only his own life but those of ten colleagues, attempting to sink a destroyer armed only with the cannon on their Hurricanes. It was the year he spent as Senior British Officer at Saint-Hippolyte and Fort de la Revère that changed him. Louis Strange was not there to guide him, and he alone found a way of dealing with the constant tension of seeking escape for the airmen under his charge while instructing soldiers to accept captivity. At 216 Group, he built on this new-found maturity and sense of responsibility. By the end of his period in command, and still aged only 32, he was in charge of almost 11,500 personnel and more than 200 aircraft. As he himself reflected when he chose civil aviation over politics, 'I have owned a situation which made BOAC possible.'[37]

15

To BOAC, Via BEA

Ironically, within weeks of VE Day, Whitney walked away from a future with BOAC. Upon learning that Alfred Critchley planned to remain as Director-General, thereby denying him the job he wanted, Whitney rang Lord Swinton, Minister of Civil Aviation, to advise him that he no longer wished to join the company. Swinton was shocked and asked for a meeting that same day, but failed to change Whitney's mind: 'I felt sure I had done the right thing,' he recalled, 'although now I am left with no post-war job.'[1]

His final months with the RAF were marked by ceremony. On a trip to Cairo to finalise arrangements for his departure from 216, he was instructed to meet General John Cannon, the new commanding general of US Air Forces in Europe. Cannon had worked with Whitney on the air operations supporting the Allied invasion of southern France, and was pleased to present him with the American Legion of Merit. This completed Whitney's unique collection of medals: the Military Cross, Distinguished Flying Cross, Norwegian War Cross, Commander of the British Empire and US Legion of Merit.

In early July, in his capacity as Air ADC to the King, he was in the guard of honour receiving the King and Queen on visits to the Isle of Man and Jersey. By then, Whitney had taken over 46 Group, and the next parades he participated in were in Berlin, in the run-up to the Potsdam Conference, where Britain, the US and the USSR attempted to reach agreement on Europe's post-war political landscape. Whitney was on the tarmac at Tempelhof when Churchill and Eden flew in for the conference on 15 July, and again on 28 July when, after Labour's landslide victory in the general election, their successors as prime minister and foreign secretary arrived. Whitney thought Clement Attlee looked 'like a frightened rabbit'[2] and considered Ernest Bevan 'a good sergeant who will make a bad officer'.[3]

He was no happier at home. He and Daphne had resumed married life together at Woods Mews, while The Aviary was being renovated. There was still a mutual fondness and respect between them, but the years apart and the affairs had taken their toll. Even the return of 8-year-old Camilla, 'a vigorous little bundle of sunshine'[4] with an American accent, could not bridge the gulf that had developed between them, and they began to talk, quite amicably, of divorce. Their bewildered daughter was packed off to Dartington, Whitney moved into The Aviary and Daphne bought her own house, overlooking Battersea Park.

In August, Whitney relieved Frederick Handley Page of his power of attorney responsibilities, thanking him profusely for the service provided while he was in Cairo: 'It has been a great source of comfort to me to know that someone of your outstanding ability was taking a fatherly interest in my affairs.'[5] Handley Page and Cox had ensured that Straight Corporation was clearly focused on the fresh challenges ahead. In the autumn of 1944, a confidential plan submitted by Britain's railway companies to the government for a reconstituted Railway Air Services to operate UK and European routes had become common knowledge. Cox felt this put a different complexion on an article in the *Weston-Super-Mare Gazette*, praising the railway companies' plans to acquire airline routes in the region once civil air traffic resumed. Handley Page agreed: 'There would appear to be a campaign by the railway companies to oust Air Commodore Straight from the Western services.'[6] He arranged for a contact at the Society of British Aircraft Manufacturers to support Cox in generating publicity for Western Airways' own plans for the routes. Out in Cairo, Whitney found the clippings Cox sent him 'most excellent'.[7]

Handley Page represented Whitney at a meeting of independent airline owners at the Ministry of Civil Aviation, where government proposals for the post-war structure of British airline operations were shared. BOAC would fly the north Atlantic and 'Empire routes' and another airline, shortly to be rebranded British South American Airlines (BSAA), would operate across central and south America and the Caribbean. Short-haul UK and European routes would be run by a new company, in which the independents could invest stakes of up to £250,000. Other shareholders would include Railway Air Services and the 'short sea' shipping lines. None could keep its current identity, no account had been taken of the independents' employees, and there was no guarantee of board representation.

Thus, when Whitney left 46 Group for Civvy Street and collected his free cigarettes and demob suit – 'a nice grey pin stripe flannel'[8] – he knew that Straight Corporation would have little or no scope to operate an independent airline. This also meant that the company's leases on its requisitioned aerodromes had little residual value. There was no choice but to focus the business on the repair, maintenance and conversion work it was continuing to generate at Weston Airport. Whitney could leave Straight Corporation in the capable hands of Stanley Cox, and seek a bigger role elsewhere. In the new year, when Sir Harold Hartley, his former rival at Railway Air Services, was made a director of BOAC, Whitney tried again to present his case for an executive position with the airline. Hartley rejected his approach, telling him he would find life in a nationalised industry too frustrating, and would be happier in private enterprise.

To a large degree, events would prove Hartley right. At 216 Group, Whitney had been part of a clearly defined command structure, leading a huge organisation in pursuit of a single objective – to support winning the war. Overwhelmingly, he had achieved that aim with American aircraft. Conversely, BOAC's managing director might report to the Minister of Civil Aviation, but any order for new aircraft had to be placed by the Ministry of Supply, while the Chancellor of the Exchequer was insistent that, with Britain's post-war balance of payments in such dire straits, the purchase of American aircraft with US dollars was out of the question. BOAC was expected to buy British, even when this meant, as Daphne had feared more than two years before, flying converted bombers that were smaller, noisier and less economic than the latest US airliners. BOAC had a fleet of more than 200 aircraft, comprising seventeen separate models, powered by sixteen different engines, operating from a plethora of bases that required an inflated workforce. Whoever was appointed its next MD would have the most frustrating job imaginable.

Whitney decided to overcome his own frustrations by training for his commercial pilot's licence, known at the time as the 'B' licence, and to share his tutor with a woman named Diana Barnato. She was the daughter of a British motor racing hero well known to Whitney, Woolf Barnato, the man who had won Le Mans on all three occasions he had entered, and who had kept Bentley afloat for several years before it was finally acquired by Rolls-Royce. Diana had flown valiantly through much of the war as a member of the Air Transport Auxiliary, delivering more than eighty different types of aircraft between factories, ferry terminals and operational airfields. She had her own reason for training for her 'B' licence. In November, her husband of eighteen months, Wing Commander Derek Walker, had been killed when his aircraft came down in severe weather, and she felt that study might numb the grief. For months, she and Whitney focused solely on mastering a slide rule and navigational instruments, and on reading meteorological charts. Only when they had secured their 'B' licences did they embark on what would be the longest affair of Whitney's life.

His search for a worthwhile role in the private sector led him back to Frederick Handley Page. Whitney was no supporter of converting bombers into airliners, but he saw merit and commercial gain in making freighter aircraft out of them. Handley Page Ltd had redundant bombers on its hands, Whitney was one of the foremost experts on air transport, and the offer of a directorship with the company seemed only logical. In search of legal advice on the details of the offer, for the first time he turned not to Dorothy's solicitor, Fred Gwatkin, but to Thomas Overy, founding partner of the leading London law firm, Allen & Overy. Here was another sign that the post-war Whitney was making his own way in the world, without the influence or financial backing of his mother and stepfather. His uncle, Almeric Paget, the first Baron Queensborough, spotted this growing maturity and financial acumen in him, and made him a trustee of over £1 million in equities. The development left Whitney wondering why his mother did not involve him in their own family's finances.

In late March, he flew out to Switzerland for his first skiing holiday in seven years, in the company of Diana Barnato and young Camilla. Upon his return, a letter from the new Civil Aviation Minister, Baron Winster, ended Whitney's interest in the Handley Page freighter. The new government had adopted a more straightforward approach to a short-haul British airline than its predecessor, and Winster wanted Whitney to take an executive position in what he called 'BOAC Europe'. Handley Page proceeded without Whitney on freighter and passenger conversions of the Halifax, but the Halton, as it was known, could carry only ten passengers; in a taste of what was to come, BOAC found it unprofitable. Whitney still rated Handley Page Ltd sufficiently that he recommended its shares at his first Paget Trust board meeting: they offered a 7.5 per cent dividend yield and were trading at 26 shillings, when he thought they were worth 40.

Britain's third state airline, British European Airways (BEA), came into being on 1 August 1946. The railway companies' machinations had been in vain, and BEA inherited Railway Air Services' disparate fleet of aircraft. Harold Hartley moved across from BOAC to become the new airline's chairman, and Gerard 'Pop' D'Erlanger, the man who had founded and commanded the Air Transport Auxiliary during the war, moved with him and took the role of managing director. Whitney was given a fascinating task as deputy chairman. Little more than a year after the war in Europe had ended, many governments were attempting to re-establish state airlines, and some turned to Britain for advice. Whitney, with his wealth of experience across Mediterranean Europe, was made the facilitator for this, in return for BEA taking minority stakes in the companies. Foremost among them was Alitalia. Discussions ahead of the formal creation of BEA had already established that Italy's new airline would have a board of ten directors, six of whom were to be nominated by the Italian government and four by BEA, reflecting the 60/40 split in equity stakes to be taken by the parties. Whitney became not only BEA's first deputy chairman, but Alitalia's too.

He hit the ground running, missing BEA's inaugural board meeting so that he could attend meetings in Rome with the British ambassador, Sir Noel Charles, and Vittorio Valletta, president of Fiat. Discussions with Italian officials and industrialists continued throughout the summer, and on 16 September, Whitney was one of the signatories to the Deed of Constitution marking the creation of Italy's new state airline. He hosted a cocktail party that evening for almost sixty people, but the hard work was just beginning. A head office was acquired, applications submitted for Alitalia's first air routes and a request made to the Italian government to lease ten Fiat G.12 aircraft. Whitney facilitated discussions between Alitalia and Bristol, the British aircraft and aero-engine manufacturer, about fitting a forthcoming Italian passenger plane, the Breda 308, with Bristol's Centaurus engines.

A target date of April 1947 for Alitalia's first scheduled operations was only just missed – its maiden flights were made on 5 May, when a pair of Fiat G.12s flew from Rome to Turin and Catania. By then, the airline had purchased no fewer than forty engines from Bristol, and five Lancastrian airliners from another British aircraft manufacturer, Avro. Alitalia aircrews spent several months in Britain, undertaking instruction on the aircraft, and made their first Lancastrian training flights to and from Rome in early May.

By then, Lord Nathan, the latest incumbent at the Ministry of Civil Aviation, had announced that Hartley would be joining BOAC on 1 July, to be succeeded as BEA chairman by Pop D'Erlanger. Whitney would be moving with him, and at his final BEA board meeting on 27 June, he was able to record significant progress at Alitalia. The Rome/Turin and Rome/Catania services had proved a great success, carrying eighty-three passengers during their first week and more than 260 in their fourth. A daily Milan/Genoa/Rome/Naples service had been introduced. Negotiations between BEA, the Treasury and the Ministry of Civil Aviation, and between Alitalia and the Italian government, on the next round of funding were at an advanced stage. 'Generally speaking,' Whitney wrote, 'progress remains satisfactory. The company is functioning on a very economic basis and the results are encouraging.'[9]

He made less rapid progress on the formation of a new Cypriot airline, simply because of the number of parties involved. By October 1946, he was pursuing the idea of a new corporation, 40 per cent owned by BEA, which would operate not only the airline but also the airfield at Tymbou (now called Ercan International). He fostered close ties with Major Ronald McCrindle, deputy director-general of BOAC, which, like BEA, used Cyprus on some of its trunk routes, and by February 1947 he had obtained agreement in principle from both the Treasury and Ministry of Civil Aviation. The Colonies Office was so focused on rising tensions in Palestine that it proved more difficult to engage with, and it was not until April that Whitney was able to instruct BEA's solicitor to draft Memoranda and Articles of Association for the new company and send them to Cyprus to take account of local company law. In another of his concluding reports to BEA's June board meeting, he was able to advise that the new company was just weeks from incorporation, and that the Cypriot government was keen to take a 20 per cent stake.

The simplest assignment on Whitney's list of European airlines was Gibraltar Airways. This had been formed in 1931 by a local shipping group, Blands, but Whitney saw the potential offered by the facilities that the RAF had developed on the rock during the war, and which he had often used. He negotiated with Blands' boss, Sir George Caggeo, over the formation of a new company, a joint venture between BEA and Blands that Caggeo would be chairman of. In an echo of Western Airways' shuttle between Weston and Cardiff, the airline would run a regular service between Gibraltar and Tangier, using a pair of de Havilland Rapides leased from BEA. When Whitney signed off in June, he was able to report that the new company had been established and a board meeting held, and that the Rapides were about to go into service.

By contrast, setting up a new Greek airline proved beyond even Whitney. TAE (Technical and Aeronautical Holdings) had flown domestic routes in Greece since 1935, but the German invasion had put it out of business. At the end of hostilities, its founder, Stephanos Zotos, sought support from the US airline, TWA, acquired three Dakotas and went back into business. Despite being late on the scene, Whitney was able to galvanise support for a joint Anglo-American-Greek company, with a complex network of shareholders. The National Bank of Greece would hold the largest stake, at 25 per cent, while BEA and TWA would have 22 per cent each, a group of influential Greek investors known to TWA 16 per cent, the Aviation Officers' Pension Fund 10 per cent and Zotos 5 per cent.

Within a month, Whitney had won support in principle from the Foreign Office, the Treasury and the Ministry of Civil Aviation, and a draft agreement had been signed between BEA, TWA and Zotos. But then Zotos refused to implement it. TWA sacked him as managing director of the existing TAE and invited BEA to acquire half its capital, so that they could jointly take control of it, liquidate it and form a new company in its place. Chaos ensued when Zotos won a claim against TWA and police ejected BEA employees from TAE's offices, but the decision was reversed on appeal and a retrial scheduled. On Whitney's final visit to Athens, he met with TWA's new chairman, Warren Lee Pierson, and was reassured to find him committed to the plan for a new company. Both men signed a Heads of Agreement in support of it, together with the Greek Ministers for Air and National Economy and the governor of the National Bank of Greece. Whitney could do no more, and was obliged to tell BEA's board, 'we may have to face further delay and litigation'.[10]

The devastation of war had left many regions in need of adequate air traffic control and navigation aids, and airlines obviously required systems of a reliable and consistent nature along their routes. International Aeradio Limited (IAL) was set up to satisfy these demands, and BEA and BOAC each took 30 per cent stakes in the company. Whitney was appointed its first chairman, and identified Air Commodore Colin Cadell, the RAF's

Director of Signals, as the man he wanted to run it. He had been impressed with Cadell when he had been Command Signals Officer, HQ Middle East, during Whitney's time with 216 Group. The RAF was reluctant to part with Cadell, so Whitney asked Lord Nathan, the Civil Aviation Minister, to intervene, and Cadell came on board in April 1947. The first IAL installation in Europe, a joint venture with Whitney's contacts at TWA and the Greek government, was signed off on 1 June, a month ahead of schedule. He stood down as IAL chairman the same day. The company went on to provide communication and navigation services along civil air routes across Europe, Africa, the Middle East and Far East, and was perhaps the greatest legacy left to civil aviation by Whitney's hectic eleven months at BEA.

Almost two years had passed since he had withdrawn from discussions to join BOAC, but now the environment there had swung much more to his liking. Critchley had retired as director-general in January 1946, and though Lord Knollys had seized the moment to become joint chairman and managing director, now he in turn was stepping down, and the roles were being split again. Hartley would become chairman, and Whitney take the newly defined position of managing director (chief executive). At their final BEA board meeting on 27 June their fellow directors placed on record their appreciation of their work, and thanked Whitney for his development of so many associated companies across the Mediterranean.

Despite his extraordinarily busy time at BEA, Whitney had not only maintained his relationship with Diana Barnato, but had become reconciled with Daphne. They had dined together often, and concluded they simply could not divorce. They even spent Christmas together at Dartington – by no means Daphne's idea of an ideal location for the festivities. It was hardly the only compromise she faced in returning to Whitney. His affair with Marcelle had been confined to Cairo, and Daphne had been in New York during his earlier extra-marital relationships. Now, though she would resume living at The Aviary, she would often see little of him during the week. Yet somehow, she and Whitney became bound together once more.

On Thursday, 3 July 1947, the 200th BOAC board meeting took place, marking the beginning of Whitney's eight-year tenure with the airline. He was given two immediate actions. First, he was to report on 'the various types of aircraft which the board have under consideration and the corporation's commitments and requirements'.[11] Second, in the light of the company's poor financial performance – it had just announced a deficit of £8 million for 1946–47, and was forecasting further losses of £7.1 million in 1947–48 – he was asked to plan a reorganisation.

The two objectives went hand in hand. Clearly, the company had too many maintenance bases and employed too many people, but the primary reason for BOAC's deficits was the severely compromised nature of its fleet, which prevented it from competing on equal terms against other international carriers. No fewer than three bomber conversions were being employed – the Halton, Liberator and Lancastrian – and a fourth aircraft, the York, used the wings and tail of the Lancaster. Each of them was uneconomic to run, noisy and uncomfortable, and BOAC was keen to withdraw all four of them as soon as practicable. Much of the rest of the fleet was made up of converted military flying boats. While these were more popular with passengers, more than thirty marine bases were needed along BOAC's trunk routes to operate them. These cost the company an additional £1.9 million each year, which rendered the flying boats hopelessly uneconomic. The only bright star among the airline's current aircraft was the US-built Lockheed Constellation, the first mass-produced civil airliner to have a pressurised cabin. Six of them flew the critical north Atlantic route in BOAC colours.

Disconcertingly, Whitney found that many of the aircraft ordered for BOAC but not yet delivered were already considered to be inferior to the competition. Avro had developed the Tudor from the Lincoln bomber, itself yet another derivative of the Lancaster. The plane had effectively been foisted on the airline by the Ministry of Supply. It still used a tailwheel, so that passengers had to negotiate a slope when embarking or disembarking, when purpose-built airliners had a 'tricycle' undercarriage and, therefore, a horizontal passenger compartment when at rest. The transatlantic version of the Tudor I could carry only twelve passengers, compared with the Constellation's forty-four. At least the Tudor II was designed to carry sixty, but its take-off characteristics made it unsuitable for some of BOAC's eastern routes, on which runways were often relatively short. The Handley Page Hermes was considered more up to date and economic to operate than either of the Tudors, but was not expected to be in service before 1951.

Two other aircraft on BOAC's order book were considered so problematic that Hartley won agreement from the Civil Aviation Ministry to have them considered 'national experiments'[12] and the costs associated with them itemised separately in the company's financial statements. Saunders-Roe had a new flying boat, the Princess, in development that Whitney considered 'primitive as a flying machine',[13] while Bristol's Brabazon was based on the outdated idea that, in order for a transatlantic airliner to compete with passenger ships offering first-class accommodation, it required a similar level of luxury. Far too large to carry only 100 passengers, Whitney thought it 'clearly not a money maker'.[14]

It seems all the more remarkable, therefore, that, between them, the Ministries of Supply and Civil Aviation had, together with two British manufacturers, come up with a pair of passenger aircraft offering BOAC a genuinely competitive future. The de Havilland company was hard at work on the Comet, which was destined to be the world's first jet-powered civil airliner, and was far ahead of anything that Boeing, Douglas or Lockheed had in the pipeline. Within six months of joining BOAC, Whitney had won board approval to increase the company's Comet order from eight aircraft to twenty-five. There were also high hopes for the Britannia, a mid-range passenger plane being developed by Bristol. Regrettably, the initial order of eight Comets was not scheduled to be satisfied for almost five years, while the Britannia would be plagued by engine design issues.

In August 1947, a month after joining the company, Whitney and Hartley visited Avro. They flew in a Tudor I and were given a guided tour of a Tudor II. They were sufficiently unimpressed that they advised Nathan that BOAC would review its requirements. Avro's chairman, Sir Roy Dobson, retaliated with a press release laying the blame for the Tudor's problems firmly at BOAC's door. Livid though BOAC's directors were – Whitney thought Dobson 'unbalanced and of that ghastly stupid vintage which plague our recovery'[15] – they refused to enter into a public spat, and instead demanded a government enquiry. Privately, Hartley warned Sir Christopher Courtney, the man put in charge of the enquiry, that Dobson's charges against BOAC's directors were so serious that civil action against him remained an option.

Late one evening in January 1948, a sombre Harold Hartley turned up at The Aviary, carrying an advance copy of the Courtney Report. Its conclusions made unhappy reading for BOAC: provided that the Tudor met its specified performance and was granted a Certificate of Airworthiness, the airline should use it on its London/Montreal service as soon as practicable. Whitney could not believe it: 'such unbelievable madness'.[16]

The next day's board meeting was a busy one. In addition to planning a response to Courtney, and reviewing lengthy correspondence between Hartley and Nathan over the Brabazon and Princess 'national experiments', there was an announcement that Sir Miles Thomas would be joining in April as deputy chairman. Born near Wrexham in north Wales, Thomas had served with the Royal Flying Corps during the First World War, winning the DFC. He had moved into automotive journalism after the war, and impressed Viscount Nuffield, founder of Morris Motors, sufficiently that he was invited to join the company. He rose steadily through the ranks until, in 1940, as he oversaw the conversion of Morris' factories to the production of munitions, tanks and gliders, he was made vice-chairman. Knighted in 1943 for his support of the war effort, he took over the group in 1946 when Nuffield stepped back.

Lord Nathan was seeking a businessman from outside aviation who could reorganise BOAC. He had a high regard for the way Thomas had led Morris first into the manufacture of military equipment and then back into the mass production of cars and trucks. There was little to tempt Thomas into taking the deputy chairmanship of a nationalised airline on lower pay, but Nathan's promise of the chairmanship fifteen months later, upon the retirement of Hartley, was much more enticing. Neither Hartley nor Whitney knew anything about this. Indeed, as requested, Whitney was already reorganising BOAC, and his initial impression of Thomas, after briefing him on the Courtney Report, was far from positive: 'there is no doubt he is an opportunist.'[17] Sixteen years later, when Thomas' autobiography was published, his recollections of first meeting Whitney damned him with faint praise: 'a dynamic, well-nourished enthusiast with whom I felt sure it would be a pleasure to work'.[18]

Whitney gained no pleasure at all from a meeting he had with Nathan on 13 January. The minister told him he expected BOAC to use the Tudor I on the north Atlantic routes, carrying just twelve passengers on each trip; according to Whitney 'spend a million of taxpayers' money, all to no purpose'.[19] Two weeks later, a meeting he was chairing was interrupted with news that a BSAA-operated Tudor en route for Bermuda from the Azores was missing over the Atlantic. No trace of the aircraft, or its twenty-five passengers and six crew, was found, nor a definite cause for their loss established. The incident marked the beginning of the Bermuda Triangle myth, but for Whitney there was a positive aspect to the tragedy – perhaps BOAC could avoid the Tudor after all.

On the eve of a major Commons debate on civil aviation, he went to Westminster and spoke to a group of MPs about BOAC and its challenges. He was disappointed in his performance, but perhaps it was this that spurred him to speak more fluently for 40 minutes to BOAC's unions the next morning. In the afternoon, he sat in the public gallery of the House of Commons to listen to the debate. It was opened by Alan Lennox-Boyd, who gave Whitney a clear indication of what a formidable Civil Aviation Minister he might make should the Conservatives return to power: 'If everybody who travelled last year by BOAC had been paid £50 not to travel, financially the country would be far better off.'[20] Whitney found himself being urged to move faster with his reorganisation. Sir Arthur Vere Harvey, the Conservative member for Macclesfield, called him 'a man with experience and a go-getter, and I believe there is a great future for him, but he must be more drastic in dealing with matters such as pruning the corporation'.[21]

Whitney's reorganisation work took him to New York in March, where he scrutinised BOAC's set-up in the US and Canada. The trip also enabled him to catch up with Biddy and Michael, whom he had seen little of since the outbreak of war. After Dartington, Biddy had returned to the US to pursue a career in acting. She was a member of the recently formed Actors' Studio in New York, and was about to star on Broadway in *The Heiress*. She and Louis Dolivet had a 3-year-old son named Willard, but Whitney could see strains in their marriage. He had his concerns about Dolivet, and he was disturbed that his brother did not share them. Michael had moved to the US after graduating from Cambridge. For a time he had worked without a salary in the European division of the US State Department, but now he was in charge of the magazine Dorothy and Willard had founded, *The New Republic*.

Over the Easter weekend, Whitney's intestinal pains and rectal bleeding became so troublesome that he sought out the advice of Dr Dana Atchley, Professor of Clinical Medicine at Columbia University's College of Physicians and Surgeons. Atchley enjoyed an enviable reputation across medical practice, research and teaching, and recommended after two days of tests that Whitney undergo an abdominal procedure. Wary of the first major operation of his life, he was grateful that he would not face the ordeal alone – Daphne flew out to be with him – but the operation, on 10 April, left him in great pain and recuperation appeared slow. A week later, his sutures burst, he lost a lot of blood, and a further operation was required. Nearly two weeks passed before he was well enough to continue his recovery back at Applegreen, the old family home, and he only returned to London at the beginning of June.

It was a critical time for BOAC, and Whitney threw himself back into work. He met with the new Civil Aviation Minister, Frank Pakenham, primarily remembered today as the prison reformer Lord Longford. Whitney had known him for years and was confident that they would enjoy a productive working relationship. He met with the US Air Attaché to discuss the implications of a novel way BOAC had found of procuring five more Constellations – not from Lockheed in US dollars, but from the Irish government in Sterling. The new *Taoiseach*, John Costello, had concluded that Ireland would take no part in transatlantic air travel, and was happy to offload the aircraft. They would go into service on the Australian route, so Whitney also met with representatives from the Australian airline, Qantas, to agree changes to its partnership agreement with BOAC.

On 18 June, a special board meeting was convened, and Whitney spent 3½ hours taking his fellow directors through his reorganisation plans in great detail. He explained that his primary objective was to create greater local autonomy, and that this would be achieved through the adoption of a regional rather than functional structure. The African and Middle East divisions would be merged into an enlarged Eastern division, and operate alongside the Western division. Whitney won unanimous board approval, and in July came two key days, when he presented his scheme to union managers, head office staff, 150 representatives of the airline's employee panels and, finally, seventy members of the press. 'I was much congratulated on all sides for my achievement, and I felt a brief glow of satisfaction. The press was very good, and I felt we had done a good deal to get over past prejudices against the corporation, and had given the impression that we were putting our house in order.'[22]

By then, Whitney had also succeeded in his other objective. He had pushed back on the Tudor – a resignation matter, had he failed – and won government approval for an alternative BOAC airliner for the period until the Comet could enter service. Pakenham had accepted Whitney's proposal that the latest version of the Tudor – the IV – be used solely as a freighter aircraft, but Whitney had endured a tougher fight with the minister, the parliamentary select committee and the press when he lobbied for the purchase of a north American passenger aircraft. This was the DC-4M North Star, based on a shortened Douglas DC-6 fuselage, and was built in Montreal by the Canadair company. Crucially, it was powered by four Rolls-Royce Merlin engines, enabling Whitney to argue that he was advocating the adoption of a Commonwealth aircraft with British engines. Even then, the *Daily Express* sneered at his American upbringing and claimed that he was anti-British. This upset him deeply: 'I, who have fought for the country and for civil aviation.'[23]

Named the Argonaut by BOAC, Miles Thomas looked upon it as the plane 'that really enabled BOAC to get out of the red and into the black'.[24] He and Whitney travelled to one key meeting at the Ministry, seeking a commitment to nineteen aircraft. They were conscious that they would be beaten down to a lower figure, but that seeking a round number might lack credibility. In the back of the car, they agreed upon twenty-three – 'a silly, odd sort of number ... [implying] ... some precise reckoning'.[25] In the end, an order for twenty-two aircraft was approved. All of them were delivered before the first Hermes arrived from Handley Page, and the Argonauts went on to deliver excellent results on BOAC's Far East routes, transforming a regular deficit of £80,000 per quarter into a surplus of £140,000 in the final quarter of 1949–50.

Whitney and Daphne left for a well-deserved holiday in the Sicilian town of Catania, scene of some 601 Group heroics five years earlier, but now the location of a secluded hotel on a terrace 1,000ft above a bay. They had grown much closer since reuniting. Daphne had seen Whitney through the long convalescence after his operation, and had offered counsel through every twist and turn of his efforts for BOAC. Now, she was expecting a baby, content to rest while Whitney enjoyed his passion for deep-sea fishing.

Two versions of the holiday exist. One lies in the letters Barnes Wallis sent home to his wife Molly from Catania. Responsible for the bouncing bomb and the geodetic structure of the Wellington, Wallis was now focused on a revolutionary design of aircraft, devoid of a tail and ailerons, and controlled solely by wing movement. Conscious that there would need to be both civil and military versions to defray the huge cost of bringing such a design to fruition, and frustrated by the negative responses he had received from his own employer, Vickers, and from the Ministry of Supply, Wallis thought Whitney was a man who could help him make a breakthrough.

He told his wife of sitting with Whitney after dinner, 'lecturing hard on future developments of aircraft, taking sips at intervals from a glass of Italian liqueur, and doubling my optimism at every sip!'[26]

When Jack Morpurgo researched his biography of Wallis, published in 1972, and came across this correspondence, he asked Whitney for his recollections of the 'lectures'. Almost a quarter-century on, Whitney had no recall of them whatsoever, and found no mention of them in his 1948 diary. His record of the holiday focused on his wife and his mistress, for on the very day Wallis described his misplaced optimism, Daphne suffered a miscarriage, while back in England Diana was pregnant with Whitney's child. Several months would pass before he could bring himself to tell Daphne; unhappy though she was at the news, still she stayed with him.

Whitney returned to London a troubled man. On top of the turmoil in his private life, his abdominal pains and rectal bleeding had resumed. The operation had given him only six months' respite, which puts a different complexion on the condition he had endured since Cairo. It appears that he was suffering from an inflammatory bowel disease – perhaps Crohn's, or ulcerative colitis – but at the time he could receive no such diagnosis, nor adequate treatment. There were problems, too, at BOAC, with Hartley reluctant to retire the following summer. Whitney: 'I told him exactly what I had told the Minister, without gloss, and I can only hope he will not feel I have betrayed him. But by July he will be nearly seventy-one, which is too old for the chairman of BOAC.'[27]

Matters were settled in a meeting with Pakenham in late September, which confirmed the arrangements Thomas had been offered by the previous minister, Lord Nathan. Hartley would retire as chairman the following summer, to be replaced by Thomas, who would assume responsibility for Whitney's reorganisation with immediate effect. At the time, Whitney felt this lifted a weight from his shoulders, and any concern he may have felt at Thomas' increasing influence were offset by Pakenham's assurance that he could look forward to taking the joint role of deputy chairman and managing director. But the chairman-designate took a tougher line on the reorganisation, removing from BOAC many senior managers, and Whitney found this difficult to implement when it meant making people he admired redundant. For the first time, he became conscious of his drinking. 'One thing I must watch is drinking. I have been doing too much and I can see that it might well become a habit.'[28]

On 17 January 1949, a second BSAA-operated Tudor was lost over the Atlantic in unexplained circumstances. The Tudor IV was grounded as a passenger aircraft with immediate effect. Over and above the tragedy itself, and the loss of seventeen passengers and crew, BSAA now had no aircraft to service its long-haul routes, and could barely function. Whitney was concerned that BOAC might have to hand over some of its hard-won Argonauts to the ailing airline.

A week later, he had a more immediate worry. His first symptom was a temperature, but then he found he could only walk with Daphne's help. By 30 January, he was gravely ill, with what he was told was jaundice or infected hepatitis. A modern interpretation of his symptoms points to ascending cholangitis. A life-threatening condition even today, in the mid-twentieth century it had a mortality rate far higher than 50 per cent, and Whitney never knew how lucky he was to survive. As it was, he felt 'a terrible sense of frustration and incapacity'[29] – unable, as he saw it, to defend BOAC against whatever remedial action Pakenham was planning over BSAA's plight.

He did not leave home for more than a month, but he felt obliged to resume work on 24 February, when Thomas arrived at The Aviary with a sheaf of documents for him to read. Chief among them was a Heads of Agreement, signed by Thomas and John Booth, chairman of BSAA, setting out the terms under which BOAC and BSAA would amalgamate. This was due to be ratified at a special BOAC board meeting the following morning, and take effect from 1 April, just six weeks away. Whitney was horrified. Given the parlous state of BSAA, its acquisition by BOAC – for that is what 'amalgamation' meant – was the logical solution. But how could a matter of such significance be driven through in a matter of days, without careful consideration of the consequences? The document also confirmed Whitney's initial view of Thomas as an opportunist: much of it read like a land grab by the Welshman. He told Thomas to expect a memorandum from him, to be distributed at the board meeting in his absence. When Thomas left, Whitney, still in his pyjamas, sat down with pen and paper, 'and finished at three in the morning, very groggy and making little sense'.[30]

Whitney's secretary rushed out to The Aviary at a more respectable hour, collected the document, typed it up and added six copies of it to the papers presented to the board. The speed with which the meeting had been called meant that, of BOAC's nine directors, only six could attend. One of them was already committed to a lunchtime engagement and would be unable to vote. Given that Hartley was by now something of a lame duck chairman, the group was barely quorate.

Whitney's document raised many questions. What was to become of BSAA's twenty grounded Tudors, and how was the 'abortive expenditure of several million pounds'[31] associated with them to be written off? How, in the absence of these aircraft, were BSAA's routes to be serviced? The deal had been presented with a sweetener, in the form of four Boeing Stratocruisers, to be purchased from a Swedish airline in Sterling, but Whitney reckoned that a further fifteen aircraft would be needed to meet BSAA's commitments. If this requirement were to be satisfied with BOAC Argonauts, it would simply move the problem elsewhere. If additional aircraft were to be purchased, an assurance that they could be bought in US dollars was required. BSAA's commitment to purchase Princess flying boats from Saunders-Roe was a further problem. It would cost in the region of £8 million, and require the continued upkeep of marine bases that would otherwise have been scrapped.

Then there were the references to an immediate move away from Whitney's revised divisional structure and increased local autonomy, and a return to a functional reporting structure. This, it was stated, had 'already been agreed as desirable'[32] by Thomas and Sir George Cribbett, deputy secretary at the Ministry of Civil Aviation. Only months had passed since the board had unanimously agreed to Whitney's proposals, they had not yet been fully implemented, and any further reorganisation would be most unsettling for the staff. 'Whatever the ultimate form may be,' wrote Whitney. 'I must make it quite plain that I am absolutely opposed to a further reorganisation of BOAC on a functional basis at the present time.'[33] And why did the Heads of Agreement raise the acquisition of BEA, and claim that only administrative problems prevented the immediate merger of all three companies? Whitney accepted the logic of the BOAC/BSAA amalgamation, but 'it seems to me that there are serious practical disadvantages in any further merger with BEA'.[34]

He concluded, 'It will be clear from the above comments that I am in disagreement with many of the intentions and views expressed in the Heads of Agreement. I believe them to be contrary to the best interest of BOAC and of British civil aviation.'[35]

Nevertheless, the five BOAC directors present throughout the meeting resolved to approve the amalgamation in principle, and to record their 'general concurrence with the Heads of Agreement as laid before them'.[36] That afternoon, Hartley visited The Aviary and harangued Whitney, in front of Daphne, for what he saw as interference. He was followed by Lord Burghley, the director who had been unable to attend the entire meeting. He gave Whitney his full support and told him he had written to Hartley, expressing his opposition to a further reorganisation and to an acquisition of BEA. Whitney's old Cambridge friend, Peter Masefield, now managing director of BEA, came by to offer support. Whitney's new lawyer, Thomas Overy, arrived to discuss not only the implications of an immediate resignation, in protest at the speed with which the acquisition was being driven through, but also the changes to his will necessitated by the impending birth of Diana's baby.

Pakenham waited until 4 March before visiting The Aviary, by which time Whitney was finally able to dress himself and walk about. They enjoyed an entirely constructive meeting. Whitney urged him to slow the process down, emphasising there was no evidence that a functional organisation would be better for the enlarged group. They agreed to remain open-minded and do whatever was best for the two companies and the industry. Whitney was leaving the next day for Switzerland to continue his convalescence, and Pakenham offered to send someone out to brief him, should a crisis arise.

In Switzerland, Whitney pondered over his next move. 'There are really basic issues involved, of self-preservation or duty to country – but perhaps duty to family should come first.'[37] That particular responsibility was about to grow more complex. A coded telegram from London prompted him to call Diana, who told him he was the father of a boy, to be named Barney. 'God knows what complications it is going to lead to for all of us, and let us pray it will involve unhappiness for no one, especially Daphne and the child.'[38]

Pilot Officer Straight of 601 Squadron with his Hurricane at Exeter, the aerodrome commandeered from Straight Corporation. (Battle of Britain Monument)

Directing local villagers laying out a runway on the frozen Lake Lesjaskog. (RAF Museum)

The consequences of invading enemy territory without at least parity in the air …

Of the eighteen 263 Squadron Gladiators that flew into Whitney's makeshift aerodrome, twelve never left the ground, while the runway was incapacitated by 130 bomb craters. (RAF Museum)

The small port of Åandalsnes, the bridgehead for Project Primrose, was subjected to continual bombing and effectively destroyed. (RAF Museum)

While Whitney recovered from the injuries he sustained in Norway, he served as ADC to the Duke of Kent. (Battle of Britain Monument)

Having taken the flak once too often, Whitney had to force-land in a Normandy field, 31 July 1941. (Laurent Viton)

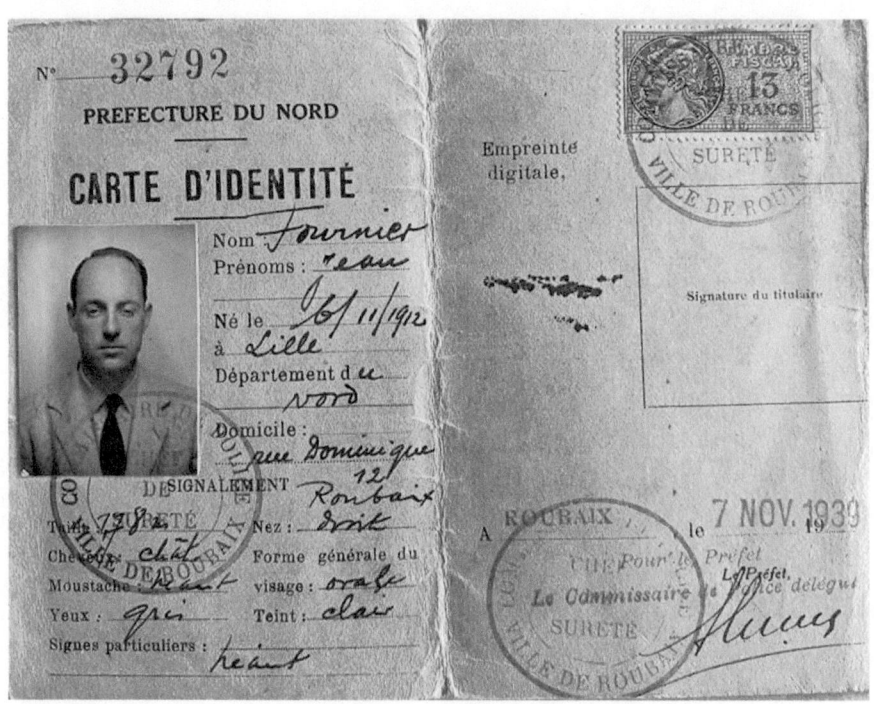

Upon escaping from captivity, Whitney was given a new identity. Jean Fournier shared Whitney's birthday. (Family collection)

On a tour of 216 Group staging posts, with Sheikh Khalifa of Bahrain. (Imperial War Museum, CM 6013)

Receiving his US Legion of Merit from Lt Gen. John Cannon, May 1945. (RAF Museum)

Diana Barnato Walker, with whom Whitney had a decades-long affair, in her days with the Air Transport Auxiliary. (Barney Walker)

The aircraft Whitney wanted BOAC to walk away from …

The Tudor: 'a million of taxpayers' money, all to no purpose'. (AirTeamImages)

The Princess: 'a fundamentally unsound project and a gross waste of public money'. (AirTeamImages)

The Argonaut helped drive BOAC into profit. (AirTeamImages)

Whitney escorting Princess Elizabeth and Prince Philip out to their Argonaut shortly before they left for Nairobi, 4 February 1952. Utilising plans first discussed with Whitney the previous year, they were back at Heathrow only three days later, at the outset of Queen Elizabeth's reign. (British Pathé)

Whitney had high hopes for the Comet, the world's first commercial jet airliner, but felt 'our neck is right out there if anything goes wrong'. (British Airways Heritage Collection)

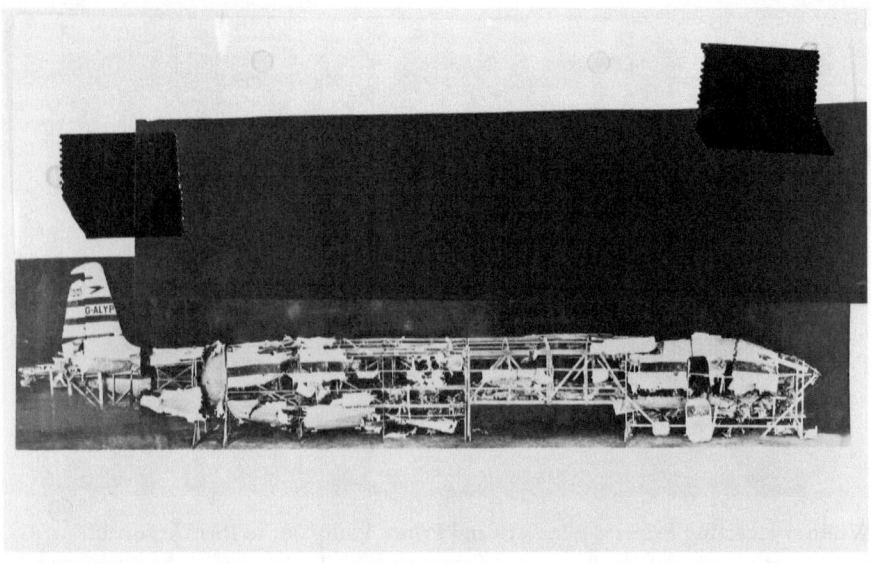

Metal fatigue proved to be the aircraft's undoing, and the Comet 4 only entered service with BOAC three years after Whitney had left the company. (SSPL/Getty Images)

Whitney ordered twenty-five Britannias for BOAC in July 1948. The aircraft finally entered service almost nine years later. (AirTeamImages)

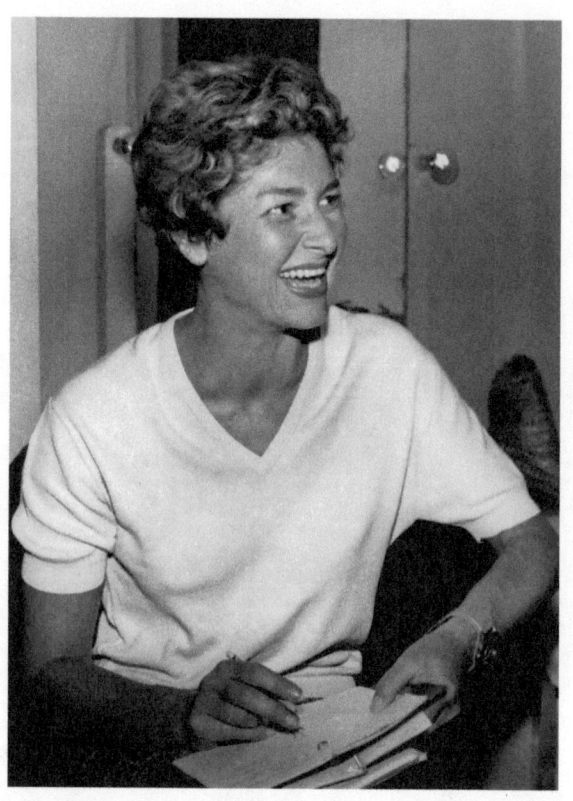

Claudine van der Stratten, about to leave for the ill-fated assault on Cho Oyu. (Keystone Press/Alamy Stock Photo)

Whitney used his Cessna for everything from trans-Saharan adventures to commuting to Airways Union board meetings at Weston-super-Mare airport. (Chris England)

Going through the motions of introducing Prince Philip to his brother-in-law, Anthony Armstrong Jones, at a Council of Industrial Design function. (Bob Hope/Mirrorpix/Getty Images)

At the press conference announcing Post Office Corporation, 22 May 1969. The enterprise's first chairman, Viscount Hall, is speaking, watched by Postmaster General John Stonehouse. (Murphy/Mirrorpix/Getty Images)

To the outside world, all seems well with Rolls-Royce. Whitney is at a reception with (centre) President of the Board of Trade Roy Mason and (right) ICI deputy chairman Peter Menzies, receiving Rolls-Royce's fifth successive Queen's Award for Industry, 23 April 1970. (PA Images/Alamy Stock Photo)

But the company has promised airline manufacturer Lockheed too much thrust from its new RB211 engine for too little revenue, and is running out of time and cash. (Rolls-Royce plc)

Whitney chairs the meeting formally taking the non-aero-engine businesses of Rolls-Royce into liquidation, 3 October 1971: 'from RR's point of view a successful exercise – but death for me, and the end of a constructive life'. (Author's collection)

Happier times, in Formentor ...

Indulging in his passion for deep-sea fishing. (Family collection)

Camanda IV sails by Villa Camanda. (Family collection)

Whitney and Daphne: neither of them could ever imagine being married to anyone else. (Family collection)

16

Breaking Up

Whitney's intervention in the amalgamation of Britain's biggest airlines had immediate effects. Booth acknowledged he could not hope to win his own board's approval for the Heads of Agreement if the clause referring to the acquisition of BEA remained in it, and Thomas agreed to its deletion. On 29 March, as Whitney flew home from Switzerland, Thomas and Booth met at the Ministry of Civil Aviation, and agreed that BSAA's commitment to the purchase of eight Princess flying boats should be reduced to three.

On 14 April, just seven weeks after the BOAC board had approved the Heads of Agreement, another board meeting demonstrated the extent to which Thomas had been reined in. Hartley presented a paper stating, 'It would be quite suicidal to attempt at this date to make a material alteration to the scheme of re-organisation that only became effective from 1 January of this year. That scheme, in its divisional aspects, must crystallise out. Already it is showing useful dividends.'[1] Instead, BSAA would be integrated within BOAC as a third division, alongside the Western and Eastern divisions set up by Whitney.

Pleased though he was that the amalgamation would now proceed in a more orderly fashion, the core element remaining of Thomas' 'land grab' still troubled Whitney: he would no longer be chief executive, but joint deputy chairman, broadly responsible for operations, alongside Booth in charge of commercial matters, while Thomas would become chairman of the enlarged group upon Hartley's forthcoming retirement. Whitney discussed his concerns with Hartley, who agreed to speak with the minister about formally recognising Whitney as Thomas' successor. Pakenham refused, stating he could not commit a future minister on the question of BOAC's next chairman. Whitney accepted his argument gracefully, oblivious to the fact that Pakenham's confirmation of Thomas as BOAC's chairman-designate had honoured his predecessor's commitment.

In May, Whitney set off on a lengthy tour of the Americas, to review the operations of the combined group. A comfortable flight aboard a Pan Am DC-6 from Buenos Aires to Lima made him realise how much BOAC still had to do if it was to compete on equal terms with America's finest airlines. In Jamaica, he found everyone he met 'universally critical of BSAA'.[2] At a meeting in Miami with Wilbur Morrison, vice president of Pan Am, he was pleased to find that the airline also employed a divisional structure.

The length of the trip meant that, for the third time, Whitney missed the wedding of a sibling. Biddy had divorced Louis Dolivet, a development that made Whitney all the more determined to establish the truth about him, and freed her to marry the man who had starred opposite her in *The Heiress*, Peter Cookson. The wedding took place a week before Whitney reached New York, but he made up for his absence by hosting a celebration at the old family home, Applegreen, and welcoming Cookson to the family.

Whitney exploited his extensive network to investigate Dolivet. For some months, he had been using Donald Fish, a senior security officer at BOAC, to look into his former brother-in-law's background, and had satisfied himself beyond doubt that Dolivet was a communist, and might well be abusing his position as editor of *United Nations World*. He shared his misgivings with Bill Stephenson, the man popularly known as Agent Intrepid, who had liaised between Churchill and Roosevelt in the early years of the war. Stephenson assured Whitney that his findings would be passed to the US State Department. Some months later, Whitney contacted the department's Chip Nolan to see what progress had been made. A Soviet expert and fluent Russian speaker, who had translated for Roosevelt at Yalta and Truman at Potsdam, Nolan assured him that he knew about Dolivet. 'This is all I can do,' wrote Whitney, 'and it is now up to them to take whatever action is considered necessary in the nation's interests.'[3]

On 14 July, at the first BOAC board meeting chaired by Miles Thomas, Whitney delivered a thought-provoking paper on the implications of the airline's enforced 'buy British' policy. He acknowledged the benefits to the nation of a successful British aircraft industry, but argued that the cost implications to BOAC were excessive. The airline was invariably the first to receive a new aircraft, burdening it with a level of risk and a share of 'snagging' costs rarely experienced by American competitors. Furthermore, the greater volumes of aircraft being produced by US manufacturers meant that they were relatively cheaper than their British equivalents. Whitney highlighted the latest-generation airliners from Douglas and Bristol: the cost per pound of gross weight of the DC-6 was 46 per cent lower than that of the Britannia. He argued that BOAC was subsidising the British aircraft industry, and he wanted the government to adopt a broader definition of 'fair market value'. His fellow directors agreed, but the government, in attempting to support a profitable national carrier and a flourishing aircraft manufacturing sector, seemed incapable of achieving either.

Two months later, Whitney took a call from an agitated George Cribbett at the Ministry of Civil Aviation, summoning him to an emergency meeting. The chancellor, Sir Stafford Cripps, was in Washington and needed to return to London with all possible haste. Whitney was asked to make the necessary arrangements, and identified American Overseas Airlines as the most expedient option, denying BOAC the opportunity to have one of its planes in the background when the chancellor spoke to the press. The reason for the urgency soon became clear: Cripps had agreed to a swingeing devaluation of Sterling against the US dollar, from $4.03 to $2.80. Whitney was torn on the subject. As the director campaigning hardest for BOAC to fly the best available aircraft, he knew that the case for buying US airliners had become still harder, but, as an individual, he had been handed a windfall. His share of the family trust, and his income from it, were denominated in dollars, and were now worth far more to a man who had made his home in Britain. The timing suited him too, as he had just bought The Aviary outright, but still he wondered why Dorothy did not invite him to participate in the running of the family's finances. Even Diana Barnato's mother used him for financial advice.

In April 1950, John Booth became the first of BOAC's triumvirate of senior executives to step back, resigning as deputy chairman and assuming a non-executive role so that he could devote more time to his family business. Thomas assumed responsibility for Booth's duties and, when BOAC's accounts for the year to 31 March 1950 were published – still showing an accumulated deficit of £4.38 million – Thomas was described as chairman and chief executive, and Whitney as deputy chairman. Thomas' land grab was complete.

Whitney focused on what he could still influence. The board accepted a paper of his, proposing a novel solution to the mounting costs associated with the Princess flying boats on order. New hangars and slipways would be needed at BOAC's base at Hythe, on the Hampshire coast, but he was reluctant to commit £100,000 of BOAC money to the project when so much uncertainty surrounded it. His solution was to request the Ministry to foot the bill, on the basis that BOAC would repay the money if the Princess went into service. An October trip to Cowes, where the first of the planes was under construction, left him dismayed that public money was being spent on it at all: 'a vast bulk being built on ship principles – the dreadful part is that no one knows what to do with it'.[4]

Whitney was much more convinced of the return to be generated from the £260,000 order he placed with Rolls-Royce. BOAC's Argonauts were fitted with Rolls' famous Merlin engine, which had powered the Spitfire, Hurricane and Lancaster to such success in the war, but an aero engine designed for military use was uncomfortably noisy when fitted to a civil airliner. Rolls had devised a 'crossover' arrangement that took the inboard exhaust outlets over the top of each engine to the far side of the cabin. This not only reduced the engine noise experienced by passengers, but also increased the power of the engines, and Whitney argued successfully that quieter, faster Argonauts would be good for business.

The next man Whitney turned to in his desire to expose Louis Dolivet was a Hungarian military historian named Ladislas Faragó. Today, his reputation is somewhat tarnished, but Whitney found what he had to say explosive. 'Louis Dolivet' was one of at least seven aliases used by the Rumanian-born Ludovic Ulianu. He had been the USSR's press representative at the League of Nations in 1923; in the early 1930s he had organised a communist cell in Grenoble and been a member of the communist 'shock troops' in Geneva; he had taken part in 1934's Asturias uprising in Spain, which began as a miners' strike but escalated into the destruction of churches; and he had spent the following winter in Russia and become the paymaster of a Soviet spy named Willi Münzenberg. Whitney gave what he had learned to Donald Fish, who in turn passed it to Guy Poston, his contact at MI5. Poston ran B4E branch, responsible for counter-espionage within Britain's commercial, banking and transport companies, and soon MI6, the British Embassy in Washington and the FBI knew about 'Dolivet' too.

When Whitney shared the news with his family, Dorothy was stunned and Biddy embarrassed, though she could see one benefit. She and her former husband had been locked in a dispute over the custody of their son, Willard, but when 'Dolivet' left New York on a brief trip to France and Switzerland, he found he was unable to return. While he was away, his contract with the UN, the source of his privileged status, expired and was not renewed, and the State Department instructed the US consulates in Paris and Geneva to refuse him a visa. 'Dolivet' had been made *persona non grata*, and was never able to enter the US again.

The family was, therefore, not in the best of spirits when it gathered at Dartington in April 1951. Whitney had finally been granted his wish – there was to be a family council about its finances and how they were managed. Dorothy still looked upon him as the headstrong young man who had frequently called upon her to support his racing and aerodrome ventures, and had needed baling out of severe personal cashflow problems. She seemed oblivious to the mature man of almost 40, entrusted to spend millions of pounds of taxpayers' money in the running of a nationalised industry. His trusteeship of her brother-in-law Almeric Paget's fortune counted for nothing. She had already decided that Whitney's brother Michael and the US family lawyer, Milton Rose, would be her new trustees.

The meeting began well enough from Whitney's perspective. Reasoned, objective discussions about Applegreen led to a unanimous decision to sell it. None of the family lived there, and the annual running costs could not be justified. Whitney was less impressed when he learned the results of Michael's stewardship of *The New Republic*. The magazine had accumulated losses of $150,000, and trust funds were to be used to wipe them out. Far worse, he discovered that the same amount had been invested in *UN World*, the publication 'Dolivet' had edited.

Whitney was appalled: 'I have to pay a fifth of this, and have never been consulted.'[5] He saw no justification for Michael's appointment as a trustee, and felt he had only one course of action. The trust would have to be broken up, and his interests split from those of the rest of the family. He would have to bear the costs of reconstruction, but at least he would then be able to manage his own affairs and take full responsibility for the futures of his wife and children. The process took several years. His relationships with his mother and sister healed well and permanently, but the gulf between himself and Michael, which had first begun to emerge after Whitney's wedding, became unbridgeable.

Whitney set about developing The Aviary. He sought the advice of the famous ornithologist Peter Scott as to how his home might live up to its historic name, and soon the lake was populated with ducks, swans and – his favourites – cranes: 'quite divine – they go in at night like cattle'.[6] Next came the final vestige of any Dartington influence on him. Whitney created a small farm, with a chicken battery generating 120 eggs a day and a piggery with a boar and half a dozen sows. Then Daphne gave him the best news of all: she was pregnant, and the baby was due in the new year.

In late May, Lord Ogmore replaced Lord Pakenham at the Ministry of Civil Aviation, but served only until October, when the Conservatives' narrow election victory presented BOAC with a fresh challenge. The new government wanted greater competition and merged the ministries of Transport and Civil Aviation. The man given this extended portfolio, John Maclay, lasted just seven months and was replaced by Alan Lennox Boyd, who, as an opposition MP, had told the Commons that if everyone flying BOAC had been given £50 not to, then the country would have been better off. Whitney feared a more difficult environment, in which BOAC might be prevented from competing on an even playing field with private airlines, some of whom enjoyed the financial support of the shipping companies.

Still, he had much to be proud of. Months of practice in a Link trainer and late-night revision enabled him to gain his instrument rating, meteorological and flight planning qualifications, granting him the freedom to fly in all kinds of weather, day or night. BOAC's half-year results revealed a profit of almost £1 million and, though he felt a certain frustration that Miles Thomas was taking the credit, 'I sit quietly back, knowing that the real reason was my own work on the overall reorganisation of the aircraft and bases.'[7] And he took personal responsibility for the travel arrangements for the forthcoming royal trip to Canada.

This was to be undertaken by Their Royal Highnesses, Princess Elizabeth and Prince Philip, on account of the poor health of the King. His frailty meant that the couple needed to fly rather than make a lengthy voyage by sea and, since the RAF's King's Flight had no suitable aircraft to cross the Atlantic, BOAC was given the prestigious job of flying the royal couple to Montreal. To represent the airline in the detailed arrangements,

Whitney appointed charter superintendent Graham Bell, while he liaised with Lieutenant Michael Parker, Prince Philip's private secretary, and with Lieutenant General Frederick 'Boy' Browning, Comptroller of the Household at Clarence House, and the man said to have coined the phrase 'a bridge too far' of the disastrous Operation Market Garden. Two subjects dominated the preparations. One was the flight schedule. The only certainty was the requirement to arrive at Dorval airport, now known as Montreal-Trudeau, at noon on Monday, 8 October. Alternative flight paths had to be mapped, via Keflavik in Iceland and Gander on Newfoundland, and Whitney could only advise Parker on the chosen option, and therefore the departure time, on the Sunday morning, once the latest forecasts on prevailing winds were known. The second topic was more sensitive: 'What would be fixed if the King died suddenly?'[8] Whitney was the sole BOAC representative at a discreet meeting at Clarence House to address the question, but the arrangements put in place were not required on this occasion.

Whitney woke to fine weather on the Sunday morning, though fog was expected later. The Atlantic winds seemed set fair, and a departure time of 00.30 on the Monday was agreed. The royal party arrived at midnight, and the BOAC Stratocruiser left precisely 30 minutes later, when the visibility was still good, at 200 yards. A quarter of an hour later, it was down to 15 yards, and Whitney was a relieved man, and happier still when he learned that the plane had touched down in Montreal on schedule. The next day, he received a personal letter of thanks from Boy Browning: 'Before Their Royal Highnesses left for Canada, they desired me to write and thank you most sincerely for all the hard work and excellent organisation you had achieved in planning Their Royal Highnesses' flight.'[9]

Princess Elizabeth was so pleased with the flight that she asked Bell, who had travelled with the party, pilot Captain Jones and his crew to line up outside the aircraft at Dorval, so that she could thank them personally. Whitney was particularly gratified to receive a letter from Lieutenant Parker a week later: 'For everything to go so well on this first flight that Their Royal Highnesses made by an airline speaks exceptionally well for your organisation ... and I hope that circumstances in the future are such that it may be repeated.'[10]

Indeed it would. After Whitney and Daphne – now eight months into a trouble-free pregnancy – had enjoyed a peaceful Christmas at The Aviary, free of the usual tensions at Dartington, Whitney pitched straight back into work on Their Royal Highnesses' next journey. They were due to leave for Kenya at the end of January, on the first leg of a lengthy tour that would take in Australia and New Zealand. Whitney hoped that a Comet could be used to fly them home, but selected a trusty Argonaut for the flight to Nairobi. Since November, he had been in contact with Denning Pearson, head of Rolls-Royce's aero-engine division, to ensure that the plane's engines were fitted with the new 'crossover' exhausts, thus ensuring a swifter, quieter flight. It was agreed that a pair of conversion kits would be fitted to the chosen aircraft on 7 January for testing. The second pair had originally been due for delivery on 30 January, but this was the day before the royal party was due to depart, and the kits were now needed ten days earlier. Pearson thought changing the programme like this would be a difficult task but promised they would do all they could.

This time, the itinerary was set well in advance. The Argonaut would depart from London at noon on Thursday, 31 January, refuel and change crews at El Adem in northern Libya and land at Nairobi at 1015 local time the next day. The more amenable departure time meant that the press and a large crowd of onlookers were present when Miles Thomas walked Their Majesties The King and Queen out to the aircraft, duly fitted with four crossover kits. Princess Elizabeth and Prince Philip followed, accompanied by Whitney. Their Majesties inspected their daughter's accommodation on board the Argonaut, then left to wave her off from the tarmac. 'It was a great relief to see the Argonaut get off on time – actually one minute late,' recorded Whitney, 'and a real thrill to have it arrive dead on time.'[11]

The first intimation that something might be wrong came that same afternoon, when Whitney received a message that Boy Browning was required back in London urgently. The Treasury refused to pay for his flight, as it had already budgeted for him to return by sea, so Whitney offered him a complementary BOAC ticket, and left as scheduled on Saturday, 2 February for a tour of BOAC's operations in the Mediterranean and Middle East. On Monday, in Tripoli, he wondered whether the forthcoming Libyan elections might lead to King Idris stepping down, but in Jerusalem two days later, he learned of a change of monarch elsewhere – King George had died in his sleep during the early hours, and the plans to rush Queen Elizabeth home, first discussed with Whitney the previous October, were already in play. When she walked down the steps from her BOAC Argonaut the next day, to be met by Winston Churchill and a host of other dignitaries, Whitney was in Nicosia with Sir Andrew Wright, governor of what was known at the time as British Cyprus. He was struck by the lengthy queue of people waiting quietly to sign the book of condolence, and by the many flags flying at half-mast across the city.

It was not until 25 February that he flew home, and dashed immediately to The Aviary to be reunited with one of the Queen's youngest subjects. Amanda Betsy Straight had been born on 27 January, and for the next few days the most common word in Whitney's diary was 'divine'. He had become a less frequent visitor to his other family, in hope that Diana might marry, ideally an accommodating man who would not object to Barney, now 3 years old, continuing to see 'Uncle Whitney'. There were candidates, even talk of marriage, but never more than that.

On 18 April, Whitney was among a party of BOAC executives and senior trade unionists who were flown to Edinburgh and back in under 2 hours on board a Comet. Thereafter, Miles Thomas became the public face of the aircraft. He led a Comet flight for the press, he was on its final training flight and first commercial flight, he was aboard an MPs' high-speed tour of Britain and the trip to Switzerland for members of the royal family. Whitney wondered if Thomas had overdone the PR: 'The Comet publicity has been too much – our neck is right out there if anything goes wrong.'[12] His concerns seemed justified when a problem emerged with the early aircraft. They were 'over-rotating' on take-off so that their tails hit the runway, and de Havilland was obliged to design and fit new leading edges to the wings.

Whitney's summer holiday was notable for the pilgrimage with Daphne and Camilla, retracing the path he had taken from Normandy to the Spanish border after being shot down in 1941. Afterwards, they toured along the Mediterranean coast to Portofino, where he enjoyed some deep-sea fishing. While they were away, The Aviary briefly hosted another famous resident: Anthony Eden and Clarissa Churchill celebrated their wedding night there. On Whitney's return to London, the man who had most closely supported him over the BOAC/BSAA Heads of Agreement, David Burghley, did him another service, introducing him to Vane Ivanović, a successful shipping magnate and former Olympic hurdler. More important from Whitney's perspective, he was another passionate deep-sea fisherman, who would write what became regarded as *the* textbook on the subject.

A fresh disagreement between Whitney and Thomas blew up when Alan Lennox Boyd sought Thomas' assurance that BOAC would not bid for freight licences from the Air Transport Advisory Council. This left the council free to discuss a ten-year, all-freight licence for the Atlantic route with Airwork, a company with a broad range of interests in chartered flights, air transport and training. Once more, Whitney confronted Thomas, in writing at a board meeting, arguing that the arrangement was fundamentally at odds with BOAC's statutory rights. He accepted that freight work was not a major revenue generator, but he saw it as an integral part of the airline's structure and he was keen to avoid sharing certain airline routes with Airwork unless BOAC was given its own transatlantic freight licence. Thomas agreed to write to Lennox Boyd, suggesting that BOAC's projected purchase of the Series 200 freighter version of the Britannia might be in jeopardy. In the end, it took an age for a clear ministerial policy to emerge, and it was not until June 1954 that an agreement was reached. Early the following year, Airwork's transatlantic cargo service was launched, then terminated shortly afterwards. The whole argument had been a waste of time, but Whitney had found himself at odds with Thomas and Whitehall once more.

On Saturday, 2 May 1953, a month to the day before Whitney and Daphne watched Queen Elizabeth's coronation celebrations from the Carlton House Terrace home of John Astor, owner of *The Times*, Whitney ran in from the garden to answer the phone. A BOAC Comet en route from Calcutta to Delhi was late. With each phone call through the night, the position became more and more hopeless, and a Sunday morning meeting in the office was interrupted with news that wreckage had been located 20 miles north-west of Calcutta, and all forty-three passengers and crew were dead. When an enquiry established that the Comet had broken up in a thunder squall, shortly after take-off, it was not considered particularly untoward – no passenger airliner of the time could expect to fly through a severe tropical storm and survive.

In August, at the invitation of Vane Ivanović, Whitney and his family holidayed in Formentor, on the northern tip of Mallorca. Whitney was transfixed by the pine trees running to the edge of cliffs plunging into deep, clear water teeming with fish. After a week of fishing trips on Vane's boat and dining on their catches, he had up made his mind: 'I think I shall build a home here. This is by far the most perfect place we have seen, and a good site which will I am sure be a worthwhile investment.'[13] Free to spend his own trust money without reference to his mother, he bought a parcel of land next to Vane's home, facing south-east over the sea, and brought in a Palma-based architect named José Alcover to design a villa that would exploit the summer sun and collect the winter rains. To oversee the work, he also employed Sir Hugh Casson, recently knighted for his work as director of architecture at the Festival of Britain site on London's South Bank. The pair had known each other since Casson was a junior partner in the firm that had designed BEA's ticket offices. Casson's role was to sign off on each phase of the work for Whitney's trustees, but in due course he and his wife Reta simply became regular guests each summer.

A foreman and a team of forty builders set to work, at what Alcover called 'American speed'.[14] The villa and garden were completed on schedule with few problems. An all-weather tennis court incorporated the slightest of falls, imperceptible to players, so that rainwater could run off into one of the many underground storage tanks on the site. In all, the property could store more than 300,000 litres of drinkable water and almost 900,000 litres of garden water.

The most difficult aspect of the project proved to be the dock. Whitney's specification for it was onerous enough, with men's and women's changing rooms to accommodate ten people each; a room for his air bottles, storage cylinder and electric pump; a bathing pool for young children; a separate bathing facility and diving board for adults; a discreet sunbathing platform; and protected waters in which boats of up to 20ft in length could be moored. All this had to be carried out in deep water, susceptible to rapid changes in sea conditions. In due course, the property, named Villa Camanda after Whitney's daughters, became the family's home-from-home for more than twenty years. Each summer, they would host friends and business and political associates of Whitney's. It was where he satiated his love of deep-water fishing, and where a new passion developed. The dock became home to a succession of motor yachts, each named *Camanda*.

The only thing that spoiled that first holiday in Formentor, in the summer of 1953, was a letter that arrived from Miles Thomas advising that he had ordered the Comet IA, in spite of Whitney's advice not to. Again, Whitney considered quitting. On 1 October, he lunched with George Cribbett, deputy secretary at the Ministry of Transport and Civil Aviation, to explain how intolerable life at BOAC had become. The irony of the meeting is that, the day after Thomas' eventual departure, Cribbett would leave Whitehall to become deputy chairman of BOAC. All he could advise Whitney at the time was that Thomas' close relationship with the press made his position impregnable. Whitney met next with Jack Profumo, parliamentary secretary at the Ministry. He explained that he planned to meet the minister, Lennox Boyd, on 8 October to 'tell him the whole story ... Miles was running BOAC as a one-man-band, without regard for the machinery of administration or government policy, or the real interests of the corporation'.[15] In the end, Lennox Boyd talked Whitney out of resignation, and undertook to speak with Thomas and to strengthen BOAC's board.

That process was already under way. With Thomas away on business, Whitney chaired the following day's board meeting, and it fell to him to declare Basil Smallpiece's appointment as a director. Smallpiece had joined BOAC in January 1950 as financial comptroller, implementing new accounting systems and improving the quality of financial and statistical information provided to the board. Today, it seems extraordinary that such a large and complex nationalised company should not have had a financial director, and his appointment should have been welcomed. As it was, the existing directors were concerned that they had not been consulted – another symptom of Thomas' 'one-man-band'.

The same board meeting approved plans for a further streamlining of the airline's future fleet around the Comet and the Britannia. Negotiations for five Comet 3s were proceeding, and an option on five more approved. The Britannia arrangement was revised: the last ten of the relatively short Series 100 passenger aircraft on order would be replaced with ten of the relatively longer Series 300s, and five Series 250 hybrid passenger/freighter and two Series 200 freighter aircraft would be added to the order.

Later in the month, Whitney met the new chairman of London Transport, John Elliot, to discuss ways of getting passengers from the capital to London airport quickly and safely. They dismissed the idea of a monorail as too expensive, and agreed that a tram track, laid from Paddington or Waterloo stations into the airport terminal, might allow the trip to be made in 35 minutes. Neither man lived to see the Heathrow Express taking passengers from Paddington to Terminals 2 and 3 in 15 minutes, and another transport route west out of London would have more effect on Whitney. He had recently attended a consultation meeting at Middlesex County

Council, 'and came up against the horrible situation that a main road is going to go right through my land'.[16] When the first section of the M4 was eventually opened in 1959, it cut The Aviary and the lake in front of it from the woods beyond, though a tunnel under the road offered access. Only one member of the family benefitted from the development – in the weeks between the laying of the road surface and the opening of the motorway, 7-year-old Amanda had a bicycle track all to herself.

BOAC's *annus horribilis*, 1954, started badly and grew worse. On the morning of 10 January, the crew of a fishing boat south of the Mediterranean island of Elba heard several explosions and looked up to see the debris of an aircraft falling towards the sea. A second BOAC Comet had broken up in mid-air, 20 minutes after leaving Rome for London. All thirty-five passengers and crew perished, and this time the weather could not be blamed. Thomas and Lennox Boyd agreed that BOAC should temporarily suspend the use of its seven remaining Comets. More than fifty minor modifications were made to them and in late March they were back in the air.

On 4 February, a prototype Britannia – still only the second to fly – encountered engine problems and force-landed in the mud of the Severn estuary, fortunately without injury to the fourteen people on board. Though the accident had nothing to do with BOAC, the aircraft was clad in the airline's livery, and the sight of its Speedbird logo on the tailplane jutting above the incoming tide hardly helped the airline's public profile. Worse, the incident set back the Britannia's delivery schedule still further. Five weeks later, a BOAC Constellation landing at Singapore hit the sea wall in front of the runway, killing thirty-three of the forty passengers and crew.

Then, on the evening of 8 April, a BOAC Comet leased to South African Airways on its way to Cairo from Rome vanished south-east of Naples. The next day, six bodies were recovered from the sea, along with some light wreckage, but no trace of the aircraft or the other fifteen people on board was found. There was little to go on, but the Elba and Naples aircraft had flown similar numbers of hours and were presumed to have met disaster at similar altitudes. There was no choice but to bring all the remaining Comets back to England – flown by volunteer crews over short legs at low altitude – and withdraw the aircraft's Certificate of Airworthiness.

The Royal Navy did sterling work in recovering some 70 per cent of the Elba Comet from the seabed. The wreckage was brought to the Royal Aircraft Establishment at Farnborough, and reassembled as far as possible for examination. A second Comet was taken to the site and placed in a huge tank. Water was pumped in and out of the cabin to replicate the changes in pressure experienced in taking off, climbing to 40,000ft, descending and landing. The two avenues of investigation pointed to the same conclusion: metal fatigue. The Comet's cabin could not cope with frequent, repeated pressurisation and depressurisation, and would have to be redesigned. Far from gaining a competitive advantage at the outset of the jet age, BOAC now faced a difficult future. It was of little consolation to the airline, to de Havilland or to the families of the ninety-nine passengers and crew who lost their lives in the three Comet accidents that every manufacturer of civil jet airliners would benefit from the accident findings, and that metal fatigue would never cause the mid-air break-up of a passenger aircraft again.

With its Comets grounded, BOAC had lost a fifth of its capacity. It suspended its South American operations. These were generally long, infrequent routes, the Argonauts working them were rarely full, and currency problems made the region even less profitable. Elsewhere, shorter turnaround times and speedier maintenance work delivered an extraordinary 12 per cent improvement in Argonaut utilisation in the first year without Comets. A Constellation was acquired from TWA to replace the one destroyed in Singapore. Australian partner Qantas was upgrading to Super Constellations, and BOAC was able to acquire four of its standard examples. It picked up seven more from Capital Airlines in part-exchange for cash and BOAC's seven older aircraft.

At the June 1954 board meeting, just eight months after he was elected to the board, Basil Smallpiece was made deputy chief executive, further sidelining Whitney, who nonetheless went into battle with both Thomas and Smallpiece at the following month's meeting, this time over the Princess flying boat. Hopelessly out of date though it was, Thomas and his new deputy chief executive wanted to maintain BOAC's order for the three aircraft because the Ministry now had an offer for them from Britavia, an independent airline focused on tour and charter work, and backed by the P&O shipping line. If BOAC finally dropped its order for the Princess, then the Ministry would be obliged to accept the bid from Britavia and grant it a licence for the routes BOAC would otherwise have used. Thomas and Smallpiece preferred to avoid this risk by persevering with the Princess.

The loss of routes to a rival airline was the same argument that Whitney had made about Airwork's north Atlantic freight licence, but he saw freight as an integral part of BOAC's business and the Princess as anything but. He introduced his paper, 'The awkward political situation described by the chairman has arisen because those in authority have either failed to appreciate, or lacked the courage to admit, that the Princess is a fundamentally unsound project and a gross waste of public money.'[17] He concluded, 'I do not agree with the chairman or deputy chief executive. My recommendation is now the same as it was in 1947, namely, that we should tell the Ministry that we do not require this aircraft because it cannot be operated commercially.'[18] The board went ahead and approved Thomas' approach, duly noting Whitney's vote of dissent. Just seven months later, Whitney won his lengthy battle over the Princess when BOAC finally withdrew its support for the aircraft. The three seaplanes were completed, then put into storage, then broken up. None of this brought any consolation to Whitney. He had been the lone voice of reason on the matter for eight years, and wondered what future he had with the company when its chairman and deputy chief executive could willingly do what he saw as the unreasonable bidding of Westminster.

A dreadful year ended in disarray. In the early hours of Christmas Day, a BOAC Stratocruiser making a scheduled stop at Glasgow's Prestwick airport landed short of the runway and burst into flames, killing twenty-eight. BOAC and de Havilland remained locked in an argument over compensation for the airline's remaining Comet I aircraft. The government wanted BOAC to commit to the Comet II, but how could it when the Cohen report into the Elba and Naples accidents would not be published until February, and longer-range versions were already on the drawing board?

In the circumstances, Whitney flew to the US to establish what aircraft BOAC could fly in the 1956–58 period. After visiting Boeing, Douglas and Lockheed, he concluded that the best option was Douglas' DC-7C. It was the only aircraft capable of flying the Atlantic non-stop in either direction, it was 30mph faster than the competition and Pan Am, SAS and Swissair had already placed orders for it. He went so far as to discuss a price for nineteen aircraft, and a delivery schedule stretching from October 1956 to June 1957. Coming from Douglas, this was a timetable that could be depended upon and planned for – unlike Bristol's for the Britannia.

This time, the board backed Whitney, and the request to purchase nineteen airliners from Douglas was duly made to John Boyd Carpenter, the new Minister of Transport and Civil Aviation, and the last of the six ministers whom Whitney worked with during his time at BEA and BOAC. Simultaneously, BOAC issued a press release in response to the usual criticisms of buying American, and failing to commit further to the Britannia. It pointed out that, since the original contract for twenty-five Britannias was signed in July 1949, never once had any order been cancelled or reduced. Nor had BOAC ever asked for material changes to the airframe, though it had requested additional pressurised test flying in light of the Comet accidents. Conversely, Bristol had redesigned the Britannia no fewer than four times to incorporate different engines, and had now raised the prospect of a fifth, the Orion. This was the first time that the prospect of a transatlantic Britannia had been raised – though the Orion was destined never to go into production. Little wonder that BOAC felt obliged to turn to Douglas.

The accepted version of how Whitney came to leave BOAC for Rolls-Royce was first told by Miles Thomas when he published his memoirs nine years later. In September 1955, Peter Masefield resigned from BEA to join Bristol in a bid to sort out the Britannia once and for all. The day before Whitney and Thomas visited the Farnborough Air Show, the *Evening Standard* reported that Whitney would be replacing Masefield. At the show, they bumped into Lord Hives, chairman of Rolls-Royce, who asked for a quiet word with Whitney. 'Lord Hives thought that if Whitney was fluid currency, so to speak, he might be interested in the deputy chairmanship of Rolls-Royce, a post which was then or was likely soon to be vacant. Within 24 hours of not dreaming of any change, Whitney found two offers on his desk.'[19]

In truth, Whitney had already had to be talked out of resignation two years earlier, and throughout 1955 he did rather more than dream about change. Uncannily, he first thought about the role he eventually took as early as 17 January. 'I think I will try and get out of BOAC via Rolls-Royce – cars and aeroplanes are my two main interests and obviously I can fill a gap there. But it ought to be more than just a directorship – V Ch or something.'[20] A month later, Masefield suggested he should come back to BEA as a non-executive director, and the idea grew on him when, later in the week, he met with Jack Profumo in Westminster and read the statement that Boyd Carpenter was about to make in the House of Commons: BOAC would be getting only ten Douglas DC-7s, too few to be operated economically. The minister walked in on the pair and laughed, but Whitney failed to find it funny. He met with Sholto Douglas, the man who had done so much to support his rise through the ranks during the war. Douglas had been BEA chairman since 1949, when D'Erlanger resigned in an argument over government subsidies. He was frank with Whitney: he wanted two more years as chairman, and perhaps two more after that. Whitney replied that he had 'no territorial ambitions'[21] – which was just as well, as Douglas would not retire until 1964. Over lunch on 5 April, the day when Churchill finally stood down as prime minister, to be succeeded by Anthony Eden, Whitney thanked Douglas but told him he would fight on at BOAC.

Eden called a snap election for 16 May, and Whitney enjoyed the parties he attended into the small hours, first at *The Times* and then the *Telegraph*. He was pleased too at the outcome: 'The Tories will have a workable majority yet not enough to enable them to be careless about the opposition.'[22] In August he recharged his batteries in Formentor. Work on the Villa Camanda was progressing smoothly. The first pair of the boats to be named *Camanda* performed well in choppy seas, Camilla learned to water ski and Whitney had a productive time fishing.

Upon his return, matters moved quickly. Masefield sent his letter of resignation from BEA to Boyd Carpenter on 29 August, advising that he would join Bristol in November. On 9 September, Cribbett told Whitney that he was rusting at BOAC and should replace Masefield, who said much the same thing over dinner at The Aviary that evening. The following week, during a visit to de Havilland to discuss the Comet 3, a call was put through to him: it was Lord Hives, offering him the precise position he had thought about nine months earlier – executive vice chairman at Rolls-Royce. The next day, both Boyd Carpenter and Douglas urged Whitney to take the job at BEA, and he flew off to Mallorca for a few days, to check again on the villa, fish with Vane and consider his options.

To the end, Whitney fulfilled his obligations to BOAC. Late on the night of 21 September, the pilot of one of its Argonauts was coping with poor visibility and strong winds on his descent into Tripoli. Three times, he pulled out of his approach and circled round, but on his fourth attempt he focused too much on the runway lights and too little on his instruments, clipping trees 1,200ft short of the runway. Of the forty-seven people on board, fifteen were killed in the ensuing accident. Whitney flew down to represent BOAC at a funeral service, and met with the captain in a bid to boost his morale. The next morning, he wrote his letter of resignation to Boyd Carpenter and flew back to London with it.

On Saturday, 1 October, Whitney flew to the East Midlands town of Derby, where Rolls-Royce's operations were headquartered, and met with Lord Hives to discuss the offer. He found the 69-year-old difficult, noting, 'He is rather vague and repeats himself',[23] yet he found the idea of Hives and Rolls-Royce preferable to Douglas and BEA, a man and a company he knew far better. Rolls-Royce's huge profile and the private sector salary it offered were influential. He also saw the restricted focus of BEA's operations as something of a step down from BOAC's global reach, ignoring the fact that the managing director role he was rejecting held more influence than the relatively ostracised position he was leaving. Then again, he would still have faced ministerial interference at BEA. On Sunday morning, after one final phone conversation with Hives, he rang Thomas to tell him he was leaving BOAC for Rolls-Royce. Whitney found himself front-page news on the Tuesday morning, and for once the coverage was positive.

His final BOAC board meeting was on 13 October: 'On behalf of the board the chairman expressed warm appreciation of Mr Straight's valuable contribution to civil aviation and to the affairs of the corporation over so many years and wished him every success in his new appointment.'[24] Ironically, Thomas stepped down from BOAC only six months later. Ground down by trying to run a profitable business while the government sought to give some of the airline's routes to independent carriers, by 'the failure of successive "world beaters" to beat anything at all – the Tudors, the Hermes, the Brabazon, the Princess'[25] – by the lateness of the Britannia and by the Comet accidents, he left to manage the UK subsidiary of the chemicals company Monsanto. When he told his fellow directors, the response from John Booth was telling. The man who, by stepping back to a non-executive role, had outlasted both Whitney and Thomas and would serve BOAC until 1965, said, 'I know exactly how you feel, Miles, enough is enough.'[26]

Had Whitney stuck it out for another six months, would he have succeeded Thomas? It seems unlikely. He was too diligent in seeking to do his best by BOAC, too unwilling to compromise with the ministers he served, for Westminster to have promoted him. Perhaps Harold Hartley had been right nine years earlier, when he told Whitney that he was not cut out for life in a nationalised industry, and would be happier in private enterprise. Besides, when Thomas' resignation sparked an ineffective game of musical chairs in British aviation, Whitney declined to play.

Breaking Up

Only two months after the then minister, John Boyd Carpenter, had encouraged him to move to BEA, and just weeks into Masefield's tenure at Bristol, Thomas visited Masefield to tell him of his forthcoming move to Monsanto and to propose that he succeed him at BOAC. He had done this with the authority of Boyd Carpenter's successor, Harold Watkinson, who rang to reaffirm the offer. Lord Beaverbrook invited Masefield to lunch, and told him that even Anthony Eden wanted him at BOAC. Masefield was flattered but felt obliged to stay at Bristol. Watkinson eventually appointed Pop D'Erlanger, seven years after he had quit BEA. So ineffective was he that, just six months later, George Cribbett, who had left Whitehall to become BOAC's deputy chairman, asked Whitney over lunch whether he might be persuaded to return as chairman. The answer was a resounding no.

17

Non-Exec

The Hon. Charles Rolls was born in 1877, third son of the future Baron Llangattock. Schooled at Eton, an interest in engineering led him to Trinity College, Cambridge, and a degree in the subject Whitney wished he had read, mechanical sciences. He set up a car sales and repair business in Fulham in south-west London, with a showroom on Mayfair's Conduit Street. A friend took him to Manchester to meet the man who had built the prototype car he was driving. The meeting took place in the Midland Hotel on 4 May 1904, thirty-six years before Whitney and Daphne dined there while he recovered from the injuries he had sustained in Norway. The car manufacturer's name was Henry Royce.

Born in 1863, Royce was just 14 when an aunt paid for him to become an apprentice with the Great Northern Railway. When she could no longer afford to support him, he joined an electrical engineering firm and became so enthused by the potential in the field that he set up his own company, manufacturing everything from electric cranes and motors to doorbells. He treated himself to a second-hand car, a Decauville, stripped it, rebuilt it and concluded he could do better. Five weeks after completing the first of three prototype cars, he was lunching with Charles Rolls.

By the end of that fateful meeting, Rolls had agreed to become the exclusive sales agent for a range of four production cars to be built by Royce and marketed as Rolls-Royces. In 1906, Rolls won the second-ever Tourist Trophy race at the wheel of a Rolls-Royce Light Twenty, and the company launched the car that sealed its reputation – the Silver Ghost. Rolls resigned to focus on flight in April 1910, and won national acclaim in June for the first return crossing of the English Channel by air. A month later he was dead, aged just 32. As he came in to land at an airshow in Bournemouth, the tailplane of his aircraft collapsed, pitching him into the ground and killing him instantly.

Royce's health, already precarious through overwork, collapsed altogether upon the news, and he was encouraged to continue his design work from his homes in West Wittering on the Sussex coast and La Canadel on the French Riviera. He never saw his company's new works in Derby, in England's East Midlands, yet the arrangement worked well. The Silver Ghost continued to sell for a premium price until production ceased in 1925 and it was superseded by the Phantom and the Wraith.

Where Royce had pushed back on Rolls' ambitions to move into aero engines, the imperatives of the First World War forced his hand. The 200hp Eagle was the first of several air-cooled Rolls-Royce engines that powered British aircraft through the conflict and, in 1919, hummed reliably during the 16 hours it took Alcock and Brown to make the first transatlantic flight.

Competition improved the breed still further, Rolls-Royce's R engine powering Supermarine seaplanes to victories in the Schneider Trophy competitions of 1929 and 1931, enabling Britain to win the trophy outright. On the ground, Rolls-Royce's creation of a manufacturing plant in Springfield, Massachusetts, and its acquisition of Bentley in 1931, broadened the reach of its car range. Before his death in 1933, Royce designed the prototype Merlin, which would prove so influential in helping the Allies to win the Second World War. It was an engine Whitney knew well, for he had sat behind it in his 601 and 242 Squadron Hurricanes, and it was still doing BOAC proud, fitted with crossover exhausts, in the Argonaut on the famous royal flights of 1952.

The engine also led, indirectly, to Rolls-Royce stealing an early lead in the development of the jet engine. In 1942, while the Rover car company was struggling to put Frank Whittle's revolutionary invention into production, a variant of the Merlin powered the Meteor tanks being built by Rolls-Royce. A simple swap was arranged: in return for Rover acquiring the Meteor tank factory, Rolls-Royce took responsibility for Whittle's design. This momentous switch was marked by a change in the naming convention for the company's aero engines: out went the birds of prey, from the Kestrel to the Merlin, and in came rivers, to represent the flow of air through a gas turbine. Rolls-Royce's first production jet engine, the Welland, powered 616 Squadron's Meteors in their interception of Germany's V1 flying bomb.

The company's first peacetime jet engines, the Nene and the Derwent, were even more successful, and within a year of VE Day 150 Meteors had flown more than 20,000 hours for the RAF. At this point, Rolls-Royce was the world leader in jet engine technology. The Soviet Union had no understanding of composite metals, and a prototype engine employing captured German designs was heavier and less fuel-efficient than a Nene or Derwent, and had ruinously short turbine blade life. US manufacturers also lagged behind Rolls-Royce, prompting Pratt & Whitney to sign a licensing deal that enabled them to manufacture more than 1,100 Nene engines, rebadged the J42. By the time the last of them rolled off the production line, any advantage Rolls-Royce enjoyed over American competition was gone.

And this was the great challenge for the company Whitney joined in the autumn of 1955. Rolls-Royce had developed the Dart, a turboprop engine, with the turbine driving a propeller, and four of them were slung from the wings of Britain's most successful airliner ever, the Viscount. The move into axial jet engines, employing a compressor to push gases through the turbine, led to de Havilland choosing the Rolls-Royce Avon for its Comet 4, but the years spent redesigning the Comet after its catastrophic setbacks had cost it dear. Now, it was up against the Boeing 707 and the McDonald Douglas DC-8, and only seventy Comet 4s were ever sold. In his authoritative history of Rolls-Royce, *The Magic of a Name*, Peter Pugh calculated that between 1956 and the year of Whitney's death, 1979, more than three-quarters of the 8,500 airliners built or on order were or would be manufactured in America. Rolls-Royce was still a presence in the luxury car market with its Phantom, and its Oil Engine Division offered effective solutions for the even smaller crawler tractor and earth-moving sector. But if the company was to flourish, it would have to break into the US civil aviation jet engine market.

The man with ultimate responsibility for meeting this challenge was Lord Ernest Hives. Born in 1886, he had joined Rolls-Royce in 1908 as a road tester and driver. He had worked on the Eagle, and had led the development of the 'R' and Merlin engines, overseeing Merlin production too. Promoted to the board in 1937, he had been made managing director in 1946 and chairman in 1950.

Whitney joined Rolls-Royce as executive vice-chairman on an initial four-year contract. Approaching his 43rd birthday, he felt ready to embrace what he saw as a wonderful opportunity. He knew Hives would retire shortly, at which point fellow deputy chairman Lord Kindersley would take over, but he expected promotion for himself in due course. He threw himself into his new role with a passion. Whenever he was based in the London office on Conduit Street, he made a point of going down to the car showroom. Tom Purves, a future chief executive of Rolls-Royce Motors, was working there, in the last phase of his Rolls-Royce apprenticeship. 'I have happy memories of this larger-than-life character coming in and asking me, "Who's been in today?" and, "What have we sold?" WS really cared about what we were doing.'[1]

An early visit to Rotol's factory concerned Whitney. The company was jointly owned by Rolls-Royce and Bristol – hence its name – and had manufactured propellers for them since before the war. Now, however, Whitney saw 'many small projects – I think we would be well out',[2] and indeed Rotol was sold two years later. He flew to Paris to discuss Air France's plans: whether they bought Boeing or McDonald Douglas, he argued that their new aircraft should be powered by Rolls-Royce Conways. He also met with airliner manufacturer SNCASE, whose Caravelle was fitted with a pair of Rolls-Royce Avons. In June 1956, he was on an early Comet 4 flight to Toulouse with representatives of BOAC, BEA, Capital Airlines and All Nippon Airlines, extolling the benefits of the Comet and its Conways over the Britannia and its Bristol engines.

But just a month later, Whitney's ambitions were dashed. Over a breakfast meeting, Hives explained that when he retired in the new year and Kindersley succeeded him, Denning 'Jim' Pearson, the head of the Aero Engine Division, with whom Whitney had liaised over the 'crossover' exhausts for the Argonaut, would not only be made deputy chairman, but chief executive too. Whitney was stunned, and the vagueness of his conversations with Hives before accepting the Rolls-Royce offer came back to haunt him. He would never have joined the company had he known that he would report in due course to Pearson. He compared himself with Anthony Eden, whose premiership would shortly unravel over the Suez crisis and who would also depart in the new year: 'Perhaps he has been too long a no 2, which is a thing I must watch too.'[3] Nevertheless, by the time the changes were announced in

October, Whitney had accepted the situation, and found that there were benefits to being, in the words of Miles Thomas, 'free currency'.[4] He was invited by Sir Walter Warboys, the man who modernised Britain's road signs, to become a director of the Council of Industrial Design, forerunner of today's Design Council. More significantly, Sir Alexander Roger, chairman of one of Britain's leading retail banks, Midland Bank, asked Whitney to join its board.

Roger was diligent in ensuring Whitney's appointment received the unanimous support of his colleagues. He raised the matter at the bank's September board meeting, telling them that he proposed to recommend Whitney's appointment the following month. Then he instructed his company secretary, Kenneth Barber, to write individually to those directors who had not been present, including Field Marshal Viscount Alanbrooke:

> Mr Whitney Straight is just under 44 years old. His war record and his services to British aviation will, I am sure, be well known to you all. In particular, you will remember that he was, until recently, Deputy-Chairman of British Overseas Airways Corporation. Mr Whitney Straight is now Executive Vice-Chairman of our greatly valued customer, Rolls-Royce Limited, and I have no doubt you will have seen the recent announcement that he is to become a Deputy Chairman when Lord Kindersley, who at present occupies that position, takes over the chairmanship from Lord Hives in January next. I consider that Mr Whitney Straight's wide experience and ability will be most useful to us on our board. At the same time his appointment will undoubtedly help to reinforce our long and close association with Rolls-Royce and I recommend him confidently to you.[5]

Alanbrooke's 'Yes, certainly'[6] was one vote in the board's unanimous agreement to Whitney's appointment. He would remain a Midland Bank director for the rest of his life.

Whitney's reduced role at Rolls-Royce also gave him more time for his own business. The re-licensing of Western Airways' service between Weston and Cardiff had enabled a left-wing Labour MP, Ian Mikardo, to provide the *Daily Express* with a lurid headline – 'Whitney Straight given an airline'[7] – and Whitney found it prudent to rename Straight Corporation. As Airways Union, it found that the proximity of its base in Weston-super-Mare to Bristol's factory at Filton gave it new sources of revenue. Bristol's 170 Freighter aircraft, famously used by Silver City Airways to ferry passengers and their cars across the English Channel, typically made several heavily laden flights per day. They therefore needed frequent, regular maintenance and Airways Union won a long-term contract for this lucrative business, its workforce swelling to 400. Then, just as the Freighter maintenance work began to dry up, the Britannia finally went into production, and Airways Union won a contract to fit the planes out. They were the largest aircraft ever to use Weston, and tests had to be carried out on the strength of the runway before the first Britannia could land there, on 14 January 1957. Each fitting out took some four months to complete, and Airways Union grew in prosperity. The ever-loyal Stanley Cox continued to serve as general manager, and Whitney flew down to Weston each month to chair the board meetings.

He first recorded his fears about Rolls-Royce's future as early as June 1957, fourteen years before it was forced into liquidation. He found an Aero Engine Division meeting 'the usual monologue from the chair of Pearson – he is bright and objective but just not enough of a businessman to deal with problems of this magnitude. I was told that the Conway was not going well. I feel in my bones that disaster is ahead for R-R and I want to be clear by then.'[8] The issue of too many engineers and not enough businessmen became a common theme in Whitney's diary. True, Rolls-Royce's new chairman, Lord Kindersley, was steeped in finance. He was also chairman of the company's merchant bankers, Lazards, and a governor of both the Bank of England and Royal Exchange Assurance. He would stay on as a Rolls-Royce director after passing the chairmanship to Pearson, yet he never managed to address the problem. Whitney had far less influence, but he came to regret bitterly his failure to encourage the company to broaden its focus on excellence to include business prowess.

He contributed where he could. A month before Pearson's monologue, he had discussed his frustrations over lunch with advertising guru David Ogilvy, and noted in his diary: 'He is the best man there is and would be wonderful for us in the USA, but I can't get our people to see sense or accept any contemporary commercial approach.'[9] Fortunately, Whitney found Frederick Llewellyn 'Doc' Smith, managing director of the Motor Car Division, perfectly open to new ideas. He arranged for Smith to meet Ogilvy in New York, and the outcome was one of the most famous advertising slogans in history. Ogilvy did not actually write the line, 'At 60 miles an hour the loudest noise in this new Rolls-Royce comes from the electric clock'. He lifted it from a road test for the Silver Cloud II he had read in *The Motor*. But the advertisement set him on the way to becoming the most creative advertising executive of the twentieth century, and generated an increase in year-on-year sales of the Silver Cloud of 50 per cent.

By then, Whitney had learned of a regrettable aero-engine order Rolls-Royce had fulfilled more than a decade earlier. In September 1946, at a Kremlin meeting on the state of Soviet aviation, an exasperated Joseph Stalin, impatient at the lack of progress in Russian jet engine technology, sanctioned an attempt to buy Rolls-Royce jet engines. He was astonished when the company agreed to the sale of thirty Derwents and twenty-five Nenes, remarking, 'What a fool one must be to sell one's own secrets,'[10] but prime minister Clement Attlee and Stafford Cripps, then President of the Board of Trade, still looked upon the USSR as an ally that had helped defeat Germany, and even sanctioned a visit to Rolls-Royce's aero-engine factory by a Soviet delegation. One member of the group wore shoes with extra-soft soles, to pick up metal sward for analysis, while another stole a turbine blade. Incredulous members of the US State Department and Department of Commerce protested furiously to Lord Inverchapel, Britain's ambassador in Washington, but it was too late. By the time that the first engine was shipped to Murmansk, Soviet orders had already been issued for the copying and mass production of the Derwent and Nene. Thousands were manufactured in the USSR, and thousands more in China. Some of them powered the MiG fighters faced by pilots of the US Air Force and Royal Navy during the Korean War.

Whitney was flabbergasted to learn of the story, and in late 1957, in pursuit of compensation for the unlicensed copying, added Chinese and Russian legs to a lengthy business trip out through India and Singapore to Australia, and back via Manilla and Hong Kong. He learned little in China to support his case, though he did locate his parents' first marital home in Beijing. A Tupolev Tu-104 – in the Comet's continued absence the only jet airliner then in active service – carried him as far as Irkutsk in Siberia, but it encountered mechanical problems and he made the long flight to Moscow on board a small, prop-driven Ilyushin Il-14. There, he dined with British Ambassador, Sir Patrick Reilly, who gave him little chance of securing compensation for the copied engines, and so it proved. Whitney's first meeting was with a Soviet official who claimed not to have been in service at the time of the Rolls-Royce deal. He agreed to check the relevant file and host a second meeting, but this proved no more productive. Whitney left Moscow empty-handed, and flew home via Helsinki and Copenhagen. His board colleagues thanked him for his efforts but clearly felt he had wasted his time, and Whitney finally accepted that compensation was out of the question when the Comptroller of the Patent Office informed him that Rolls-Royce had failed to take out patents in Moscow for its engines.

He was more fulfilled in his private life. On a skiing holiday in Cervinia in the spring of 1957, he had met a Belgian woman, Claudine van der Straten Panthoz. Her father had played in goal for Belgium's ice hockey team, but her sporting passions were mountaineering and skiing. When Whitney arrived at Villa Camanda a month later for his usual 'spring maintenance' visit, he was intrigued to find a letter from her: 'Strange how just a brief contact like this can set off a chain reaction.'[11] They became better acquainted during a trip Whitney made to Amsterdam for meetings with KLM, and he realised he had deep feelings for her when she returned gaunt from two months climbing in the Andes. She moved into Whitney's London *pied-à-terre* in Hyde Park Gardens Mews for a time, ostensibly to improve her English, but the arrangement ended when she grew jealous of Whitney returning to The Aviary each weekend. Hitherto, if any woman had encroached too far into his marriage and home life, he had ended the relationship, yet with Claudine he found himself speaking of marriage and a child. The relationship had become that important to him.

In May 1959, Whitney and Daphne flew to Paris to sign documents for a pair of cars they had purchased for the villa, and returned a few weeks later to drive them down through France and Spain, to take across on the ferry to Mallorca. He had a much more romantic trip in mind for Claudine. She would shortly be leaving for the Himalayas to participate in a unique, all-woman ascent of Cho Oyu, the world's sixth-highest mountain. Whitney's latest motor yacht, the *Camanda III*, had recently been completed by Fairey Marine in Southampton, and he had it brought to Paris, so that he and Claudine could navigate it through the canals of France, down the Spanish coast and across the sea to Mallorca. They would bid each other farewell in Palma, Whitney to sail back up the coast to Villa Camanda, and Claudine to head off for Kathmandu, the starting point of the long overland trek to the foot of Cho Oyu.

Their trip began badly. On 22 July, only a day out of Paris, Claudine was at the helm and Whitney below deck when the boat struck a canal bank so firmly that the propeller shaft was damaged. He managed to manoeuvre the *Camanda* as far as a lock basin, and spent much of the next day under the water, trying to detach the propeller and shaft. A local factory was able to repair the damage and the pair made Toulouse late on 25 July. 'This is not a romantic business at this speed,'[12] recorded Whitney. They set off early the next morning down the Canal du Midi and reached the coast at La Nouvelle, below Narbonne, in three days. The *Camanda* held the water well in a heavy swell as they headed down the coast as far as Blanes on the Costa Brava, some 40 miles north-east of Barcelona.

At 5.30 a.m. on Saturday, 1 August, with tanks full to the brim with diesel, Whitney and Claudine set off across 112 miles of open sea, heading due south for the port of Soller, on Mallorca's north-west coast. Everything went to schedule: the switch to reserve tanks, the first sighting of land and, 7 hours and 40 minutes after leaving Blanes, mooring briefly for a meal and refuelling in Soller. After a week-and-a-half on board the *Camanda*, the couple enjoyed two days of luxury in Palma, before a tearful farewell at the airport. Claudine left a white scarf in the top drawer of the *Camanda*'s dressing table, 'and it will always stay there', wrote Whitney, 'exactly as it is — she and I are joint owners in this boat and I feel it belongs to her also'.[13] As ever, marriage was out of the question, unless anything should happen to Daphne, but he was now ready to father Claudine's child.

Back home, Whitney expected his old friend Max Aitken, now proprietor of the *Daily Express*, to keep him regularly updated on her progress on Cho Oyu. The newspaper was sponsoring the expedition and its reporter, Stephen Harper, was loosely attached to it. Expedition leader Claude Kogan had climbed within 1,400ft of the mountain's summit five years earlier, and remained bitter that her colleague, Raymond Lambert, had insisted that they must turn back or risk death. Now, she was determined that her all-woman team would succeed on the mountain where a man had failed. Male sherpas were a necessity, but Harper was not, and he would have to file his reports based on the messages sent to him by runner.

Tragically, discipline broke down on the mountain. On 30 September, ignoring warnings that an apparent break in the weather would not last, Kogan and Claudine established their Camp Four, a half-day's climb from the summit, in a slight hollow set back from cliffs plunging thousands of feet into a crevasse. They took the highly unusual step of staying there. They had even taken the tent from Camp Three with them, rendering it inoperable. Their colleagues at Base Camp became so concerned for their safety – spending too long at high altitude as rising temperatures triggered avalanches – that they sent two sherpas to bring them back down and wait for a proper break in the weather. The two men were themselves caught in an avalanche and only one survived, and it was not until 11 October that a party reached the site of Camp Four and found no trace of it. Claudine, Kogan and the sherpa supporting them had been swept away.

Oblivious to all this, Whitney was still buoyed by a letter from Claudine that had arrived at The Aviary four days earlier: 'I pray for her, in my own godless way.'[14] On Thursday, 14 October, he had taken comfort from Harper's latest report in the *Express*, but a day later, a call from Aitken crushed him. The *Daily Mail* had stolen a march on its rival by the simple expedient of bribing the runners carrying messages to Harper, and Aitken had learned that it would break the news of the disaster the next morning, a day ahead of the *Express*.

Whitney received all the weekend papers at the Aviary, and he was horrified by the front page of the *Mail*. He rang the news desk at the *Express*, in hope that Harper had sent more positive news. They had no word, but rang back later in the day to tell him they now had Harper's copy, and there was no hope of Claudine having survived. Whitney's mind was in a whirl. He hoped against hope that she was still alive and descending the Chinese side of Cho Oyu. He cursed her for her recklessness – she and the obsessed Kogan had made fatally poor climbing partners. He thought of the child he and Claudine had spoken of. 'Perhaps I should have reached out and grasped this situation, whatever the consequences for my family.'[15] He would carry a photograph of her in his wallet for years, and whenever he flew over the south of France and spotted the Garonne or the Canal du Midi, he thought of their extraordinary journey together aboard *Camanda III*. Her scarf remained a permanent fixture on the boat. Yet, just as thoughts of his family had always pulled him away from any woman who grew too close to him, so they pulled him out of his grief for Claudine: 'Daphne, Camilla, Amanda – I have tried and must more than ever now do the best for them.'[16] The remarkable Daphne reciprocated, comforting him in his anguish and even sending Claudine's mother a letter of condolence.

Claudine's death coincided with the fourth anniversary of Whitney joining Rolls-Royce. Kindersley and Whitney agreed that he would continue to serve as deputy chairman, both men confident that he could make a contribution to the company. In June, for example, he met with Bob Gross, chairman and chief executive of Lockheed. If Rolls-Royce had failed with Boeing and McDonnell Douglas, he reasoned, might Gross consider Rolls-Royce engines for Lockheed's next airliner? The talks led nowhere, and it would take the most concerted effort by Rolls-Royce to change Lockheed's mind in the future. The real problem, Whitney mused, were his fellow directors: 'so terribly un-businesslike and so reckless. It is rare that someone who is 100% engineer can also have good judgement in business matters. They tend to be too influenced by the enthusiasms of their trade – and care little for the realities.'[17] He was no happier with the company's divisional boards. He felt too much influence rested with them, and that they might be a filter – were discussions and decisions at main board level based on all the facts? A road test in a 3.8-litre Jaguar depressed him further. Noting its performance and road-holding capabilities, he wondered why anyone would pay a premium for a Bentley Continental.

In the spring of 1960, Camilla introduced Whitney and Daphne to Michael Bowater, or Mikey as he became known to the family. Educated at Sandhurst and commissioned in the Scots Guards, he was now a major in the Pathfinders unit of 16th Parachute Brigade. On an early visit to The Aviary, Whitney took him rowing on the lake for a man-to-man chat. Mikey navigated Whitney's chief concern – 'How long do you plan to jump out of aircraft for a living?'[18] – by explaining his plans for a career in Civvy Street (he subsequently enjoyed executive roles with the Bowater paper group on both sides of the Atlantic). He was more surprised when Whitney started talking about his own family: 'My brother's a bloody spy.'[19]

It will be remembered that Michael had been the only member of the family not at Raquette Lake in August 1935 to welcome the honeymooning Whitney and Daphne. He was in Moscow with a group of students led by Anthony Blunt. He became a member of Cambridge's left-leaning Apostles Group and was recruited into the Communist party. After graduating in Economics, he was instructed to return to the US. There, he took an unpaid role in the State Department's European division, and passed confidential files to a Soviet agent he knew only as 'Michael Green'. That, he claimed, was the extent of his work for the USSR, but the chief criticism against him is that in Washington, during the spring of 1951, he saw Guy Burgess, well known to him as another member of the Cambridge spy ring, and learned that he had been working since the previous October on the British Embassy's Far East desk. Burgess had, therefore, been in a position to disclose to the Soviets America's plans to send troops into North Korea – where they were ambushed by overwhelmingly larger Chinese forces, acting, it is widely believed, on Soviet intelligence.

Michael did nothing to expose Burgess, who left Washington two months later to return to Britain, and who then fled, with Donald Maclean, to Moscow shortly afterwards. Indeed, he remained silent until 1963, when the Kennedy administration offered him the chairmanship of the National Endowment for the Arts. Knowing that he would face a security check, he voluntarily told the FBI all he knew, an action that led to Blunt confessing his role as chief recruiter of the Cambridge spy ring. Quite when Whitney learned all this is not clear. As far back as January 1953, Douglas Hyde, a former *Daily Worker* editor who had become a leading critic of communism, had told him that Michael had been a Communist party member while working in the US State Department – 'a really nasty situation'[20] – and clearly by 1960 Whitney had become fully informed, and even less enamoured with his brother. He had no such qualms about Mikey. St Margaret's, Westminster, scene of Whitney and Daphne's wedding twenty-five years earlier, played host to Mikey and Camilla marrying on 22 June.

That summer, Whitney decided to treat himself to the ultimate executive toy, a light aircraft. After a thorough analysis of the market, he settled on a Cessna 310, considering it convenient and safe: its twin-engine configuration was inherently less risky than a single-engine model, and the 50-gallon 'tip tanks' at the end of each wing were designed to shear off in the event of an accident. Actually, since he claimed a range of 1,400 statute miles in still air for the aircraft he purchased, G-ARMK, it must have been fitted with several auxiliary tanks. At £37,000, it would stretch even his finances, but he looked upon it as an investment. When he was not flying it – something that became increasingly frequent as his health problems mounted – he could rent it out to other pilots, just as he did with Villa Camanda when the family was not using it. The purchase was finally completed in June 1961.

The Cessna was located in Boston, Massachusetts, and Whitney hired a pilot/navigator named Johnson to help map out the most appropriate way of flying it back across the Atlantic. The two men flew to New York on

30 June, and on to Boston to collect the aircraft the next morning. After checking it over, Whitney and Johnson left for Torbay, Newfoundland, the easternmost tip of Canada, that afternoon. The next leg was exceedingly hazardous, and Whitney must have had great confidence in both Johnson's flight plan and the weather forecast to have attempted it. It involved flying south-east across the Atlantic from Newfoundland to the Azores, a distance of approximately 1,250 statute miles. This gave the pair a margin of perhaps 10 per cent – barely acceptable with a tail wind but downright dangerous if the wind direction were to change – yet Whitney's only comment about the flight was, 'We made the Azores nicely.'[21] The final leg, to Hurn aerodrome, just north of Bournemouth in Dorset, was much more straightforward, and completed bang on schedule. So fresh was Whitney after his transatlantic flight that he was up bright and early the next morning to fly to Weston for an Airways Union board meeting.

His proudest engagement with the Cessna was a trans-Saharan trip, part-sponsored by the BBC, made during March 1963. The Sudanese Embassy in London and the Aéro Club de France in Paris assisted Whitney in his meticulous planning, and he required the permission of the military governor in El Fasher, Darfur, to fly over his territory. Sandstorms were a regular problem but the Cessna flew trouble-free throughout the trip, and Whitney was delighted with the end result – a documentary narrated by him and broadcast by the BBC on 14 October. An episode in the corporation's *Adventure* series called 'When the Sea Ran Dry', it tracked not only his trip but also a much larger-scale expedition made by a French team. Producer Brian Branston previewed the programme in the *Radio Times*. He described the French team, 'equipped like a regiment ... nine huge lorries, a refrigerator truck, a helicopter and fifty personnel', then continued, 'going the same way was a tiny British expedition flying a small plane, its leader one-time racing driver and wartime pilot ace Whitney Straight. And the encounters of the British party, whether with Tuaregs [a Saharan group of nomadic pastoralists], with strange "desert roses" or with the rock paintings of Tassili, were no less rewarding than those of the more spectacular professional explorers.'[22]

Another overseas trip, made a month before the Saharan expedition, also led to Whitney appearing on television, but this time in the most embarrassing of circumstances. He was part of a delegation of businessmen visiting Moscow, led by newspaper magnate Roy Thomson. While

Thomson discussed Russo-Chinese relations with Soviet premier Nikita Khrushchev, Whitney's meetings on the Russian automotive and aeronautic sectors were rendered ineffective by a poor interpreter. On what should have been the last day of the trip, he paid a brief visit to the exiled spy, Guy Burgess, but the flight home was cancelled and he spent the evening at yet another reception. Burgess joined it and, recorded Whitney, 'got rather tight'.[23]

The delegates flew home the next morning, Whitney pondering whether the trip had been worthwhile. It was only when he collected his baggage at London Airport and was confronted by a barrage of microphones and camera flashes that he realised that some loose comments about Burgess the night before – he was not even sure what he had said – had been picked up by the press and now he was headline news. The television reporter obliged to conduct a staid interview with Thomson on the merits of the trip had more sport with a mortified Whitney:

> Interviewer: 'What is Guy Burgess doing now?'
> Whitney: 'I don't really know.'
> Interviewer: 'What are his views on a return to England. You must have asked him that.'
> Whitney: 'I am afraid that I didn't ask him that question.'
> Interviewer: 'What did you talk about?'
> Whitney: 'We talked about Cambridge and about life in general and domestic things in Moscow.'
> Interviewer: 'Did you gather he was quite happy with his lot there after twelve years?'
> Whitney: 'I thought he seemed very happy, yes.'
> Interviewer: 'Has he got a lot of Russian friends.'
> Whitney: 'So he says. I didn't meet any.'[24]

'I was horrified,' he recorded the next day. 'The press have taken me apart based on one chance remark – a good lesson which I will certainly not forget.'[25] Keen to move swiftly on, he made sure that he was on top form three days later, at Midland Bank's annual general meeting. Addressing 300 shareholders in front of his fellow directors, his ostensible task was to formally request that the meeting express it thanks 'to all members of the staff, both at head office and at the branches, for the conscientious and enthusiastic manner in which they have served the bank during the past year'.[26] He also took the opportunity to tell shareholders about the bank's new computer, KDP.10; the diligent way in which staff had gone about implementing it; and 'substantially more success'[27] for Midland employees in the Institute of Bankers examinations than for those working for other UK banks. Whitney generated as many 'hear hears' as he did laughs, and he put the embarrassment of Moscow firmly behind him.

In late April, he caught the sleeper train west so that he could see his mother receive an honorary doctorate at the University of Exeter. Never the easiest of train passengers, nevertheless he was 'soon asleep after a good dose of Fleming'.[28] The eleventh James Bond book, *On Her Majesty's Secret Service*, had just been published, and featured the return of Ernst Stavro Blofeld, the man who had organised the theft of two nuclear bombs in the ninth book, *Thunderball*. He is now posing as Comte Balthazar de Bleuville, running what is claimed to be an allergy clinic in an exclusive alpine resort called Piz Gloria. Bond journeys there under the guise of a genealogical expert, Sir Hilary Bray, to conduct research into the Comte's family.

In chapter 12, 'Two Near Misses', Bond is invited to lunch on the terrace by Blofeld's assistant, Irma Blunt.

> She waved a hand towards the crowded tables around them. 'A most interesting crowd, do you not find, Sair [stet] Hilary? Everybody who is anybody. We have quite taken the international set away from Gstaad and St Moritz. That is your Duke of Marlborough over there with such a gay party of young things. And nearby that is Mr Whitney and Lady Daphne Straight. Is she not chic? They are both wonderful skiers.'[29]

If Whitney was reading a first impression copy of the first edition, he would have been still more impressed – Fleming had known his wife as Lady Daphne for almost thirty years and had inadvertently knighted him in the manuscript, an error corrected in the second impression onwards.

The name check was Fleming's way of thanking Whitney for help given six years earlier. He had written to Whitney at Rolls-Royce's Conduit Street offices in July 1957, seeking advice on a new car for his hero, 'a cross between a Continental Bentley and a Ford Thunderbird

– i.e. a smallish cockpit with a long bonnet line in front and a large boot behind'.[30] Fleming also wanted input on a villain's car, 'an armour-plated Rolls Royce [he never used the hyphen] of rather statuesque vintage with armour-plated glass windows.'[31] He sought specifications of the grand Silver Ghosts that Rolls-Royce had sold to Indian maharajas in the inter-war period, and was particularly keen to understand how the suspension and brakes of such cars had been upgraded to cope with their extra weight.

He wrote again to Whitney in December: 'Conduit Street were as helpful as they could be over my rather incoherent requirements for James Bond's new motor car, but I'm not sure how it is likely to feature in the new book. It rather looks as if the villain is going to be equipped with an armour-plated Silver Ghost.'[32] Sure enough, in 1959's *Goldfinger*, Bond uses a pool car, an Aston Martin DB III, and he cannot help but be impressed when he sees Auric Goldfinger's Silver Ghost cruising up the drive of the Royal St Mark's golf club (a *very* thinly disguised Royal St George's). The car is key to the book's plot, in that the real reason for its immense weight is not its armour plating and reinforced glass, but the gold hidden within its armour plates, which Goldfinger is smuggling out of the country. The information Rolls-Royce had provided to Fleming shines through when Goldfinger proudly tells Bond of the modifications he has made to the car. 'I have added five leaves to the springs and fitted disk brakes to the rear wheels to increase the braking power. The Servo-operated front-wheel brakes were not sufficient.'[33]

It was not until *Thunderball* was published in 1961 that Fleming finally gave James Bond:

> the most selfish car in England. It was a Mark II Continental Bentley that some rich idiot had married to a telegraph pole on the Great West Road. Bond had bought the bits for £1,500 and Rolls had straightened the bend in the chassis and fitted new clockwork – the Mark IV engine with 9.5 compression. Then Bond had gone to Mulliners with £3,000, which was half his total capital, and they had sawn off the old cramped sports saloon body and had fitted a trim, rather square convertible two-seater affair, power-operated, with only two large armed bucket seats in black leather.[34]

In thanking Whitney for his help, Fleming told him that he feared Goldfinger's Silver Ghost might not be particularly good for Rolls-Royce business. In truth, by the 1960s, no car, real or fictional, could materially affect the company's fortunes. All that mattered was breaking into the US aero-engine market.

18

Liquidation

The challenge of establishing a sustainable presence in the global aero-engine market was a daunting one for Rolls-Royce. The General Electric engine chosen by McDonnell Douglas for its DC-10 had begun life powering Lockheed's giant Galaxy military transport aircraft. This had been funded by the Pentagon and, as Tory grandee Michael Heseltine memorably put it, 'Rolls-Royce effectively decided to compete with the US taxpayer.'[1] The news from Boeing was no better. When Pan Am became the first airline to order the most famous of the wide-bodied airbuses, the 747, it specified Pratt & Whitney's JT9D engines.

Worse, UK rival Bristol Siddeley, the company created when Bristol and Armstrong Siddeley merged their engine interests, was due to take a stake in the Airbus A300 alongside the French company Sud Aviation and a German consortium. It seemed likely that this too would use the JT9D, though it would be built under licence by Bristol Siddeley and another French manufacturer. Faced with a substantial loss of business on its own doorstep, Rolls-Royce concluded it had no option but to acquire Bristol Siddeley, and the deal was completed in October 1966. Whitney had wanted this for years. In April 1962, he had met with Bristol chairman Sir Reginald Verdon Smith, to see if he would be agreeable to acquisition. 'He seemed willing,' recorded Whitney, 'but there are clearly lots of problems.'[2] In January 1964, he and Kindersley had discussed the matter with Rolls-Royce's financial advisers, Lazards.

But while the commercial logic of creating a single British jet aero-engine manufacturer was sound, the terms and execution of the deal were anything but. Rolls-Royce paid a premium price of £63.6 million, apparently unaware that Bristol was so short of cash that it was withholding payments to suppliers totalling £4 million. Bristol's tangible assets were worth only £42 million. The remaining third of the acquisition price was, in accounting terms, 'goodwill', but very little of it would ever be realised. An Anglo-French development of Bristol's Olympus engine would power the Concorde, for example, but only sixteen production aircraft ever flew. Whitney visited Bristol Siddeley four months after the acquisition and concluded, 'It will be a big problem to combine the best features of both companies.'[3] So it proved. Bristol Siddeley was permitted to retain its identity, and even compete with Rolls-Royce. The delay in implementing any meaningful economies across the enlarged group hit Rolls-Royce's cashflow so hard that Midland Bank's new chairman, Sir Archibald Forbes, took Whitney aside after a board meeting to express his concerns about the company's growing overdraft.

In July 1967, Rolls-Royce proposed an ambitious new engine to Lockheed, which was working on its own wide-bodied airliner, the Tristar. The RB211's three-shaft design offered easier maintenance and lower noise levels; extensive use of a composite material, Hyfil, made it lighter; its fan diameter and thrust would be twice that of the Conway; and, promised Rolls-Royce, it would be in service by 1971, only four years away. By cruel coincidence, that same month, the company's brilliant director of aero-engineering, Adrian Lombard, who had played a key role in the design of the Nene, Derwent, Avon and Conway, died suddenly of a brain haemorrhage, aged only 52. 'Very sad for the company,' wrote Whitney the next day. 'A good technical man who will be hard to replace.'[4] Indeed, the failure to replace him at all would have profound consequences for Rolls-Royce.

That autumn, as negotiations with Lockheed progressed, David Huddie, managing director of Rolls-Royce's Aero Engine Division, decamped to New York. Obliged to win Lockheed's business come what may, he pledged more and more thrust for less and less money. November's decision by Harold Wilson's government to devalue Sterling, from $2.80 to $2.40, gave him some much-needed room for manoeuvre. Just as with the 1948 devaluation, Whitney benefitted too, making it easier for him to commission the finest of his motor yachts, *Camanda IV*. Its hull was built by Michael Souter at Cowes on the Isle of Wight, and a unique cockpit and cabin with accommodation for eight was designed by Whitney's old friend, Sir Hugh Casson.

It was the smallest of Casson's nautical projects – he had already designed the interiors of the Royal Yacht *Britannia* and the P&O liner *Canberra*.

A Rolls-Royce board sub-committee meeting on 19 February 1968 reviewed the negotiations with Lockheed. Pearson considered the deal won, and Whitney found his attitude 'rather shocking – i.e. "I have made a good deal. It is up to you to find the money"'.[5] This was a deeply held belief of Pearson's: when the man appointed Rolls-Royce's receiver three years later, Rupert Nicholson, published his record of the company's collapse, he recalled him 'saying, among other surprises, that the duty of a company was to concentrate on technical excellence and leave profits to come, as they would, as a sure reward'.[6] The Lockheed contract was finally secured, to great fanfare, on 29 March, and earned Huddie a knighthood for services to export. Tony Benn (still referred to by *Hansard* at the time as Anthony Wedgwood Benn), Wilson's Minister of Technology, proclaimed in the House of Commons, 'We can be justly proud of the company's achievement in designing the RB211 and in winning the order in the face of determined competition.'[7] Whitney's reaction to the deal was more measured; 'Little do they realise the big problems ahead, of actually making the thing work – and this is where I fear we may fail.'[8] Just like Rolls-Royce's acquisition of Bristol Siddeley, the commercial imperative of the sale of the RB211 to Lockheed was clear. This time, its terms and execution would prove fatal.

Whitney had problems of his own. On 5 February, he was being driven into London by his long-term chauffeur, Hanshaw, when his heart started racing. His pulse remained high all day, and when he was admitted to the King Edward VII hospital in Marylebone the following morning, it was still 140bpm. He was suffering from atrial fibrillation, and placed on medication. He was not discharged until 16 February, just in time for Pearson's sub-committee meeting. He found the advice he received in hospital sobering: no more diving, skiing, smoking or drinking. 'All this adds up to a no-good life.'[9] He was still only 55, but he came to accept the idea of a less active life, and managed to get the smoking down to a cigar after lunch and supper. Abstaining from alcohol would prove a much tougher challenge, but what upset him most was the loss of his pilot's licence, and the far higher insurance bill on the Cessna when he was permitted to resume flying.

Sadly, Whitney was obliged to submit an insurance claim for the aircraft just months later. He was contacted over the summer by a 30-year-old pilot named R.S. Ducker, a former RAF officer who had piloted Boeing 707s for Pan Am, and was now operations manager at Aircruise (Operating) Ltd. His pilot's licence was not yet endorsed for the Cessna 310F, but he was being trained on it and he made a test flight in Whitney's aircraft down to Weston-super-Mare and back on 18 September. He arranged with Whitney to rent the Cessna again on 29 September for a trip to Blackpool. He never arrived, and a large-scale search found the wreckage of the plane on high ground near Bethesda in Snowdonia. Ducker was dead and the Cessna was written off. No reason for his navigational error could be established.

Whitney took to chartering Cessnas himself, but he found some were not maintained as well as his own aircraft and he suffered several scares. The worst came as he approached Leavesden in Hertfordshire, with a cloud base of 500ft and visibility of 1,000 yards, and an electrical fault caused the instruments to fail. That was the final straw, and he concluded that flying had to go the same way as deep-sea diving.

He was consoled by *Camanda IV*. Camilla and Amanda had the honour of smashing a bottle against her hull when she was launched from Souter's slipway in Cowes on 14 July, and after several weeks of trials Whitney was pleased with her. She could glide through rough waves, and her pair of Cummins diesels generated a steady speed of 20.5 knots at 2,200rpm. When he opened her throttles up, he saw 28 knots at 3,100rpm. Wanting no reminders of the journey he had made with Claudine in *Camanda III*, Whitney chose to take his latest vessel out to Villa Camanda via the Bay of Biscay and the Straits of Gibraltar – a hazardous undertaking in a boat with no keel. This required a tough crew, and Whitney took with him Arthur 'Jumbo' Preston, long-time Arena Master of the Royal Tournament; Peter Lucy, a retired lieutenant commander in the Royal Navy who had recently taken a stake in Airways Union; and son-in-law Mikey Bowater – each a courageous man with a military background.

They set off early on Wednesday, 14 August but a storm blew in quite suddenly and Whitney and his crew found themselves in trouble. The cockpit window was shattered by mountainous seas and the boat took on water. Lucy considered their plight so serious that he told Whitney they should put out a 'mayday', but the winds dropped, the sea conditions improved and Whitney was able to steer the damaged vessel into Dartmouth. Souters repaired *Camanda* swiftly, and the crew set off again two days later, only to be driven back to port by a gale warning and a faulty regulator. After a test run on the Sunday evening, Whitney neglected to turn the starter switch off and the starter motor burned out. He and Mikey consoled themselves each evening in a small hotel on Dartmouth's quayside, but it was not until Tuesday morning that they were finally able to set off.

Off Brest, Whitney put a reassuring call on his radio telephone into Souters, and then came the long grind across the Bay of Biscay. There was a regular rota of watchkeepers, the men grew accustomed to identifying the speed and direction of other vessels, and the night passed quickly. Dawn brought a sea fog and *Camanda* was held at a steady 14 knots, but the weather cleared and the crew made good time to Cascais, outside Lisbon. At dawn on the Saturday, Whitney proudly took *Camanda* through the Straits of Gibraltar, where they were greeted by an officer sent out by the governor, Sir Gerald Lathbury. As Whitney approached Formentor, he opened the throttles wide and tore round the bay. Vane Ivanović and another neighbour, the art collector Kitty Miller, came to the cliff edges of their properties to welcome him in, and then he tied up on up Villa Camanda's dock. That night, he recorded his feelings at the end of a great adventure. 'The boat has really been wonderful – she seems able to take any sea and any load without a murmur and she is so comfortable to be with. The crew have been wonderful, and we have certainly been through some difficult moments.'[10]

It was some time before *Camanda IV* regularly gave as much joy as she had on her maiden voyage. The next afternoon, villa residents enjoying a siesta were woken by Daphne shouting. They rushed out on to the terrace and looked down to find Whitney sitting astride the upright bow of the boat, which was sitting vertically at her mooring. Vane arrived in his boat and threw Whitney a line, and the two men somehow managed to beach her. Mercifully, she had sprung a serious leak only after sailing down the English Channel, across the Bay of Biscay and on to Mallorca. The unfortunate saga continued when the lorry carrying replacement engines was involved in a serious accident, but once *Camanda IV* was cleaned up and fitted with a third pair of Cummins, she became the centrepiece of Villa Camanda summers.

The year ended sadly. On the evening of Saturday, 14 December, Whitney received a phone call from a sombre Jerry – Dorothy had felt poorly that morning and stayed in bed, and when he and their son Bill returned from a school Christmas dinner, they found she had died, aged 81. Daphne and Camilla joined Whitney two days later for her funeral at St Mary's Church, Dartington, and cremation in Torquay. Whitney, not normally a fan of funerals, found the day very moving, but he was less impressed by his mother's memorial service in January: 'a mixture of Dartington long hair and rather bad church procedure – a dreary cello played Bach in hoarse tones.'[11]

Late in the evening of 4 February 1969, Whitney took a phone call from John Stonehouse, Postmaster General in Harold Wilson's government. The Post Office was to be nationalised, and he wanted Whitney to become its first chairman. Whitney was flattered: alongside his long-term directorship at Midland Bank, this would give him an enviable profile in the City. It would also give him an honourable way out of Rolls-Royce. He had told himself for years that the company was in danger of going bust and that he must leave before that happened, yet now he felt a growing commitment, and a sense of responsibility as pressure grew to deliver the RB211 on schedule. Kindersley had stepped back, and Pearson was now chair as well as managing director, something Whitney had never supported, but Pearson seemed to want more of him and he was keen to do more. Even Stonehouse's blandishments of a knighthood followed by a peerage did not move him – 'gongs' had long since stopped being of any importance to him.

Whitney concluded that another deputy chairmanship might be possible, provided that Archie Forbes, his chairman at Midland Bank, approved. Giro Bank would be a subsidiary of the newly incorporated Post Office. It had been set up the previous autumn as a retail bank, the first to employ optical character recognition in its processing, and using Post Office counters instead of branches. Whitney received Forbes' assurance that taking the Post Office role would not represent a conflict of interest, on which basis he agreed to become one of two deputy chairmen. Viscount Hall, a qualified surgeon who had moved into business during his time with Powell Duffryn, the coal mine and seaport group, was appointed chairman, and William Ryland, formerly managing director of Telecommunications, was made chief executive and the second deputy chairman.

Vesting Day, the date on which the Post Office went from being a government department to a publicly owned corporation, was set for 1 October 1969, and by then Whitney was already looking at the loss-making Giro Bank, to establish whether it could operate successfully in such a competitive market. He reported that its current executive team – three Post Office members and three non-Post Office members reporting into Geoffrey

Vieler, who also sat on the Post Office Board as MD, Posts and Giro – was appropriate but that its marketing needed to be strengthened. Giro Bank was in negotiations with finance house Mercantile Credit about providing an unsecured personal loan product that would sit alongside its current account, and Whitney felt confident about its future.

He also turned his attention to the new organisation's many brands, from the Post Office and Telecommunications to Royal Mail and Girobank, and sought to bring a corporate conformity to them. He set up a Design Advisory Committee, and invited his old friend Hugh Casson and Sir Paul Reilly, long-term director at the Council of Industrial Design, to sit on it with him, together with senior marketing, public relations and design representatives from each Post Office division. They established a brief for a visual design programme and invited four consultancy firms to pitch for the business. A design and typography house called Banks and Mills was chosen, and embarked on a decade-long project to devise an integrated set of identities across the group. Central to the work was the creation of a unique double-line alphabet, a version of which can still be seen on Royal Mail vans fifty years later.

Edward Heath's Conservative party won a narrow majority in the June 1970 election, and the new Minister of Posts and Telecommunications, Christopher Chataway, decided to replace Hall with Ryland, who was in due course awarded the knighthood that could have been Whitney's. Ryland asked Whitney to take full responsibility for Girobank, but this would have meant stepping down from Midland's board and Whitney was not prepared to do this. He was content for his Post Office work to be confined to weekly conference calls with Ryland, chairmanship of the Design Advisory Committee and attendance at board meetings.

Meanwhile, at Rolls-Royce, problems with the RB211 were mounting. Soon after the contract was signed, Lockheed requested that the mounting point of the engine be moved, arguing that this would lighten the overall weight of the Tristar. This necessitated numerous detail changes to the engine, but the work was undertaken at no extra charge. The Hyfil fan blades failed a bird impact test, then an open-air test bed suffered a failure so serious that the fan disk and shaft assembly flew out of the engine and landed 60 yards away. Heavier, more expensive titanium blades had to be adopted. There were concerns over fuel consumption and vibrations, and test running fell behind schedule.

In November 1969, Tom Metcalfe, RB211 Programme Director, wrote to Huddie:

> I am convinced that unless we take some very special steps right away, we will not have an engine that works at all, we will be seriously late in deliveries, and eventually we will be the cause of delay to the aircraft programme and the aircraft deliveries to the airlines.[12]

Quite what Huddie did with this information is not clear – Pearson claimed later that he did not see Metcalfe's report until Rolls-Royce was in receivership. In February 1970, Whitney requested a meeting directly with Huddie and established the truth for himself: 'I only hope that we don't get landed without the right engine – this is really the test for RR and if we fail there will be no further engine business in the US.'[13]

By July, it was concluded that delivery of the engine to Lockheed at the specified thrust and on schedule was no longer possible. Worse, launch costs had grown to almost £150 million, an increase of £20 million in just three months, barely leaving any margin in the deal. That same month, Huddie was obliged to take extended sick leave, and never returned to the company. Sir Ronnie Melville, who had enjoyed a long career in Whitehall focused on aviation, and at the time was permanent secretary at the short-lived Ministry of Aviation Supply, took Whitney to lunch. He had concluded that Pearson could no longer steer Rolls-Royce through the crisis, and sounded Whitney out about taking over. Whitney replied that he was willing to consider this, but only if the corporate troubleshooter Ian Morrow came on board.

By the autumn, it was clear to Whitney that he was no longer being considered as a replacement for Pearson, but he still had a significant role to play. He met with Morrow on 1 October and told him frankly that Pearson must go, yet left the meeting far from clear that Morrow should replace him. Prompted by an increasingly worried Archie Forbes, Whitney arranged for Pearson to meet both of Rolls-Royce's principal bankers, Midland and Lloyds. On 27 October, after the briefest of board meetings in Derby, he accompanied Pearson back to London, preparing him for the worst: 'The state of tension is considerable.'[14] At the Bank of England the next day, the two men met with the governor, Sir Leslie O'Brien, who informed Pearson that his chairmanship of Rolls-Royce 'was no longer acceptable'.[15] On 11 November, with Lord Cole, formerly the long-term chairman of international conglomerate Unilever, poised to become chairman and Morrow managing director, Whitney was at Lazards when 'Jim Pearson handed over the chair and with it his life ambitions – and with a permanent black mark against his name.'[16]

Into the new year, the pressure on Whitney was growing intolerable. At the Post Office, he tried in vain to prevent a strike. He admired both his chairman, Bill Ryland, and the general secretary of the Union of Post Office Workers, Tom Jackson, but felt they were on a collision course. In a time of high inflation, Jackson was demanding a 15 per cent pay rise for his members, Ryland was offering 7 per cent and Whitney argued through two board meetings that a 10 per cent offer would avoid a strike. He found himself in a minority of one on both occasions, and on 20 January Jackson led all 230,000 UPW members out on a ruinous strike, the longest since the General Strike of 1925. Their resolve finally collapsed on 8 March without resolution, but two months later a Commission of Enquiry awarded them a rise of 9 per cent, backdated to 1 January.

Worse, the new executive team at Rolls-Royce were unable to reverse Rolls-Royce's fortunes, and on 4 February, after Heath and the US president Richard Nixon had discussed the implications on the phone, Rupert Nicholson of Peat Marwick McLintock was called in as receiver. He met with the directors for a working lunch that same day, noting that Whitney appeared 'extremely sullen'.[17] Whitney's mood was no better on 9 February, when Nicholson joined a board meeting chaired by Morrow: 'This great company is being run by nobody – Ian Morrow may be an expert juggler with accounts but he is not a leader in any way.'[18]

It seems likely that Whitney was unaware of the most pressing issue at this point. Heath's government was willing to break its principles and rescue Rolls-Royce's Aero Engine Division, but only to ensure that the company's defence contracts were honoured. Indeed, Defence Minister Lord Carrington brusquely informed Nicholson that he must repudiate the RB211 contract altogether. Nicholson did nothing of the sort, ringing Lockheed's chairman, Dan Houghton, the next day to assure him that RB211 research, development and testing continued apace. On 11 February, while Archie Forbes was refusing to accept Whitney's letter of resignation from Midland's board, Frederick Corfield, Minister of Aviation Supply, was in the House of Commons, giving the Rolls-Royce (Purchase) Bill its second reading. The government would form a new company to acquire Rolls-Royce's aero-engine and defence interests from Nicholson.

On 22 February, Lord Cole informed Whitney that there would be no place for him in the new company and that he had to leave, but Whitney took the precaution of phoning Nicholson, who told him 'to do nothing precipitate'.[18] Sure enough, just two days later, Cole learned that he could not be chairman of both the new aero-engine company and the company in receivership, and he asked Whitney to take formal responsibility for steering the car and diesel operations into liquidation. Whitney's old sense of responsibility kicked in. There were shareholders to consider, and 8,500 employees. There was danger of a run on Derbyshire Building Society, where many employees held their savings. He accepted the unpaid role without hesitation.

It took more than a month for Whitney's depression to lift, with him of the opinion, 'I am now just chairman of a rotting corpse',[19] but as he formed a clearer understanding of his objectives and how to meet them, so his spirit returned. His immediate responsibility was to chair an Extraordinary General Meeting on 19 April. Ostensibly, its purpose was to seek shareholders' agreement to a Department of Trade investigation into the collapse of the company. But the meeting would be shareholders' first opportunity to air their grievances, and Whitney knew full well that it would be a most trying day: 'This will have to be impeccable and there are so many possible snags – I have to be very clear cut about the drill ... and I will have to be on good form and precise.'[20]

He was expecting 100 shareholders to attend, but six times that number squeezed into Covent Garden's Connaught Rooms. To his right sat Pearson, the man he blamed for Rolls-Royce's collapse, and company secretary J.W. Reader Harris. Doc Smith sat on his left. The vote for a DoT enquiry was never in doubt, simply because of the volume of proxy votes from institutional shareholders, but Whitney was obliged to answer questions for 90 minutes, and found the meeting 'my worst ordeal'.[21] Over lunch the following week, he readily agreed to Nicholson's proposal that he should take on the chairmanship of Rolls-Royce Motors, but it soon emerged that the decision taken at the EGM prevented this: all the original company's directors, including Whitney, would be interviewed by the DoT investigators, and unless and until they were cleared of any responsibility, they could not serve on the board of either company.

Liquidation

Rolls-Royce Motors began trading without Whitney that same week. Ian Frazer, director general of the Takeover Panel, was appointed its chairman in the autumn. Whitney would have permitted himself a wry chuckle had he known of Frazer's initial conversation with Nicholson. When Frazer said he knew nothing about cars, Nicholson replied, 'We don't want an engineer. We've got plenty of those.'[22] In mid-May, after days of meetings between the directors of the new company, Lockheed, TWA, Eastern Airlines, Delta and Air Canada, and agreement between the Heath and Nixon administrations that the US government would guarantee the loan needed by Lockheed, a deal was done that increased the price of each RB211 engine purchased by Lockheed by more than 30 per cent. At midnight on 22 May, Rolls-Royce (1971) began trading.

Whitney had just one act left to perform for the old company. On 4 October, he went back to the Connaught Rooms to chair the meeting sending it into liquidation. Again, he faced a barrage of questions from irate shareholders, and even a proposal to reconstruct the company rather than liquidate it. 'I had a terrible day' recorded Whitney, 'but ran things well, and from RR's point of view a successful exercise – but death for me, and the end of a constructive life.'[23]

On Sunday 24 October, he cleared out his office at Conduit Street and, after dusting the cupboards and shelves, he permitted himself a single drink, musing on whether he had wasted the last sixteen years of his career. The following day, he dropped his company car off and gave substantial presents to his administrative staff and to Hanshaw, who was also leaving Rolls-Royce. Nicholson marked the role Whitney had played in the orderly creation of new directions for the various Rolls-Royce operations by hosting a lunch for him, and he was granted Companionship of the Royal Aircraft Establishment. But as he left Conduit Street for the last time, he knew that the door was closing on twenty-five years on the front line of civil aviation.

Other players in the drama seemed to fare better. Cole and Morrow were each awarded a knighthood two years later. Pearson maintained his belief that an engineering education was the best preparation for management, serving on the universities/industry joint committee of the Confederation of British Industry. Huddie's health recovered. In old age he summed up perhaps the most catastrophic corporate failure in British history thus: 'We had promised a bit more than we could perform. Things were not deplorable. Flight engines were four months late. Four months is four months but it is not deplorable. The deplorable thing was the cost ... The accountants never got cash flow into our heads.'[24]

When Lockheed left the civil aviation market after building 250 Tristars, Rolls-Royce continued to manufacture RB211 engines for both the aviation and industrial sectors. Its derivative, the Trent, has become the most successful aero-engine family in history. At the time of writing, the company, which returned to the London stock market as Rolls-Royce plc in 1987, enjoys a market capitalisation of £48 billion and a one-third market share of the large aero engines in service, worldwide. Rolls-Royce Motors endured a more difficult recovery. It floated as early as 1973, but Tony Benn's threat of renationalisation hurt the issue, and underwriters were obliged to take most of the shares. The company was acquired by engineering firm Vickers in 1980, and it was not until 1988 that a complex set of agreements was put in place whereby Vickers disposed of Rolls-Royce Motors; Rolls-Royce plc received £40 million for permitting luxury cars to be built by BMW as Rolls-Royces; and Volkswagen acquired the right to manufacture and sell Bentleys.

As for Whitney, he still had what most would have considered an enviable portfolio career, with positions on the Midland Bank and Post Office boards, and Airways Union continuing to enjoy success at Weston. The nearby factory at Filton, now operated by British Aircraft Corporation, was under pressure to meet production deadlines on Concorde, and Airways Union provided a working party of twenty operatives each day, including an inspector and a foreman. A most ironic piece of sub-contract work came in a little later, to manufacture acoustic side panels for an aero engine – the RB211.

Yet Whitney remained mired in depression. Some eight months after the Rolls-Royce liquidation meeting, he wrote, 'Pretty clearly, I have come to the end of my life. It is now a question of tidying up and keeping what I have left.'[25] His drinking became more of a problem. Daphne and Amanda spoke to him regularly about it, and Camilla wrote him a stern letter, but none of them were able to stop him adding a shot of vodka to his morning orange juice. Disk trouble landed him back in the King Edward VII hospital at the beginning of 1972, and that autumn he started to retch and vomit in the mornings. Every doctor he consulted told him to give up alcohol, yet he could not. A sure sign that he was losing his discipline came when he gave up on the diary he had written up each day since the war.

At least the reduction in his workload enabled him to spend more time with the family at Villa Camanda, although his 'spring maintenance' visit of 1973 almost ended in disaster. Completing his tasks early, he was able to book the only seat left on a BEA flight from Palma to Heathrow. The Iberia flight he was scheduled to be on the next morning collided over Nantes with a second Spanish airliner. This aircraft sustained minor damage to a wing and landed safely, but the Iberia plane exploded, killing all sixty-eight passengers and crew. Someone suggested to Whitney that God had been on his side and that he should renounce his atheism. His curt reply was that God had not been on the side of the sixty-eight!

Summers at the villa became extended family affairs. Whitney enjoyed Camilla and Mikey bringing their daughters: 'It is great fun to have them, and they are wonderful children of whom I am very proud – I really am so very lucky with my wife and family when one looks at all the disasters in other people's lives – mine on balance has been remarkably successful.'[26] Jerry was another regular visitor in the early 1970s, and Whitney was delighted when his stepfather told him that he was to remarry and move to sunnier climes permanently. Sue Isaacs had been a Dartington pupil in the 1930s and had come to know Jerry and Dorothy well when she became the school's consultant child psychologist. She and Jerry were to move to the US, where she had taken a position at the University of Southern California. 'Daphne and I send warmest congratulations to you on your forthcoming marriage,' wrote Whitney. 'This is a good thing, and we hope that you both will be very happy for many years to come.'[27] Jerry used his remaining time well, writing a slim volume called *The Straight and Its Origins* about his time at Cornell and his early encounters with Dorothy. He died just weeks after submitting the manuscript, and his ashes were brought back to Dartington and interred alongside those of Dorothy.

Whitney's contract with the Post Office was due to expire in July 1974, but February's general election was such a close-run thing – Labour won just four more seats than the Conservatives and formed a minority government – that another election was considered an inevitability. Just days before Whitney was due to leave, Tony Benn, now Secretary of State for Industry, asked him to stay on until the end of the year. Sure enough, when Labour emerged from the October election with the slimmest of majorities, Benn had another word with him, and he stepped down in December. His departure was positioned as retirement, but the 62-year-old Whitney looked forward to another eight years before reaching Midland Bank's automatic retiring age. For almost twenty years now, he had found every board meeting stimulating, and he had been grateful for Archie Forbes' support of him over Rolls-Royce's collapse (similarly, the DoT inspectors found no fault on his part when they reported their findings). In the spring of 1975, Forbes stepped down as chairman and was replaced by William Armstrong, recently made a life peer for his work as head of the Civil Service. He and his wife Gwendoline were friends of Whitney and Daphne, and Whitney came to enjoy his association with Midland Bank all the more.

In 1978, he called time on Airways Union. As fewer aircraft came to be manufactured and maintained in Britain, so the mainstay of the company's business dried up. It diversified into all manner of metalwork, including the manufacture of prams for mother-and-toddler retailer Mothercare, but the final straw came when the Civil Aviation Authority informed Whitney that the runway required resurfacing, at a cost of £150,000. He issued redundancy notices on his ten remaining staff and terminated the lease on Weston Airport. His life as an entrepreneur, which had begun in the heady days of 1935, was at an end.

That autumn, Whitney noticed a significant deterioration in his eyesight, and he learned that he had cataracts in both eyes. In September, he went into London's famous eye hospital, Moorfields, to have the more damaged eye repaired. Only when the results of the operation could be confirmed would a decision be taken on whether he needed a procedure on his other eye. The treatment was judged a success and Whitney was discharged after four days, having cheerfully demolished the bowl of fruit Armstrong had sent to him with Midland Bank's best wishes.

In the new year, it was decided that Whitney would have the same procedure on his other eye, and that this time it would take place at the Wellington Hospital, on the north-west corner of Regent's Park. He would check in on the afternoon of Friday, 16 February, and have the operation the next day. Before leaving The Aviary, he dictated a letter to Brenda Farrell, his private secretary since leaving Rolls-Royce. He was keen to explain the procedure to his sister Biddy, recent winner of the Best Supporting Actress Oscar for her performance in the movie *Network*. After complaining about what would become known as the Winter of Discontent, with rubbish piling up on snow-covered streets because of a binmen's strike, he told her, 'I shall be out on Sunday, fully implanted!'[28]

His doctor was less optimistic, advising that a chest cold meant that the operation should be postponed, but Whitney would not hear of it: he wanted his sight fully restored.

By the time Biddy read her brother's letter, he was critically ill. The eye procedure had gone well, but when Whitney was brought round from the anaesthetic, it was found that his chest cold had developed into double pneumonia. He was rushed by ambulance from the Wellington to the Charing Cross Hospital in Fulham, and placed in an iron lung in intensive care. Daphne and the family were warned that the situation was grave, and to expect that Whitney would need to remain in the iron lung for two weeks. In fact, twenty days passed before he was first removed from the machine, then promptly placed back in it because he found breathing on his own so exhausting.

On 28 March, almost six weeks after the operation, he was oblivious to the news from Westminster. Harold Wilson's successor as prime minister, James Callaghan, had lost a vote of no confidence, and an election had been called for 3 May. Whitney had been born at the conclusion of a US presidential election, and would continue his fight for life during a UK general election campaign. Two days later, Airey Neave, Margaret Thatcher's shadow Northern Ireland Secretary, and the man who as head of MI9 had supported Whitney's escape from captivity during the war, was assassinated by a car bomb planted by the Irish National Liberation Army. There seemed no end to the sadness, but over the next few days Whitney rallied. A second attempt to take him off the lung machine was more successful, he grew in strength and on 3 April he was moved from intensive care to a private room. The hope was that he would be home for the Easter weekend, two weeks away.

On the evening of 5 April, Daphne took a phone call from the hospital. Whitney had been found, slumped and unconscious, outside his room. He had suffered a heart attack, and been rushed back into intensive care. Daphne rang Amanda, who was at a dinner party on the other side of London, then left for the hospital. Amanda remembers nothing of her mad-dash drive across town, but when she arrived she took up vigil in the intensive care waiting room while her mother took a short break. As she anxiously paced up and down, Amanda found herself looking out of one window and in through another, and realised she was watching medics fighting to save her father's life. Then she watched them stop working on him. As Daphne rejoined her and the intensive care doors swung open, she already knew the worst. Whitney was dead.

One of the first letters of condolence to arrive at The Aviary was from Isaiah Berlin, who had seen something of the complexities in Daphne's life when she worked for him in New York and there were effectively four people in her marriage. 'Dearest and best friend,' she replied, 'I have to answer your dear little letter at once as it touched me so deeply and in which all you said about my dear Whitney was all true. Only you, I think, understood my feelings for him, and realised as I went through those difficult war days that there never was and never could be anyone else for me.'[29]

19

A Good Sport and Afraid of Nothing

When Whitney left for England aged 13, he did not take his father's 'if anything should happen to me' letter with him. He did not visit Willard's grave, or read Herbert Croly's biography of his father, until he was 40. It seems he grew up unaware of the advice Willard left him, and yet the emotions that swept over him that day in the military cemetery in Suresnes – 'deeply moved and somehow conscious of some spiritual element – wish he had survived'[1] – point to a certain bond between father and son, one of moral courage and a sense of obligation.

The loss of his father at just 6 affected Whitney profoundly. He developed such a decidedly English stiff upper lip, years before Jerry ever thought of 'the English experiment', that Dorothy was oblivious to his grief and the way he bottled up his emotions. A New York upbringing in which his closest friends were his future stepfather and his tutor, followed by the four years he spent as Dartington's oldest junior, left him with a lifelong inability to form male friendships – only Dick Seaman, Max Aitken and Hugh Casson penetrated the wall he formed around himself, and he lost Dick before he was 27.

Whitney's unique education at The Lincoln and Dartington, where he mixed easily with children of all classes, served him well in adulthood in one respect. Even if the perception in others that he had been born with a silver spoon in his mouth preceded him throughout his various careers, he was able to disabuse that notion in an instant, and he enjoyed cordial relations with the shopfloor workers and trade union representatives he worked with throughout his BOAC and Rolls-Royce years. Had the advice he gave to his fellow Post Office directors been followed in the early weeks of 1971, Britain's longest industrial strike for forty-six years may have been avoided.

A similar presumption perhaps affected some observers' reactions to Whitney's startling arrival in motor sport. No other teenager could have afforded Tim Birkin's Maserati, yet the very fact that he was immediately able to go faster in it than Birkin demonstrated that here was a rare talent indeed. Nor was he content merely to enjoy regular success at Brooklands and Shelsley Walsh. From the outset, he wanted to escape the club atmosphere of British motor racing and go head to head with Europe's finest. His timing was unfortunate – the best car he could spend his mother's money on, the 8CM Maserati, was no match for those of Mercedes, Auto Union and Alfa Romeo – but even in those two brief seasons of full-time racing, he established a legitimate claim to being Europe's finest independent driver, and second only to Enzo Ferrari as a privateer team entrant.

Whitney's unique, multi-faceted vision of bringing flying to the middle classes, incorporating municipal aerodromes, flying clubs, short-haul airlines and a light aircraft developed to his own specification, achieved real substance in just four years. The Ministry of Civil Aviation fully supported his objectives and how he went about them, and only war brought his efforts to a halt. He may have needed his mother's financial support, but as aviation writer Lewis Selby put it at the time, 'If only everybody with a fortune would make something so constructive out of their lives, the world would be a better place.'[2]

War was the making of Whitney. At Dartington, one of his first teachers, the prescient Wyatt Rawson, thought that he would 'always find it difficult to unify his impulses'.[3] At Tangmere eleven years later, Whitney effectively defined those impulses when he looked beyond the war and wondered what he might do with his life. 'Shall I become an adventurer, buccaneering through life, living as my pleasure dictates and riding roughshod over people? I'm strongly inclined towards this, but I feel I have a power inside of me to do good in this world which it is my duty above all else to honour.'[4] It was the buccaneer in him that made him demand 'a nasty job somewhere'[5] from the Air Ministry, and end up being shipped home from Norway, deaf and with a wound in his back the size of a fist. It was the buccaneer in him that led him to take on a destroyer and flak ships with no bombers in attendance, and get shot down.

But, through the year as Senior British Officer in Saint-Hippolyte and Fort de la Revère, and the two-and-a-half years in command of 216 Group, a sense of responsibility and that power to do good by his adoptive country kicked in, and Whitney emerged from the war ready to run BOAC. Throughout his tenure there, Whitney never wavered in his single-minded objective to create and maintain a national airline to be proud of, capable of competing on the world stage against America's finest carriers. Again and again, he went up against his own chairman and successive governments, arguing his case coherently and objectively, and often winning – but all the while being marginalised. At BOAC too, his timing was off – how he would have excelled as chairman of the privatised British Airways in the 1980s and '90s.

Sadly, Whitney was unable to be so objective about his route out of BOAC. BEA and Sholto Douglas would at the very least have provided a safe haven in troubled times, but he paid a heavy price for failing to perform due diligence on Rolls-Royce. His understanding upon joining the company (even if Lord Hives had meant no such thing) was that he would, in the fullness of time, become its chairman. He should have left the company as soon as it became clear to him that Jim Pearson would in due course succeed Lord Kindersley as chairman, in addition to being chief executive. Whitney had always been uneasy about the two most senior executive offices of a great company being held by the same person.

But he did not leave, even when, after barely eighteen months with Rolls-Royce, he first recorded that the company was heading for disaster. To this point, throughout his post-war career as an industrialist, he had managed to unify his impulses. Now, unable to exert influence over the direction of Rolls-Royce, he complained only in the privacy of his diary about what was happening to the company; he enjoyed being deputy chairman, his Conduit Street office and his chauffeur-driven car; and he became something of a part-time buccaneer, embarking on affairs, trans-Saharan expeditions and adventurous boat voyages. Worse, as he struggled with those conflicting impulses, he found solace in drink. John Stonehouse's repeated offers of the chairmanship of the newly incorporated Post Office through the spring of 1969 gave him one last chance to quit Rolls-Royce with dignity. Instead, he watched on as the company went into receivership, his sense of responsibility only re-emerging when he stayed on to chair the shareholders' meetings assigning the non-aero-engine businesses to liquidation. For the only time in his life, he felt a profound sense of failure. It is no exaggeration to say that it killed him.

Whitney chose his own path in life. His family were socialists, and his brother, for a time, a communist. His own political inclinations were right of centre, yet he preferred working with Labour ministers. Michael was instructed to return to the US and Biddy chose to pursue her acting career there, but Whitney alone decided to make England his permanent home. Taking British citizenship may, in part, have been prompted by the need for Straight Corporation to enjoy simpler administration of its aircraft fleet, but he already felt the deepest of attachments to Britain, and he served his adopted country with distinction over four decades, in peace and war.

Clearly, one particular piece of advice his father left for him, 'Save yourself ... that you may go clean and unashamed to her who will be your wife',[6] went unheeded even by the teenage Whitney; yet another of Willard's instructions, 'Treat all women with real chivalry',[7] came entirely naturally to him. Whitney and Daphne found perfect life partners in one another, and could never imagine being married to anyone else. He was as open and honest with the other great loves of his life – Marcelle, Diana and Claudine – as he was with Daphne. The terms on which each of these relationships were based were largely his, yet each woman accepted them and loved him unconditionally.

The last word goes to young Charlie Potter, one of the little boys who took part in Whitney's war games on the beach in the summer of 1918. As he told his mother, 'Whitney Straight was a good sport and afraid of nothing'.[8]

Notes

Chapter 1: New York

1. W.A. Swanberg, *Whitney Father, Whitney Heiress* (Charles Scribner's Sons, 1980).
2. Division of Rare and Manuscript Collections, Cornell University Library, Dorothy Whitney Straight Elmhirst papers, #3725, Dorothy Whitney, letter to Willard Straight, 17 November 1909.
3. Ibid.
4. Cornell, #3725, Dorothy Straight's diary, 4 February 1913.
5. Cornell, #3725, Dorothy Straight, letter to Willard Straight, 13 July 1913.
6. Peter Pennoyer and Anne Walker, *The Architecture of Delano & Aldrich* (W.W. Norton & Company, 2003).
7. Swanberg, *Whitney Father, Whitney Heiress*.
8. Cornell, #3725, Willard Straight, letter to Whitney, 17 April 1918.
9. Ibid.
10. Cornell, #3725, Whitney, letter to Willard Straight, 29 March 1918.
11. Cornell, #3725, Willard Straight, postcard to Whitney, undated.
12. Cornell, #3725, Dorothy Straight, letter to Willard Straight dictated by Whitney, 1 July 1918.
13. Cornell, #3725, Dorothy Straight, letter to Willard Straight dictated by Whitney, 5 July 1918.
14. Cornell, #3725, Dorothy Straight, letter to Willard Straight, 6 August 1918.
15. Cornell, #3725, Dorothy Straight, letter to Willard Straight, 4 August 1918.
16. Ibid.
17. Ibid.
18. Cornell, #3725, Willard Straight, letter to Dorothy Straight, 6 August 1918.
19. Cornell, #3725, Willard Straight, letter to Whitney, Beatrice and Michael Straight, 18 July 1918.
20. Cornell, #3725, Willard Straight, letter to Whitney, 6 November 1918.
21. Cornell, #3725, Willard Straight, letter to Dorothy Straight, 4–11 November 1918.
22. Cornell, #3725, Willard Straight, letter to Dorothy Straight, 13–14 October 1918.

23. Cornell, #3725, Willard Straight, letter to Dorothy Straight, 11–17 November 1918.
24. Jane Brown, *Angel Dorothy: How an American Progressive Came to Devon* (Unbound, 2017).
25. www.cdc.gov/flu/pandemic-resources/1918-pandemic-h1n1.html.
26. Cornell, #3725, Willard Straight, letter to Whitney, 10 December 1917.

Chapter 2: After Willard

1. 'Bishop Brent's Remarks at the Grave of Willard Straight, *The New Republic*, 11 January 1919.
2. Cornell, #3725, Willard Straight, undated letter to Whitney, postmarked 11 December 1918.
3. Ibid.
4. Cornell, #3725, Louisa Weinstein, letter to George Bennett, 1 January 1919.
5. Elmer Davis, 'Four-Year-Old Educational Experiment', *New York Times*, 28 August 1921.
6. Devon Heritage Centre, Papers of Leonard Knight Elmhirst, LKE/DWE, Personal letters, Dorothy Straight, letter to Leonard Elmhirst, 7 November 1924.
7. Ibid.
8. Cornell, #3725, Dorothy Straight's diary, 19 July 1919.
9. Ibid., 30 July 1919.
10. Ibid., 5 September 1919.
11. Michael Young with Anthea Williams and Robin Johnson, *The Elmhirsts of Dartington* (Dartington Hall Trust, 1996).
12. Ibid.
13. Cornell, #3725, Willard Straight, letter to Whitney, 6 November 1918.
14. Michael Straight, *After Long Silence* (W.W. Norton and Company, 1985).
15. Cornell, #3725, Willard Straight's final will, 26 June 1917.
16. Leonard Elmhirst, *The Straight and Its Origin* (Willard Straight Hall, 1975).
17. Jane Brown, *Angel Dorothy: How an American Progressive Came to Devon* (Unbound, 2017).
18. Dartington Hall Trust Archives, LKE/FAM/24, Leonard Elmhirst, letter to Whitney, 21 August 1919.
19. Ibid.
20. Devon Heritage Centre, LKE/DWE, Dorothy Straight, letter to Leonard Elmhirst, 14 August 1923.
21. Devon Heritage Centre, LKE/DWE, Dorothy Straight, letter to Leonard Elmhirst, 17 August 1924.
22. Devon Heritage Centre, LKE/DWE, Dorothy Straight, letter to Leonard Elmhirst, 2 September 1924.
23. Ibid.
24. Devon Heritage Centre, LKE/DWE, Leonard Elmhirst, letter to Dorothy Straight, 6 March 1925.
25. Devon Heritage Centre, DWE, Dorothy Elmhirst's diary, 30 May 1925.
26. Ibid.
27. Devon Heritage Centre, LKE/DWE, letter to Leonard Elmhirst, 7 November 1925.

28. Ibid.
29. Ibid.
30. Devon Heritage Centre, DWE, Dorothy Elmhirst's travel diary, America to Dartington Hall, 19 May 1926.

Chapter 3: Dartington

1. Devon Heritage Centre, T/DHS/A/5/F, *Outline of an Educational Experiment* (Dartington Hall, 1926).
2. Devon Heritage Centre, T/DHS/A/5/E, *Prospectus* (Dartington Hall, 1926).
3. Ibid.
4. Devon Heritage Centre, T/DWE/LKE/DWE/11, Dorothy Straight, letter to Leonard Elmhirst, 17 August 1924.
5. Devon Heritage Centre, T/DHS/A/5/E, *Prospectus*.
6. Devon Heritage Centre, T/DHS/A/1/A, Minutes of conference chaired by Eduard Lindeman, 11–15 September 1926.
7. Ibid.
8. Ibid.
9. Ibid.
10. Ibid.
11. Ibid.
12. Ibid.
13. Devon Heritage Centre, DWE/G/S7/E/007, Dorothy Elmhirst, 'Early Days of Dartington Hall School' notebook, 1926.
14. Ibid.
15. Dartington Hall Trust, T/DHS/N/1/554, Dartington Hall School pupil file, Whitney's school report, 7 April 1927.
16. Devon Heritage Centre, T/DHS/A/1/C, Leonard Elmhirst, 'Report on Educational Experiment, Dartington Hall, September to December 1926', 16 December 1926.
17. Devon Heritage Centre, T/DHS/A/1/F, Early School Rules, undated.
18. Devon Heritage Centre, T/DHS/A/1/C, Dr S.R. Williams, 'Observations, Criticisms and Suggestions', May 1930.
19. Ibid.
20. Ibid.
21. Devon Heritage Centre, T/DHS/A/3/F, Dorothy Elmhirst, letter to Vic Elmhirst, 29 March 1929.
22. Devon Heritage Centre, T/DHS/A/1/G, Frederick Bonser and Virginia Bonser, 'Observations and Suggestions Relative to the Educational Experiment At Dartington Hall, June 1 – June 20 1928', 20 June 1928.
23. Ibid.
24. Devon Heritage Centre, T/DHS/A/1/G, Dorothy Elmhirst, letter to Mrs Bonser, 30 July 1928.
25. Devon Heritage Centre, T/DHS/N/1/554, Whitney's school report, week ending 28 September 1928.
26. Ibid., week ending 20 October 1928.
27. Ibid.

28. Devon Heritage Centre, T/DHS/A/1/B, Wyatt Rawson, remarks on Dartington School pupils and their families, 1929.
29. Ibid.
30. Ibid.
31. Teignmouth and Shaldon Museum. Bill Parkhouse personal reminiscences, 20 January 1956.
32. Ibid.
33. Ibid.
34. *Dartington Voice*, No. 28, June 1979.
35. Churchill Archives Centre, Churchill College, Cambridge University, The Papers of Michael Young, GBR/0014/YUNG 10/6/4: 'Audio tape of Phyllis Willmott's oral history interviews with Michael Young about his early life, 1929–33'.
36. *Dartington Voice*, ibid.
37. Devon Heritage Centre, T/DHS/A/2/F, John Wales, 'The Present Position of the School', 1 March 1930.
38. Devon Heritage Centre, T/DHS/A/2/F, John Wales, letter to Dorothy and Leonard Elmhirst, 6 March 1930.
39. Devon Heritage Centre, T.DHS/A/2/F, Leonard Elmhirst, letter to John Wales, 21 March 1930.
40. Young, Williams and Johnson, *The Elmhirsts of Dartington*.
41. Devon Heritage Centre, T/DWE/LKE/DWE/12, Leonard Elmhirst, letter to Dorothy Elmhirst, 7 April 1930.
42. Whitney's diary, 30 July 1950.
43. Young, Williams and Johnson, *The Elmhirsts of Dartington*.
44. Devon Heritage Centre, *Outline of an Educational Experiment*.
45. Devon Heritage Centre, T/DHS/A/1/C, Leslie Burrowes' Report on the Juniors' dancing class, Autumn Term 1928.

Chapter 4: Cambridge or Racing?

1. Dartington Hall Trust, LKE/FAM/34, Donald Guy, letter to Leonard Elmhirst, 30 April 1930.
2. Dartington Hall Trust, LKE/FAM/34, Leonard Elmhirst, letter to E.A. Benyons, St John's College, Cambridge University, 12 June 1930.
3. 'Shelsley Autumn Meeting', 'The Sport' by 'Casque', *Autocar*, 14 September 1934.
4. Brooklands Automobile Racing Club Official Race Card, 3 August 1931.
5. Ibid.
6. 'Scandinavia', 'The Sport' by 'Casque', *Autocar*, 1 January 1932.
7. 'Whitsun at Brooklands', *Motor Sport*, June 1932.
8. 'Mountain Lap Record', 'The Sport' by 'Casque', *Autocar*, 3 June 1932.
9. Trinity College, Cambridge, 'List of Freshmen, 1932'.

Chapter 5: A Brief, Busy Attempt at Both

1. 'Straight's Record', 'Rumblings' by 'Boanerges', *Motor Sport*, May 1933.
2. 'The International Trophy', *Motor Sport*, June 1933.

3. 'The JCC International Trophy', *The Light Car Cyclecar*, 12 May 1933.
4. 'Success Well Merited', 'The Sport' by 'Casque', *Autocar*, 12 May 1933.
5. Eoin Young, 'The Intense Talents of Whitney Straight', *The Bulletin of the Vintage Sports-Car Club*, Autumn 1978.
6. 'Single-handed on an Alfa' 'The Sport' by 'Casque', *Autocar*, 1 September 1933.
7. S.C.H. Davis, *A Racing Motorist: His Adventures at the Wheel in Peace and War* (Ilffe & Sons, 1949).
8. National Motoring Library, Beaulieu, Straight 1/2/3, Whitney, letter to Steve Parry of the Midland Automobile Club, 28 April 1975.
9. 'Whitney Straight', 'Rumblings' by 'Boanerges', *Motor Sport*, August 1933.

Chapter 6: Racing Wins Out

1. 'The Monza Races', *Autocar*, 15 September 1933.
2. 'Shelsley's Record Day', *Autocar*, 6 October 1933.
3. 'Records Fall at Shelsley Walsh', *Motor Sport*, November 1933.
4. Ibid.
5. 'Shelsley's Record Day', *Autocar*, 6 October 1933.
6. British Movietone, 'Record Is Smashed at Shelsley Walsh', www.youtube.com/watch?v=2N0MdYLhDZ4.
7. British Pathé, 'The Famous Shelsley Walsh Hill Climb (1933)', www.youtube.com/watch?v=3yOnD3dcXjw.
8. Ibid.
9. Eoin Young, 'Whitney Straight: Making It Look Easy', *Motor Sport*, February 2002.
10. Dartington Hall Trust, LKE/FAM/34, Donald Guy, letter to Leonard Elmhurst, 30 April 1930.
11. 'The Sport' by 'Casque', *Autocar*, 20 October 1933.
12. Raymond Mays, *Split Seconds: My Racing Years* (G.T. Foulis & Co., 1951).
13. 'Nuvolari at Brooklands', 'Rumblings' by 'Boanerges', *Motor Sport*, November 1933.
14. Dartington Hall Trust, LKE/FAM/34, Leonard Elmhurst, letter to Whitney, 27 October 1933.
15. Ibid.

Chapter 7: The Straight Stable

1. 'Why I drive foreign racing cars' by Whitney, *The Motor*, 5 December 1933.
2. National Motor Museum Reference Library, Beaulieu, Richard Seaman Collection, Seaman/6/32, Whitney, letter to Dick Seaman, 5 March 1934.
3. 'On Road and Track', by 'Grand Vitesse', *The Motor*, 8 May 1934.
4. 'A Four Seconds Win: Whitney Straight Wins International Trophy Race by a Narrow Margin, With Front Tyre in Ribbons', *Autocar*, 4 May 1934.
5. Ibid.

Chapter 8: From Brooklands to Bremgarten

1. Dartington Hall Trust, LKE/FAM/34, Bill Lambert, letter to William Elmhirst, 17 May 1934.
2. 'A Motor Racing Stable' by Whitney, *Mine*, October 1935.
3. 'The Shelsley Record', 'The Sport' by 'Casque', *Autocar*, 15 June 1934.
4. 'Prince Nicholas to Race at Le Mans: Whitney Straight as Partner', *Daily Telegraph*, 9 June 1934.
5. Surrey Historical Centre, 606 / 2 / box 7 / file 10, John Houldsworth inquest, 26 June 1934.
6. 'Driving at 150mph is easy ... says Whitney Straight', *The Motor*, 11 September 1934.

Chapter 9: Facing Facts

1. 'Hugh Caufield Hamilton', *Autocar*, 31 August 1934.
2. Beaulieu, Seaman/6/32, Dick Seaman, letter to Whitney, 28 August 1934.
3. Dartington Hall Trust, LKE/FAM/34, Bill Lambert, letter to Fred Gwatkin, 13 September 1934.
4. 'The Final Meeting', *Autocar*, 19 October 1934.
5. A.F. Rivers Fletcher, *Mostly Motor Racing* (Foulis, 1986).
6. Beaulieu, Straight/1/4, Whitney, letter to Dick Seaman, 1 November 1934.
7. 'Whitney Straight: Making it Look Easy', by Eoin Young, *Motor Sport*, February 2002.
8. 'Straight's Car Tried Out', *Natal Mercury*, 18 December 1934.
9. Whitney's diary, 6 May 1964.
10. Beaulieu, Straight/2/16, unpublished draft by Barré Lyndon, 1935.
11. Beaulieu, Straight/1/5/9, Whitney, letter to Hans Tanner, 24 December 1951.
12. 'A Motor Racing Stable' by Whitney, *Mine*, October 1935.
13. Dartington Hall Trust, LKE/FAM/34, Fred Gwatkin, letter to Leonard Elmhirst, 17 September 1934.
14. Dartington Hall Trust, LKE/FAM/34, Bill Lambert, letter to Fred Gwatkin, 15 September 1934.
15. 'Whitney Straight's Plans, 'Rumblings' by 'Boanerges', *Motor Sport*, December 1934.
16. 'Only German Drivers Need Apply, 'On Road and Track', by 'Grand Vitesse', *The Motor*, 6 November 1934.
17. 'On Road and Track', by 'Grand Vitesse', *The Motor*, 15 January 1935.
18. 'Whitney Straight, Airman', *Autocar*, 29 March 1935.
19. 'Who's Who in Motor Racing', *The Motor*, 16 April 1935.
20. 'Straight's Activities', 'Rumblings', *Motor Sport*, May 1935.
21. 'Mountain Lap Record', 'The Sport' by 'Casque', *Autocar*, 3 June 1932.
22. Raymond Mays, *Split Seconds: My Racing Years* (G.T. Foulis & Co., 1951).
23. 'Looking back on 1934', *Motor Sport*, December 1934.
24. 'Driving at 150mph is easy ... says Whitney Straight', *The Motor*, 11 September 1934.
25. 'Whitney Straight: two legends in his lifetime' by Eoin Young, *Thoroughbred & Classic Cars*, October 1975.

Chapter 10: Daphne

1. *The Times*, 11 April 1935, 'Forthcoming Marriages'.
2. Andrew Lycett, *Ian Fleming* (Weidenfeld & Nicholson, 1995).
3. Nicholas Shakespeare, *Ian Fleming: The Complete Man* (Harvill Secker, 2023).
4. Lilian Beattie-Seaman, *Richard Seaman: His Life and Death* (private manuscript).
5. Bill Elmhirst, conversation with the author, 11 January 2014.
6. Devon Heritage Centre, T/W/8/A, 'An account of the London visit to attend Whitney's wedding of a group of estate employees, written by Anne and Jack Collingbourne'.
7. Ibid.
8. Whitney's diary, 22 January 1950.

Chapter 11: High Flyer

1. *Evening News*, 6 April 1934, 'US Millionaire in King's Cup Air Race'.
2. Beaulieu, Straight/1/4, Whitney, letter to Dick Seaman, 19 August 1935.
3. Beaulieu, Straight/1/4, Dick Seaman, letter to Whitney, 27 July 1935.
4. Dartington Hall Trust, LKE/FAM/34, Osmer Gorton, letter to Dorothy Elmhurst, 4 September 1935.
5. Dartington Hall Trust, LKE/FAM/34, Fred Gwatkin, letter to Leonard Elmhirst, 2 October 1935.
6. Dartington Hall Trust, LKE/FAM/34, Fred Gwatkin, letter to Leonard Elmhirst, 6 October 1935.
7. Dartington Hall Trust, LKE/FAM/34, Whitney, letter to Leonard Elmhirst, 8 October 1935.
8. Dartington Hall Trust, LKE/FAM/34, Leonard Elmhirst, letter to Whitney, 7 February 1936.
9. British Airways Heritage Collection, N247, Railway Air Services superintendent, letter to Sir Harold Hartley, 18 July 1936.
10. Dartington Hall Trust, LKE/FAM/34, Fred Gwatkin, letter to Leonard Elmhirst, 22 July 1936.
11. Charles Gray, letter to Whitney, 13 August 1936.
12. Dartington Hall Trust, LKE/FAM/34, Fred Gwatkin, letter to Whitney, 10 September 1936.
13. Mary de Bunsen, *Mount Up With Wings* (Hutchinson, 1960).
14. Lewis Selby, 'Rough Stuff', *Aeropilot*, September 1937.
15. Devon Air Day souvenir programme, 24 July 1937.
16. Dartington Hall Trust, LKE/FAM/34, Leonard Elmhirst, letter to Whitney, 20 September 1937.
17. Ibid.
18. Dartington Hall Trust, LKE/FAM/34, Fred Gwatkin, letter to Whitney, 2 March 1938.
19. 'The Aerodrome Owners' German Tour', *Straightaway*, No. 9, June 1938.
20. 'Twelve Months Reviewed', *Straightaway*, No. 12, September 1938.
21. Ibid.
22. 'Whitsun Traffic: A World's Record for Western Airways', *Straightaway*, No. 15, June 1939.

23. 'Hard thinking', *Straightaway*, No. 13, April 1939.
24. Dorothy Whitney Straight Elmhirst papers, Willard Straight, letter to Dorothy Straight, 18 July 1918.
25. 'Chamberlain announces Britain is at war with Germany', www.bbc.com/historyofthebbc/anniversaries/september/war-announced.

Chapter 12: War

1. RAF Museum Archives, Whitney's RAF log book, 26 August 1939.
2. Whitney's diary, 23 March 1940.
3. Ibid., 21 March 1940.
4. Ibid., 17 March 1940.
5. Tom Moulson, *The Flying Sword: The Story of 601 Squadron* (Macdonald & Co., 1964).
6. Lord Apsley, 'Western Airways to Close', *Flight*, 11 April 1940.
7. Whitney's diary, 3 May 1940.
8. Ibid.
9. Ibid., 4 June 1940.
10. Dartington Hall Trust, LKE/FAM/34, Whitney, letter to Leonard Elmhirst, undated.
11. Peter Hearn, *Flying Rebel: The Story of Louis Strange* (HMSO, 1994).
12. Whitney's diary, 5 June 1940.
13. Ibid., 16 June 1940.
14. Ibid., 15 July 1940.
15. Ibid., 12 August 1940.
16. Ibid., 16 August 1940.
17. Ibid., 18 August 1940.
18. Royal Archives – Windsor Castle, PS/PSO/GVI/PS/NAVY/04129/28-3C, Sir Alexander Hardinge, letter to Whitney, 4 September 1940, by permission of His Majesty King Charles III.
19. Ibid., Whitney, letter to Air Marshal Leslie Gossage, 20 September 1940, by permission of His Majesty King Charles III.
20. Whitney's diary, 27 August 1940.
21. Moulson, ibid.
22. Young, *The Elmhirsts of Dartington*.
23. Sholto Douglas, *Years of Command* (Collins, 1966).
24. Ibid.
25. Ibid.
26. Whitney's diary, 19 July 1941.
27. Ibid., 23 July 1941.
28. Ibid., 27 July 1941.
29. Ibid., 26 July 1941.
30. Ibid., 30 July 1941.

Chapter 13: Captivity

1. RAF Museum Archives, 'Whitney Straight forced down over France', Air Ministry Bulletin No. 4646, 1 August 1941.

2. Ibid.
3. 'Wing Cdr Whitney Straight Shot Down Over Channel', *The Times*, 1 August 1941.
4. National Archives, WO 208/3309/787, Whitney's debriefs with MI9, 25 and 28 July 1942.
5. Whitney's diary, 30 July 1952.
6. Ibid., 1 August 1952.
7. Ibid.
8. National Archives, WO 208/3309/787, ibid.
9. Whitney's diary, 16 January 1942.
10. Ibid., 15 February 1942.
11. Ibid., 5 March 1942.
12. Ibid.
13. Ibid.
14. Ibid., 6 March 1942.
15. Ibid.
16. Ibid., 18 March 1942.
17. Ibid., 27 March 1942.
18. Ibid., 19 May 1942.
19. Vincent Brome, *The Way Back: The Story of Lieut.-Commander Pat O'Leary, GC, DSO, RN* (The Companion Book Club, 1958).
20. Ronald Stephens, Sue and Andy Parlour, *HMS Tarana: Under Two Flags* (Ten Bells Publishing, 2009).
21. Anthony Deane-Drummond, *Return Ticket* (Collins, 1953).
22. Airey Neave, *Saturday at MI9: The Classic Account of the WWII Allied Escape Organisation* (Pen & Sword, 1969).
23. RAF Museum Archives, Whitney Straight's RAF log book.
24. RAF Museum Archives, 'Record of Service of Air Commodore Whitney Willard STRAIGHT, CBE, MC, DFC'.

Chapter 14: Expanding Horizons

1. The Isaiah Berlin Papers, Bodleian Library, University of Oxford, Isaiah Berlin, letter to Daphne Straight, 26 November 1942.
2. Whitney's diary, 29 August 1942.
3. Ibid., 11 September 1943 (reminiscence on the anniversary of his arrival in Cairo).
4. Ibid.
5. Ibid., 19 October 1942.
6. Ibid., 6 November 1942.
7. Ibid.
8. Ibid., 3 February 1943.
9. Isaiah Berlin Papers, Daphne Straight, letter to Isaiah Berlin, 13 May 1943.
10. National Archives, AIR/25/867, Operations Record Book for Advanced 216 Group, Wing Commander G.G. Cradock-Watson, 30 July 1943.
11. *Dartington Voice*, No. 28, June 1979.
12. National Archives, AIR/25/872, Squadron Leader A.R.H. Downing, 'Brief Summary of 216 Group During Operation "Husky"', 13 August 1943.

13. Ibid.
14. Whitney's diary, 9 September 1943.
15. Ibid., 26 September 1943.
16. Ibid., 17 November 1943.
17. Ibid., 26 November 1943.
18. National Archives, AIR/25/879, Squadron Leader W. Townson, 'Evacuation from Yugoslavia', 4 January 1945.
19. National Archives, AIR/25/881, Squadron Leader W. Townson, 'No. 216 Review of 1944'.
20. 'King George VI's speech on D-Day', www.royal.uk/king-george-vis-speech-d-day.
21. National Archives, AIR/2/9003, 'Decorations, Medals, Honours and Awards (Code B, 30): Birthday Honours list 1944 – higher awards', 'Birthday Honours List – Non-Operational Commands: Summary of Recommendations for the CB'.
22. Whitney's diary, 8 June 1944.
23. Ibid., 26 September 1944.
24. Isaiah Berlin Papers, letter from Daphne Straight to Isaiah Berlin, 18 October 1944.
25. Whitney's diary, 18 January 1945.
26. Ibid., 2 February 1945.
27. Ibid., 3 February 1945.
28. Ibid., 19 February 1945.
29. Ibid., 27 February 1945.
30. Ibid., 3 March 1945.
31. Churchill Archive Centre, CHAR 20/200/59, letter from Whitney Straight to Winston Churchill, 5 March 1945.
32. British Airways Heritage Collection, N247, letter from Railway Air Services superintendent to Sir Harold Hartley, 18 July 1936.
33. Whitney's diary, 5 March 1945.
34. Churchill Archives, CHAR 20/200/62, Winston Churchill, note to Whitney Straight, 10 March 1945.
35. Whitney's diary, 8 May 1945.
36. Ibid.
37. Ibid., 8 March 1945.

Chapter 15: To BOAC, Via BEA

1. Whitney's diary, 1 June 1945.
2. Ibid., 28 July 1945.
3. Ibid.
4. Ibid., 7 November 1945.
5. RAF Museum, Frederick Handley Page papers, Box 219, Straight Corporation correspondence 1942–45, Whitney, letter to Frederick Handley Page, 11 August 1945.
6. Ibid., Frederick Handley Page, letter to Stanley Cox, 15 November 1944.
7. Ibid., Whitney, letter to Frederick Handley Page, 26 January 1945.
8. Whitney's diary, 1 November 1945.
9. British Airways Heritage Collection, N4117, 'Alitalia', Whitney, report to the BEA board, 25 June 1947.

10. Ibid., N4117, 'Greek Company', Whitney, report to the BEA board, 25 June 1947.
11. Ibid., N4034, minutes of BOAC board meeting, 3 July 1947.
12. Ibid., N4056, Sir Harold Hartley, letter to Lord Nathan, 27 November 1947.
13. Whitney's diary, 21 January 1948.
14. Ibid., 1 March 1948.
15. Ibid., 18 January 1948.
16. Ibid., 7 January 1948.
17. Ibid., 9 January 1948.
18. Sir Miles Thomas, *Out on a Wing* (Michael Joseph, 1964).
19. Whitney's diary, 13 January 1948.
20. Hansard, Vol. 447, columns 2137–261, 'Civil Aviation', 26 April 1948.
21. Ibid.
22. Whitney's diary, 23 July 1948.
23. Ibid., 3 July 1948.
24. Thomas, *Out on a Wing*.
25. Ibid.
26. J.E. Morpurgo, *Barnes Wallis: A Biography* (Longman, 1972), quoting Barnes Wallis' letter to Molly Wallis, 23 August 1948.
27. Whitney's diary, 24 September 1948.
28. Ibid., 1 October 1948.
29. Ibid., 31 January 1949.
30. Ibid., 24 February 1949.
31. British Airways Heritage Collection, N4058, 'Chief Executive's Comments on Heads of Agreement dated 22.2.49', memorandum to the BOAC board, 25 February 1949.
32. Ibid., N4058, 'Heads of Agreement, signed by Miles Thomas and John Booth', 22 February 1949.
33. Ibid., N4058, 'Chief Executive's Comments on Heads of Agreement dated 22.2.49', 25 February 1949.
34. Ibid.
35. Ibid.
36. Ibid., N4058, 'Minutes of a Special Board Meeting held on Friday, 25 February 1949'.
37. Whitney's diary, 11 March 1949.
38. Ibid., 12 March 1949.

Chapter 16: Breaking Up

1. British Airways Heritage Collection, N4059, 'Forward Organisation', Harold Hartley's memorandum to the BOAC board, 13 April 1949.
2. Whitney's diary, 3 June 1949.
3. Ibid., 14 June 1949.
4. Ibid., 13 October 1950.
5. Ibid., 6 April 1951.
6. Ibid., 17 June 1951.
7. Ibid., 4 June 1951.
8. Ibid., 29 August 1951.

9. British Airways Heritage Collection, AW/1/6881, Sir Frederick Browning, letter to Whitney, 8 October 1951.
10. Ibid., Lieutenant Michael Parker, letter to Whitney, 9 October 1951.
11. Whitney's diary, 31 January 1952.
12. Ibid., 6 May 1952.
13. Ibid., 5 August 1953.
14. Victoria and Albert Museum Archive of Art and Design, Sir Hugh Casson papers, 1867–2007: AAD/2008/2/1/1/1, Villa at Formetor, Mallorca, 1954: José Alcover, letter to Sir Hugh Casson, 16 September 1954.
15. Whitney's diary, 5 October 1953.
16. Ibid., 13 April 1953.
17. British Airways Heritage Collection, N4068, 'Comments on Chairman's note of 24 June', Whitney Straight.
18. Ibid.
19. Thomas, *Out on a Wing*.
20. Whitney's diary, 17 January 1955.
21. Ibid., 3 March 1955.
22. Ibid., 27 May 1955.
23. Ibid., 1 October 1955.
24. British Airways Heritage Collection, N4070, minutes of BOAC board meeting, 13 October 1955.
25. Thomas, *Out on a Wing*.
26. Ibid.

Chapter 17: Non-Exec

1. Tom Purves, conversation with the author, 27 September 2017.
2. Whitney's diary, 11 November 1955.
3. Whitney's diary, 20 August 1956.
4. Thomas, *Out on a Wing*.
5. HSBC Archives, London, UK GCS-0101, File relating to W. Straight, letter from Kenneth Barber of Midland Bank to Lord Alanbrooke, 5 October 1956.
6. Ibid.
7. Roy Nash, '"Whitney Straight given an airline": airport man's charges denied', *Daily Express*, 7 June 1948.
8. Whitney's diary, 28 June 1957.
9. Ibid., 1 May 1957.
10. Vladimir Kotelnikov and Tony Buttler, *Early Russian Jet Engines: The Nene and Derwent in the Soviet Union, and the evolution of the VK-1* (Rolls-Royce Historical Trust, 2003).
11. Whitney's diary, 22 April 1957.
12. Ibid., 25 July 1959.
13. Ibid., 19 August 1959.
14. Ibid., 7 October 1959.
15. Ibid., 3 November 1959.
16. Ibid.

17. Ibid., 14 July 1959.
18. Michael Bowater, conversation with the author, 15 July 2014.
19. Ibid.
20. Whitney's diary, 2 January 1953.
21. Ibid., 2 July 1961.
22. Royal Geographical Society, WST: Correspondence and papers relating to Socotra and Sahara, 1962–65, 'Sahara, Adventure in the Desert', Brian Branston, *Radio Times*, 10 October 1963.
23. Whitney's diary, 10 February 1963.
24. British Pathé, abridged record of Whitney's television interview at London, Airport, 11 February 1963, 'UK, London: Roy Thomson and Whitney Straight SOF Interviews on Return From Moscow Tour (1963)', www.britishpathe.com/asset/247018.
25. Whitney's diary, 12 February 1963.
26. HSBC Archives London, UK GCS-0059, Verbatim reports of AGMs and EGMs, 1930–1976, 'Proceedings of the one hundred and twenty-seventh annual general meeting of the company, held at the head office, Poultry, London EC2 on Friday, the 15th day of February 1963'.
27. Ibid.
28. Whitney's diary, 30 April 1963.
29. Reproduced with permission of Ian Fleming Publications Ltd, London. *On Her Majesty's Secret Service*, © Ian Fleming Publications Ltd 1963 (www.ianfleming.com).
30. Lilly Library, Indiana University, Russell, L. mss., 1908–1967, Ian Fleming, letter to Whitney, 23 July 1957 © The Ian Fleming Estate.
31. Ibid.
32. Lilly Library, Ian Fleming, letter to Whitney, 10 December 1957 © The Ian Fleming Estate.
33. Reproduced with permission of Ian Fleming Publications Ltd, London. *Goldfinger* © Ian Fleming Publications Ltd 1959 (www.ianfleming.com).
34. Reproduced with permission of Ian Fleming Publications Ltd, London. *Thunderball* © Ian Fleming Publications Ltd 1961 (www.ianfleming.com).

Chapter 18: Liquidation

1. Michael Heseltine, *Life in the Jungle: My Autobiography* (Hodder and Stoughton, 2000).
2. Whitney's diary, 17 April 1962.
3. Ibid., 12 January 1967.
4. Ibid., 14 July 1967.
5. Ibid., 19 February 1968.
6. Rupert Nicholson, *Rolls-Royce Limited: Recollections of the Receiver and Manager* (KPMG, 1993).
7. *Hansard*, Vol. 762, 'Rolls-Royce Ltd (United States Order)', 1 April 1968.
8. Whitney's diary, 14 April 1968.
9. Ibid., 15 February 1968.
10. Whitney's diary, 25 August 1968.

11. Ibid., 21 January 1969.
12. Peter Pugh, *The Magic of a Name: The Rolls-Royce Story, Part Two: The Power Behind the Jets* (Icon Books, 2001), letter from Tom Metcalfe to David Huddie, 28 November 1969.
13. Whitney's diary, 26 February 1970.
14. Ibid., 27 October 1970
15. Ibid., 28 October 1970.
16. Ibid., 11 November 1970.
17. Nicholson, *Rolls-Royce Limited: Recollections of the Receiver and Manager*.
18. Whitney's diary, 22 February 1971.
19. Ibid., 29 March 1971.
20. Ibid., 4 April 1971.
21. Ibid., 19 April 1971.
22. Pugh, *The Magic of a Name: The Rolls-Royce Story, Part Two: The Power Behind the Jets*.
23. Whitney's diary, 4 October 1971.
24. Pugh, *The Magic of a Name: The Rolls-Royce Story, Part Two: The Power Behind the Jets*.
25. Whitney's diary, 27 June 1972.
26. Ibid., 30 July 1974.
27. Dartington Hall Trust, LKE/FAM/34, Whitney Straight, letter to Leonard Elmhirst, 10 November 1972.
28. Beatrice Straight papers, #4496, Division of Rare and Manuscript Collections, Cornell University Library, Whitney Straight, letter to Beatrice Straight, 16 February 1979.
29. The Isaiah Berlin Papers, Bodleian Library, University of Oxford, Daphne Straight, letter to Isaiah Berlin, 9 April, 1979.

CHAPTER 19: A GOOD SPORT AND AFRAID OF NOTHING

1. Whitney's diary, 23 August 1953.
2. Lewis Selby, 'Rough Stuff', *Aeropilot*, September 1937.
3. Devon Heritage Centre, T/DHS/A/1/B, Wyatt Rawson, remarks on Dartington School pupils and their families, 1929.
4. Whitney's diary, 14 March 1940.
5. Moulson, *The Flying Sword: The Story of 601 Squadron*.
6. Cornell, #3725, Willard Straight, letter to Whitney, 10 December 1917.
7. Ibid.
8. Cornell, #3725, Dorothy Straight, letter to Willard Straight, 4 August 1918.

Bibliography

Primary Sources

Phil Lo Bao, *An Illustrated History of British European Airways* (Browcom Group, 1989).
Lilian Beattie-Seaman, *Richard Seaman: His Life and Death* (private manuscript).
William Boddy, *The History of Brooklands Motor Course* (Grenville Publishing Company, 1957).
——, 'The Brooklands Duesenberg', *Veteran and Vintage Magazine*, July 1974.
——, 'Atlantic Crossing', *Motor Sport*, December 2002.
Winston Bray, 'The History of BOAC: 1939–1945' (unpublished).
British Airways Heritage Collection, AW/1/6881, 'Royal Flight: Princess Elizabeth and Duke of Edinburgh UK/Kenya'.
——, N4028 BEA Board Minutes 1946–1954.
——, N4416 BEA Board Papers August 1946–March 1947.
——, N4117 BEA Board Papers April–July 1947.
——, N4034 BOAC Board Minutes February 1947–February 1957.
——, N4056 BOAC Board Documents, October 1947–March 1948.
——, N4058, BOAC Board Documents, November 1948–March 1949.
——, N4059 BOAC Board Documents, April–September 1949.
——, N4061 BOAC Board Document, May–November 1950.
——, N4063 BOAC Board Documents, June–December 1951.
——, N4065 BOAC Board Documents, July 1952–January 1953.
——, N4066 BOAC Board Documents, February–July 1953.
——, N4068 BOAC Board Documents, March–July 1954.
——, N4069 BOAC Board Documents, July–December 1954.
——, N4070 BOAC Board Documents, January–June 1955.
Vincent Brome, *The Way Back: The story of Lieut.-Commander Pat O'Leary, GC, DSO, RN* (Cassell & Co., 1957).
Jane Brown, *Angel Dorothy: How an American Progressive Came to Devon* (Unbound, 2017).
Graeme Cocks, *The Mighty MG Magnettes of 33: The Cars, the Drivers, the Mystery* (Motoring Past Vintage Publishing, 2014).

Lord Cohen, *Civil Aircraft Accident: Report of the Court of Enquiry into the Accidents to Comet G-ALYP on 10 January 1954 and Comet G-ALYY on 8 April 1954* (HMSO, 1955).
Herbert Croly, *Willard Straight* (The Macmillan Company, 1925).
Dartington Hall, *Outline of an Educational Establishment* (Dartington Hall, 1926).
——, *Prospectus* (Dartington Hall, 1926).
——, *Prospectus* (Dartington Hall, 1929).
Dartington Hall Trust papers, Leonard Elmhirst, 'Report on Educational Experiment, Dartington Hall, September to December 1926'.
Anthony Deane-Drummond, *Return Ticket* (Collins, 1953).
Dorothy Whitney Straight Elmhirst papers, #3725, Division of Rare and Manuscript Collections, Cornell University Library.
'Driving at 150mph is easy ... says Whitney Straight', *The Motor*, 11 September 1934.
Roger Dudley and Ted Johnson, *Weston-super-Mare and the Aeroplane* (Amberley Publishing, 2010).
Leonard K. Elmhirst, *The Straight and Its Origin* (Willard Straight Hall, 1975).
Norman L.R. Franks, *Royal Air Force Fighter Command Losses of the Second World War, Vol. 1, 1939–1941* (Midland, 2008).
Jon Gilbert, *Ian Fleming: The Bibliography* (Queen Anne Press, 2012).
Lewis L. Gould, *Four Hats in The Ring: The 1912 Election and the Birth of Modern American Politics* (University Press of Kansas, 2008).
Geirr H. Haarr, *The Battle for Norway: April–June 1940* (Seaforth, 2010).
Hugh Halliday, *242 Squadron, the Canadian Years: The Story of the RAF's 'All-Canadian' Fighter Squadron* (Canada's Wings Inc., 1981).
A. Cecil Hampshire, *On Hazardous Service* (Purnell Book Services, 1974).
Stephen Harper, *A Fatal Obsession: The Women of Cho Oyu – A Reporting Saga* (Book Guild Publishing, 2007).
Peter Hearn, *Flying Rebel: The Story of Louis Strange* (HMSO, 1994).
Robert Hening and Anthony M. Chitty, 'Design for Expansion', *Flight*, 2 February 1939.
Richard Hough, *Tourist Trophy: The History of Britain's Greatest Motor Race* (Hutchinson of London, 1957).
Hypermetropia, 'Air Transport in War', *Flight*, 11 April 1940.
C.G. Jefford, *RAF Squadrons: A Comprehensive Record of the Movement and Equipment of all RAF Squadrons and their Antecedents since 1912* (Airlife, 1988).
Denis Jenkinson, *Maserati 3011: The Story of a Racing Car* (Aries Press, 1987).
Paul Kenny, *The Man Who Supercharged Bond* (Haynes, 2009).
Vladimir Kotelnikov and Tony Buttler, *Early Russian Jet Engines: The Nene and Derwent in the Soviet Union, and the evolution of the VK-1* (Rolls-Royce Historical Trust, 2003).
A.L. Lloyd, 'BOAC's Boss: The Fabulous Mr Straight', *Picture Post*, 4 December 1948.
Karl Ludwigsen, *Reid Railton: Man of Speed* (Evro Publishing, 2018).
Barré Lyndon, *Grand Prix* (John Miles Ltd, 1935).
R.A. MacCrindle QC and P. Godfrey FCA, *Rolls-Royce Limited: Investigation under Section 165 (a) (i) of the Companies Act 1948* (HMSO, 1973).
'Marriages: Mr Whitney Straight and Lady Daphne Finch-Hatton', *The Times*, 18 July 1935.
Raymond Mays, *Split Seconds: My Racing Years* (G.T. Foulis & Co., 1951).

Bibliography

Anthony John Moor, *Ramsgate Municipal Airport: A Pictorial History* (Fonthill, 2019).
J.E. Morpurgo, *Barnes Wallis: A Biography* (Longman, 1972).
'Motoring Sportsmen VII – Whitney Straight', *Motor Sport* (December 1933).
Tom Moulson, *The Millionaires' Squadron: The Remarkable Story of 601 Squadron and the Flying Sword* (Pen & Sword Aviation, 2014).
National Archives, AIR/25/867, Operations Record Books for 216 (Air Transport and Ferry) Group, 1 September 1942–31 December 1943.
——, AIR/25/868, Ibid., 1944.
——, AIR/25/871, Operations Record Book Appendices, 216 (Air Transport and Ferry) group, 1 September 1942–30 June 1943.
——, AIR/25/872, Ibid., 1 September 1942–31 December 1943.
——, AIR/25/874, Ibid., 1 April 1944–30 June 1944.
——, AIR/25/877, Ibid., 1 September 1944–31 October 1944.
—— AIR/25/879, Ibid., January 1945.
——, AIR/25/881, Ibid., March 1945.
——, AIR/25/882, Ibid., April 1945.
——, AIR/27/1471, Detail of work carried out for 242 Squadron, July 1941.
——, AIR/27/1471, Operations Record Book for 242 Squadron.
——, AIR/50/165, Whitney's Combat Report, 12 December 1940.
——, AIR/50/165, Whitney's Combat Report, 2 February 1941.
——, AIR/50/165, Whitney's Combat Report, 14 May 1941.
——, AIR/50/165, 242 Squadron's Combat Report, 23 June 1941 (regarding the activities of 12/13 June).
——, AIR/50/165, Whitney's Combat Report, 17 June 1941.
——, KV 2/4366, 'Louis DOLIVET alias DOLIVEUX, Ludovic BRECHER, ULIANU, BOVET: Romanian, Czecj, French, Swiss', 18 December 1937–22 March 1951.
——, WO 208/3309/787, Whitney's debriefs with MI9, 25 and 28 July 1942.
——, WO 208/3309/790, Sergeant T.G. Johnson's debrief with MI9, 31 July 1942.
——, WO 208/3309/795 and 796, Sergeant J. Beecroft and Sergeant H.P. Hanwell's debriefs with MI9, 31 July 1942.
——, WO 208/3309/797, Sergeant Stefan Miniakowski's debrief with MI9, 31 July 1942.
——, WO 208/3309/798, Private Charles Knight's debriefs with MI9, 31 July and 1 August 1942.
——, WO 208/3309/799, Lance Corporal E. Prady's debrief with MI9, 31 July 1942.
——, WO 208/3309/800, Private Sydney Fullager's debrief with MI9, 31 July 1942.
——, WO 208/3309/801, Lieutenant A.J. Deane-Drummond's debriefs with MI9, 31 July and 4 and 5 August 1942.
Airey Neave, *Saturday at MI9: The Classic Account of the WWII Allied Escape Organisation* (Pen & Sword, 1969).
Mary Bride Nicholson, *A Life at Dartington* (Mary Bride Nicholson, 2015).
Rupert Nicholson, *Rolls-Royce Limited: Recollections of the Receiver and Manager* (KPMG Peat Marwick, 1993).
Chris Nixon, *Shooting Star: The Life of Richard Seaman* (Transport Bookman Publications, 2000).

Matt Perry, 'Bombing Billancourt: Labour Agency and the Limitations of the Public Opinion Model of Wartime France', *Labour History Review*, Vol. 77, No. 1, April 2012 (Liverpool University Press).
Peter Pugh, *The Magic of a Name: The Rolls Royce Story, Part One: The First Forty Years* (Icon Books, 2000).
——, *The Magic of a Name: The Rolls Royce Story, Part Two: The Power Behind the Jets* (Icon Books, 2001).
——, *The Magic of a Name: The Rolls Royce Story, Part Three: A Family of Engines* (Icon Books, 2002).
RAF Museum Archive, 'The Duke of Kent: Visit to a North-West Military Hospital', *Mansfield Guardian*, 27 September 1940.
——, Whitney's RAAF log book.
Derek Richardson, *Detachment W* (Paul Mould Publishing, 2004).
A.F. Rivers Fletcher, *Mostly Motor Racing: A Vivid Account of Life, Motoring, the Motor Industry and Motor Racing in the Vintage Years* (Haynes, 1986).
Royal Archives – Windsor Castle PS/PSO/GVI/PS/NAVY/04129/28-3C, letter from Whitney Straight to Sir Alexander Hardinge, 2 September 1940.
Keith A. Saunders, *Teignmouth's Haldon Aerodrome* (Teignmouth Museum & Historical Society, 1999).
Graham M. Simons, *Western Airways: The West Country Airline* (Redcliffe, 1988).
Quentin Spurring, *Le Mans: The Official History of The World's Greatest Motor Race, 1930–39* (Evro Publishing, 2017).
Ronald Stephens, Sue and Andy Parlour, *HMS Tarana: Under Two Flags* (Ten Bells Publishing, 2009).
Michael Straight, *After Long Silence* (W.W. Norton & Company, 1983).
Whitney Straight, 'A Motor Racing Stable', *Mine*, October 1935.
John Stroud, *Railway Air Services* (Ian Allan Ltd, 1987).
Surrey Historical Centre, 606 / 2 / box 7 / file 10, John Houldsworth inquest, 26 June 1934.
W.A. Swanberg, *Whitney Father, Whitney Heiress* (Charles Scribner's Sons, 1980).
Kevin Taylor, *Central Cambridge: A Guide to the University and Colleges* (Cambridge University Press, 2008).
Simon Taylor, *The Shelsley Walsh Story: A Century of Motorsport* (Haynes, 2005).
Julian C. Temple, *Wings Over Woodley: The Story of Miles Aircraft and the Adwest Group* (Aston Publications, 1987).
Sir Miles Thomas, *Out on a Wing: An Autobiography* (Michael Joseph, 1964).
David Venables, *Brooklands: The Official Centenary History* (Haynes Publishing, 2007).
Victoria and Albert Museum Archive of Art and Design, Sir Hugh Casson papers, 1867–2007: AAD/2008/2/1/1/1-5, Villa at Formetor, Mallorca, 1954–1965.
Captain Dacre Watson, 'British Overseas Airways Corporation 1940–1950 and its legacy', *Journal of Aeronautical History*, paper number 2013/03.
'Wedding Presents: Mr Whitney Straight and Lady Daphne Finch-Hatton', *The Times*, 17 July 1935.
Whitney Museum of American Art, *Flora Whitney Miller: Her Life, Her World* (Whitney Museum of American Art, 1987).

Bibliography

Maurice Wickstead, 'Whitney Straight – A Full Life', part one, *AIR Pictorial*, July 2000.
——, 'Whitney Straight – A Full Life', part two, *AIR Pictorial*, August 2000.
——, 'Forgotten Fields: Haldon Aerodrome, Teignmouth', *Devon Strut News*, May 2006.
Eoin Young, 'Whitney Straight: two legends in his lifetime', *Thoroughbred & Classic Cars*, October 1975.
——, 'Whitney Straight: Making It Look Easy', *Motor Sport*, February 2002.
Helen Young, *Safe House are Dangerous* (Abson Books, 1985).
Michael Young with Anthea Williams and Robin Johnson, *The Elmhirsts of Dartington*, (Dartington Hall Trust, 1996).

Further Reading

Isaiah Berlin, *Flourishing: Letters, 1928–1946* (Pimlico, 2005).
'Business Profile: Whitney Straight', *Future*, Vol. V, No. 2, April 1950.
John Chenery, *Styling the Post Office: Corporate Brand Evolution* (Light Straw, 2022).
Noël Coward, *Middle East Diary* (Doubleday, Doran & Co., 1944).
Donald Darling, *Sunday at Large: Assignments of a Secret Agent* (William Kimber & Co., 1977).
'A Descriptive Booklet' (The Lincoln School of Teachers College, 1922).
John Dewey, *The Child and the Curriculum* (University of Chicago Press, 1902).
Robert Edwards, 'Team Managers: Lofty England', *Motor Sport*, June 1999.
K.D. Ewing, Joan Mahoney and Andrew Moretta, *MI5, the Cold War and the Rule of Law* (Oxford University Press, 2020).
Malcolm F. Fillmore, 'Whitney Straight – some additions', *AIR Pictorial*, August 2000.
Donald Fish, *Airline Detective* (Fontana Books, 1962).
Robert Goralski, *World War II Almanac 1931–1945: A Political and Military Record* (Hamish Hamilton, 1981).
Handley Page Ltd, *Forty Years On: 1909–1949* (Handley Page, 1949).
Simon Heffer (ed.), *Henry 'Chips' Channon, The Diaries: 1938–43* (Hutchinson, 2021).
——, *Henry 'Chips' Channon, The Diaries: 1943–57* (Hutchinson, 2022).
Michael Heseltine, *Life in the Jungle: My Autobiography* (Hodder & Stoughton, 2000).
Roy Jenkins, *Churchill* (Macmillan, 2001).
Howard Kroplick and Al Velocci, *The Long Island Motor Parkway* (Arcadia Publishing, 2008).
B.H. Liddell Hart, *History of the Second World War* (Cassell, 1970).
Eduard C. Lindeman, *The Meaning of Adult Education* (New Republic, 1926).
José Manser, *Hugh Casson: A Biography* (Viking, 2000).
Peter Masefield, *Flight Path* (Airlife, 2002).
Richard Mead, *General 'Boy': The Life of Lieutenant General Sir Frederick Browning* (Pen and Sword Military, 2010).
Richard Meaden, *Classic Motorsport Routes* (AA Publishing, 2007).
Charles Mosley (ed.), *Burke's Peerage, Baronetage & Knightage, Clan Chiefs, Scottish Feudal Barons, 107th Edition* (Burke's Peerage, 2003).
Tom Moulson, *The Millionaires' Squadron* (Pen and Sword, 2014).
National Archives, HO 334, Whitney Straight's Certificate of Naturalisation, 7 July 1936.
National Library of Scotland, Acc.7548, G88–G94, Papers of Rev Donald Laskie.

Chris Nixon, *Auto Union Album: 1934–1939* (Transport Bookman Publications, 1998).
Denis Rake, *Rake's Progress* (Leslie Frewin, 1968).
David Ranstead, 'Aeroplane Database: Lockheed Tristar', *Aeroplane*, June 2024.
A.F. Rivers Fletcher, *Bentley Past & Present* (Gentry Books, 1982).
Lord Rothschild, *Mediations of a Broomstick* (William Collins, 1977).
Lewis Selby, 'Rough Stuff', *Aeropilot*, September 1937.
Nicholas Shakespeare, *Ian Fleming: The Complete Man* (Harville Secker, 2023).
Andrew Simpson, 'Individual History, Gloster Gladiator MkII N5628', 2012.
Michael Straight, *On Green Spring Farm: The Life and Times of One Family in Fairfax County, Virginia, 1942–1966* (Devon Press, 2004).
Rodney Walkerley, *Moments That Made Motor Racing History* (Temple Press, 1959).
Christopher Warwick, *George and Marina: The Duke and Duchess of Kent* (Weidenfeld & Nicholson, 1988).
Charles Woodley, *The History of British European Airways, 1946–1972* (Pen & Sword, 2006).

Audio, Film and Video

British Movietone, 'Record Is Smashed at Shelsley Walsh', www.youtube.com/watch?v=2N0MdYLhDZ4.
British Pathé, 'Devaluation "The Only Way" says Sir Stafford (1949)', www.youtube.com/watch?v=YqQfecCR0TU.
——, 'London: Roy Thomson and Whitney Straight interviews on return from Moscow (1963)' www.britishpathe.com/asset/247018.
——, 'Race to Salve Britannia' (1954), www.youtube.com/watch?v=r0lJrNMfRps.
——, 'The Famous Shelsley Walsh Hill Climb (1933)', www.youtube.com/watch?v=3yOnD3dcXjw.
The Papers of Michael Young, Churchill Archives Centre, Churchill College, Cambridge University, GBR/0014/YUNG 10/6/4: 'Audio tape of Phyllis Willmott's oral history interviews with Michael Young about his early life, 1929–33, 2000'. Apply to Churchill Archives Centre for a soundcloud.com file link.
'Upscaled to Full HS 60FPS – 1933 Targa Abruzzo & Coppa Acerbo Pescara: Nuvolari, Fagioli, Hellé Nice', www.youtube.com/watch?v=gnEioUOUYwM.

Websites

ASN Wikibase #150998, Aviation Safety Network summary of Flying Officer Few's fatal accident at Brooklands, 16 September 1933. asn.flightsafety.org/wikibase/150998.
ASN Wikibase #24524, Aviation Safety Network summary of R.S. Ducker's fatal accident on Carnedd Dafydd, 29 September 1968. asn.flightsafety.org/wikibase/24524.
BBC, '130 years since Sunday drinking was banned in Wales', www.bbc.co.uk/news/uk-wales-14136013.
Bureau of Aircraft Accidents Archives, 'Crash of an Avro 685 York off Lampedusa: 15 killed', www.baaa-acro.com/crash/crash-avro-685-york-i-lampedusa-15-killed.

Bibliography

'Buzzards Bay, MA: One of the most challenging and satisfying bodies of water to navigate on the East Coast', sailing-tara.com/buzzards-bay.html.
Mark Finlay, 'The Story of Former UK Carrier Railway Air Services', simpleflying.com/railway-air-services-uk-history.
Francis Holland School, Sloane Square, 'History', www.fhs-sw1.org.uk/about-us/history.
National Army Museum, 'Battles of Imphal and Kohima', www.nam.ac.uk/explore/battle-imphal.
'Osterley Park', historicengland.org.uk/listing/the-list/list-entry/1000287.
'Sea Evacuations of 1942 – Operations Bluebottle I and II', www.conscript-heroes.com.
'The Golden Era of Grand Prix Racing', www.goldenera.fi/main.htm.
'The Honours System of the United Kingdom', honours.cabinetoffice.gov.uk/about/orders-and-medals.
The Nostalgia Forum, forums.autosport.com/forum/10-the-nostalgia-forum.
The Postal Museum, 'A brief history of national postal strikes', www.postalmuseum.org/blog/brief-history-of-national-postal-strikes.

Index

Note: *italicised* page references denote illustrations

Adam, Robert 204
Air Commerce Ltd 170, 171, 177
Airways Union 309–10, 317, 326, 334, 336
Airwork 294
Aitken, Max 197, 313, 314, 339
Alanbrooke, Field Marshal Viscount 309
Albi Grand Prix 103–4, *119*, 139–40, 156, 160
Alcover, José 295
Alfa Romeo 57, 101, 105, 110, 120, 121, 132, 133, 155, 158
   Brooklands 68, 75, 120
   Grands Prix 83–4, 99, 100, 101, 102, 103, 106–7, 123–5, 129, 130, 131, 137, 138, 139, 141, 142–3, 145, 151, 160
   and Maserati 106, 124, 125, 132, 142, 156, 340
Algerian Grand Prix (Bouzaréah) *119*, 147, 151–2, 155, 160
Alitalia 255–6
Altham, Psyche ('Peggy') 78–9, 81, 84, 109, 110, 111, 114–15
Alvis 50, 56, 63
American Airlines 171, 243
American Overseas Airlines 287
Anstey, Alfred 179
Applegreen, Long Island 14, 15, 17–18, 19, 23, 31–2, 35, 36–7, *86*, 106, 167, 181, 263, 286, 289
Apsley, Lord 199
Armstrong, Hamilton Fish 230

Armstrong, William and Gwendoline 336
Armstrong Jones, Anthony *279*
Armstrong Siddeley 79, 323
Ascari, Antonio 151
Association Internationale des Automobiles Clubs Reconnus (AIACR) 121, 131, 137, 148
Astor, John 294
Attlee, Clement 252, 311
Austin (car manufacturer) 62, 63, 67, 80, 150, 176
Auto Union 123, 125, 131, 132, 138, 139, 140, 141, 142, 145, 147, 150–1, 156, 157–8, 159, 161
Autocar 62, 65, 69, 71, 77, 83, 108, 111, 132–3, 145, 159
The Aviary *192*, *194*, 204, 222, 230, 252, 258, 266, 268, 290, 291–2, 293, 301, 312, 315, 336
   M4 296–7
   Nelli van der Brink at 207, 211, 220, 222, 230
   Whitney purchases 287
Avro 181, 230, 241, 246, 255–6, 259, 260, 261, 263, *274*, 302
   Whitney's Avro Avian 48, 50, *91*

Bader, Douglas 209
Baillie, Olive 164
Balfour, Harold 184, 237, 241, 244

Balmain, G.H.S. 108
Barbieri, Ferdinando 101, 102
Barnard Castle 199, 200
Bartlett, J.H. 68
Beaton, Cecil 122
Beaverbrook, Lord 241, 303
Belgian Grand Prix 57, 186
Bell, Graham 291
Bend family 14, 15, 16, 18–19
Benn, Tony 325, 334, 335
Bennström, Olle 100
Bentley cars 57, 62, 82, 117, 120, 129, 130, 153, 253–4, 306, 315, 319, 320, 334
Berlin, Isaiah 198, 230, 237, 338
Bermuda Triangle 261
Bertram, Oliver 80, 164
Bevan, Ernest 252
Biggin Hill 197
Birkin, Tim 57, 62, 64–5, 67, 68, 82, 99, 101, 112, 117, 120, 126, 159, 340
Bishop, Edward ('Brud') 152, 154
Bjørnstad, Eugen 100
Black, Norman 69
Blanchain, Francis 224, 227
Blixen, Karen 170
Blunt, Anthony 167, 315, 316
Boeing 260, 267, 291, 299, 307, 308, 323, 325–6
Bogue, Anna 37
Bologna 64, 120, 121, 122, *190*
Bolt, Roy 46, 50
Bonetto, Felice 107, 108
Bonser Report 45–6, 54
Boote, R.S.L. 62
Booth, John 266, 285, 287, 302
Borzacchini, Mario 99, 101, 102, 107
Boucher, Hélène 124, 170–1
Bowater, Camilla (née Straight) 179, 198, 217, 227, 252, 254, 293, 301, 314, 315, 326, 334, 335
Bowater, Michael ('Mikey') 315, 316, 326, 327, 335
Bowhill, Air Chief Marshal Sir Frederick 244
Boyd Carpenter, John 299–300, 301
Brackenbury, Charles 80, 102, 105
Braillard, Louis 103–4, 105, 139, 160
Branston, Brian 317

Brauchitsch, Manfred von 82, 132
Brighton and Hove Motor Club speed trials 109–10, 118, *119*
Bristol (aircraft and aero engine manufacturer) 255, 260, 300, 301, 303, 308, 309–10, 323, 324
Brabazon 260, 302
Britannia 260, *277*, 287, 294, 296, 297, 299, 300, 302, 308, 310
Bristol Siddeley 323–4
British Airways 171, 184
British European Airways (BEA) 255, 256, 257, 258, 268, 285, 295, 300–1, 302, 308, 335, 341
British Overseas Airways Corporation (BOAC) 56, *193*, 233, 244, 247–8, 249, 252–68, *274*, *277*, 285–8, 290–303, 308
BSAA amalgamation 266–8, 285
crashes and disappearances 261, 294, 297–8, 299, 301, 302
Elizabeth, Queen (*formerly* Princess) *193*, *275*, 290–3, 294
financial matters 258–9, 264, 290
freight 294, 296, 298–9
Qantas 263, 298
reorganisation 258–9, 261, 262, 263, 267, 285
Whitney on the board 56, *192*, 249, 258–68, *275*, 285–8, 290–3, 294, 295–6, 298–300, 302, 309, 340, 341
Whitney refuses directorship 237–8, 247, 251, 258
Whitney resigns 300–1, 302, 303
British Racing Drivers' Club 108, 136
British South American Airlines (BSAA) 252, 261, 266–8, 285, 286
Brivio, Count Antonio 99–101, 118, 151, 152
Broad, C.D. ('Charlie') 70
Brome, Vincent 224–5
Brooklands 56–69, 73, 75, 79, 80, 108, *119*, 120, 124, 160, 186
handicap system 62, 63, 67–8, 73–7, 80–1, 114, 125, 126, 133–4, 160
origins 56, 57, 58–60
records *95*, 136–7, 148, 149, 150, 159, *190*
'the right crowd and no crowding' 115
Brooklands, race meetings
Bank Holiday meeting, 3 August 1931 60–2

Index

BARC meeting, 17 October 1931 63–4
BARC meeting, 3 March 1934 122
BRDC 500 mile race, 16 September 1933 108–9
BRDC 500 mile race, 22 September 1934 147
Easter Monday meeting, 28 March 1932 65, 66–7
Easter Monday meeting, 17 April 1933 73–5
Easter Monday meeting, 2 April 1934 123
Empire Trophy race, July 1933 106
Empire Trophy race, 23 June 1934 133–6
JCC International Trophy race, 6 May 1933 75–8, 83
JCC International Trophy race, 28 April 1934 76, 125–7
October meeting, 21 October 1933 93, 112–15
October meeting, 13 October 1934 95, 148–51
Whit Monday meeting, 16 May 1932 67–8
Whit Monday meeting, 5 June 1933 80–1
Brooklands, track
  bumps 60, 109, 125, 149
  Byfleet Banking 58, *59*, 62, 75, 108, *135*, 149
  Finishing Straight *59*, 60, *61*, 74, *76*
  The Fork *59*, 60, *61*, 62, 63, 64, 67, 68, 69, 74, 80, 109, 113, 114, 133
  Fork Hairpin 74, 134, *135*
  handicap lanes 75, *76*, 77, 125, 126
  Members' Banking 58, *59*, 60, 63, 75, 77, 113, 120, 134, 137, 149, 150
  Members' Bridge Snake 134, *135*, 136
  Members' Bridge Turn 60, *61*, 64, 68, 69, 74, 78, 113, 150, 159
  Mountain Circuit 60, *61*, 67, 73, 74, 75, 80, 112, 121, 148, 150, 157, 159, *190*
  Outer Circuit *59*, 60, 62, 63, 67, 75, 80, *95*, 108, 113, 133, 137, 149, *190*
  Railway Snake 133, 134, *135*
  Railway Straight 58, *59*, 63, 75, *76*, 113, 133, 137
Browning, Lieutenant General Frederick ('Boy') 291, 292
Bugatti cars 63, 105, 110, 155
  Brooklands 62, 63, 66, 67, 74, 75, 78, 80, 106, 112, 113, 134, 136–57
  Grands Prix 66, 83, 101, 103, 106, 107, 123, 138, 151

Bunsen, Mary de 179, 181
Burgess, Guy 71, 315–16, 318
Burghley, Lord 65, 268, 293
Bury St Edmunds 182
Bushell, Flight Lieutenant Roger 197
Butler, J.R.M. ('Jim') 55, 70

Cadell, Air Commodore Colin 257–8
Cadman, Lord 183
Caggeo, Sir George 256
Cairo 16, 153, 229–37, 242, 244–6, 248, 251, 252, 297
Caldwell, Otis 37–8
Callaghan, James 337
Camanda I-IV (yachts) *195*, *284*, 295, 301, 312–13, 314, 324, 326–7
Cambridge University 32, 40, 52, 55–6, 58, 65, 69–71, 111–12, 114, 117, 122, 305, 315, 316
Campari, Giuseppe 83, 101, 102, 107, 120
Campbell, Sir Malcolm 57, 64, 75, 77, 79–80, *93*, 109, 112, 113, 150
Canada 209, 262, 263–4, 290–1, 317
Cannon, General John 251, *273*
Capital Airlines 298, 308
Caracciola, Rudi 104, 105, 110, 140, 147, 160
Cardiff 182, 184, 185, 204
Carr, Noel 74
Carrington, Lord 331
Casablanca *119*, 130–1, 132, 155, *234–5*, 236, 244
Casson, Sir Hugh and Reta *195*, *196*, 295, 324–5, 329, 339
Catchatoor, G.E.W. 63
Cecchini, Raffaele 102, 141
Cessna *194*, *278*, 316–17, 325–6
Chamberlain, Neville 186, 202
Charles, Sir Noel 255
Chataway, Christopher 329
Child, Sir Francis and Robert 204
China 15, 16–17, 18, 24, 311, 316
Chinetti, Luigi 133
Chiron, Louis 99, 100, 106, 124–5, 129, 130, 131, 132, 133, 142, 146, 151, 152, 160
Chitty, Anthony 179, 180
Cho Oyu, all-woman ascent *278*, 312, 313–14
Churchill, Clarissa 293
Churchill, Winston 164, 202, 207, 211, 236–7, 244, 246–7, 248, 251, 286, 292–3, 301

Clacton 182
Claridge's 206, 237, 244, 247
Clark, Lieutenant Commander ('Nobby') 226, 227
Clemenceau, President 24
Cleveland, President Grover 13
Cobb, John *95*, 109, 149
Cochrane, Air Marshal Sir Ralph 247–8, 249
Cole, Lord 331, 332, 333
Coleman, Satis 34–5
Columbia University 14, 28, 40, 45, 262
Comminges Grand Prix 102–3, 126, 142–3, 155
communism 286, 288, 315–16
Comotti, Gianfranco 142, 143
Concorde 324, 334
Coppa Acerbo Grand Prix (Pescara) 81, 99, 101–2, 103, *119*, 126, 141, 151, 157, 161
Coppa Ciano Grand Prix 139
Coppa Florio 58
Coppa Principessa di Piedmont Grand Prix 151
Coppins 205, 206, 207, 231
Corfield, Frederick 331–2
Cornell University *11*, 15, 32, 33, 37, 40, 335
Council of Industrial Design *279*, 309, 329
Couper, Mike 63
Courtney, Sir Christopher 260, 261
Cox, Stanley 177, 199, 230, 247, 252, 253, 310
Creasy, Noah 177
Cribbett, Sir George 267, 287, 295–6, 301, 303
Cripps, Sir Stafford 237, 241, 287, 311
Critchley, Air Commodore Arthur 238, 251, 258
Croly, Herbert 18, 31, 339
Crystal, Albert 31, 32, 35
Cumming, Jay 74
Curry, Bill 52
Curtis, Nell 31, 42
Cyprus 256, 293
Czaykowski, Stanislas 106–7
Czech Grand Prix (Brno) 109, 148, 161

Dahlin, Börje 100, 101
Daily Telegraph Trophy 68
Daimler 79, 120, 123

Darling, Donald ('Agent Sunday') 223, 227, 237
Darragh *235*, 236
Dartington Hall 35–6, 37, 38, 39–54, *91*, 164–5, 179, *188*, 204, 205, 228, 238, 252, 258, 289, 335
Dartington Hall School 39–47, 49–52, 53–4, 56, 165, 335, 339
Davies, Sir Henry Walford 165
Davis, Sammy 77–8, 132–3, 160
de Gaulle, Charles 244
de Havilland 48, 50, 153–4, 171, 174, 176, 257, 299, 301, 307
 Comet 260, *276*, 292, 293, 294, 295, 296, 297–8, 299, 301, 302, 307, 308
 engines 169, 175
Deane-Drummond, Lieutenant Anthony 225, 226
Delage 64, 80, 109, 177–8
Delano, Bill 15, 18, 33
Delcassé, Théophile 19
Derby 302, 306, 330
D'Erlanger, Gerard ('Pop') 255, 256, 301, 303
Design Advisory Committee *195*, 329
Dewdney, Percy 153, 167
Dickerman, Emma 14–15
Dieppe Grand Prix 84, 139, 166
Dierks, Barry 166
Digoine, Captain 218, 222
Divo, Albert 137
Dixon, Freddie 113, 114, 126, 134, 136
Dobson, Sir Roy 260
Dodge 120, 121, 146
Dolivet, Louis 228, 262, 286, 288–9
Don, Kaye 62, 66, 67, 78
Don, Rita 114–15
Donald, Guy 55, 112
Donaldson, Squadron Leader J.W. ('Baldy') 201, 202
Donington Park *119*, 147, 159, 160, *190*
Douglas 232, 246, 260, 299, 300, 307, 308, 323
 Argonaut *193*, 264, 266, 267, *275*, 288, 292, 298, 301
 DC-6 264, 286, 287, 299
Douglas, Sholto 209, 210, 229, 237, 300–1, 341
Downing, A.R.H. 240
Drexel, Bill 165

Index

Dreyfus, René 138, 139
Driscoll, L.P. 67, 80, 150
Drogheda, Kathleen, Countess of 112, 150, 164
Ducker, R.S. 325–6
Duesenbergs *95*, 106, 108, 125, 133, 147, 148–9, 152, 155, 156
Duller, Jack 113, 155
Dunlop Tyres 149

Ebb, Karl 66, 99, 100, 160
Ebblewhite, Albert ('Ebby') 67, 68, 73–4, 80, 114
Eccles, A.H.L. 112
Eccles, R.H. 74
Eden, Anthony 204, 211, 237, 244, 246–7, 251, 293, 301, 303, 308
Edgar, Alfred (*pseudonym* Barré Lyndon) 154–5
Edgar, Norman 182
El Alamein 232–3, *234–5*
El Aouina *234–5*, 238, 239, 240
Elizabeth, Queen (*was* Princess) *193*, *275*, 290–3, 294
Elliot, John 296
Elliot, Maxine 166
Elliott, Theyre Lee 56
Elmhirst, Bill 49, 53, 165, 167, 327
Elmhirst, Leonard Knight ('Jerry') 32–8, 48, 52–3, 55–6, 112, 115, 167, 172–3, 181, 202–3, 327, 335
  Dartington Hall and School 35–6, 38, 40–3, 44, 48, 49, 50–2, 163
  meets and marries Dorothy 33–5, *90*
  Whitney Straight Ltd 117–18, 130, 157, 158
Elmhirst, Richard 53
Elmhirst, Ruth 36, 53, 165, 167
Elmhirst, Air Vice Marshal Tommy 238–9
Elmhirst, Vic 40, 46, 47, 50
England, F.R.W. ('Lofty') 120
ERA (English Racing Automobile) 132, 148, 150, 166
Etancelin, Philippe 83, 104, 105, 130–1, 132, 133, 138, 139, 142–3, 157
Eton College 69, 118, 184, 305
Everitt, Bill 150
Exeter 173, 177, 179, 181, 184, 198, 207, 230, *269*, 319
Eyston, George 64, 136, 148

Fagioli, Luigi 101, 102–3, 106, 147–8
Falchetto, Benoît 103, 105
Faulkner, W.K. 62, 66–7
Featherstonhaugh, Rupert ('Buddy') 67, 68, 123, 125, 126, 139–40, 142, 143, 155, 156–7
Ferrari, Enzo 82, 83, 99, 101, 139, 142, 151, 340
Finch Hatton, Denys 170
Finlayson, 'Jock' 120
First World War 12, 19–20, 21–4, 48, 101, 163, 173, 176, 182, *188*, 209, 230, 261, 306
Fish, Donald 286, 288
Fleming, Ian 163–4, 168, 319–21
Forbes, Sir Archibald 324, 328, 330, 331, 336
Forsberg, John 100
Fort de la Revère *215*, 222–3, 229, 245, 249, 341
Fotheringham Parker, Philip 63, 75
Frazer, Ian 333
Freeman, Norman *95*, 149
Freeman, Air Chief Marshal Wilfrid 228
French Grand Prix (Montlhéry) 64, 82, 122, 125, 136–7, 140
Froome, Freddy 185
Furmanik, Giuseppe 101

Gallop, Clive 121
Garbett, Cyril 164
Gardner, Eric 134–6
Gardner, Major Goldie 136
Garrow, Ian 218, 219–20, 223
George VI, King 179, 231, 243, 251, 290, 291, 292
German Grand Prix (Nürburgring) 64, 66, 69, 104, *119*, 122, 131, 132, 138, 158, 161
Gibbs, Pat 218, 219
Gibraltar 167, 221, 223, 226, 227, 231, *234–5*, 237, 256–7, 327
Giles (cartoonist) *194*
Gillow, Victor 68
Giro Bank 328–9
Goodall, Morris 66, 67
Gorton, Osmer 171–2
Gossage, Air Marshal Leslie 206, 207
Gray, Charles 177
Greece 229, 231, 257
Gresham, Sir Thomas 204

Gross, Bob 315
Guinness, Loel 197
Guiver, C.L. 62
Gunning, Brigadier General Sir Charles 164
Gurney Nutting 78, 121, 155
Gwatkin, Fred 118, 157, 158, 170, 172, 176–7, 178, 182, 220, 230, 247, 254

Halahan, Air Vice Marshal Frederick 164
Haldon 48, 50, 177, 181
Hall, Viscount 279, 328, 329
Hamilton, Hugh ('Hammy') 62, 122–3, 125, 126, 155
  death 94, 109, 143, 145–6
  Grands Prix 109, 122, 129–32, 133, 137–8, 139–41, 142–3, 145–6, 156
Handley Page Ltd 254–5, 259, 264, 302
Handley Page, Sir Frederick 204, 230, 241, 244, 252, 254, 258–9
Handley, W.L. 126
Hardin, Major General Thomas 242–3
Hardinge, Sir Alexander 206–7
Harper, Stephen 313, 314
Hartley, Sir Harold 173–4, 248, 253, 255, 256, 258, 260, 261, 265, 267, 268, 285, 302
Hartnell, Norman 122
Hawker Hurricane 198, 200, 202–3, 208, 209, 210, 211, 213, 233, 236, 249, 269, 288
Harvey, Sir Arthur Vere 262
Healey, Donald 56
Heath, Edward 329, 331, 333
Heathrow 193, 275, 296, 335
Heidinger, Louis 41
Henderson, Basil 169
Hendon 73, 176, 197
Hendy Heck 169, 174
Hening, Robert 179, 180
Heseltine, Michael 323
Heston 73, 153, 154, 170, 171, 175–6, 179, 211, 227
Hillman's Airways 171
Hitler, Adolf 24, 123, 158, 183, 199, 230
Hives, Lord Ernest 300, 301, 302, 307, 308, 309
Holden, Henry 58
Horton, Ron 58, 155

Houghton, Dan 331
Houldsworth, John 134–6
House, Colonel Edward 19, 23, 24, 27
Howe, Lord 57, 64, 67, 68, 69, 75, 82, 106, 107, 110, 112, 122, 123, 159, 164
Huddie, David 324, 325, 330, 333–4
Hunter, Polly 49
Huntingdon, John Holland, Earl of 35
Hyde, Douglas 316

Imperial Airways 56, 154, 169, 173–4
India 32, 33–4, 50, 109, 122, 242–3, 311
International Aeradio Limited (IAL) 257–8
Inverchapel, Lord 311
Ipswich 173, 177, 179, 182, 184
Ireland 263
Isaacs, Sue 335
Isherwood, Margaret 52
Italian Grand Prix 106, 146–7, 161
Ivanović, Vane 293, 294, 295, 301, 327

Jackson, Tom 331
Jaguar 120, 315
Jamieson, Tom Murray 157
Japan 15, 242
Johnson, Sergeant T.G. 225

Kauffer, Edward McKnight 169
Keinänen, S.P.J. 66
Kent, Duke and Duchess of 177, 205–7, 231, 271
Kesselberg hill climb 81–2, 119, 159–60
Kindersley, Lord 308, 309, 310, 315, 323, 328, 341
Klausen hill climb 119, 139, 140, 160, 202
KLM 312
Knight, Private Charles 223, 224, 225
Knollys, Lord 238, 247, 249, 258
Kogan, Claude 313–14

Lafrenz, Erik 100
Lambert, Bill 117, 118, 123, 130, 146, 155, 156, 157, 158, 170, 177
Lambert, Raymond 313
Lancaster, W. 184
Langres 20, 29
Lathbury, Sir Gerald 327

Index

Lawson, W.H. 56
Le Mans 57, 77, 82, 108, *119*, 120, 125, 133, 157, 159
League of Nations 23, 42, 139, 288
Leeds Castle, Kent 164
Lehoux, Marcel 83, 105, 107–8, 130, 131, 133, 138, 142, 143, 147–8, 151
Lennox-Boyd, Alan 262, 290, 294, 296, 297
Lévy, Louis 224
Lewis, Brian, 2nd Baron Essendon 77, 78, 110, 112, 113, 114, 126, 127, 153, 160, 173
The Lincoln School, New York 28–9, 31, 32, 34–5, 37–8, 339
Lindberg, Einar 66
Lindbergh, Charles 31, 175
Lindeman, Professor Eduard 40–1
Locke King, Hugh 58–60
Lockheed 184, 232, 260, 299, 323
    Constellation 259, 263, 297, 298
    Rolls-Royce engines *281*, 315, 324–5, 328, 329, 330, 331, 333
    Tristar 324, 334
Lombard, Adrian 324
Longworth, Nicholas 15
Lucy, Peter 326

McCrindle, Major Ronald 256
McGillivray, Chief Wireless Instructor J. 184
Maclean, Donald 316
Malaguti, Romano 101, 145
Malta 238, 239, 240, 246, 249
Manchester 184, 202, 207, 305
Mannin Beg, Isle of Man 84
Manston 108, 180, 203, 210, 211, 213
Marne Grand Prix 82–4, 137–8
Marsala *234–5*, 239
Marseille 124, 153, 218–19, 220, 221, 224, 225, 227, 244
Marshall, David and Arthur 70, 112
Masaryk Grand Prix (Brno) *119*, 148
Masefield, Peter 70–1, 73, 74, 112, 268, 300, 301, 303
Maserati 64, *93*, 118, 120–1, 124, 129, 146, 153, 155, 156–7, 178, *190*, 340
    and Alfa Romeo 106, 124, 125, 132, 142, 156, 340

Brooklands 67–9, 73–4, 75, 80–1, 113, 125–7, 133–7, 150
    gearboxes 68, 79–80, 83, 84, 99, 105, 121, 132, 157
    Grands Prix 64, 65–6, 82–4, 101–2, 103–4, 106–8, 123, 129–32, 137, 138–9, 141, 142–3, 147, 151, 156
    order backlog 121, 123, 129, 146, 156, 178
    Whitney buys and races 64–9, 73–4, 75, 77, 79–81, 82–4, 101, 103–8, 110–11, 113, 117–18, 120–2, 123, 125–7, 129–32, 133–9, 141, 142–3, 146–7
Maserati, Alfieri 64
Mason, Roy *280*
Mathieson, Thomas ('Taso') 74, 112, 113
Matossian, Marcelle 232, 237, 241, 243, 245, 247, 342
Mays, Ray 58, 79, 110, 111, 112–14, 132, 148, 150, 166
Meeson, E.L. 63
Melville, Sir Ronnie 330
Menzies, Peter *280*
Mercedes 64, 66, 79, 99, 100, 123, 125, 131, 132, 138, 139, 140, 141, 147–8, 150–1, 156, 177–8
Mere, Robin 125, 140, 146
Metcalfe, Tom 330
MG 62, 108, 109, 122, 150
    Magnette 75, 81, 102, 104, 121, 122, 125, 126, 129, 133, 136, 139, 140, 141, 142, 146–7, 148, 150–1, 152, 156
MI5/MI6 288–9
MI9 223, 224, 225, 227, 337
Midland Automobile Club 57, 79
Midland Bank 309, 318–19, 324, 328, 329, 330, 331, 334, 335–6
Mikardo, Ian 309
Milan 106, 120, 142, 256
Miles, F.G. *97*, 174–6
Miles, George 176
Miles Whitney Straight aircraft *97*, 175–6, *191*
Mille Miglia 81, 102, 104, 120
Miller, Kitty 327
Miniakowski, Sergeant Stefan 223, 224, 225
Minozzi, Giovanni 151
Modena Grand Prix *119*, 150

Moll, Guy 105, 106–7, 124–5, 130, 131, 141–2, 151
Monaco Grand Prix 64, *94*, *119*, 123, 124–5, 132, 156, 159
Monsanto 302, 303
Mont Ventoux *93*, 104–6, 146, 147, 156, 160, *189*
Monte Carlo 56, 124–5
Montgomery, Lieutenant General Bernard 232, 233, 238, 240
Montreux Grand Prix *119*, 131–2, 160
Monza Grand Prix 106–8, *119*
Morel, Oliver 41, 42
Morgan, J.P. 16, 163
Morgan, Ruth 42
Morpurgo, Jack 265
Morris Motors 261
Morrison, George 16
Morrison, Wilbur 286
Morrow, Ian 330, 331, 333
Mortimer, A.L. 185
The Motor 118, 125, 150, 158, 159, 161, 311
Motor Sport 62, 74–5, 82, *93*, 105, 113, 158, 159, 160
Mott, Colonel Thomas 22
Mountbatten, Lord Louis 164, 242
Münzenberg, Willi 288
Mussolini, Benito 101, 158, 240

Nash, Dick 58
Nathan, Lord 256, 258, 260, 261, 265
Neave, Airey ('Agent Saturday') 227, 337
The New Republic 18, 29–30, 262, 289
Newcombe, Charles 120
Nice Grand Prix *119*, 142, 160
Nicholson, Rupert 325, 331, 332, 333
Nixon, Lorna 41
Nixon, Richard 331, 333
Nockolds, Roy 149, *188*, *191*
Nolan, Chip 286
Northolt 208, 227–8, 244
Norway 199–202, 248–9, *269*, *270*, 340
Nouveau, Louis and Renée 225, 227
Nuffield Trophy 148, 156
Nuffield, Viscount 261
Nuvolari, Tazio ('Flying Mantuan') 83, 101, 102, 104, 106, 107, 112–13, 122–3, 129, 137, 141, 142, 150–1, 157, 160–1

O'Brien, Sir Leslie 330–1
Øen, Captain Bjorn 200
Ogilvy, David 310–11
Ogmore, Lord 290
Old, General William 242–3
O'Leary, Patrick (*pseudonym of* Albert-Marie Guérlise) 218, 219–20, 223, 224, 225
Osterley Park *192*, 204
Overy, Thomas 254, 268

P&O shipping line 298, 325
Page, William 17
Paget, Almeric, 1st Baron Queensborough 17, 62, 254, 289
Paget, Caroline 164
Paget, Dorothy 62, 117–18
Paget, Pauline Payne Whitney (née Straight) 17
Paget Trust 254–5
Pakenham, Frank 263, 265, 268, 285–6, 290
Pan Am 286, 299, 323, 325–6
Paris 16, 19, 22, 23, 27, 29, 133, 166, 214–16, 221, *234–5*, 244, 312
Parkhouse, Bill 48, 50, 177
Parry Thomas, John 56, 63
Patton, Lieutenant General George 238, 240
Peake, Air Commodore Sir Harald 206
Pearson, Denning ('Jim') 292, 308, 310, 325, 328, 330–1, 332, 333, 341
Peel, Squadron Leader John 197
Peirse, Sir Richard 242–3
Penn-Hughes, Clifton 66, 148
Penya Rhin Grand Prix 133
Perrin, Commander Harold 169
Pershing, General John ('Black Jack') 22, 24, 29
Petre, Kay 114, 115
Philip, Prince, Duke of Edinburgh *193*, *275*, *279*, 290–3, 323
Phillips & Powis 175, 176, 179, 185
Phillips, Jack 175
Phillips, Captain P. 181
Pierson, Warren Lee 257
Pietsch, Paul 82
Pleydell Bouverie, Audrey 205
Pleydell Bouverie, David *98*, 179–80
Plymouth 173, 179, 181
Ponsford, Keith and Mary 41

Index

Ponte Olivio *234–5*, 239, 240
Popp, Franz Josef 186
Post Office *195*, *279*, 328–9, 331, 334, 335, 340, 341
Poston, Guy 288
Potter, Charlie 21, 342
Poulett, Lady Bridget 122
Powis, Charles 175
Powys-Lybbe, Antony 80
Pratt & Whitney 184, 307, 323
Pratt, John, Lord Brecknock ('Breckie') 118, 307
pre-selector gearboxes 79–80, 81, 83, 84, 105, 106, 110, 121, 136, 137, 157
Preston, Arthur ('Jumbo') 326
Preston, Michael 41, 42
Princess flying boat 259–60, 267, *274*, 288, 298–9, 302
Profumo, Jack 296, 300
Purves, Tom 308

Qantas 263, 298

Railton, Reid 56, 79, 118, 120–1, 125, 127, 149, 153, 157
Railway Air Services 173–4, 248, 252–3, 255
Rambert, Marie 163
Ramponi, Giulio *96*, 120, 122, 124, 136, 153, 155, 156, 157, 177–8
Ramsgate *98*, 170, 173, 176, 178, 179–80, 184
Rawson, Wyatt 40, 41–2, 45–6, 47, 340
Reilly, Sir Patrick 311
Reilly, Sir Paul 329
Reims-Gueux 82–3, 101, *119*, 122, 137, 160
Rhodes Moorhouse, Flight Lieutenant Willie 205
Rigden, Maude 41, 44
Riley 56, 58, 68, 70, 110, 111, 113, 114, 126, 132, 133, 134
  Whitney's Riley Nine 56, 57, 58, 62, 64, *92*
Roberts, Owen 184, 198
Robertson Justice, James 120, 121, 130, 139
Robinson, J.A. 63
Rockefeller, John D. 28
Rockell, Billy 120, 143, 155, 156, 177–8
Rodocanachi, Georges 219, 223
Roger, Sir Alexander 309

Rolls, Charles 305–6
Rolls-Royce 253–4, *280*, 305–12, 323–5, 340, 341
  aero engines 292, 306–7, 308, 315, 321, 323, 334
  Bristol Siddeley acquired 323–4
  cars 253–4, 305, 306, 307, 310–11, 320, 321, 332–3, 334
  collapse and liquidation *282*, 310, 323–5, 329–34, 336, 341–2
  government rescue 331–2
  Merlin 264, 288, 306, 307
  RB211 *281*, 315, 324–5, 328, 329–30, 331, 333, 334
  Russian sale 311–12
  Whitney joins 300, 301, 302, 308–9
  Whitney leaves 328, 332–3
Romanian royalty 125, 133
Rommel, Erwin 232, 233
Roosevelt, Alice 15
Roosevelt, Franklin 236, 246, 286
Roosevelt, Quentin 21–2, 29, 30, 31
Roosevelt, Theodore 13, 14, 16, 17, 18, 20–1, 24, 28
Rose, Harry 155, 159
Rose, Milton 289
Rose, Tommy 175
Rose-Richards, Tim 74, 108, 112, 113, 127
Rosemeyer, Bernd 158, 161
Rothenstein, Sir William *191*
Rothermere, Esmond Harmsworth, 2nd Viscount 168
Rotol 308
Rover 63, 306
Rowbotham, Frederick 164
Royal Aero Club 50, 169
Royal Air Force (RAF) 163, 177, 181, 225, 237, 238, 242, 243, 256, 257–8, 290, 306–7, 325–6
  216 Group 229–49, 251, 253, *272*, 341
  242 Squadron 209–12, 213, 214, 228, 306
  263 Squadron 201, 202, *270*
  601 Squadron 197–8, 202, 205, 206, 207–9, *269*, 306
Royal Auxiliary Air Force (RAAF) 197
  Whitney in 185–6, *191*, 197–212, 213–28, 229–49, 251, *269*, *270*, 271, *272*, 306, 340–1

Royal Automobile Club 35
Rubin, Bernard 82, 99, 101
Russia/Soviet Union 15, 19, 71, 167, 251, 286, 288, 311–12, 315–16, 317–18
Ryland, William 328, 329, 331

Sahara expedition 317
St Hippolyte (internment camp) *215*, 218, 219–23, 229, 230, 245, 249, 341
St Margaret's, Westminster 164, 316
Sandhurst 40, 184, 315
Saratoga Springs 167
Sayer, Flight Lieutenant Gerry 68
Scapa Flow 201–2, 248–9
Schneider Trophy competitions 306
Scott, Peter 290
Scuderia Ferrari 101, 106, 108, 117, 139, 141–2, 146, 147, 151, 156
  Grands Prix 106, 123, 124, 130, 131, 133, 137, 138, 142, 151
Seaman, Dick 70, 114, 122, 133, 134, 139, 141, 142, 145–6, 147, 148, 150–1, 164, 170, 177–8, 186, 339
Second World War 24, 115, 178, 183, 185, 197–212, 213–28, 229–49, 254, 257–8, 306–7
Segrave, Sir Henry 62–3, 118, 140
Selby, Lewis 180, 340
Shelford Hall 78
Shelmerdine, Sir Francis 180
Shelsley Walsh 57–8, 69, 70, 74, 78–9, 80, *92*, 110–11, *119*, 131, 132–3, 147, 148, 153, 156, 159
Shephard, Captain J.S. 154
Siena, Eugenio 82, 105
Silver City Airways 310
Simon, André 225
Smallpiece, Basil 296, 298, 299
Smith, Frederick Llewellyn ('Doc') 310–11, 332
Smyth, Brigadier H.E.F. 248–9
Soffietti, Luigi 147, 148, 150, 151, 152
Sommer, Raymond 83–4, 105, 124, 160
Souter, Michael 324, 326, 327
South African Grand Prix 153–4
South Africa's Border 100 *96*, 152–3, 156
Southern Airways 182
Southport 62, 63, 74, *119*

Spanish Grand Prix 147–8
Special Operations Executive (SOE) 218, 224, 225, 227
Stace, L.H. 124
Stephens, Ron 226
Stephenson, Bill ('Agent Intrepid') 286
Stisted, H.H. 79
Stone, Les 120
Stonehouse, John *279*, 327, 328, 341
Straight, Amanda Betsy *194*, 293, 297, 314, 326, 334, 337–8
Straight, Beatrice ('Biddy') 36, 165, 166, 167, 198, 337
  acting career 262, 336, 342
  birth and childhood 18–19, 20, 22, 37–8, 41, 42, 44, 47, 52, *87*
  marriages 228, 262, 286, 289
Straight Corporation Ltd *98*, 170–85, 198–9, 207–8, 230, 233, 252–3, 309–10, 342
  financial matters 172, 178, 183–4, 214
  Second World War 185, 198–9, 203, 207–8, 230, 241, 247, 248, *269*
Straight, Dorothy (Whitney's mother; née Whitney, *later* Elmhirst) 13–25, 27, 28–38, *85*, 208, 228, 247, 249
  Applegreen 14, 15, 17, 18, 23, 31, 32, 35, 36–7, 48, 167, 181
  birth and childhood 13–14
  Dartington Hall and School 36, 37, 38, 40–2, 44, 45, 48, 49, 50–3, 165, 335
  death 327–8, 335
  family finances 36, 287, 289–90
  financial assistance to Whitney 39, 69, 112, 117–18, 172, 181–2, 289, 340
  First World War 19, 21, 22–3
  marries Leonard 'Jerry' Elmhirst 33–4, 35, *90*
  marries Willard Straight 14, 15–16
  philanthropy 28, 29–30, 31, 33, 40
  Whitney's feelings, oblivious to 26–7, 30, 36–7, 38, 51, 53, 339
  and Whitney's racing 69, 73, 112, 115, 170
Straight, Hazel 15
Straight, Henry 14
Straight, Michael (Whitney's brother) 165, 166, 167, 228, 262, 289–90, 342
  birth and childhood 19, 20, 31, 32, 34, 41, 47, 52–3, *87*

Index

Border 100 race 152–3, 154
espionage 167, 315–16
Straight (née Finch Hatton), Lady Daphne
  163–8, *194*, 290, 337–8
  birth and childhood 163–4
  and Ian Fleming 164, 168, 319
  and Isaiah Berlin 198, 230, 237, 338
  marriage, affairs during 198, 204, 220, 222
  marriage, health of 167–8, 198, 203–4,
    205, 222, 252, 258, 264–5, *284*, 291–2,
    312, 314, 335, 338, 342
  meets and marries Whitney 2, *96*, 164–7
  Second World War 198, 200, 203–4, 220,
    222, 227, 230, 237
  on Whitney's political prospects 244–5
Straight, Whitney Willard ('Bill') 21,
  56, *269, 271, 272, 273, 275, 279, 280,
  282, 283*
  ADC to Duke of Kent 205–7, *271*
  ADC to George VI 243, 251
  birth 13, 17
  black cars 50, 56, 65, 81, 148, 155, 159
  Cambridge University 55–6, 65, 69–71,
    79, 81, 84, 111–12, 114, 117
  childhood 13, 17–25, 27–32, 33–8, 39–54,
    85, 87, 88, 89, 90, 187
  citizenship 121, 169, 177, 342
  death 337–8
  death of father 12, 24–5, 27–8, 37, 339
  deep-sea diving *283*, 293, 295, 325, 326
  drinking 265, 325, 334, 341
  education 28–9, 31, 37–8, 39–54, *188*
  financial situation 172–3, 222, 254, 287,
    289–90
  French language 35, 42, 43, 46, 53, 214
  health 18, 19, 45, 84, 244, 245, 262–3,
    265, 266, 316, 325, 334, 336–7, 341
  honours 202, 203, 211, 243, 251, *273*, 328
  marriage, affairs during 167, 198, 204, 205,
    220, 222–3, 232, 241, 245–6, 247, 252,
    254, 258, 265, 293, 312, 314
  marriage, health of 167–8, 198, 203–4,
    205, 222, 252, 258, 264–5, *284*, 291–2,
    312, 314, 335, 338, 342
  meets and marries Daphne 2, *96*, 163,
    164–7, 171–2
  political career (putative) 237, 244–5,
    246–7

  in RAAF 185–6, *191*, 197–212, 213–28,
    229–49, 251, *269, 270, 271, 272*, 306,
    340–1
Straight, Willard (Whitney's father) 18, 31, *86*
  career 15, 16, 17, 18, 24
  childhood 14–15
  death 23–5, 27, 33
  Dorothy Whitney, meets and marries 14,
    15–16
  First World War 12, 19–20, 22–3, 24, 27,
    28, *86*
  letters to his son 12, 19, 20, 22, 24–5, 27,
    188, 342
Strange, Louis 176–7, 198–9, 203, 210
Stuck, Hans 57, 79, 110, 111, 125, 132, 140,
  141, 145, 147, 150, 160, 161
Summers, Joseph ('Mutt') 241
Sunbeam cars 62, 75, 80, *93*, 109, 112, 113,
  114, 118, 150
Sundstedt, Knut Gustav 65–6
Surtees, Major General George 233
Swedish Grand Prix 65–6, *92*, 99–101
Swinton, Lord 247, 248, 251
Swiss Grand Prix *94*, 131, 142, 143, 145–6,
  156, 161, 268

Tangmere, Sussex 198, 200, 205, 207,
  209, 340
HMS *Tarana* 225–7, 231
Taruffi, Piero 106, 113, 114
Tavernier, Colonel 220, 221
Tedder, Air Chief Marshal Arthur 229,
  231–2
Teignmouth 48, 179
Tempelhof airport, Germany 183, 251
Thanet 173, 176, 184, 237
Thomas, Sir Miles 261, 264, 265, 266, 267,
  285–6, 287–8, 290, 292, 293, 294,
  295–6, 297, 298, 299, 300, 302, 303, 309
Thomson & Taylor 79, 81, 99, 120–1, 124
Thomson, Roy 317–18
Tito, Marshal Josip 241
Totnes 36, 41, 47, 49, 65, 245
Tourist Trophy, Northern Ireland 57, 81,
  104, 118, 305
Tower, Roderick 30, *88*
Treacy, W.P.F. ('Treacle') 209
Tree, Ronnie 164

375

Trenchard, Lord 197
Trinity College, Cambridge 32, 40, 52, 55, 65, 69–71, 111–12, 114, 117, 305
Tripoli Grand Prix 82, *119*, 126, 127, 129–30, 132
Trossi, Count ('Didi') 106, 108, 124, 125, 131, 138–9, 142, 147, 155, 160
Tunis Grand Prix 161
TWA 243, 257, 258, 298

University Motors 62, 109

Valletta, Vittorio 255
van der Brink, Nellie 204, 205, 207, 211, 220, 222–3, 230
van der Stratten Panthoz, Claudine *278*, 312–15, 342
Vanderbilt, Gladys 13–14
Varzi, Achille 129, 130, 131, 133, 137, 141, 142, 160
Veyron, Pierre 103, 145
Vichy Grand Prix *119*, 138–9, 155, 156, 160
Vickers 108, 241, 264, 334
Villa Camanda *194*, *196*, *284*, 294–5, 301, 312, 316, 326, 327, 335
Villiers, Amherst 58, 62, 79, 157, 175–6
Villiers Supercharge 58, 79, 110, 111, 176

Wales, John ('Pop') 43, 44–5, 46, 47, 50–1, 52
Walker, Barney 268, 293
Walker, Diana Barnato 253–4, 258, 265, 268, *273*, 287, 293, 342
Walkerley, Rodney 125, 126, 158
Wallenius, Asser 100
Wallis, Barnes 264–5
Warboys, Sir Walter 309
Waterlow, Tom 207–8

Watkinson, Harold 303
Watson, M.B. 109
Western Airways 182, 184, 185, 199, 252, 309
Westminster, Duke of 230
Weston-super-Mare 181–2, 184, 185, 199, 230, 253, 309, 317, 325–6, 334, 336
Whitney, Flora (Dorothy's mother) 14, 24
Whitney, Flora (Dorothy's niece) 22, 29, 30, *88*
Whitney, Harry 14
Whitney, William 13, 14, 24, 167
Whitney Straight Ltd 117–27, 129–43, 145–57
Whittle, Frank 306
Wickberg, Oscar 100
Widengren, Henken and Per Victor 65, 66, 100
Wilde, Oscar 78
Willard Straight Hall, Cornell University 11–12, *11*, 37
Wilson, Harold 324, 327, 337
Wilson, Woodrow 13, 18, 19, 23, 24
Wimille, Jean-Pierre 83, 151, 152
Winchilsea, Guy Finch-Hatton, Earl of 163, 164
Winchilsea, Margaretta, Countess of (née Drexel) 163, 200, 204
Wise, Marjorie 40, 41, 45–6
Wodehouse, P.G. 152
Woking 113–15
Woods Hole, Massachusetts 30–1, 32, 33, 34

Yalta *234–5*, 246, 286
Yellow Peril (Whitney's Model T Ford) 49
Young, Michael 49–50

Zehender, Goffredo 143
Zotos, Stephanos 257